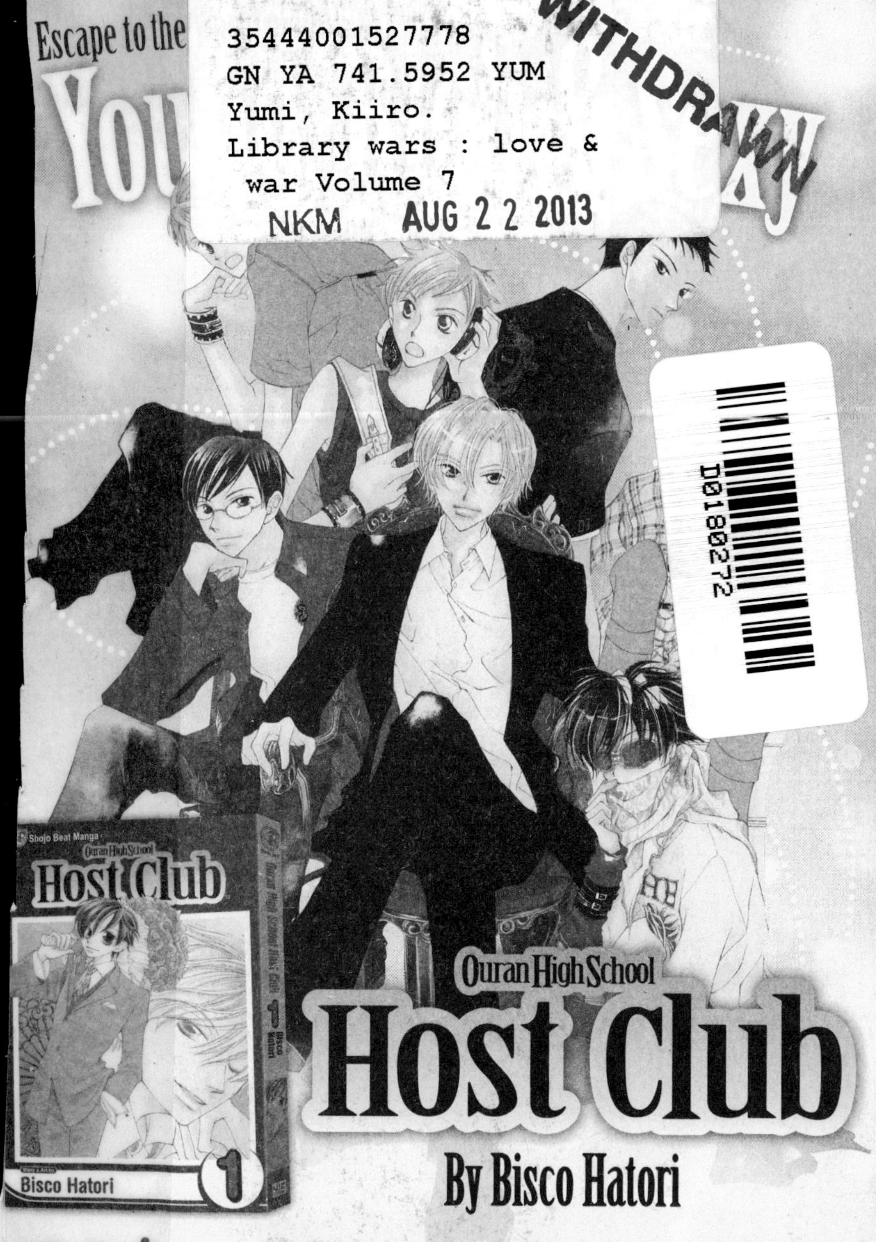
Escape to the
You
Shojo Beat Manga
Ouran High School
Host Club
1
Bisco Hatori

Don't Hide What's *Inside*

OTOMEN
by AYA KANNO

Despite his tough jock exterior, Asuka Masamune harbors a secret love for sewing, shojo manga, and all things girly. But when he finds himself drawn to his domestically inept classmate Ryo, his carefully crafted persona is put to the test. Can Asuka ever show his true self to anyone, much less to the girl he's falling for?

Find out in the *Otomen* manga—buy yours today!

library wars

Volume 7
Shojo Beat Edition

Story & Art by **Kiiro Yumi**
Original Concept by **Hiro Arikawa**

ENGLISH TRANSLATION Kinami Watabe
ADAPTATION & LETTERING Sean McCoy
DESIGN Amy Martin
EDITOR Megan Bates

Toshokan Sensou LOVE&WAR by Kiiro Yumi and Hiro Arikawa
© Kiiro Yumi 2011
© Hiro Arikawa 2011
All rights reserved.
First published in Japan in 2011 by HAKUSENSHA, Inc., Tokyo.
English language translation rights arranged with HAKUSENSHA,
Inc., Tokyo.

Printed in the U.S.A.

Published by VIZ Media, LLC
P.O. Box 77010
San Francisco, CA 94107

10 9 8 7 6 5 4 3 2 1
First printing, February 2012

www.shojobeat.com   www.viz.com

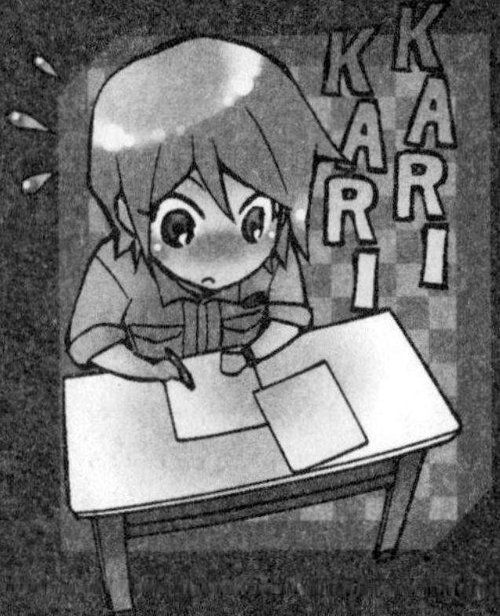
KARI
KARI

Kiiro Yumi won the 42nd *LaLa* Manga Grand Prix Fresh Debut award for her manga *Billy Bocchan no Yuutsu* (Little Billy's Depression). Her latest series is *Toshokan Senso Love&War (Library Wars: Love & War)*, which runs in *LaLa* magazine in Japan and is published in English by VIZ Media.

Hiro Arikawa won the 10th Dengeki Novel Prize for her work *Shio no Machi: Wish on My Precious* in 2003 and debuted with the same novel in 2004. Of her many works, Arikawa is best known for the *Library Wars* series and her *Jieitai Sanbusaku* trilogy, which consists of *Sora no Naka* (In the Sky), *Umi no Soko* (The Bottom of the Sea) and *Shio no Machi* (City of Salt).

Library Wars

Love & War

7

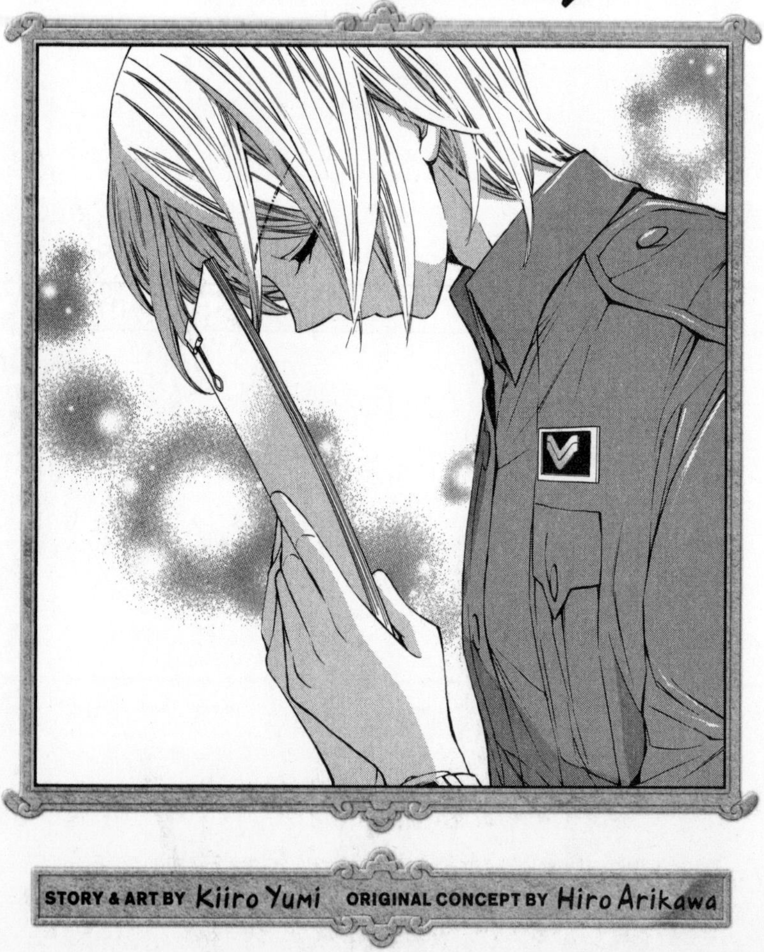

STORY & ART BY Kiiro Yumi ORIGINAL CONCEPT BY Hiro Arikawa

Library Wars

Love & War

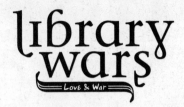

Contents

The Library Freedom Act

Libraries have the freedom to acquire their collections.

Libraries have the freedom to circulate
materials in their collections.

Libraries guarantee the privacy of their patrons.

Libraries oppose any type of censorship.

When libraries are imperiled,
librarians will join together
to secure their freedom.

library wars
Love & War

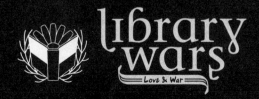

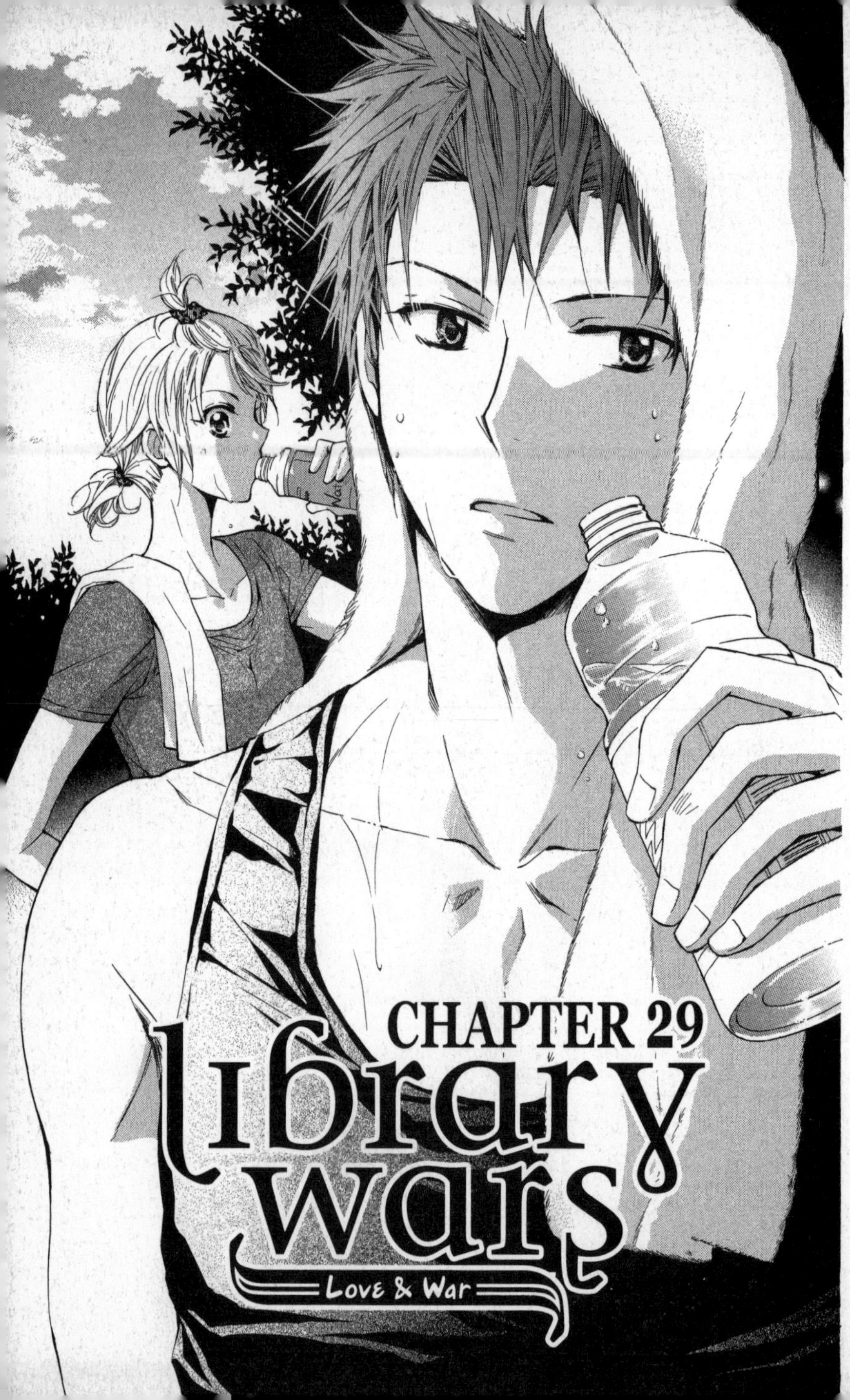
CHAPTER 29
library wars
Love & War

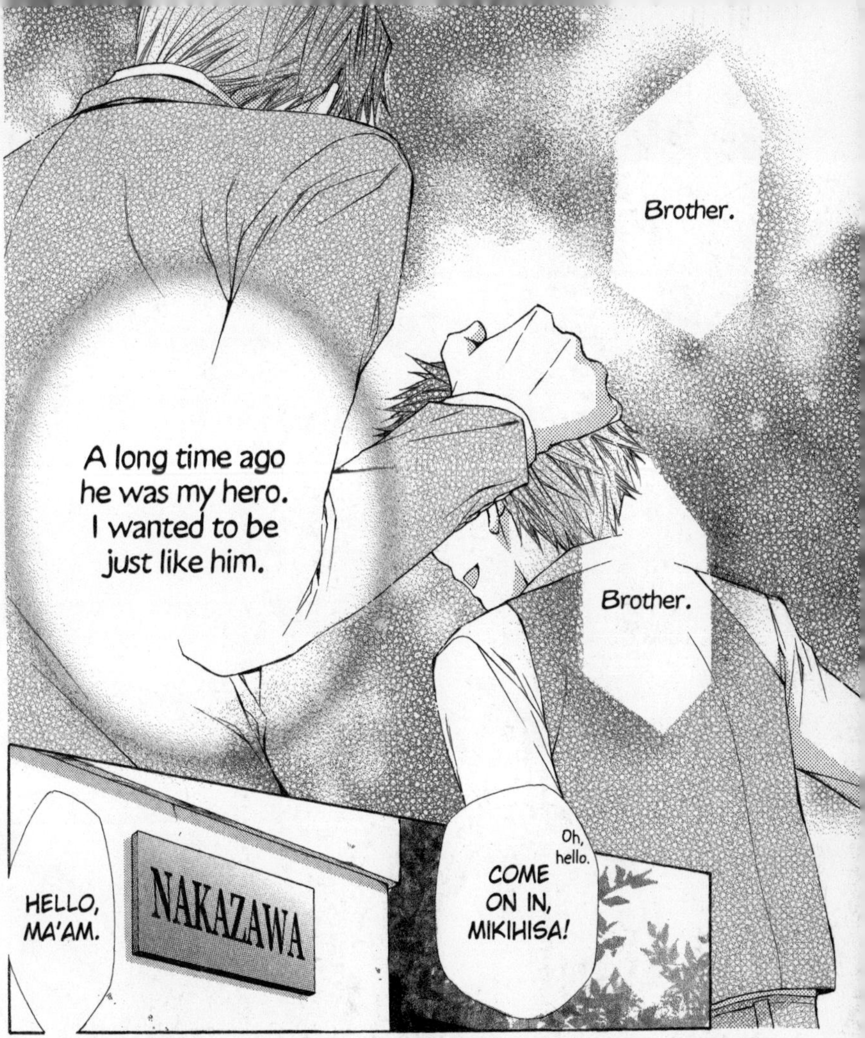
Brother.
Brother.
A long time ago he was my hero. I wanted to be just like him.
Oh, hello.
COME ON IN, MIKIHISA!
NAKAZAWA
HELLO, MA'AM.

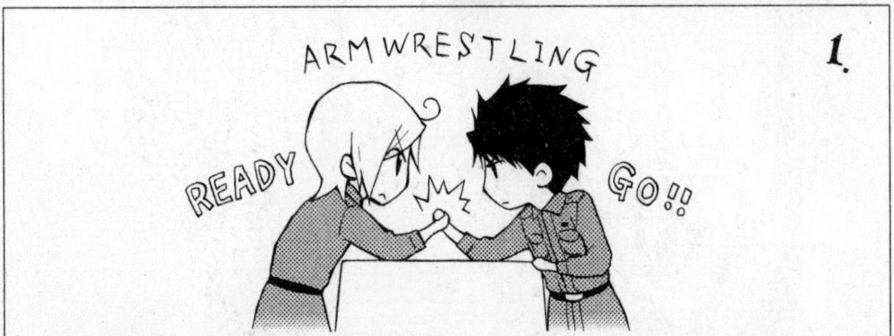
1.
ARM WRESTLING
READY
GO!!

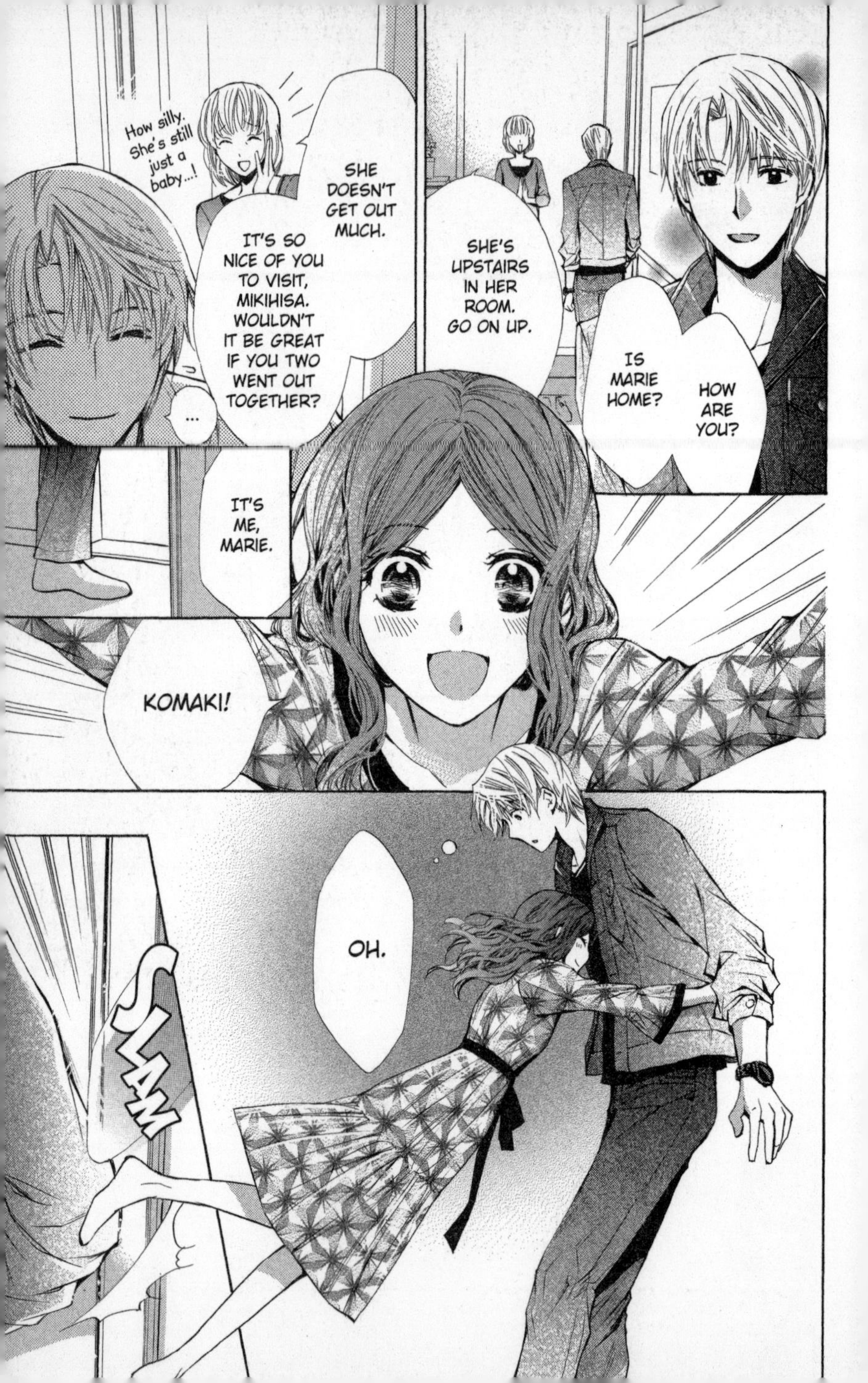
HOW ARE YOU?
IS MARIE HOME?
SHE'S UPSTAIRS IN HER ROOM. GO ON UP.
SHE DOESN'T GET OUT MUCH.
IT'S SO NICE OF YOU TO VISIT, MIKIHISA. WOULDN'T IT BE GREAT IF YOU TWO WENT OUT TOGETHER?
How silly. She's still just a baby...!
...
IT'S ME, MARIE.
KOMAKI!
OH.
SLAM

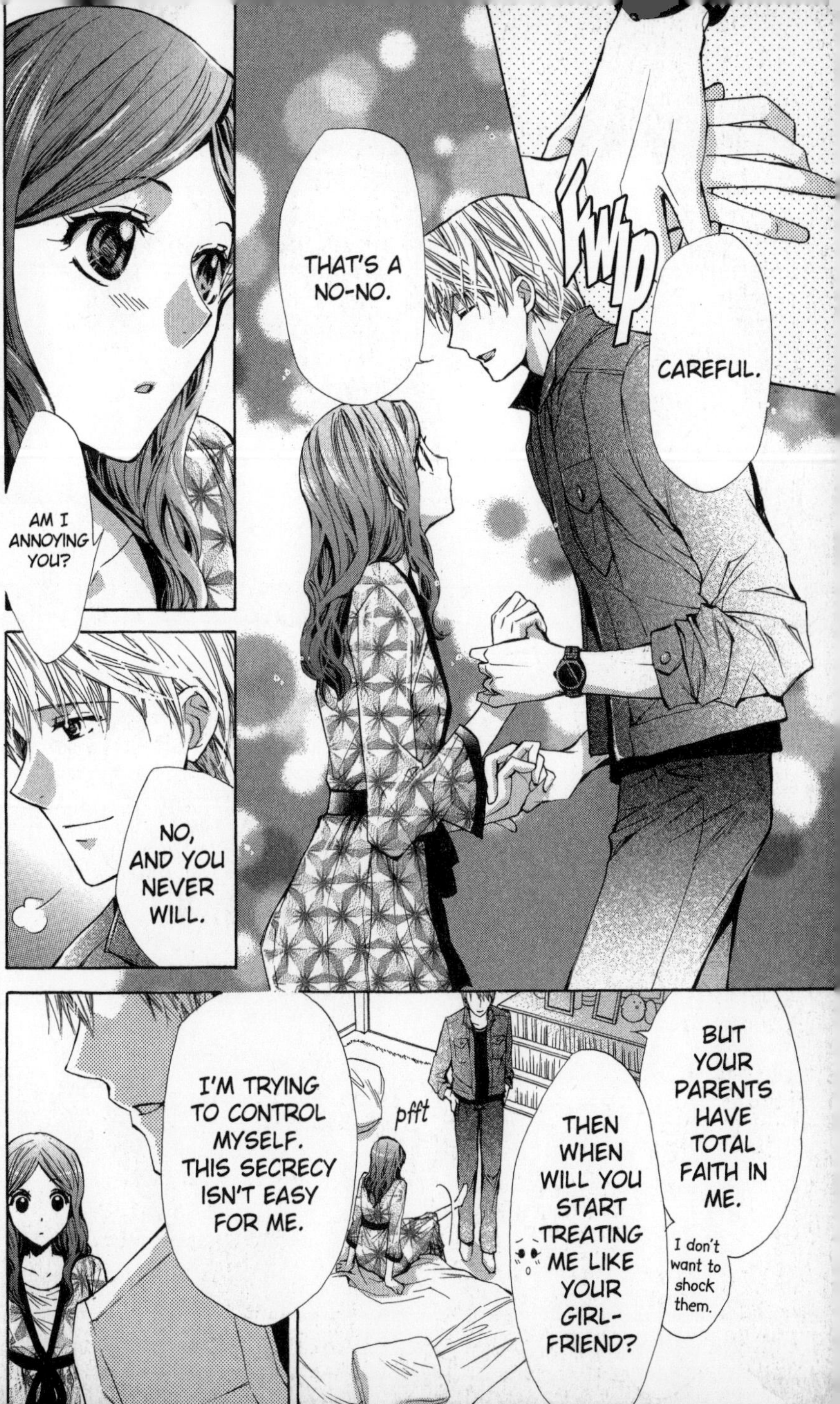
TWIP
CAREFUL.
THAT'S A NO-NO.
AM I ANNOYING YOU?
NO, AND YOU NEVER WILL.
BUT YOUR PARENTS HAVE TOTAL FAITH IN ME.
I don't want to shock them.
THEN WHEN WILL YOU START TREATING ME LIKE YOUR GIRL-FRIEND?
pfft
I'M TRYING TO CONTROL MYSELF. THIS SECRECY ISN'T EASY FOR ME.

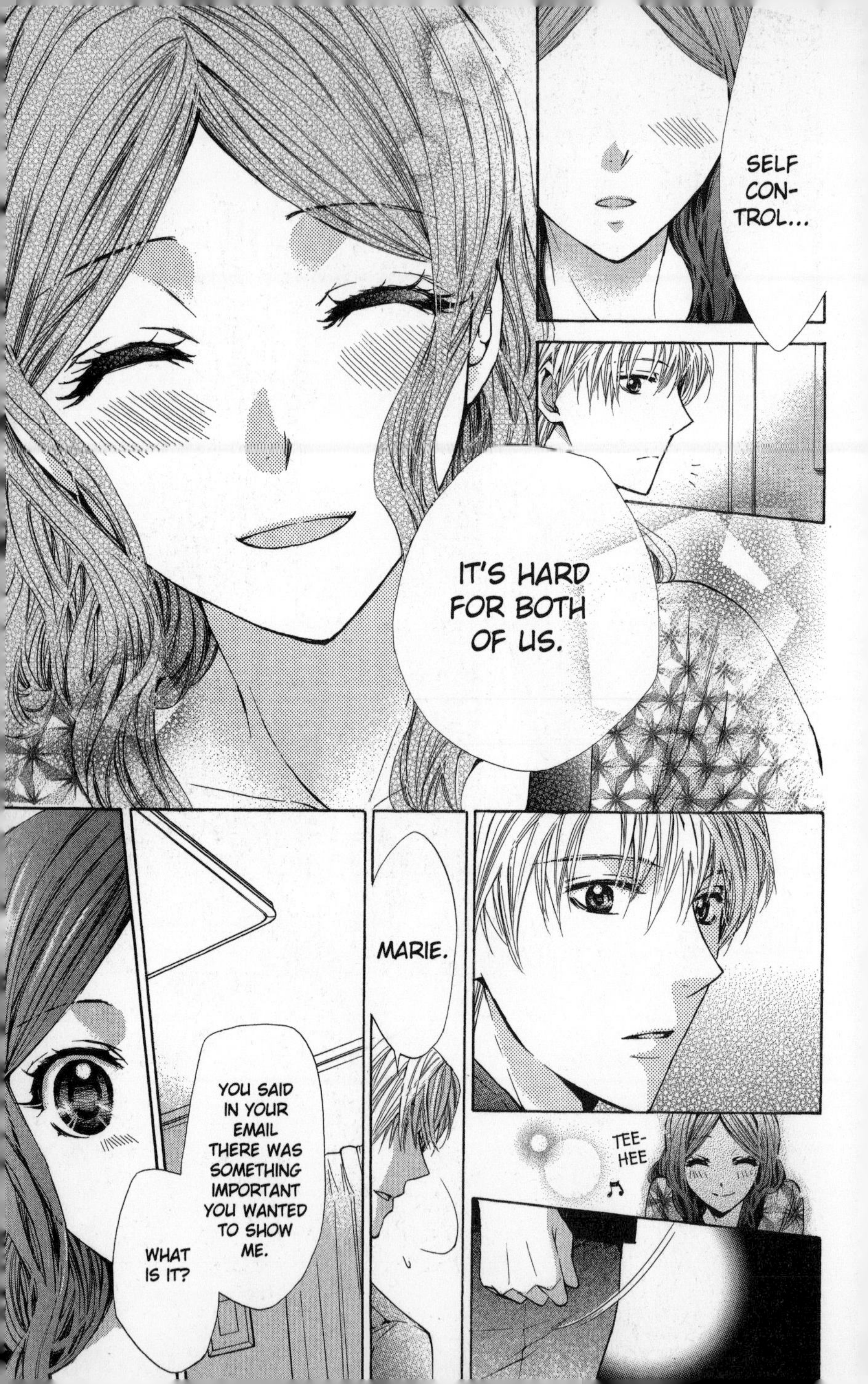
SELF CON-TROL...
IT'S HARD FOR BOTH OF US.
TEE-HEE ♪
MARIE.
YOU SAID IN YOUR EMAIL THERE WAS SOMETHING IMPORTANT YOU WANTED TO SHOW ME.
WHAT IS IT?

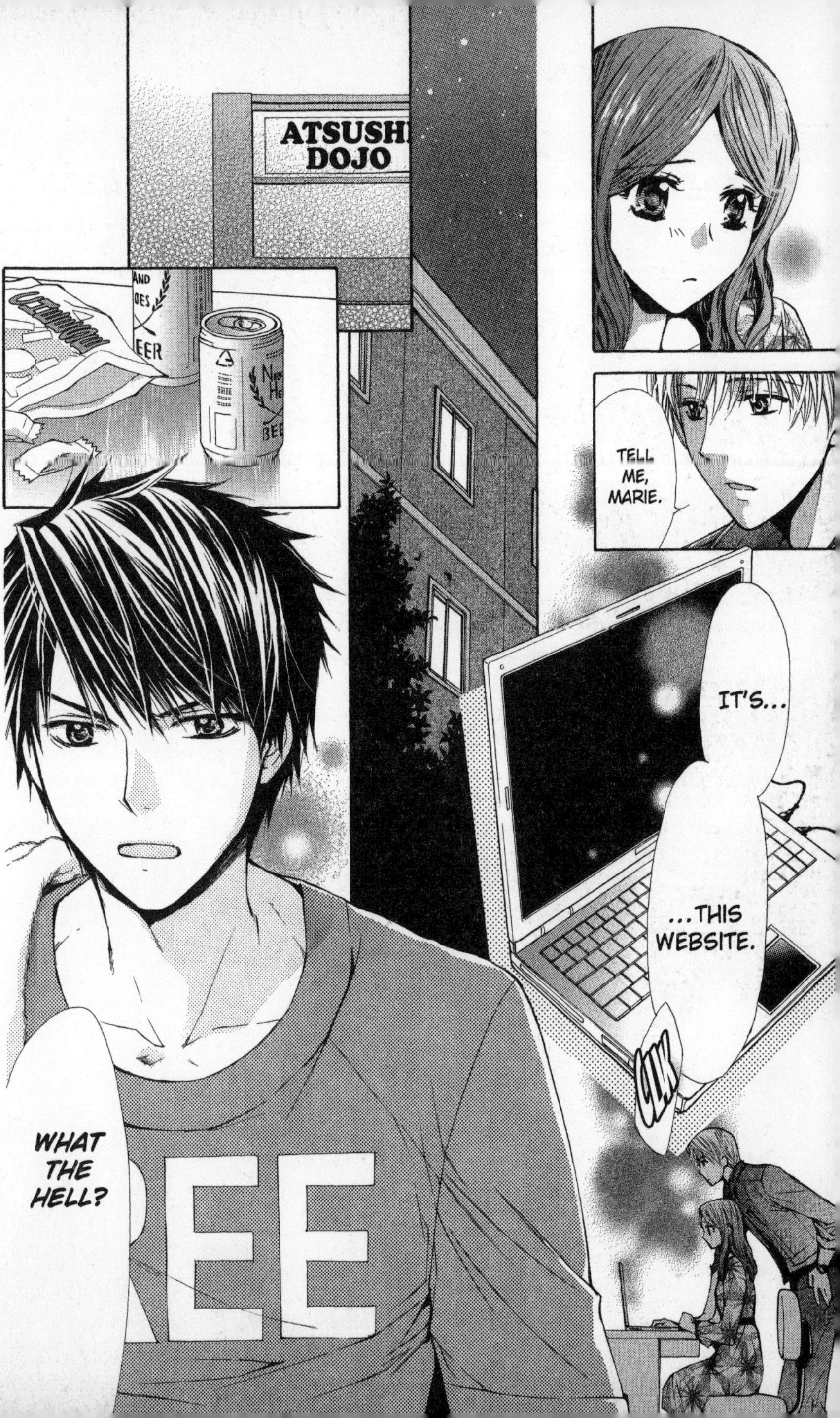
TELL ME, MARIE.
ATSUSHI DOJO
IT'S...
...THIS WEBSITE.
WHAT THE HELL?

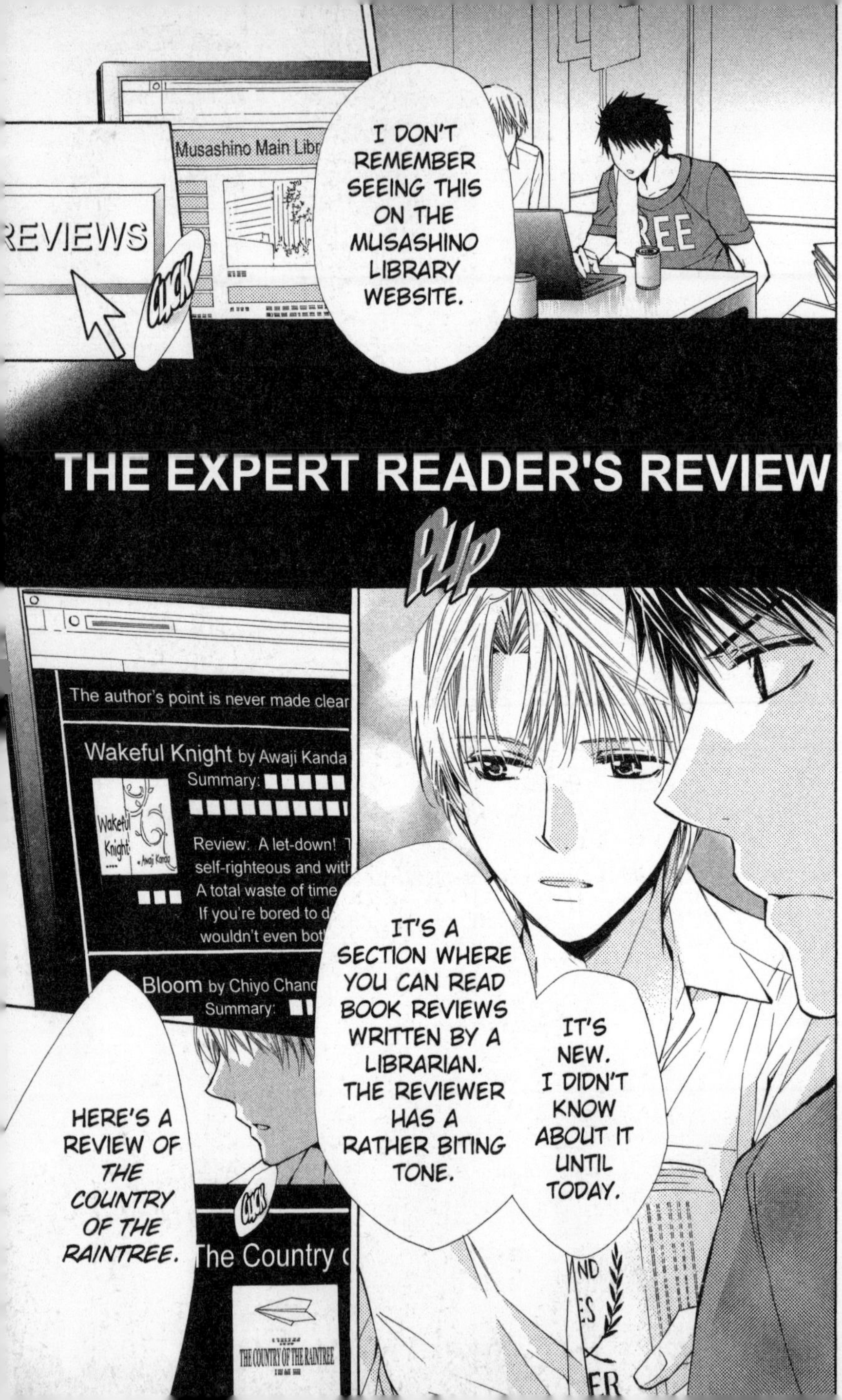
Musashino Main Libr
REVIEWS
CLICK
I DON'T REMEMBER SEEING THIS ON THE MUSASHINO LIBRARY WEBSITE.
THE EXPERT READER'S REVIEW
FLIP
IT'S NEW. I DIDN'T KNOW ABOUT IT UNTIL TODAY.
IT'S A SECTION WHERE YOU CAN READ BOOK REVIEWS WRITTEN BY A LIBRARIAN. THE REVIEWER HAS A RATHER BITING TONE.
The author's point is never made clear
Wakeful Knight by Awaji Kanda
Summary:
Wakeful Knight
Awaji Kanda
Review: A let-down!
self-righteous and with
A total waste of time
If you're bored to d
wouldn't even bot
Bloom by Chiyo Chanc
Summary:
HERE'S A REVIEW OF THE COUNTRY OF THE RAINTREE.
CLICK
The Country c
THE COUNTRY OF THE RAINTREE

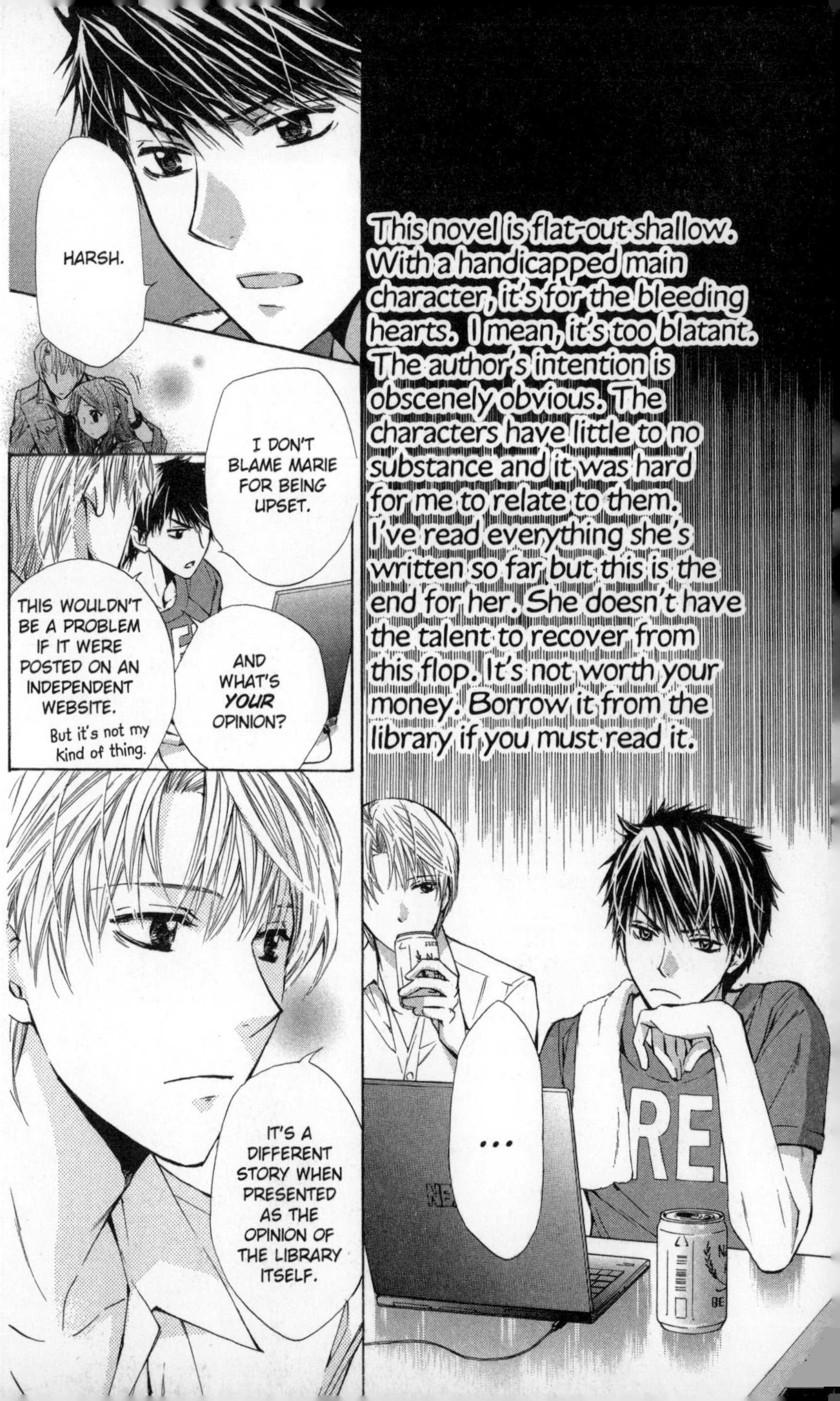
This novel is flat-out shallow. With a handicapped main character, it's for the bleeding hearts. I mean, it's too blatant. The author's intention is obscenely obvious. The characters have little to no substance and it was hard for me to relate to them. I've read everything she's written so far but this is the end for her. She doesn't have the talent to recover from this flop. It's not worth your money. Borrow it from the library if you must read it.
...
HARSH.
I DON'T BLAME MARIE FOR BEING UPSET.
AND WHAT'S *YOUR* OPINION?
THIS WOULDN'T BE A PROBLEM IF IT WERE POSTED ON AN INDEPENDENT WEBSITE.
But it's not my kind of thing.
IT'S A DIFFERENT STORY WHEN PRESENTED AS THE OPINION OF THE LIBRARY ITSELF.

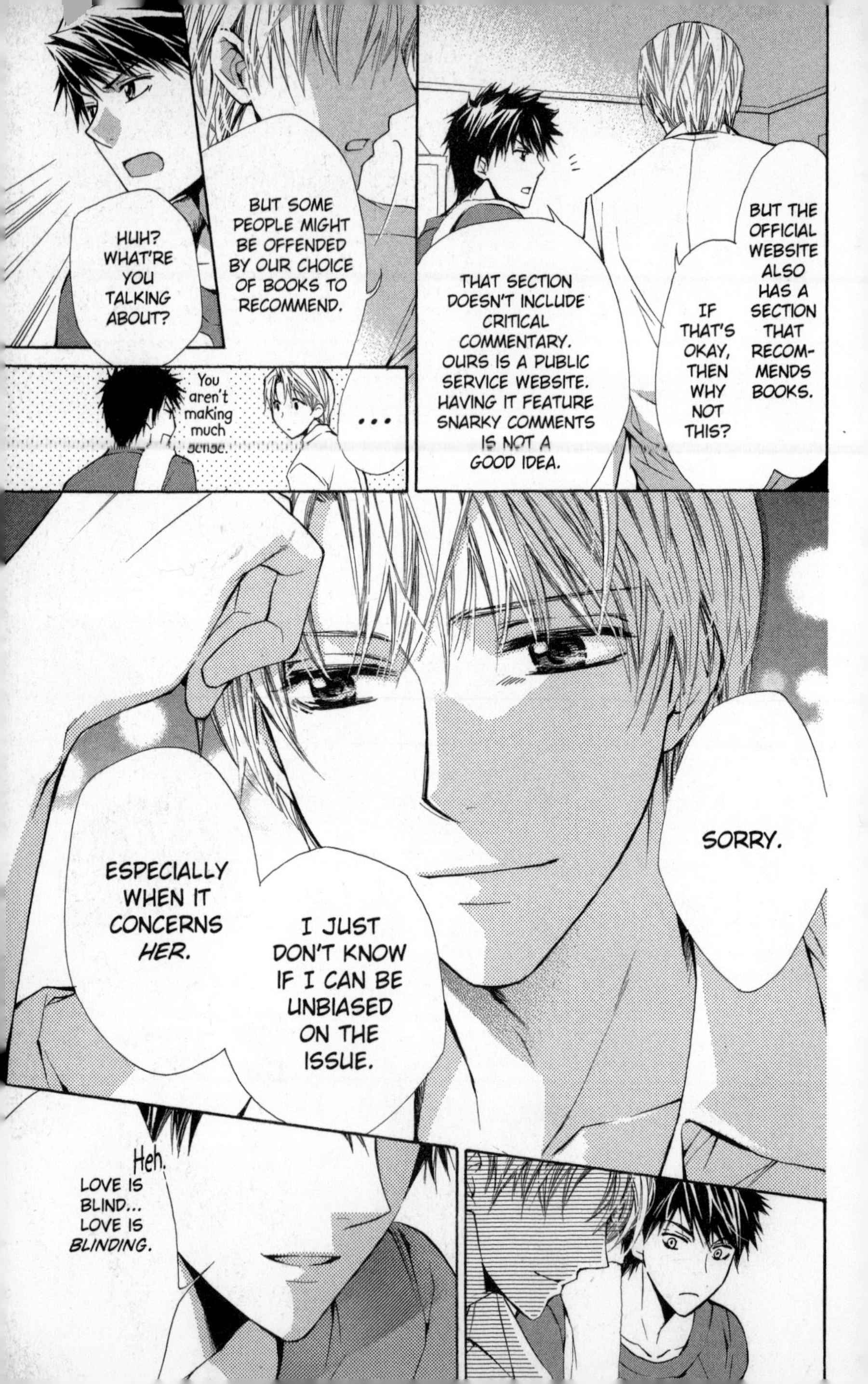
BUT THE OFFICIAL WEBSITE ALSO HAS A SECTION THAT RECOMMENDS BOOKS.
IF THAT'S OKAY, THEN WHY NOT THIS?
THAT SECTION DOESN'T INCLUDE CRITICAL COMMENTARY. OURS IS A PUBLIC SERVICE WEBSITE. HAVING IT FEATURE SNARKY COMMENTS IS NOT A GOOD IDEA.
BUT SOME PEOPLE MIGHT BE OFFENDED BY OUR CHOICE OF BOOKS TO RECOMMEND.
HUH? WHAT'RE YOU TALKING ABOUT?
...
You aren't making much sense.
SORRY.
I JUST DON'T KNOW IF I CAN BE UNBIASED ON THE ISSUE.
ESPECIALLY WHEN IT CONCERNS *HER*.
Heh.
LOVE IS BLIND... LOVE IS *BLINDING*.

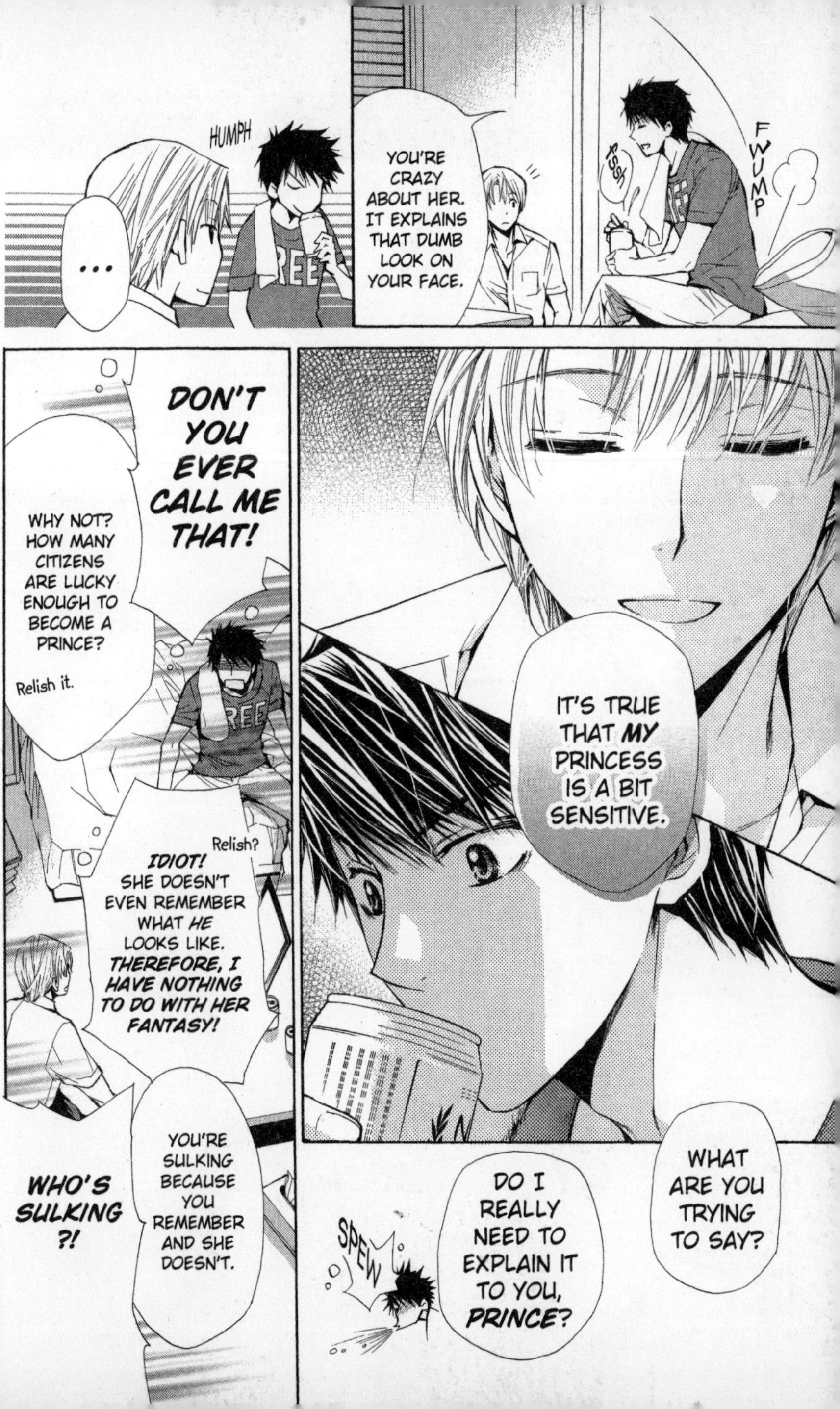
FWUMP
fssh
YOU'RE CRAZY ABOUT HER. IT EXPLAINS THAT DUMB LOOK ON YOUR FACE.
HUMPH
...
IT'S TRUE THAT *MY* PRINCESS IS A BIT SENSITIVE.
WHAT ARE YOU TRYING TO SAY?
DO I REALLY NEED TO EXPLAIN IT TO YOU, *PRINCE*?
SPEW
DON'T YOU EVER CALL ME THAT!
WHY NOT? HOW MANY CITIZENS ARE LUCKY ENOUGH TO BECOME A PRINCE?
Relish it.
Relish?
IDIOT! SHE DOESN'T EVEN REMEMBER WHAT *HE* LOOKS LIKE. THEREFORE, I HAVE NOTHING TO DO WITH HER FANTASY!
YOU'RE SULKING BECAUSE YOU REMEMBER AND SHE DOESN'T.
WHO'S SULKING ?!

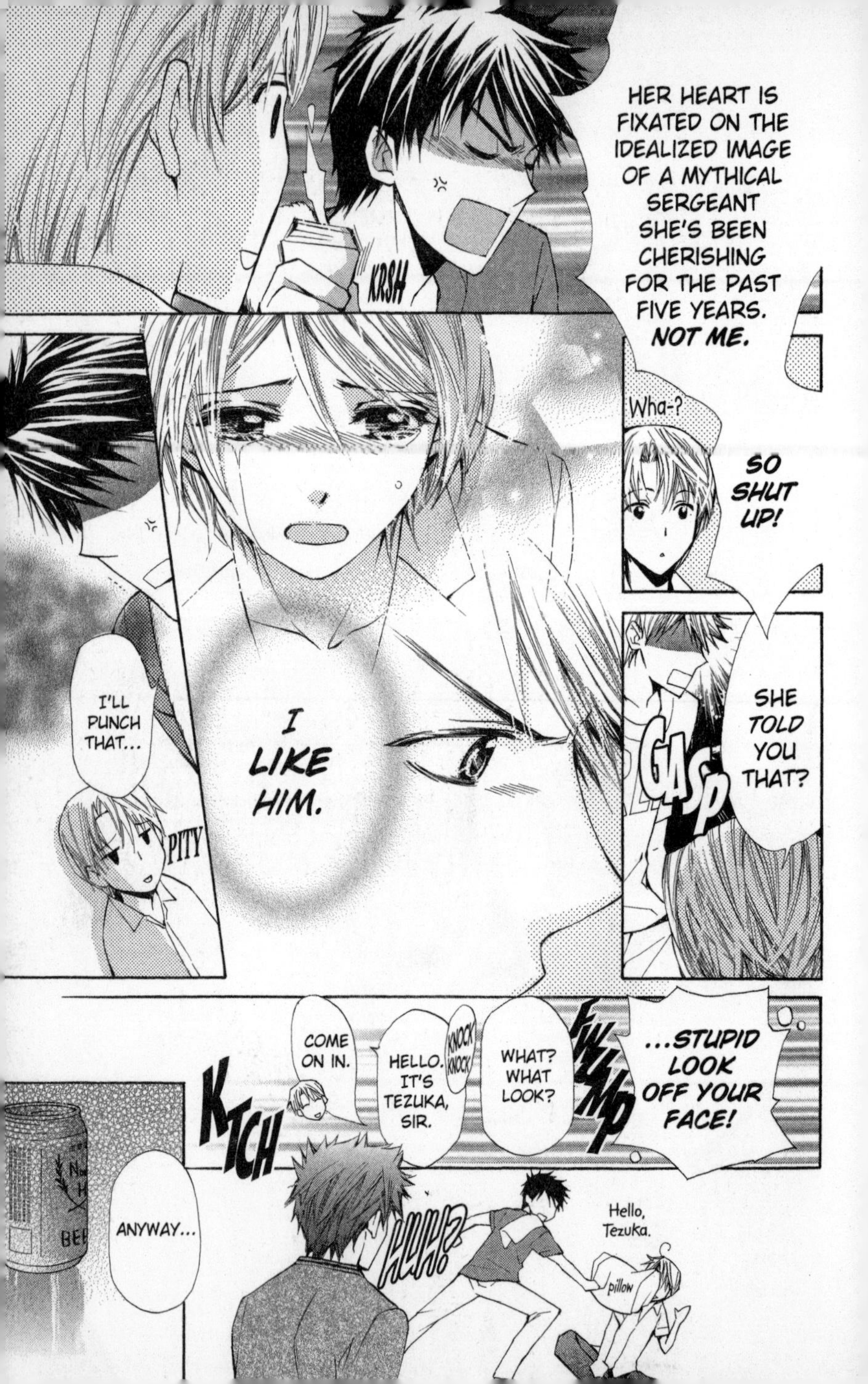
HER HEART IS FIXATED ON THE IDEALIZED IMAGE OF A MYTHICAL SERGEANT SHE'S BEEN CHERISHING FOR THE PAST FIVE YEARS. NOT ME.
KRSH
Wha-?
SO SHUT UP!
SHE TOLD YOU THAT?
GASP
I LIKE HIM.
I'LL PUNCH THAT...
PITY
...STUPID LOOK OFF YOUR FACE!
FWUMP
WHAT? WHAT LOOK?
KNOCK KNOCK
HELLO. IT'S TEZUKA, SIR.
COME ON IN.
KTCH
Hello, Tezuka.
pillow
ANYWAY...

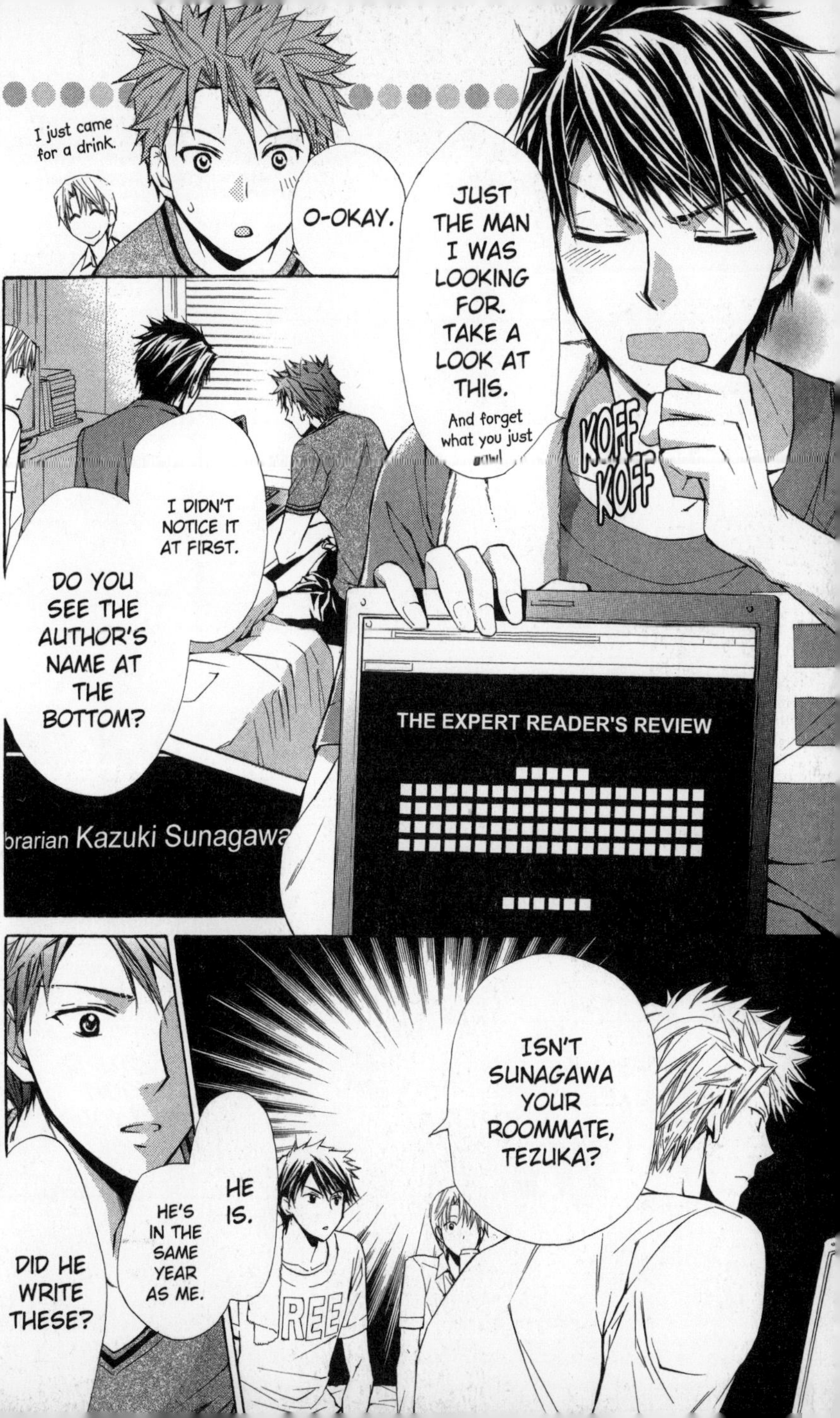
JUST THE MAN I WAS LOOKING FOR. TAKE A LOOK AT THIS.
And forget what you just
KOFF KOFF
O-OKAY.
I just came for a drink.
I DIDN'T NOTICE IT AT FIRST.
DO YOU SEE THE AUTHOR'S NAME AT THE BOTTOM?
THE EXPERT READER'S REVIEW
brarian Kazuki Sunagawa
ISN'T SUNAGAWA YOUR ROOMMATE, TEZUKA?
HE IS.
HE'S IN THE SAME YEAR AS ME.
DID HE WRITE THESE?
REE

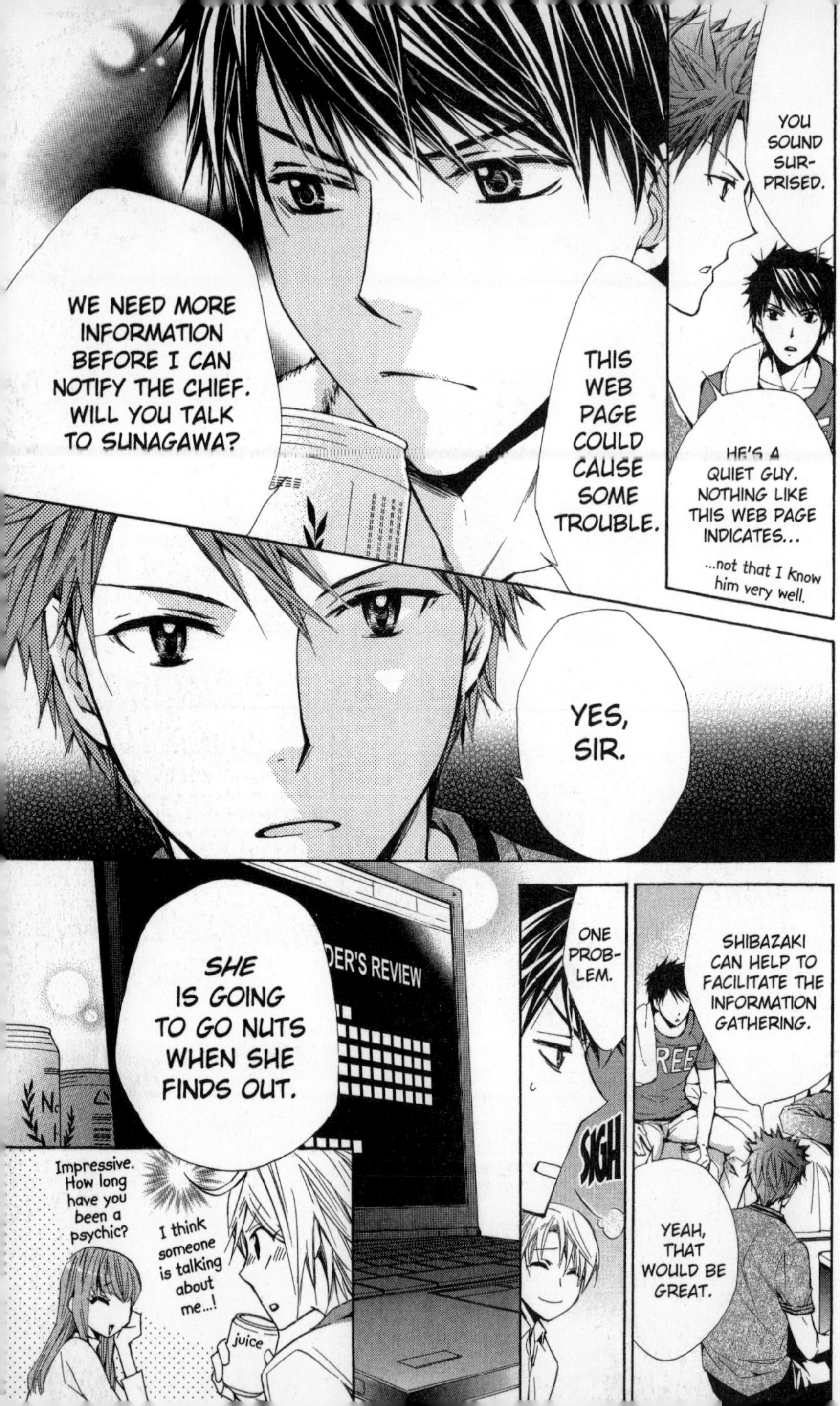
YOU SOUND SUR-PRISED.
HE'S A QUIET GUY. NOTHING LIKE THIS WEB PAGE INDICATES...
...not that I know him very well.
THIS WEB PAGE COULD CAUSE SOME TROUBLE.
WE NEED MORE INFORMATION BEFORE I CAN NOTIFY THE CHIEF. WILL YOU TALK TO SUNAGAWA?
YES, SIR.
SHIBAZAKI CAN HELP TO FACILITATE THE INFORMATION GATHERING.
ONE PROB-LEM.
SIGH
YEAH, THAT WOULD BE GREAT.
SHE IS GOING TO GO NUTS WHEN SHE FINDS OUT.
DER'S REVIEW
I think someone is talking about me...!
Impressive. How long have you been a psychic?
juice

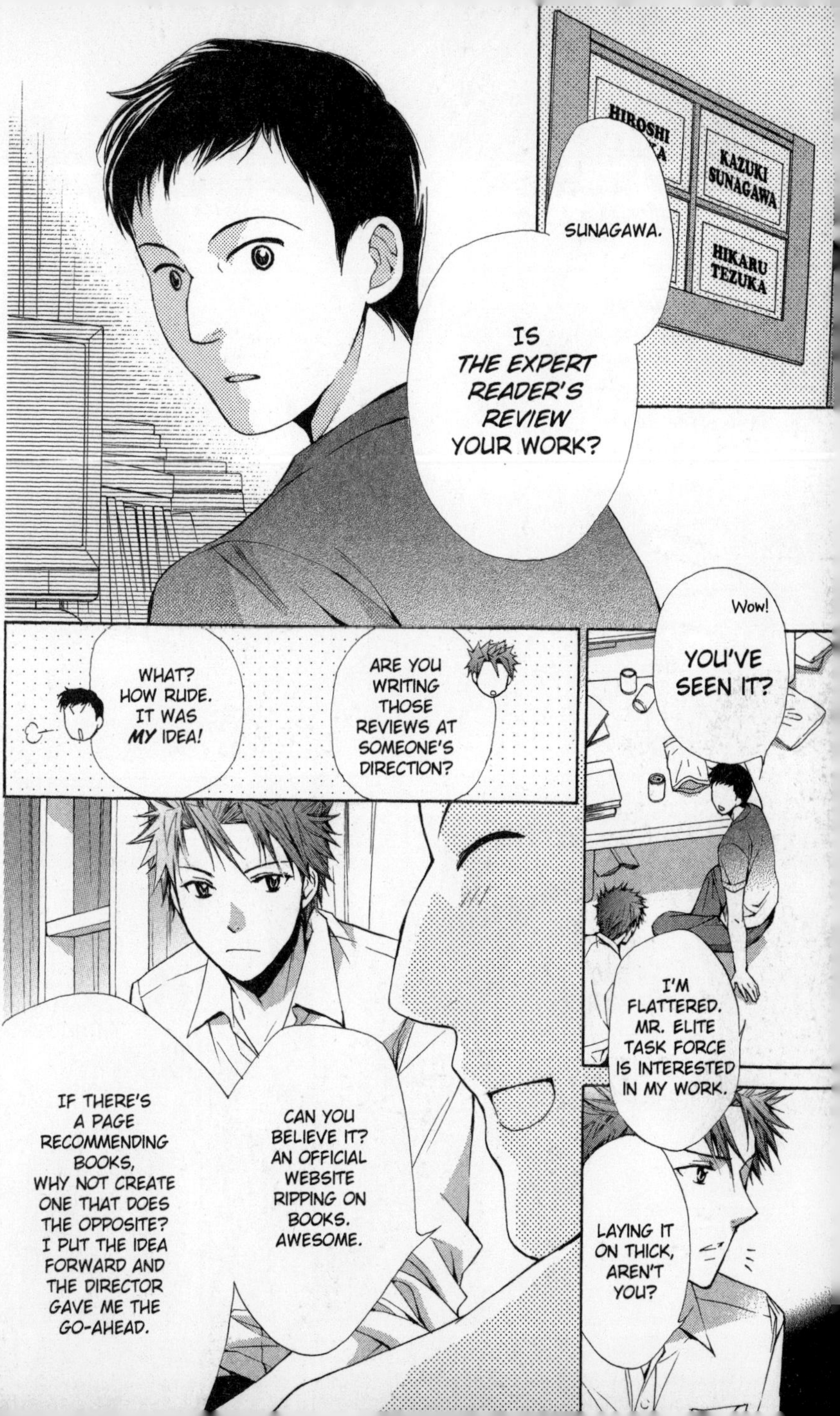
HIROSHI
KAZUKI SUNAGAWA
HIKARU TEZUKA
SUNAGAWA.
IS *THE EXPERT READER'S REVIEW* YOUR WORK?
Wow!
YOU'VE SEEN IT?
I'M FLATTERED. MR. ELITE TASK FORCE IS INTERESTED IN MY WORK.
LAYING IT ON THICK, AREN'T YOU?
ARE YOU WRITING THOSE REVIEWS AT SOMEONE'S DIRECTION?
WHAT? HOW RUDE. IT WAS *MY* IDEA!
CAN YOU BELIEVE IT? AN OFFICIAL WEBSITE RIPPING ON BOOKS. AWESOME.
IF THERE'S A PAGE RECOMMENDING BOOKS, WHY NOT CREATE ONE THAT DOES THE OPPOSITE? I PUT THE IDEA FORWARD AND THE DIRECTOR GAVE ME THE GO-AHEAD.

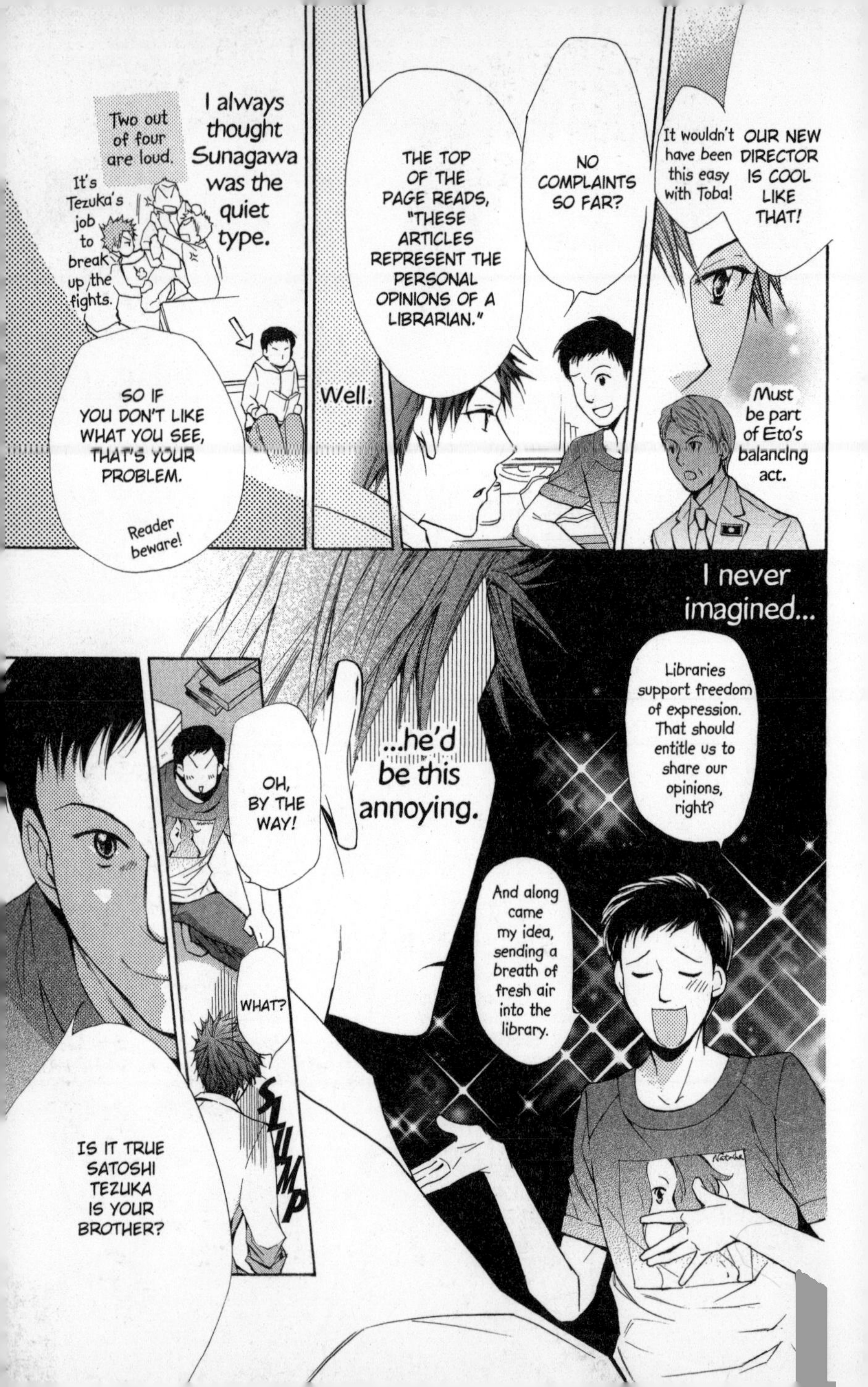
OUR NEW DIRECTOR IS COOL LIKE THAT!
It wouldn't have been this easy with Toba!
Must be part of Eto's balancing act.
NO COMPLAINTS SO FAR?
THE TOP OF THE PAGE READS, "THESE ARTICLES REPRESENT THE PERSONAL OPINIONS OF A LIBRARIAN."
Well.
I always thought Sunagawa was the quiet type.
Two out of four are loud.
It's Tezuka's job to break up the fights.
SO IF YOU DON'T LIKE WHAT YOU SEE, THAT'S YOUR PROBLEM.
Reader beware!
I never imagined...
Libraries support freedom of expression. That should entitle us to share our opinions, right?
And along came my idea, sending a breath of fresh air into the library.
...he'd be this annoying.
OH, BY THE WAY!
WHAT?
SLUMP
IS IT TRUE SATOSHI TEZUKA IS YOUR BROTHER?

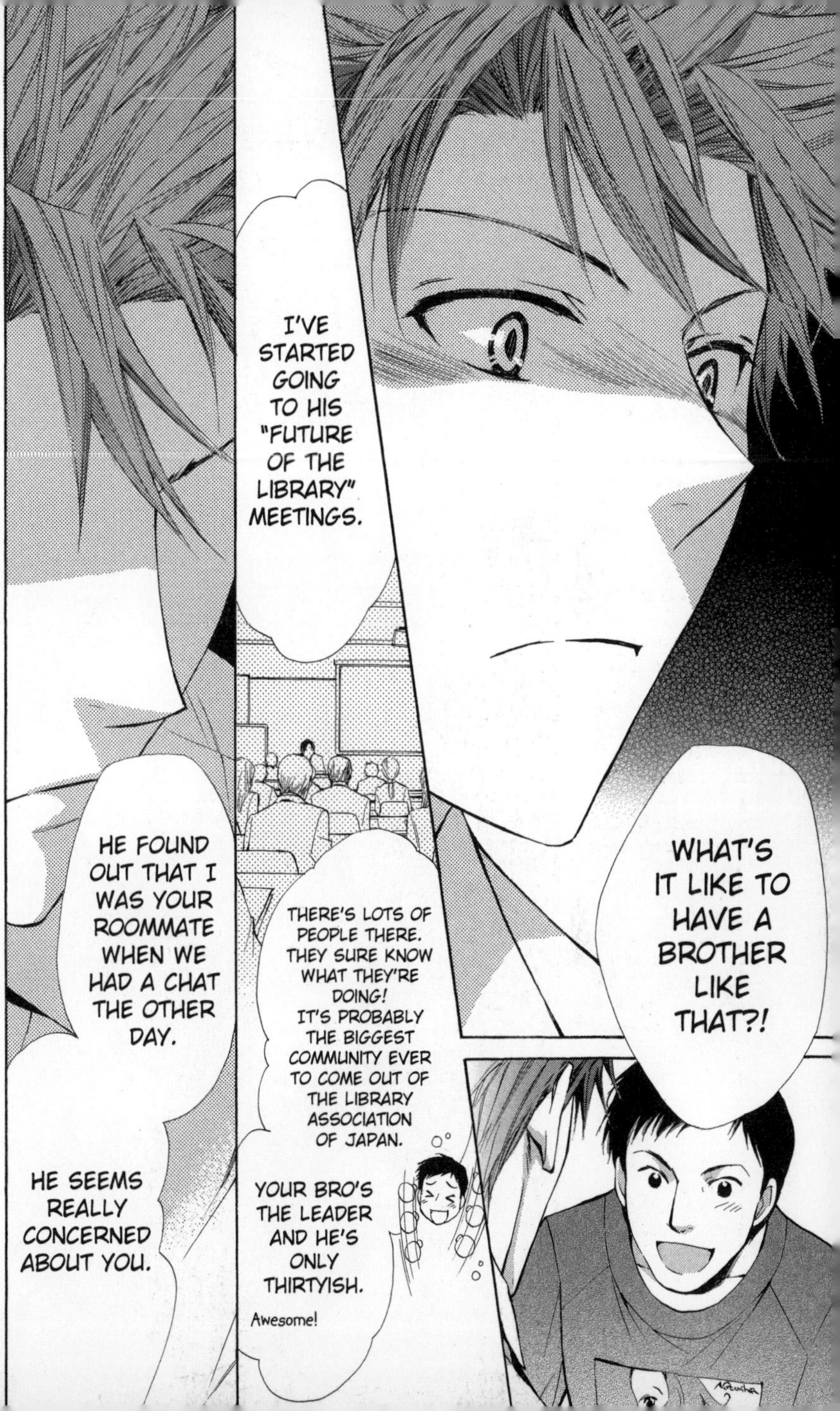
I'VE STARTED GOING TO HIS "FUTURE OF THE LIBRARY" MEETINGS.
THERE'S LOTS OF PEOPLE THERE. THEY SURE KNOW WHAT THEY'RE DOING! IT'S PROBABLY THE BIGGEST COMMUNITY EVER TO COME OUT OF THE LIBRARY ASSOCIATION OF JAPAN.
YOUR BRO'S THE LEADER AND HE'S ONLY THIRTYISH.
Awesome!
WHAT'S IT LIKE TO HAVE A BROTHER LIKE THAT?!
HE FOUND OUT THAT I WAS YOUR ROOMMATE WHEN WE HAD A CHAT THE OTHER DAY.
HE SEEMS REALLY CONCERNED ABOUT YOU.

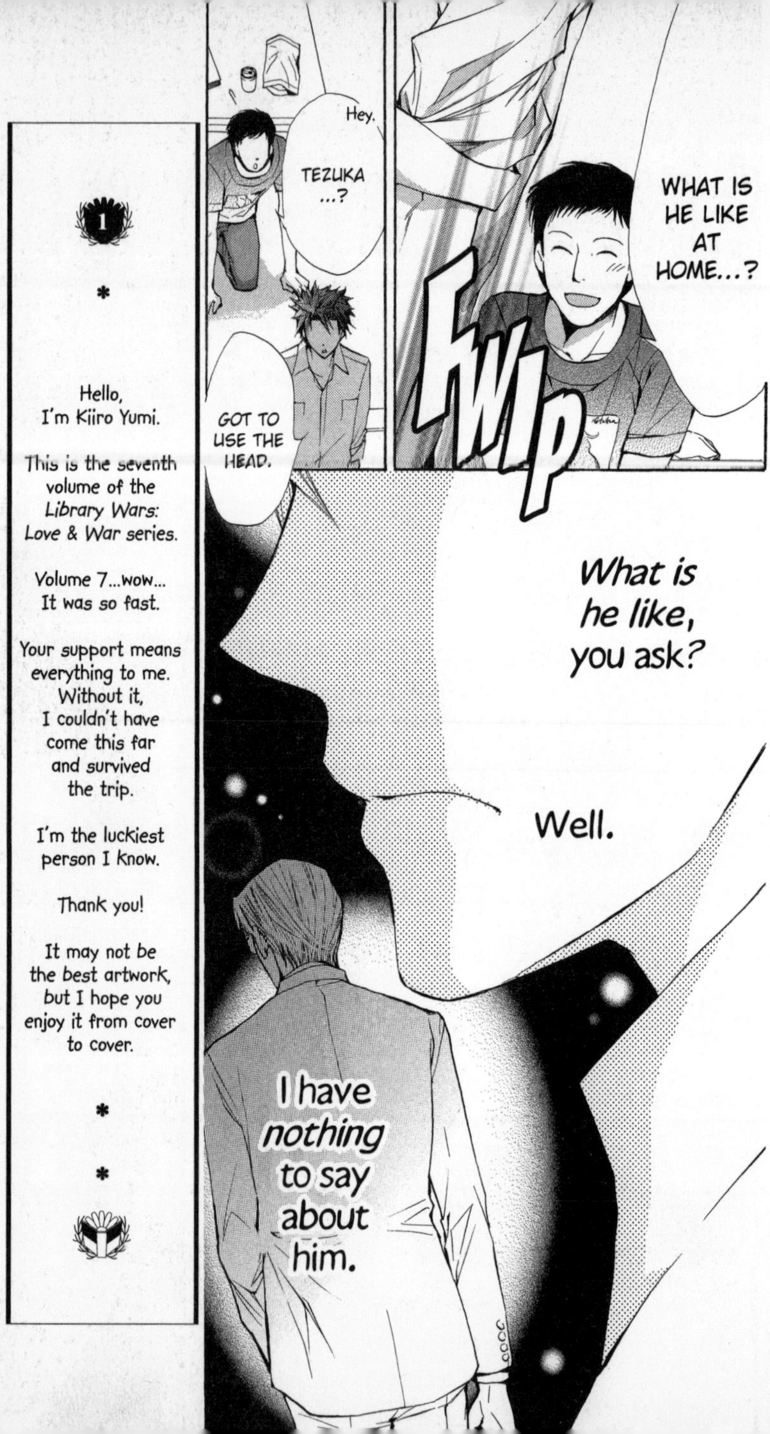
WHAT IS HE LIKE AT HOME...?
FWIP
Hey.
TEZUKA ...?
GOT TO USE THE HEAD.
What is he like, you ask?
Well.
I have *nothing* to say about him.

1

*

Hello,
I'm Kiiro Yumi.

This is the seventh volume of the *Library Wars: Love & War* series.

Volume 7...wow... It was so fast.

Your support means everything to me. Without it, I couldn't have come this far and survived the trip.

I'm the luckiest person I know.

Thank you!

It may not be the best artwork, but I hope you enjoy it from cover to cover.

*

*

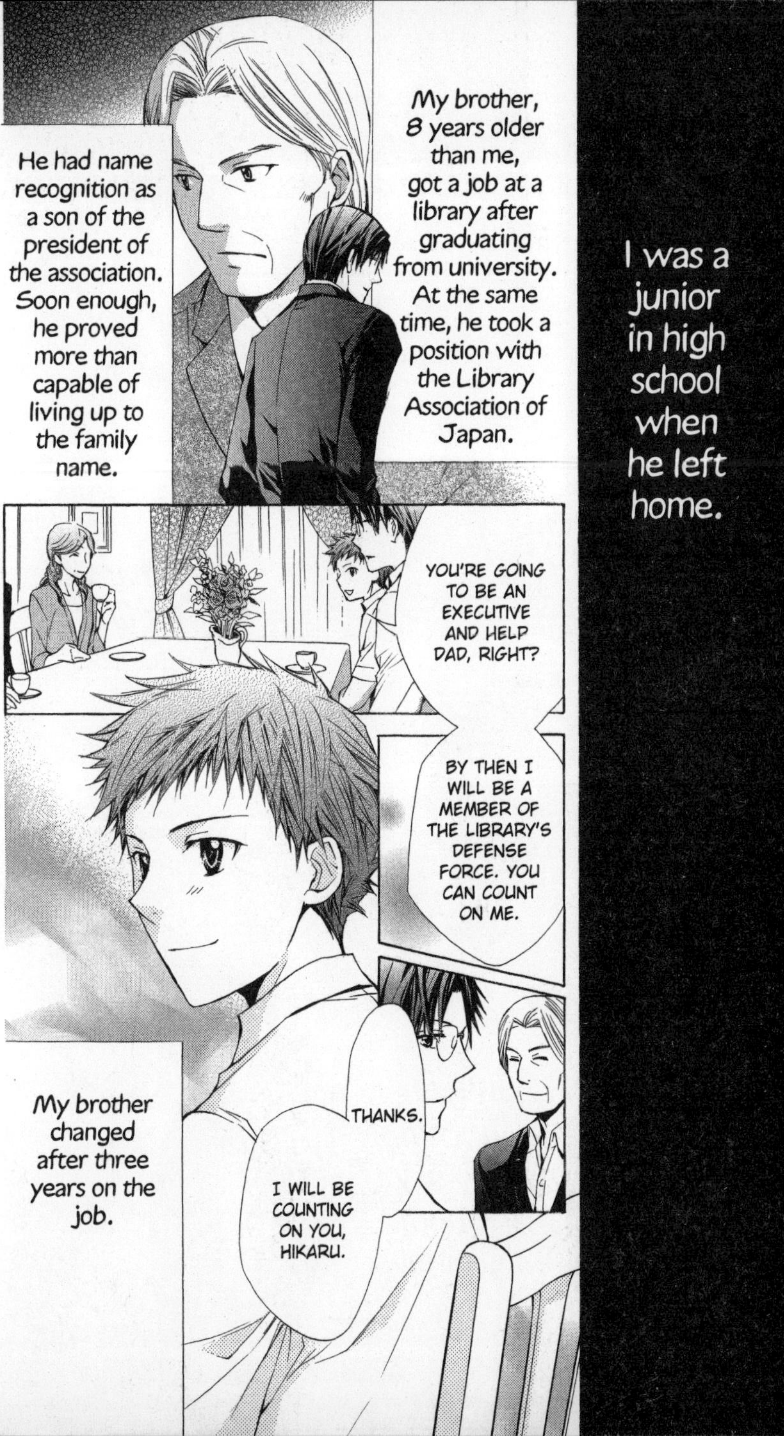
I was a junior in high school when he left home.
My brother, 8 years older than me, got a job at a library after graduating from university. At the same time, he took a position with the Library Association of Japan.
He had name recognition as a son of the president of the association. Soon enough, he proved more than capable of living up to the family name.
YOU'RE GOING TO BE AN EXECUTIVE AND HELP DAD, RIGHT?
BY THEN I WILL BE A MEMBER OF THE LIBRARY'S DEFENSE FORCE. YOU CAN COUNT ON ME.
THANKS.
I WILL BE COUNTING ON YOU, HIKARU.
My brother changed after three years on the job.

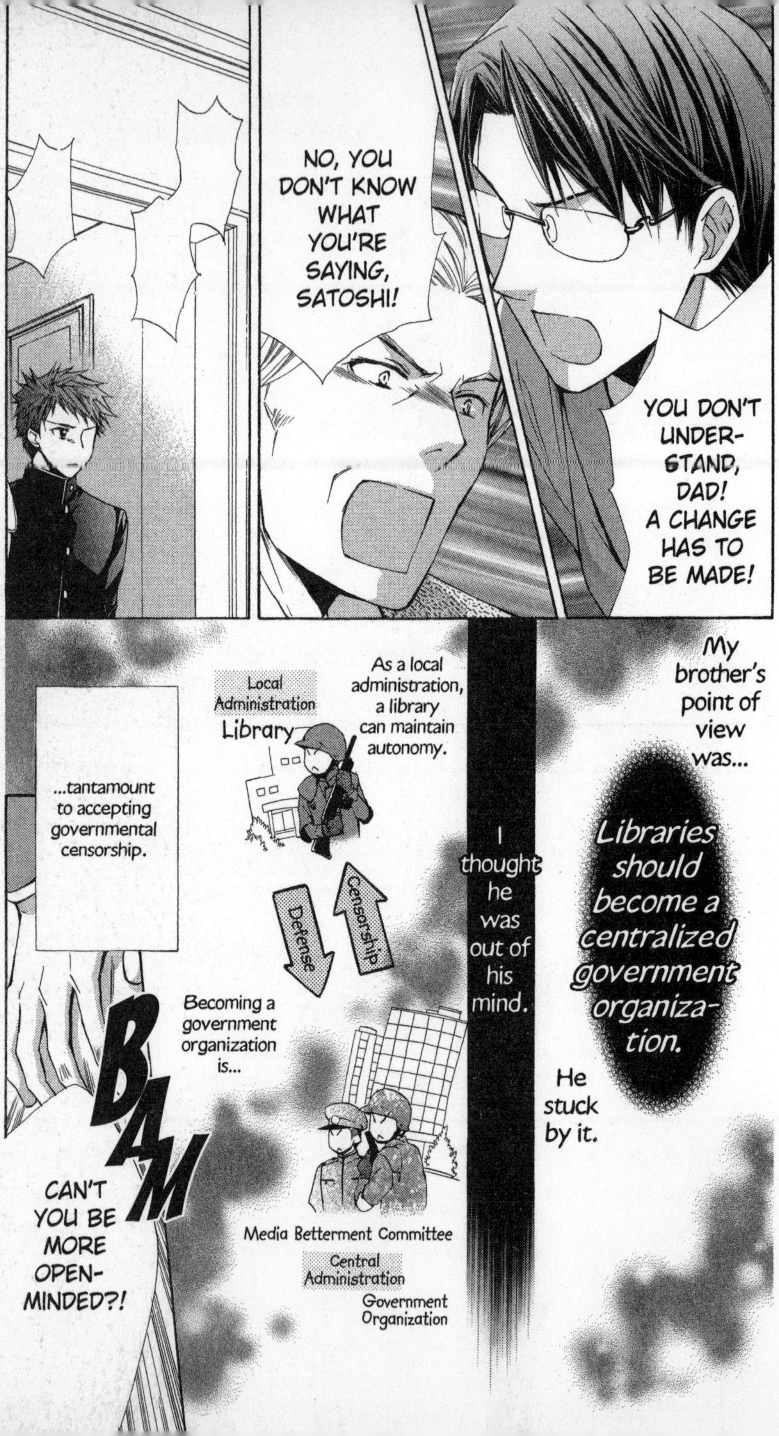
YOU DON'T UNDER-STAND, DAD! A CHANGE HAS TO BE MADE!
NO, YOU DON'T KNOW WHAT YOU'RE SAYING, SATOSHI!
My brother's point of view was...
Libraries should become a centralized government organiza-tion.
He stuck by it.
I thought he was out of his mind.
As a local administration, a library can maintain autonomy.
Local Administration
Library
Censorship
Defense
Becoming a government organization is...
Media Betterment Committee
Central Administration
Government Organization
...tantamount to accepting governmental censorship.
BAM
CAN'T YOU BE MORE OPEN-MINDED?!

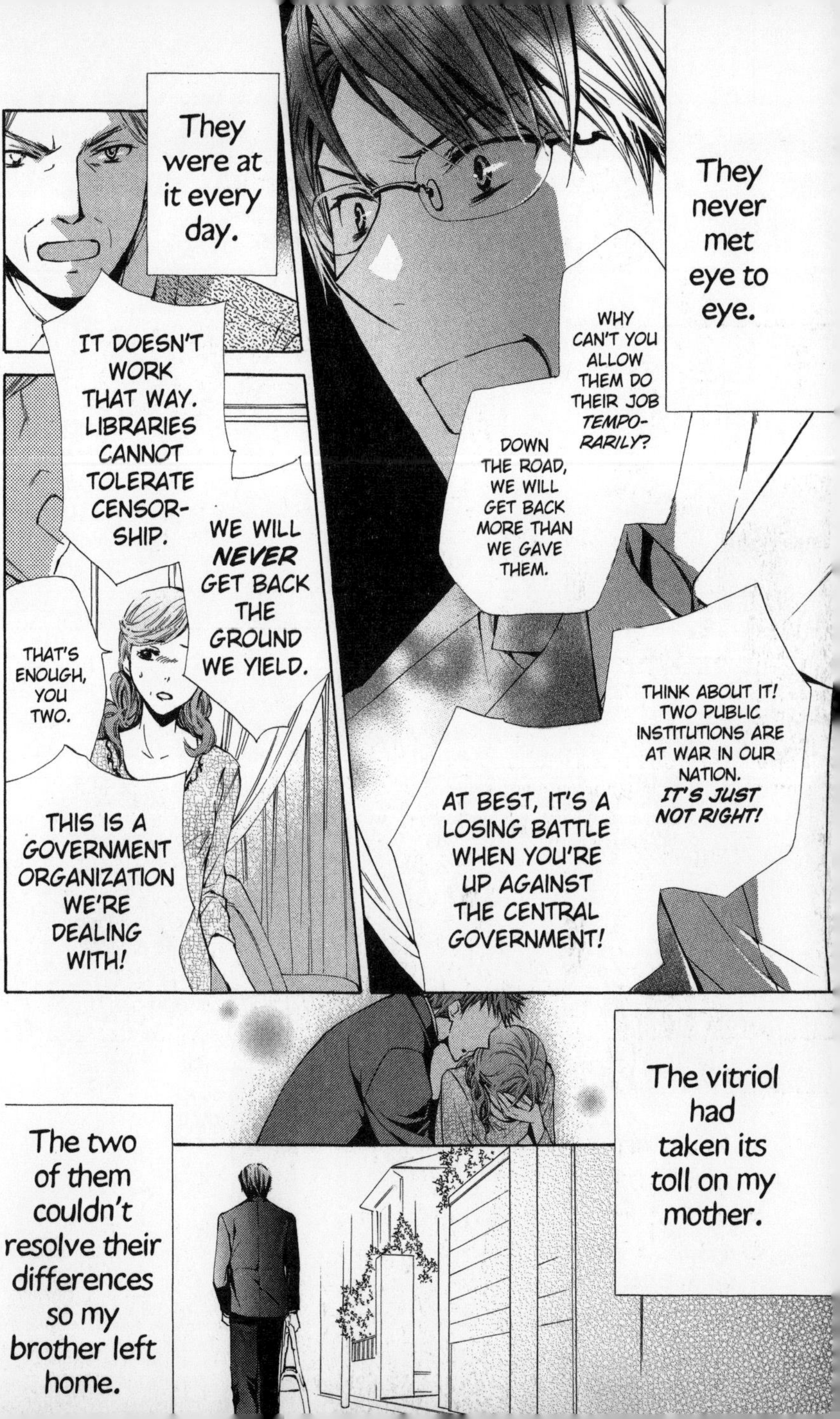
They never met eye to eye.
WHY CAN'T YOU ALLOW THEM DO THEIR JOB *TEMPO-RARILY?*
DOWN THE ROAD, WE WILL GET BACK MORE THAN WE GAVE THEM.
THINK ABOUT IT! TWO PUBLIC INSTITUTIONS ARE AT WAR IN OUR NATION. *IT'S JUST NOT RIGHT!*
AT BEST, IT'S A LOSING BATTLE WHEN YOU'RE UP AGAINST THE CENTRAL GOVERNMENT!
They were at it every day.
IT DOESN'T WORK THAT WAY. LIBRARIES CANNOT TOLERATE CENSOR-SHIP.
WE WILL ***NEVER*** GET BACK THE GROUND WE YIELD.
THAT'S ENOUGH, YOU TWO.
THIS IS A GOVERNMENT ORGANIZATION WE'RE DEALING WITH!
The vitriol had taken its toll on my mother.
The two of them couldn't resolve their differences so my brother left home.

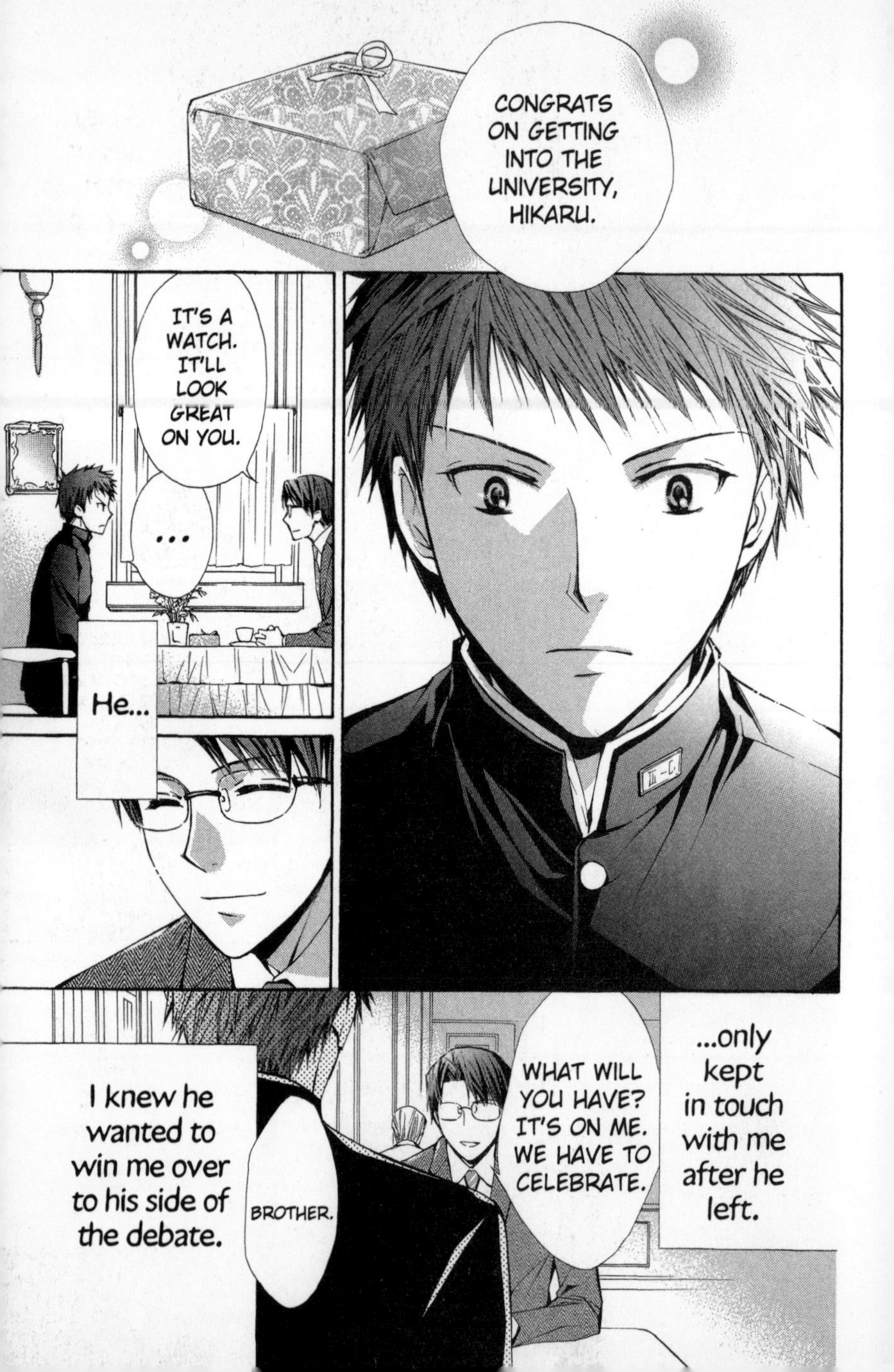
CONGRATS ON GETTING INTO THE UNIVERSITY, HIKARU.
IT'S A WATCH. IT'LL LOOK GREAT ON YOU.
...
He...
...only kept in touch with me after he left.
WHAT WILL YOU HAVE? IT'S ON ME. WE HAVE TO CELEBRATE.
BROTHER.
I knew he wanted to win me over to his side of the debate.

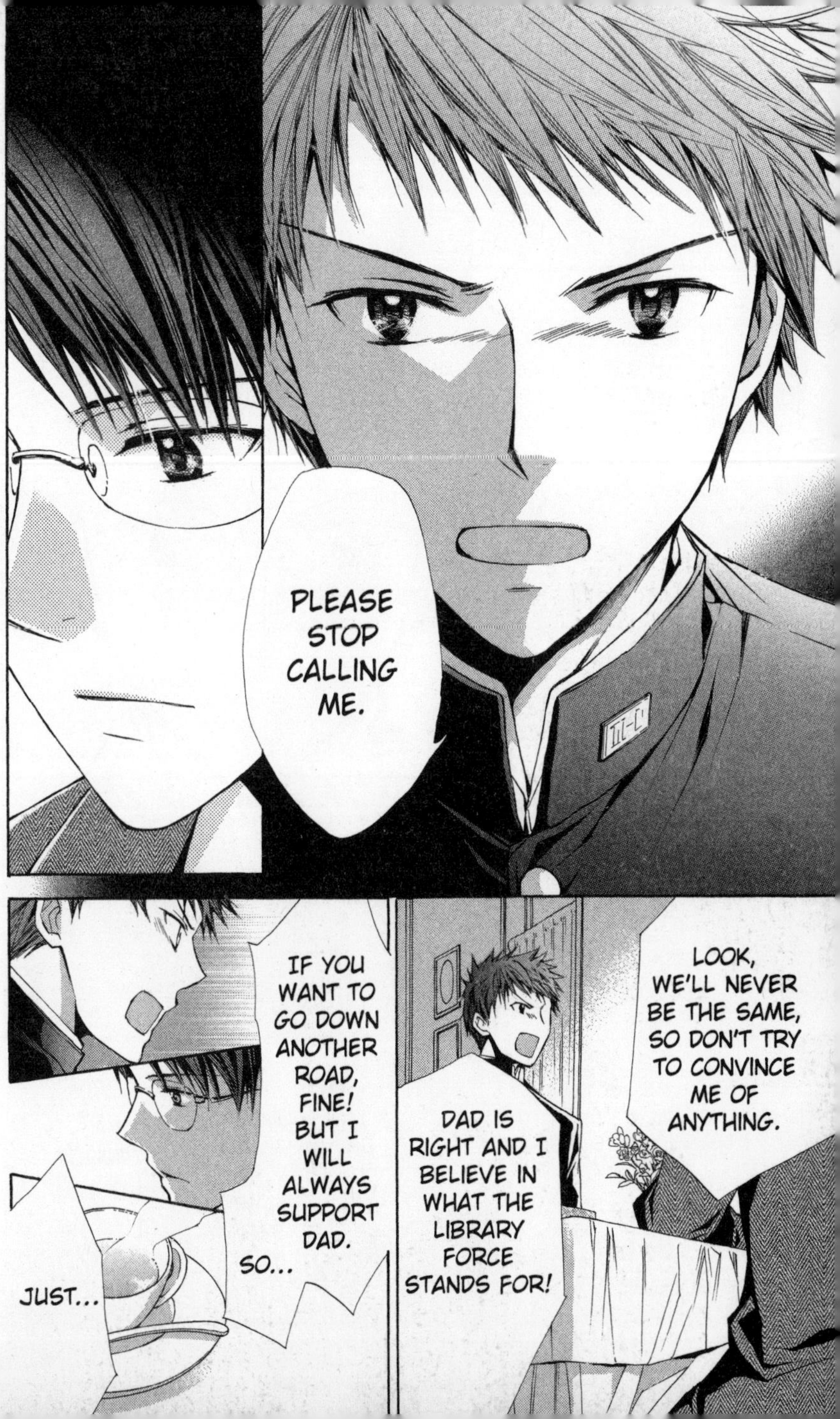
PLEASE STOP CALLING ME.
LOOK, WE'LL NEVER BE THE SAME, SO DON'T TRY TO CONVINCE ME OF ANYTHING.
DAD IS RIGHT AND I BELIEVE IN WHAT THE LIBRARY FORCE STANDS FOR!
IF YOU WANT TO GO DOWN ANOTHER ROAD, FINE! BUT I WILL ALWAYS SUPPORT DAD.
SO...
JUST...

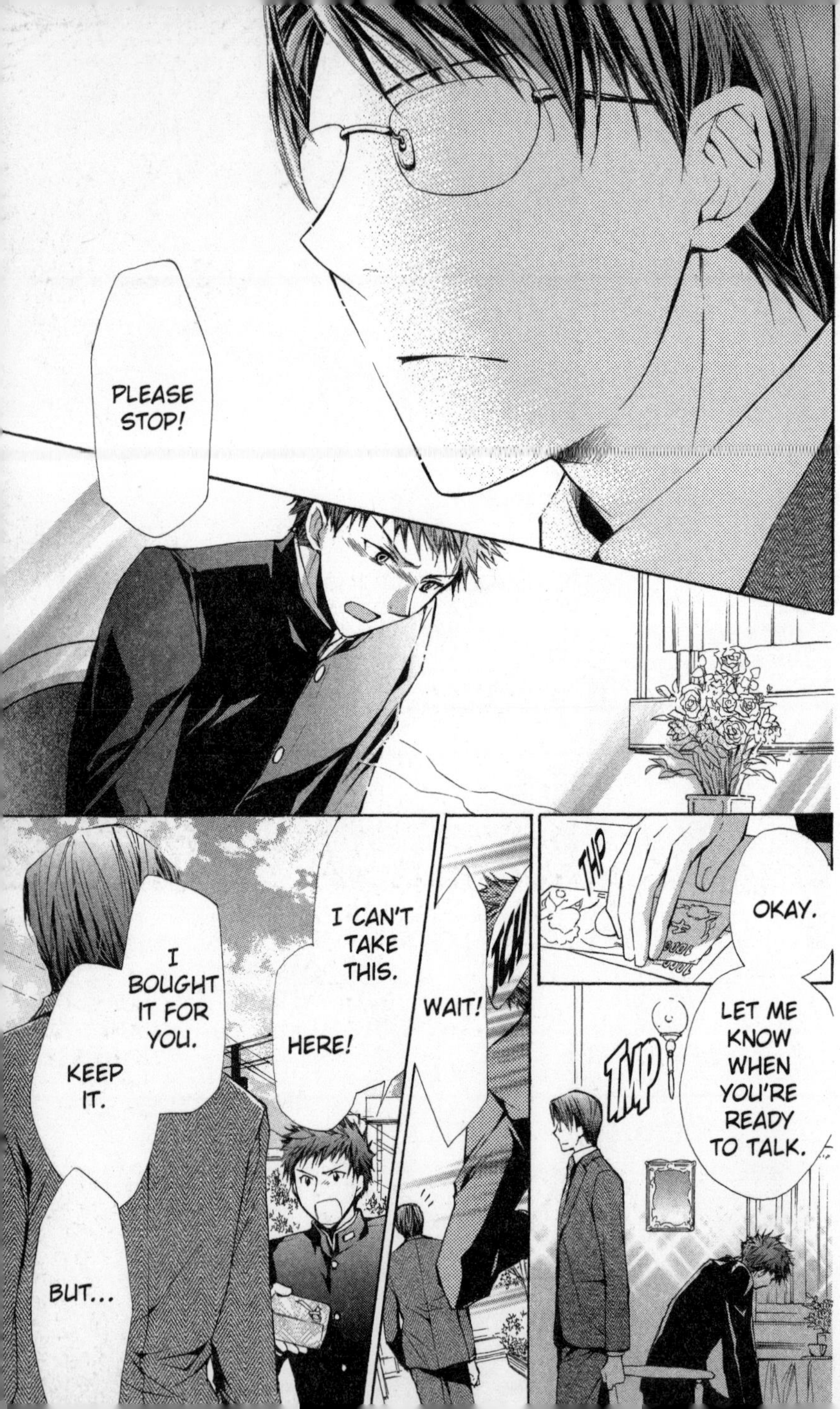
PLEASE STOP!
THP
OKAY.
TMP
LET ME KNOW WHEN YOU'RE READY TO TALK.
WAIT!
I CAN'T TAKE THIS.
HERE!
I BOUGHT IT FOR YOU.
KEEP IT.
BUT...

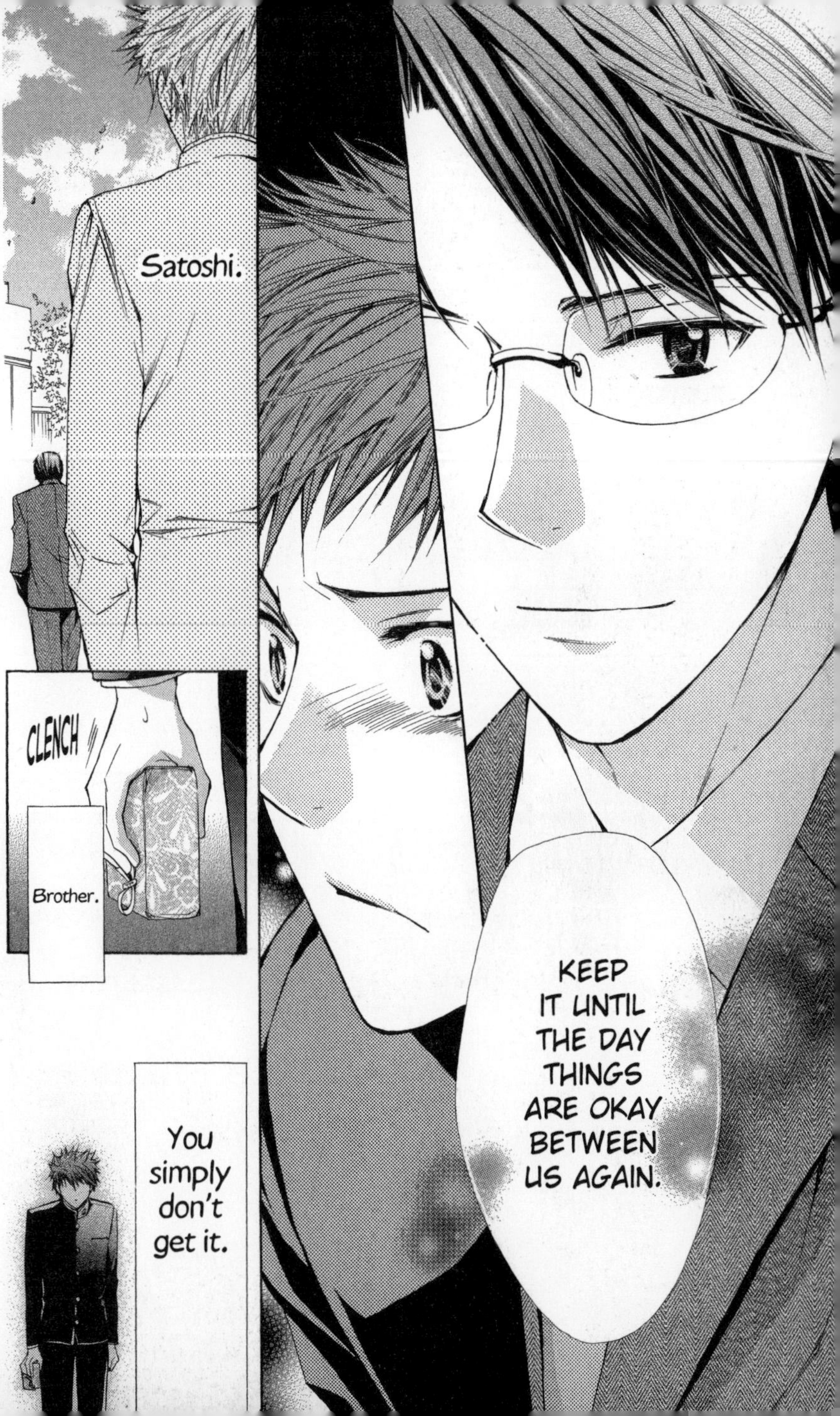
KEEP IT UNTIL THE DAY THINGS ARE OKAY BETWEEN US AGAIN.
Satoshi.
CLENCH
Brother.
You simply don't get it.

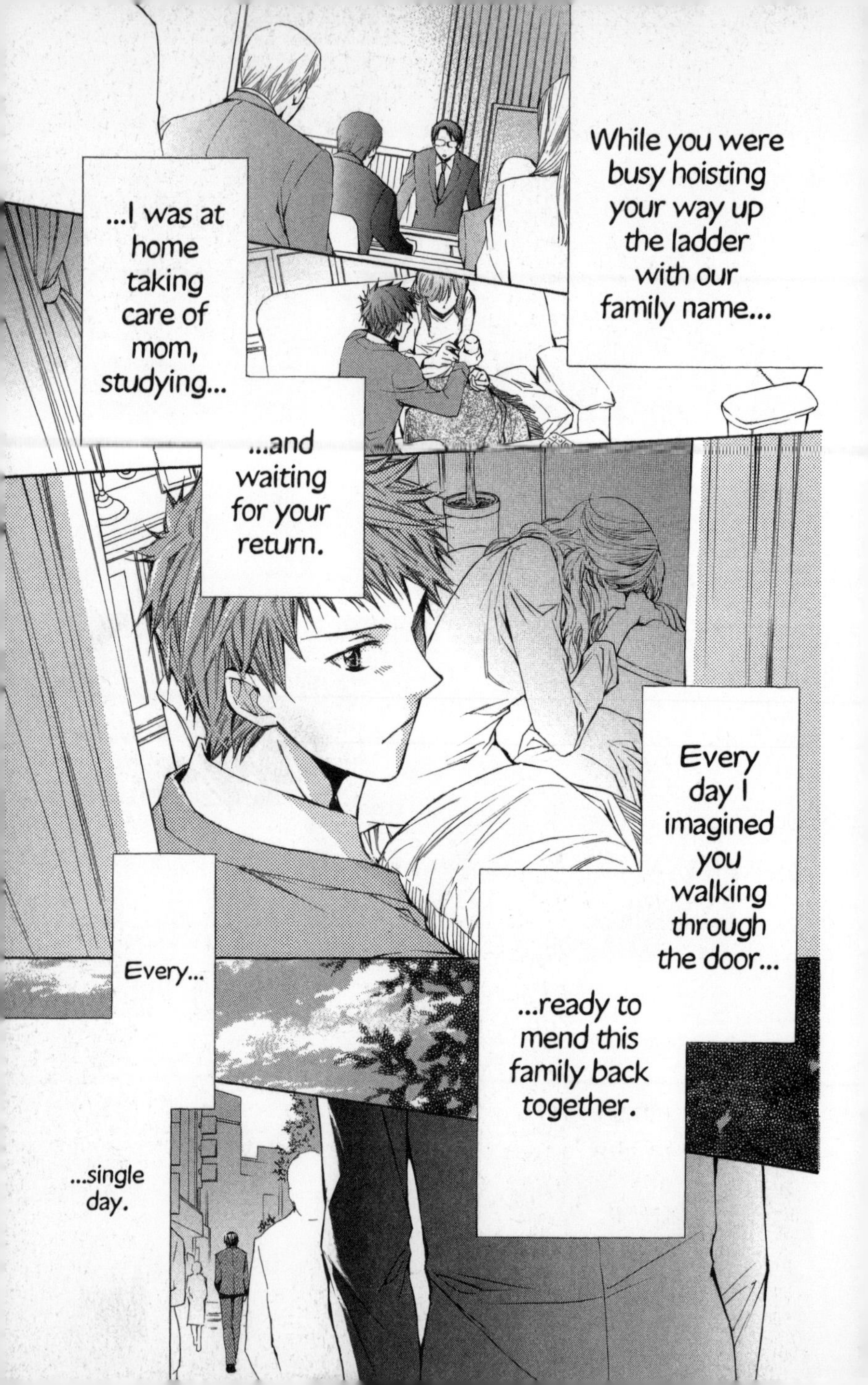
While you were busy hoisting your way up the ladder with our family name...
...I was at home taking care of mom, studying...
...and waiting for your return.
Every day I imagined you walking through the door...
...ready to mend this family back together.
Every...
...single day.

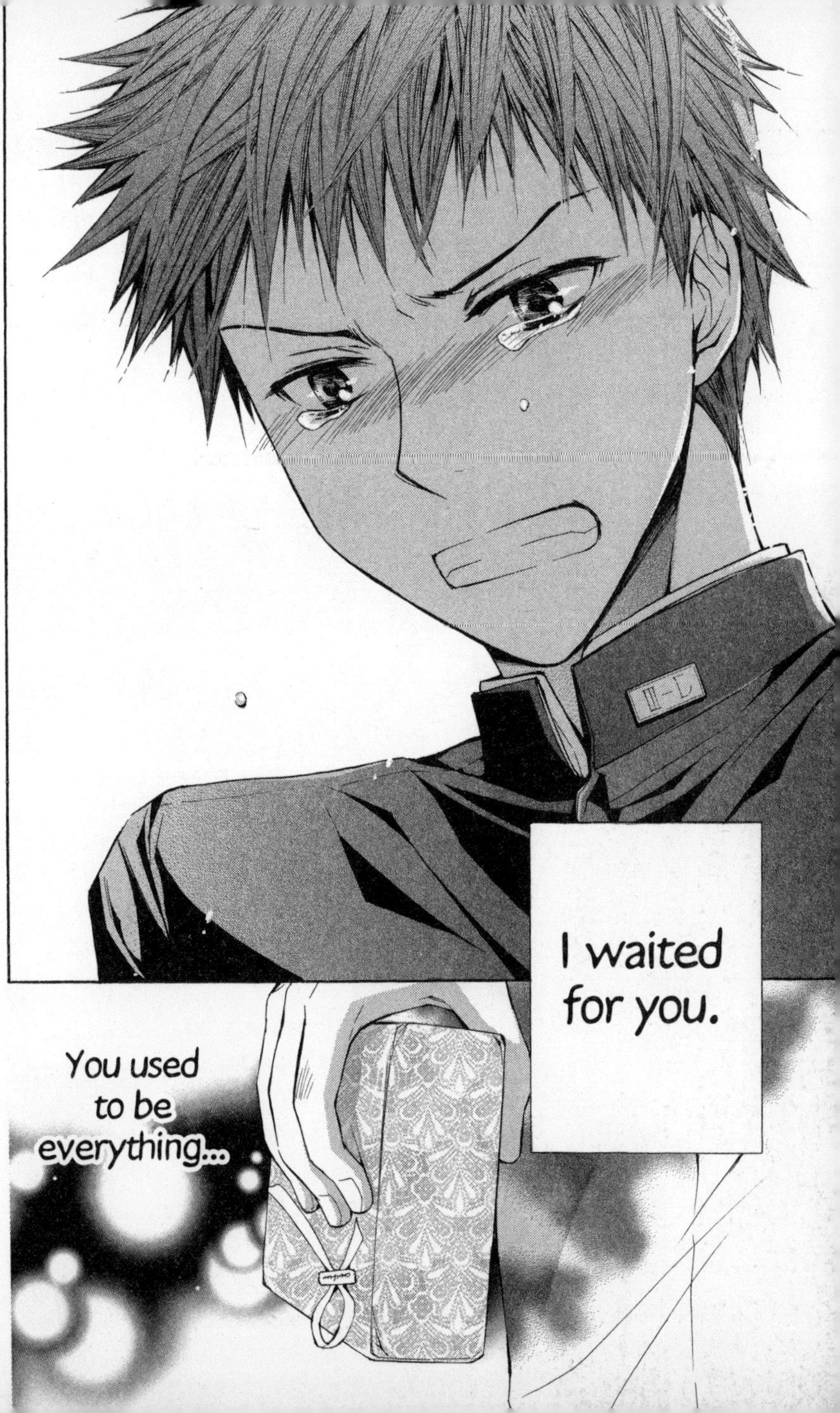
I waited for you.
You used to be everything...

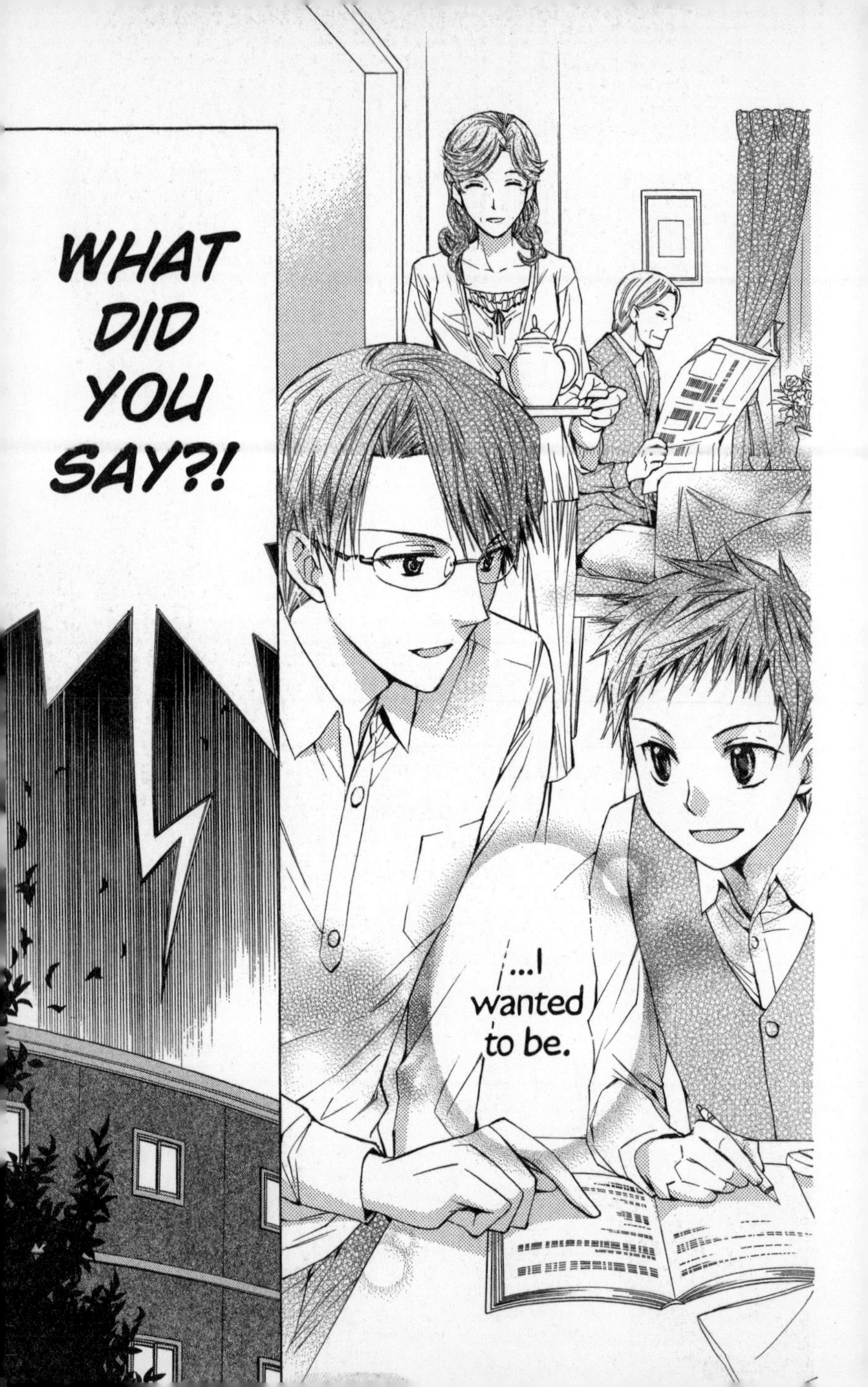
...I wanted to be.
WHAT DID YOU SAY?!

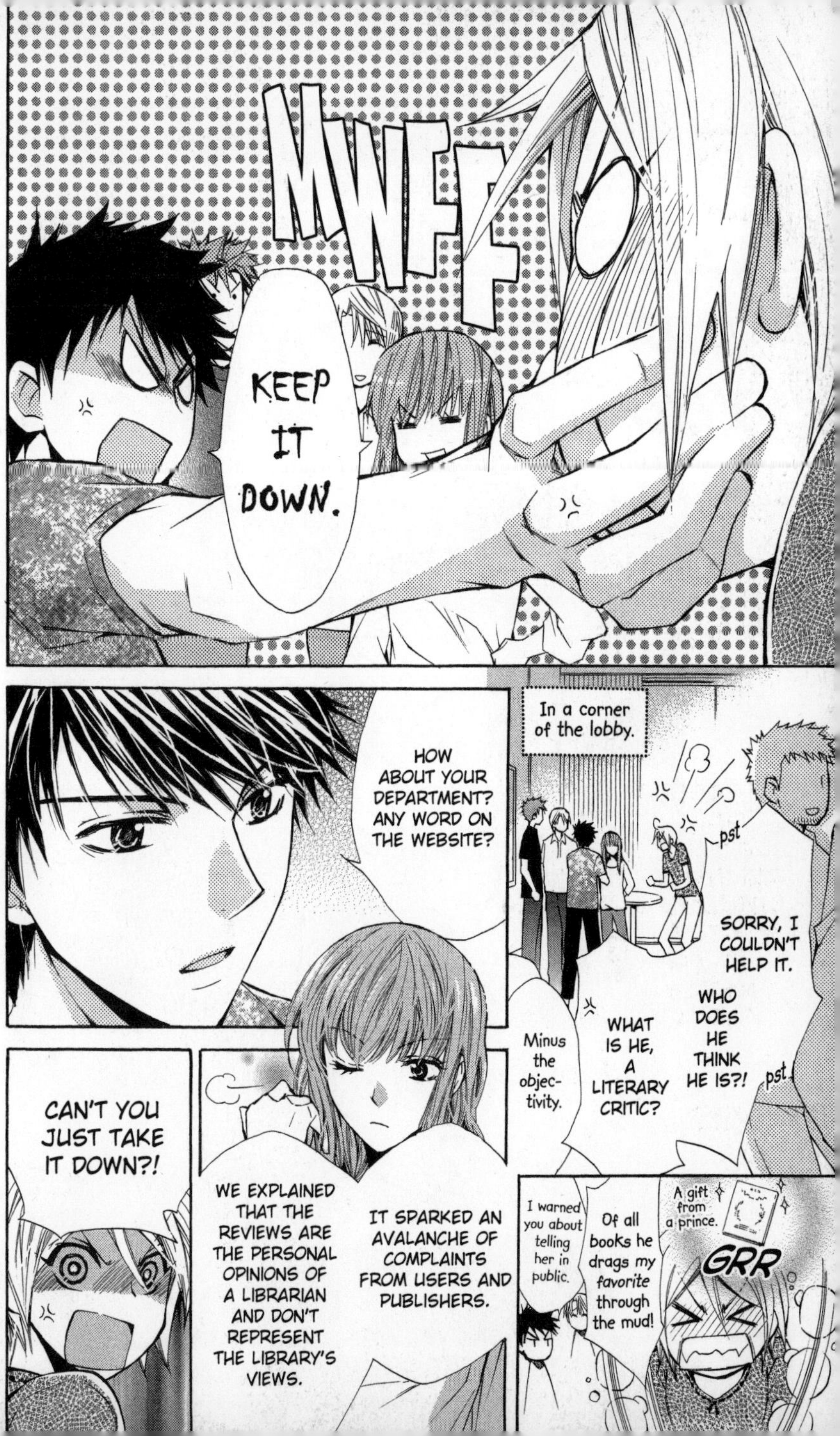
MWFF
KEEP IT DOWN.
In a corner of the lobby.
pst
SORRY, I COULDN'T HELP IT.
WHO DOES HE THINK HE IS?!
pst
WHAT IS HE, A LITERARY CRITIC?
Minus the objectivity.
A gift from a prince.
GRR
Of all books he drags my favorite through the mud!
I warned you about telling her in public.
HOW ABOUT YOUR DEPARTMENT? ANY WORD ON THE WEBSITE?
WE EXPLAINED THAT THE REVIEWS ARE THE PERSONAL OPINIONS OF A LIBRARIAN AND DON'T REPRESENT THE LIBRARY'S VIEWS.
IT SPARKED AN AVALANCHE OF COMPLAINTS FROM USERS AND PUBLISHERS.
CAN'T YOU JUST TAKE IT DOWN?!

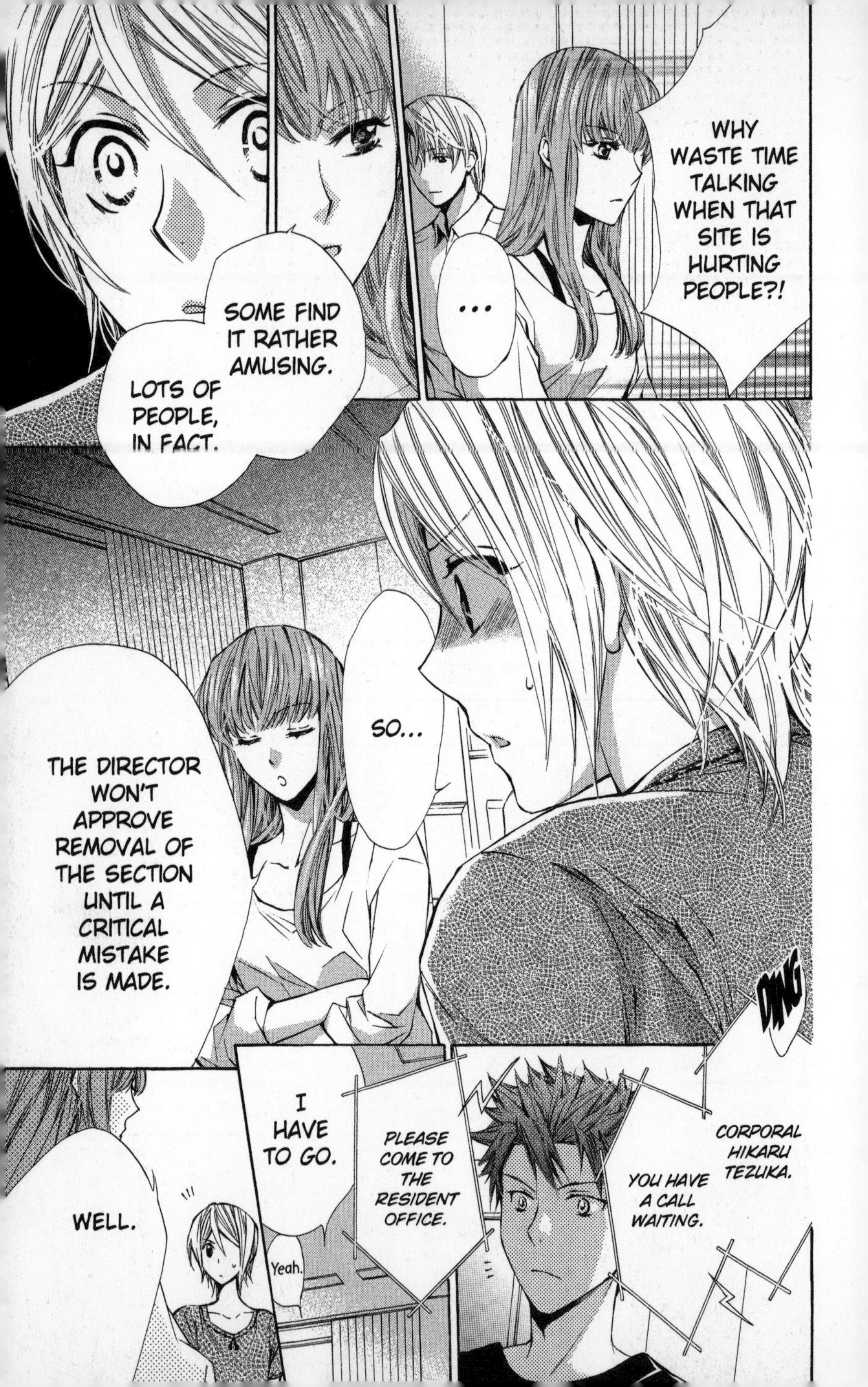
WHY WASTE TIME TALKING WHEN THAT SITE IS HURTING PEOPLE?!
...
SOME FIND IT RATHER AMUSING.
LOTS OF PEOPLE, IN FACT.
SO...
THE DIRECTOR WON'T APPROVE REMOVAL OF THE SECTION UNTIL A CRITICAL MISTAKE IS MADE.
DING
CORPORAL HIKARU TEZUKA.
YOU HAVE A CALL WAITING.
PLEASE COME TO THE RESIDENT OFFICE.
I HAVE TO GO.
WELL.
Yeah.

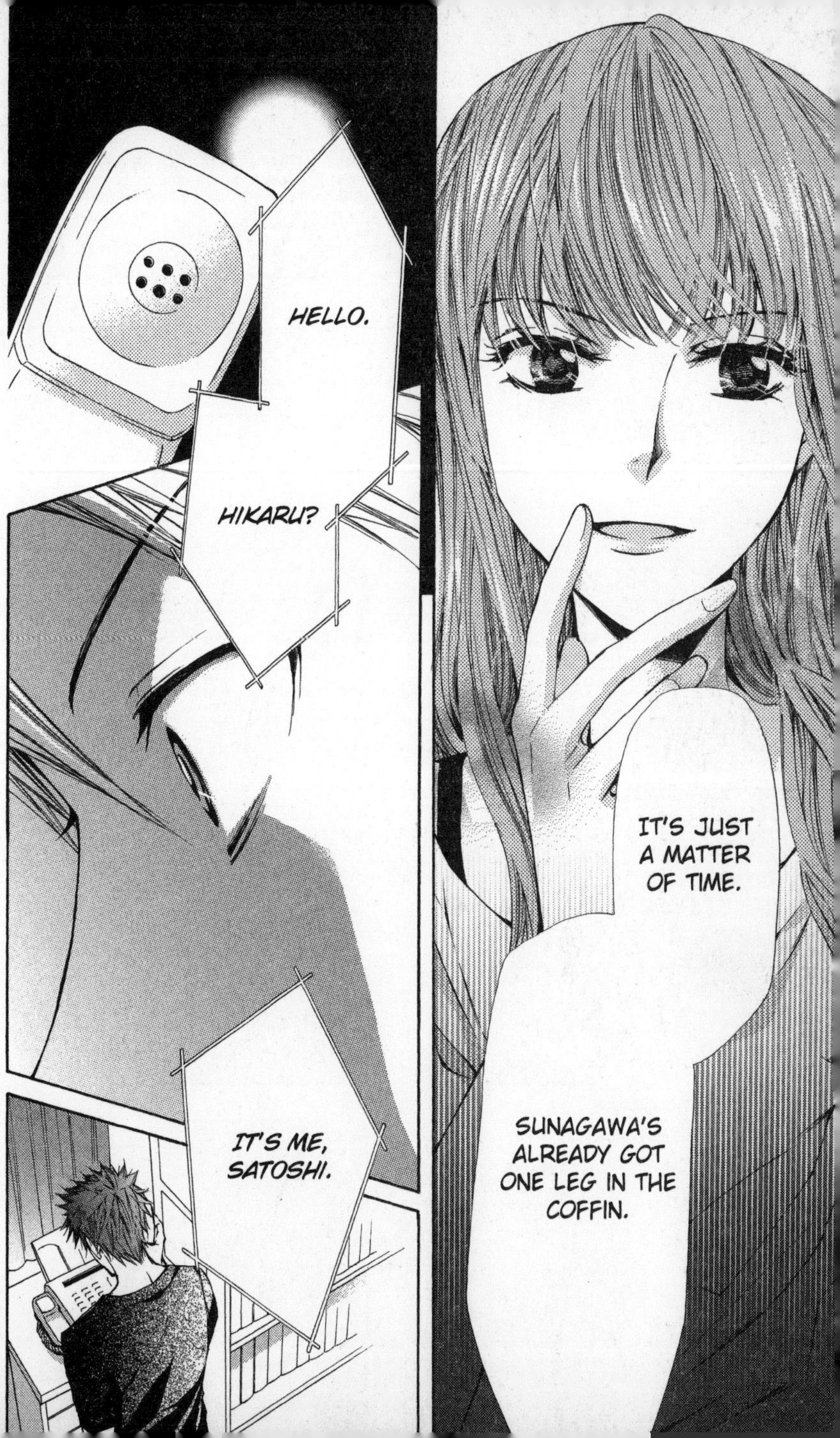
IT'S JUST A MATTER OF TIME.
SUNAGAWA'S ALREADY GOT ONE LEG IN THE COFFIN.
HELLO.
HIKARU?
IT'S ME, SATOSHI.

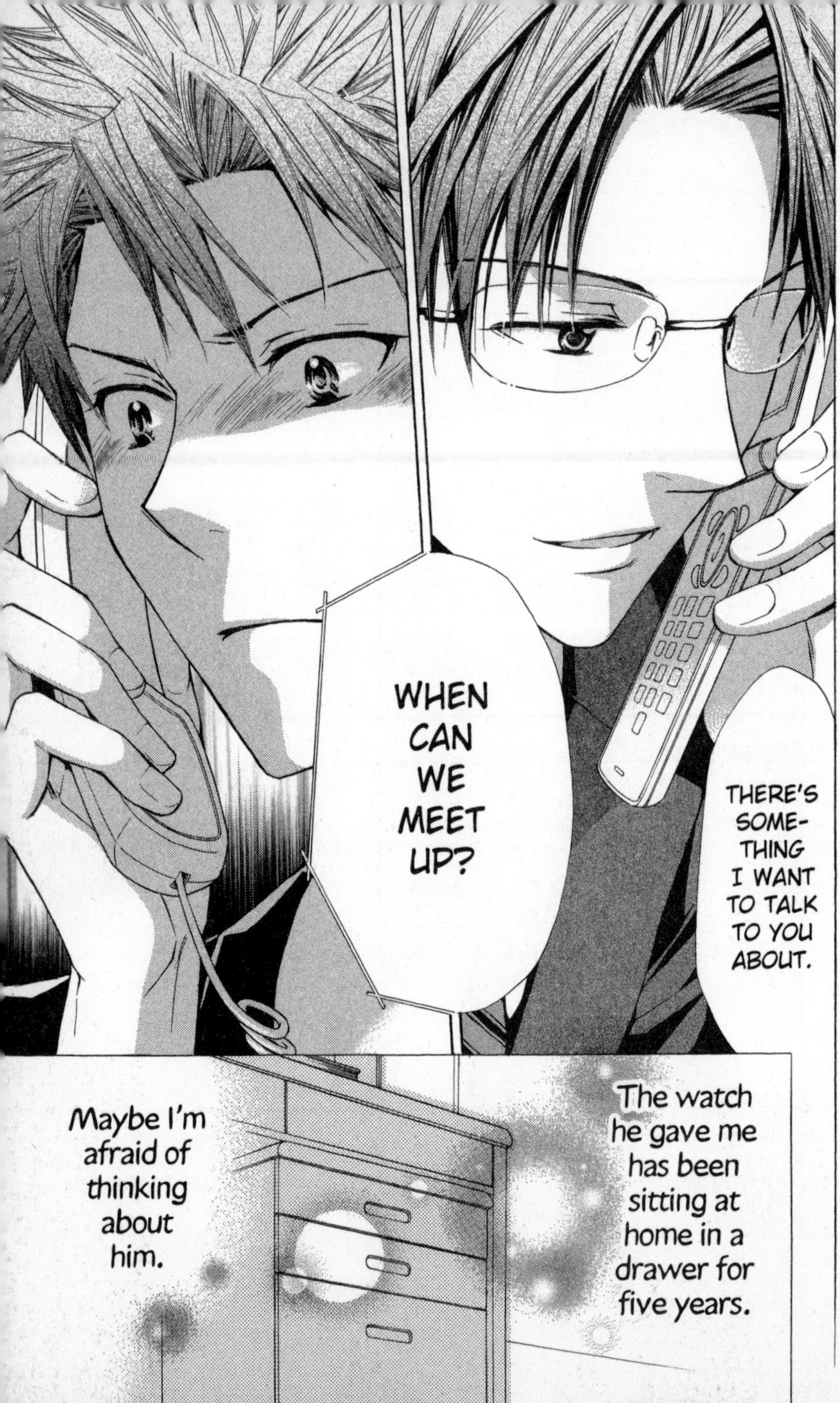
THERE'S SOME-THING I WANT TO TALK TO YOU ABOUT.
WHEN CAN WE MEET UP?
The watch he gave me has been sitting at home in a drawer for five years.
Maybe I'm afraid of thinking about him.

Haunting Memory of the Boss

Reporting on Sunagawa
What did he say?
He said the idea was his, not an order.
He thought it would spice things up.
What about the aggres-sive tone he uses?
A warning is posted at the top of the page.
Viewers are advised to use discretion. So it's their responsibility if they get offended, according to him.
WHROOSH
...?
...
Is that so...?
What is he, a literary critic?
Can't you just take it down?!
Tezuka knows Iku's desire for revenge can be fulfilled if he unleashes Komaki upon Sunagawa.
...
But he can't bring himself to do it.
Some find it rather amusing.

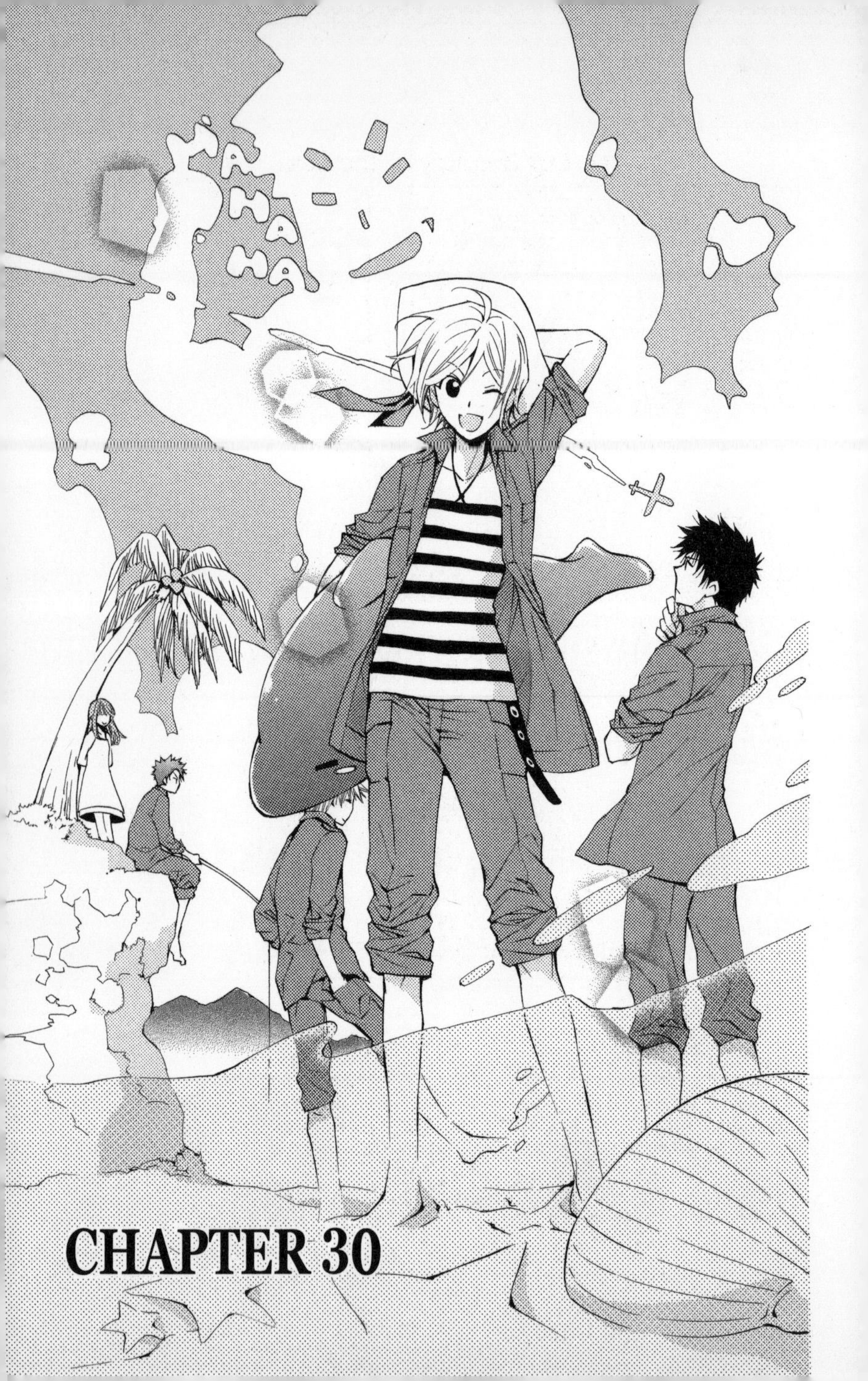

HA HA HA

CHAPTER 30

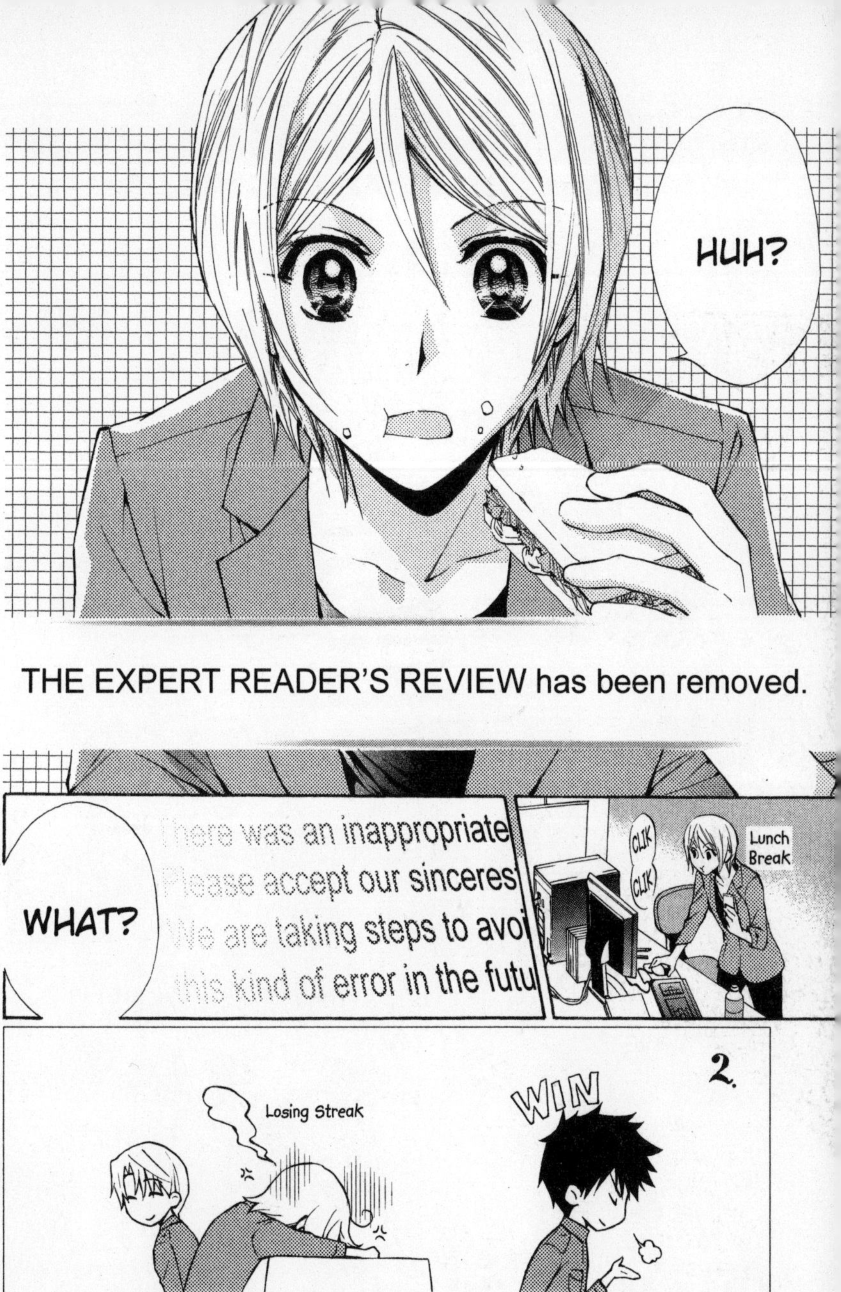
HUH?
THE EXPERT READER'S REVIEW has been removed.
CLIK
CLIK
Lunch Break
WHAT?
There was an inappropriate
Please accept our sinceres
We are taking steps to avoi
this kind of error in the futu
2.
WIN
Losing Streak

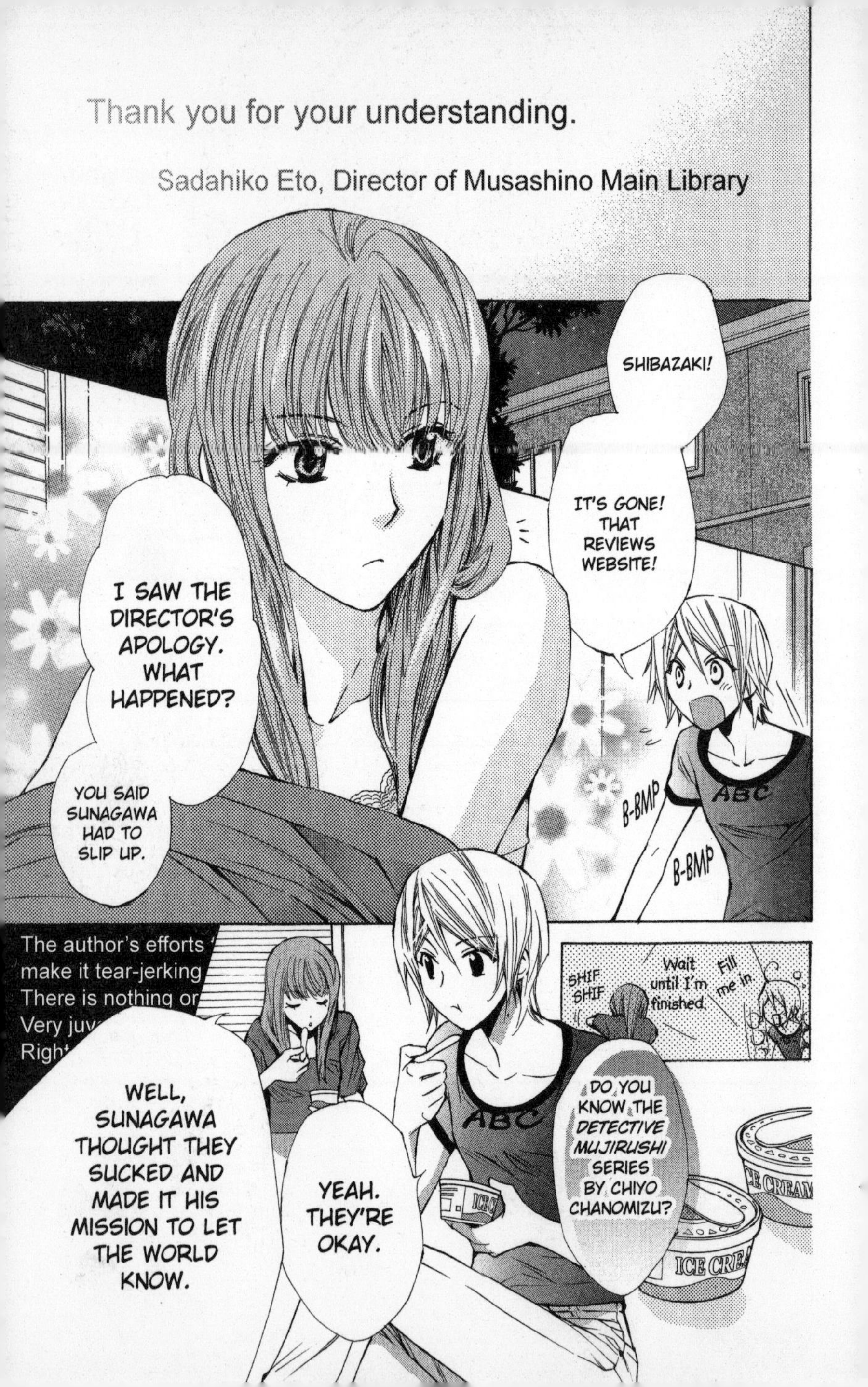
Thank you for your understanding.
Sadahiko Eto, Director of Musashino Main Library
SHIBAZAKI!
IT'S GONE! THAT REVIEWS WEBSITE!
B-BMP
B-BMP
I SAW THE DIRECTOR'S APOLOGY. WHAT HAPPENED?
YOU SAID SUNAGAWA HAD TO SLIP UP.
Fill me in
Wait until I'm finished.
SHIF SHIF
The author's efforts
make it tear-jerking
There is nothing
DO YOU KNOW THE *DETECTIVE MUJIRUSHI* SERIES BY CHIYO CHANOMIZU?
YEAH. THEY'RE OKAY.
WELL, SUNAGAWA THOUGHT THEY SUCKED AND MADE IT HIS MISSION TO LET THE WORLD KNOW.
ICE CREAM
ICE CREAM
ABC
ABC

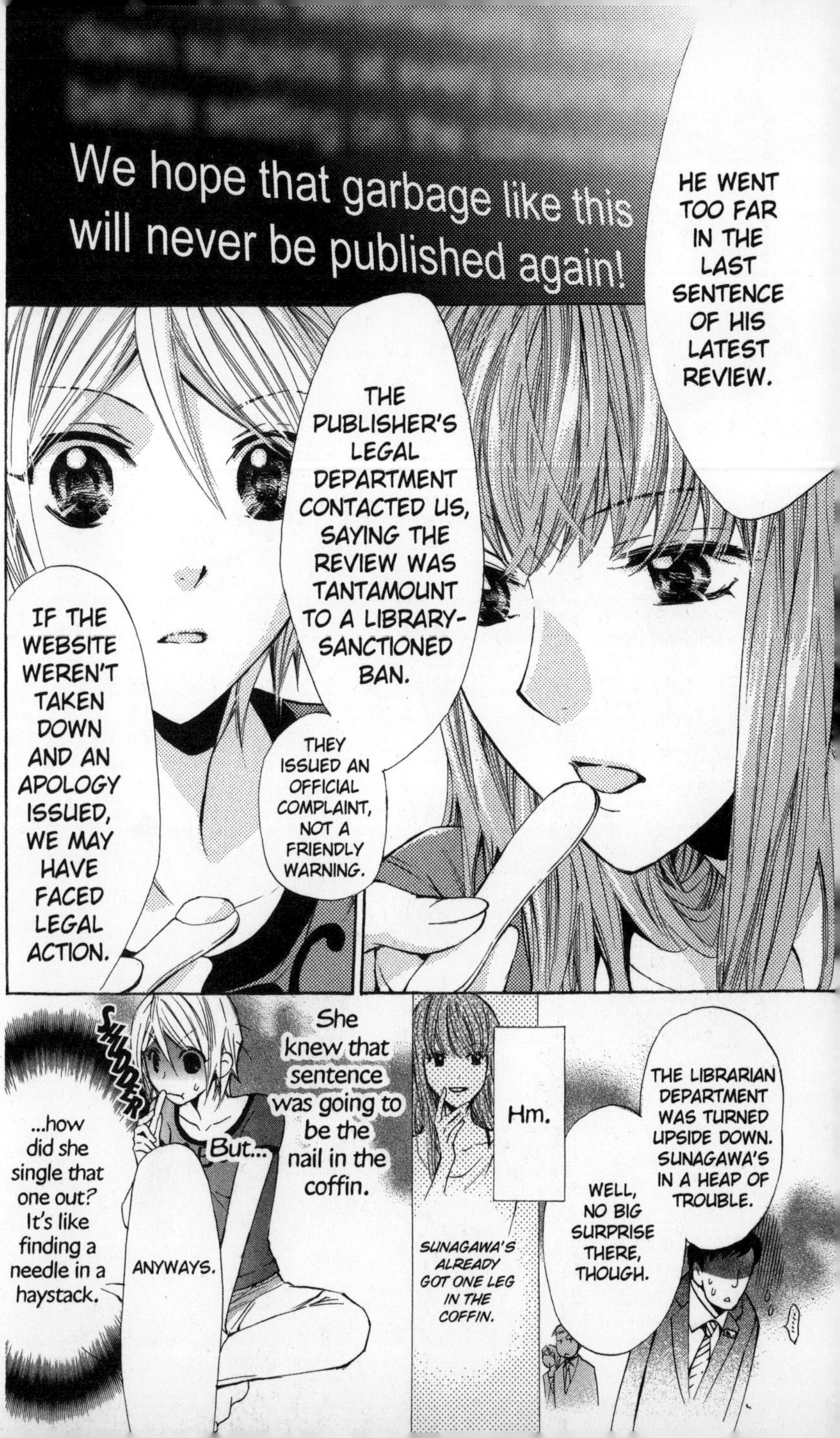

We hope that garbage like this will never be published again!
HE WENT TOO FAR IN THE LAST SENTENCE OF HIS LATEST REVIEW.
THE PUBLISHER'S LEGAL DEPARTMENT CONTACTED US, SAYING THE REVIEW WAS TANTAMOUNT TO A LIBRARY-SANCTIONED BAN.
THEY ISSUED AN OFFICIAL COMPLAINT, NOT A FRIENDLY WARNING.
IF THE WEBSITE WEREN'T TAKEN DOWN AND AN APOLOGY ISSUED, WE MAY HAVE FACED LEGAL ACTION.
THE LIBRARIAN DEPARTMENT WAS TURNED UPSIDE DOWN. SUNAGAWA'S IN A HEAP OF TROUBLE.
WELL, NO BIG SURPRISE THERE, THOUGH.
Hm.
SUNAGAWA'S ALREADY GOT ONE LEG IN THE COFFIN.
She knew that sentence was going to be the nail in the coffin.
SHUDDER
But...
...how did she single that one out? It's like finding a needle in a haystack.
ANYWAYS.

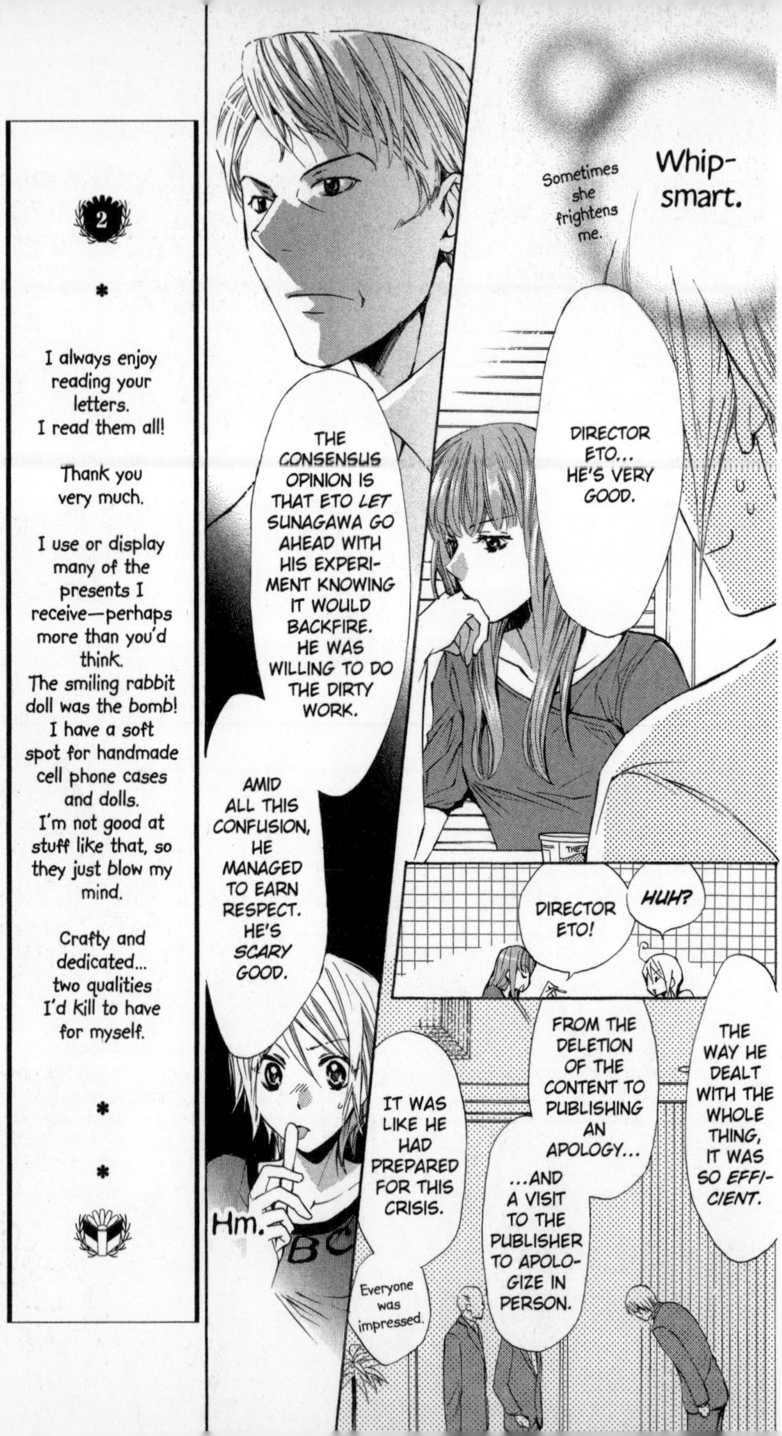
Whip-smart.
Sometimes she frightens me.
DIRECTOR ETO... HE'S VERY GOOD.
HUH?
DIRECTOR ETO!
THE WAY HE DEALT WITH THE WHOLE THING, IT WAS SO *EFFICIENT*.
FROM THE DELETION OF THE CONTENT TO PUBLISHING AN APOLOGY...
...AND A VISIT TO THE PUBLISHER TO APOLOGIZE IN PERSON.
IT WAS LIKE HE HAD PREPARED FOR THIS CRISIS.
Everyone was impressed.
Hm.
THE CONSENSUS OPINION IS THAT ETO *LET* SUNAGAWA GO AHEAD WITH HIS EXPERIMENT KNOWING IT WOULD BACKFIRE. HE WAS WILLING TO DO THE DIRTY WORK.
AMID ALL THIS CONFUSION, HE MANAGED TO EARN RESPECT. HE'S *SCARY* GOOD.

2

*

I always enjoy reading your letters.
I read them all!

Thank you very much.

I use or display many of the presents I receive—perhaps more than you'd think.
The smiling rabbit doll was the *bomb*!
I have a soft spot for handmade cell phone cases and dolls.
I'm not good at stuff like that, so they just blow my mind.

Crafty and dedicated... two qualities I'd kill to have for myself.

*

*

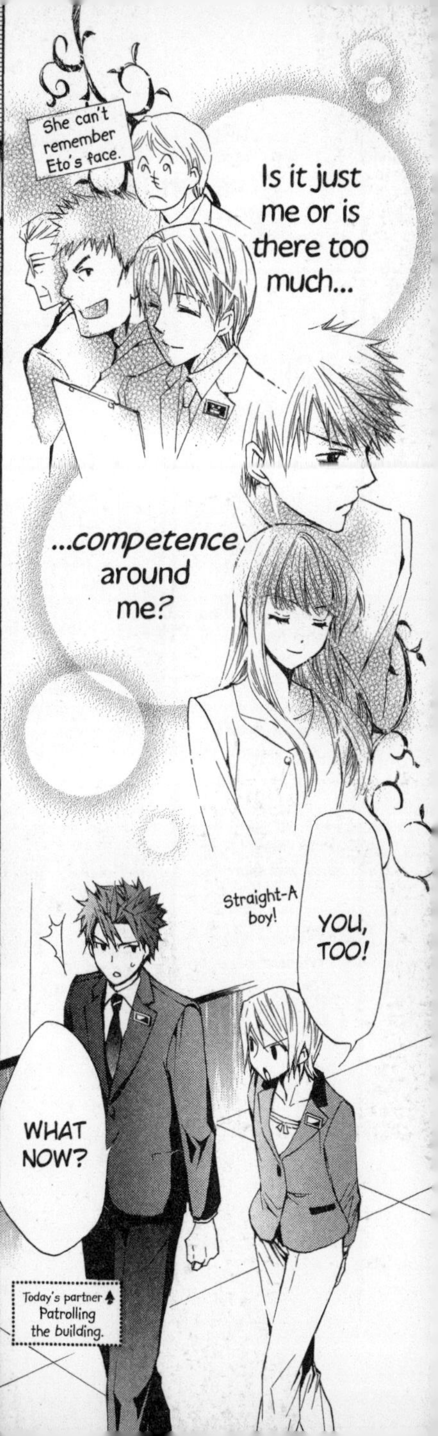
She can't remember Eto's face.
Is it just me or is there too much...
...competence around me?
YOU, TOO!
Straight-A boy!
WHAT NOW?
Today's partner ▲ Patrolling the building.

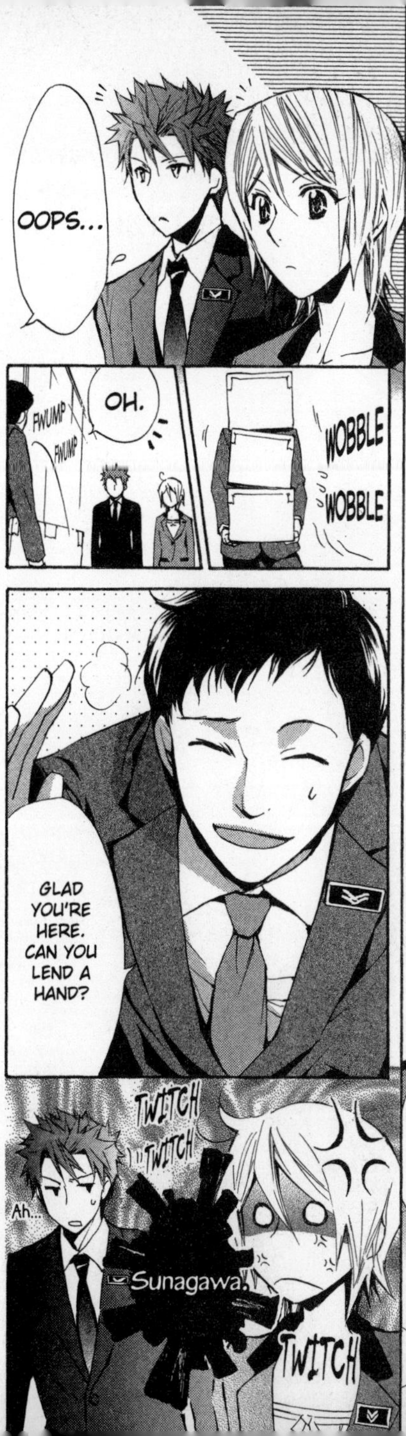
OOPS...
WOBBLE WOBBLE
OH.
FWUMP FWUMP
GLAD YOU'RE HERE. CAN YOU LEND A HAND?
TWITCH TWITCH
Ah...
Sunagawa.
TWITCH

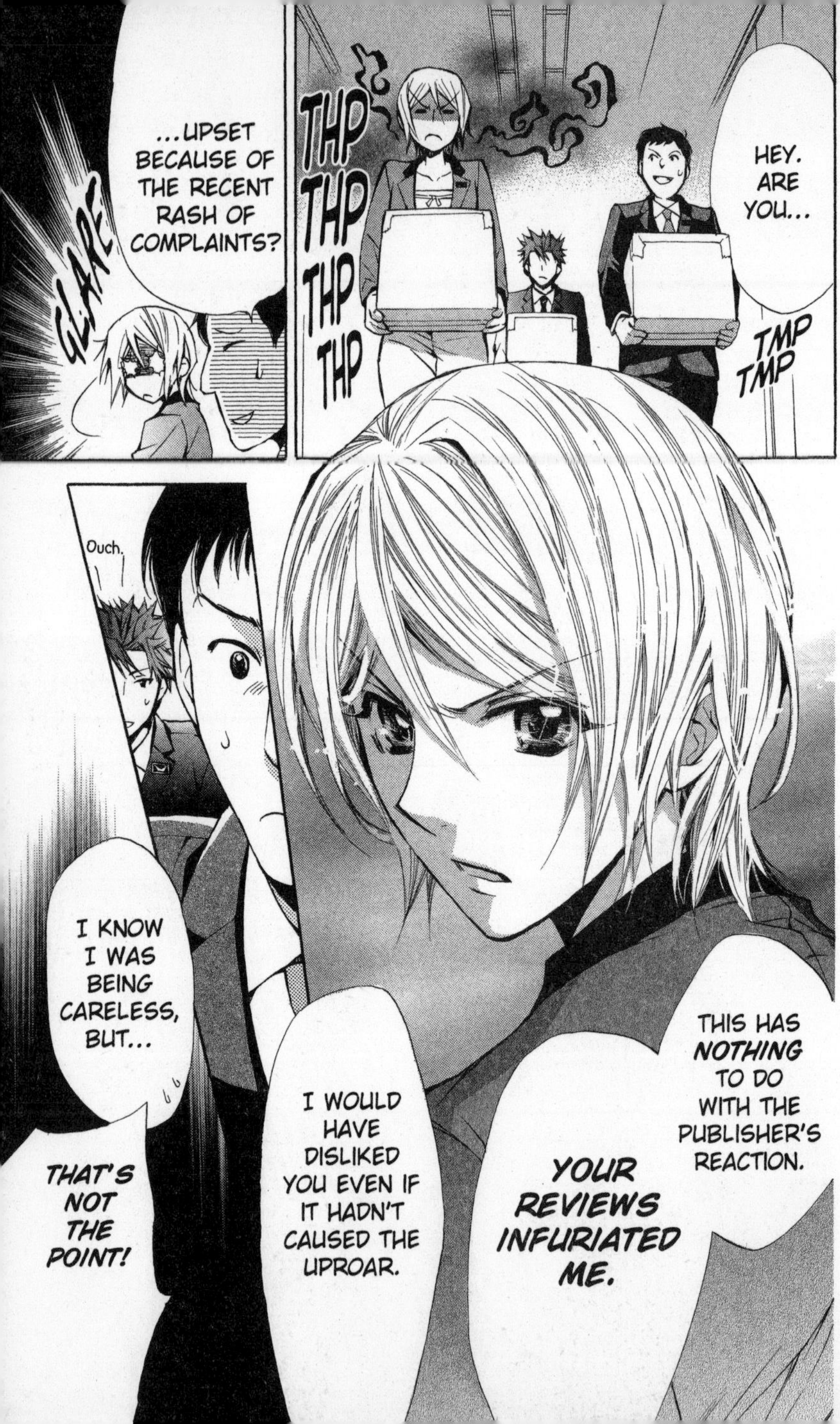
HEY. ARE YOU...
THP THP THP THP
TMP TMP
...UPSET BECAUSE OF THE RECENT RASH OF COMPLAINTS?
GLARE
THIS HAS *NOTHING* TO DO WITH THE PUBLISHER'S REACTION.
YOUR REVIEWS INFURIATED ME.
I WOULD HAVE DISLIKED YOU EVEN IF IT HADN'T CAUSED THE UPROAR.
Ouch.
I KNOW I WAS BEING CARELESS, BUT...
THAT'S NOT THE POINT!

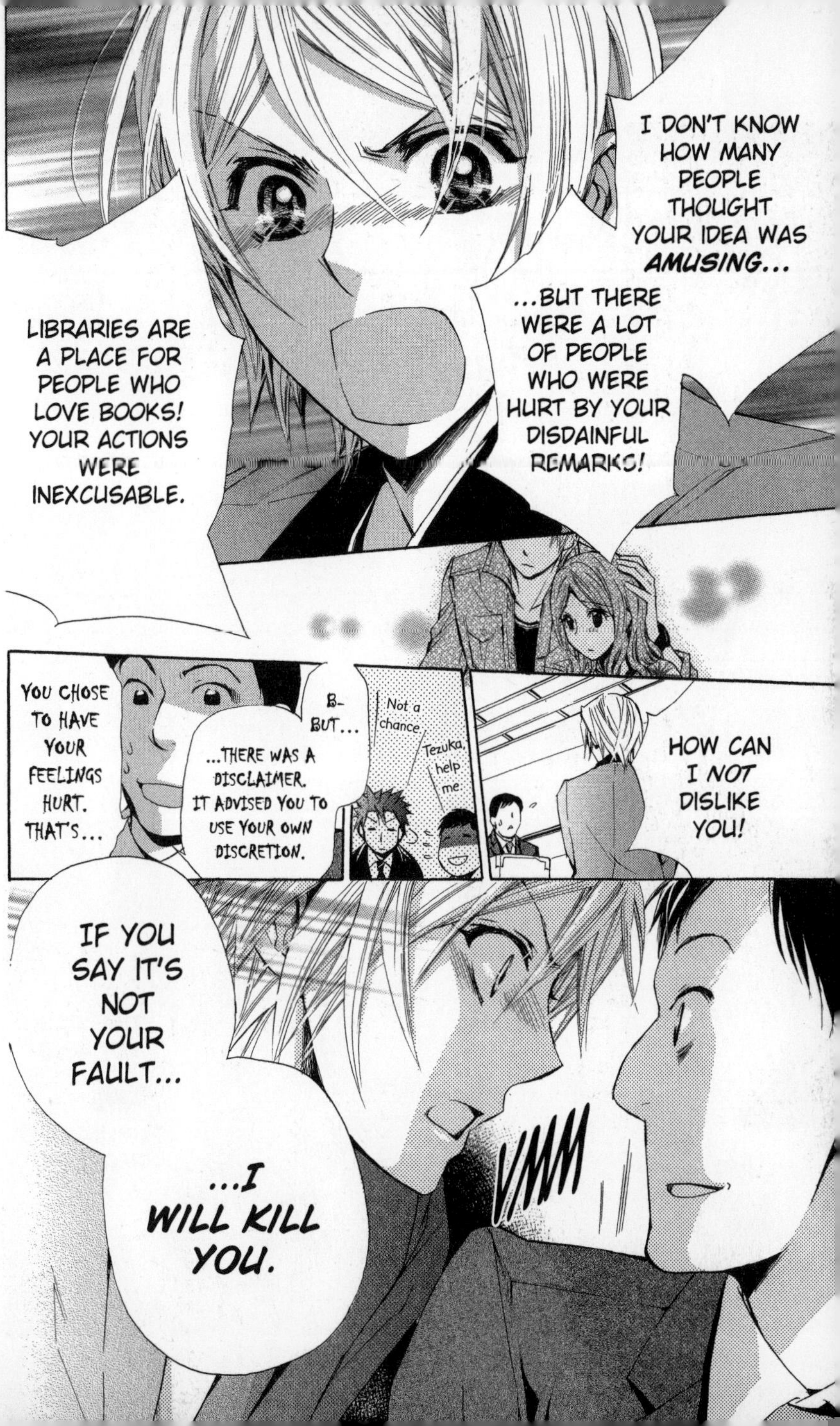
I DON'T KNOW HOW MANY PEOPLE THOUGHT YOUR IDEA WAS ***AMUSING...***
...BUT THERE WERE A LOT OF PEOPLE WHO WERE HURT BY YOUR DISDAINFUL REMARKS!
LIBRARIES ARE A PLACE FOR PEOPLE WHO LOVE BOOKS! YOUR ACTIONS WERE INEXCUSABLE.
HOW CAN I *NOT* DISLIKE YOU!
Not a chance.
Tezuka, help me
B-BUT...
...THERE WAS A DISCLAIMER. IT ADVISED YOU TO USE YOUR OWN DISCRETION.
YOU CHOSE TO HAVE YOUR FEELINGS HURT. THAT'S...
IF YOU SAY IT'S NOT YOUR FAULT...
...I WILL KILL YOU.
VMM

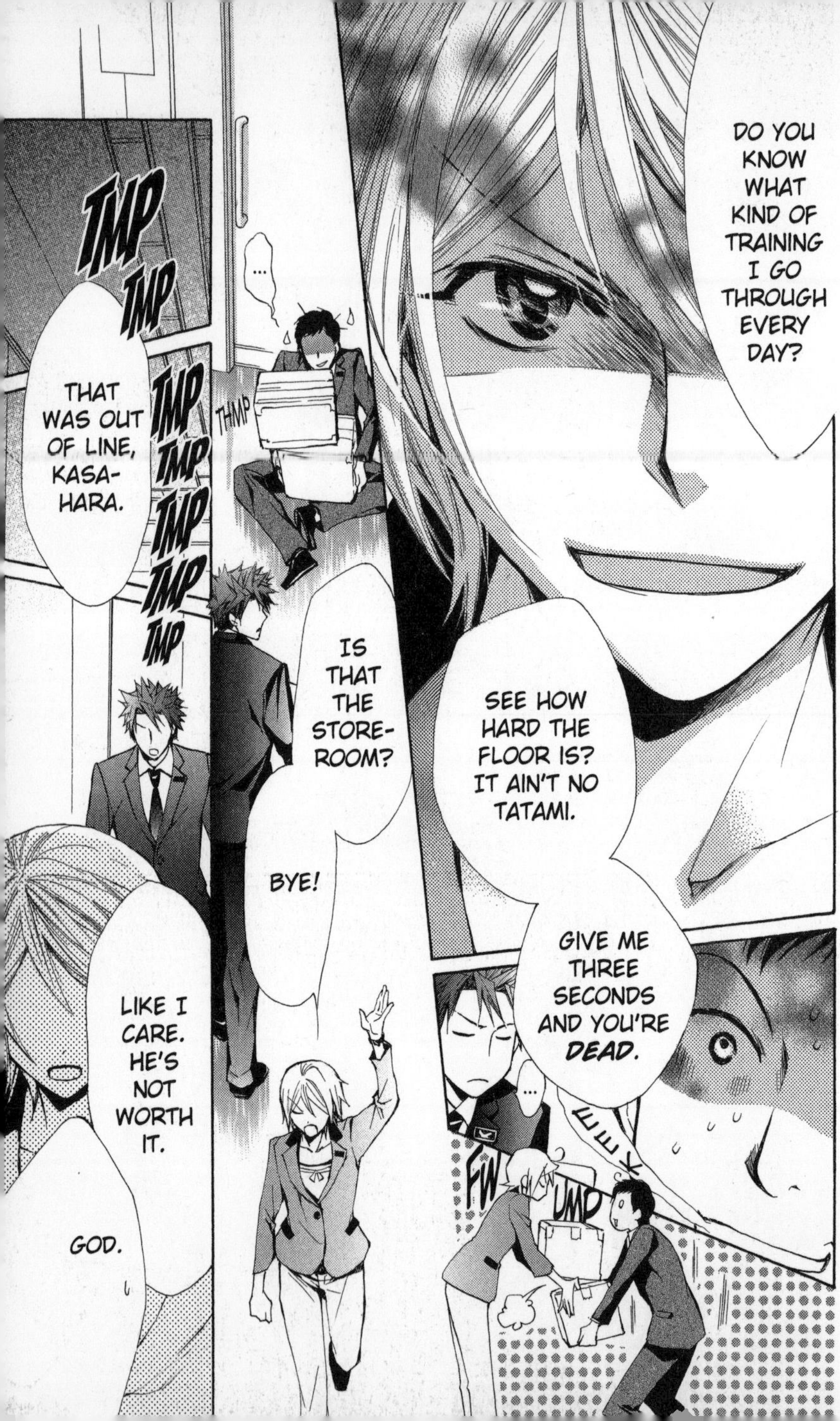
DO YOU KNOW WHAT KIND OF TRAINING I GO THROUGH EVERY DAY?
SEE HOW HARD THE FLOOR IS? IT AIN'T NO TATAMI.
GIVE ME THREE SECONDS AND YOU'RE *DEAD*.
...
FWUMP
...
THMP
IS THAT THE STOREROOM?
BYE!
TMP TMP TMP TMP TMP TMP TMP
THAT WAS OUT OF LINE, KASA-HARA.
LIKE I CARE. HE'S NOT WORTH IT.
GOD.

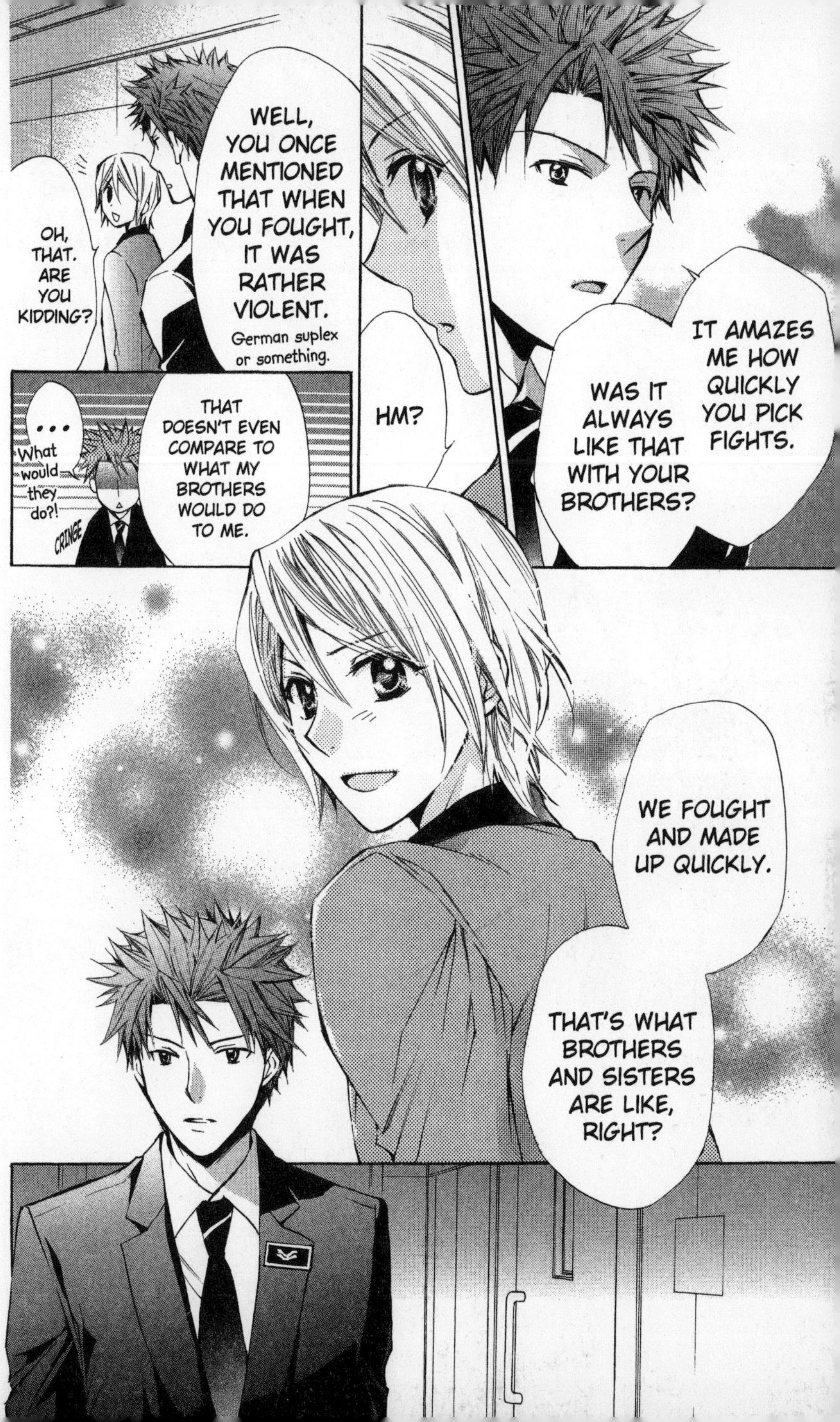
IT AMAZES ME HOW QUICKLY YOU PICK FIGHTS.
WAS IT ALWAYS LIKE THAT WITH YOUR BROTHERS?
HM?
WELL, YOU ONCE MENTIONED THAT WHEN YOU FOUGHT, IT WAS RATHER VIOLENT.
German suplex or something.
OH, THAT. ARE YOU KIDDING?
THAT DOESN'T EVEN COMPARE TO WHAT MY BROTHERS WOULD DO TO ME.
...
What would they do?!
CRINGE
WE FOUGHT AND MADE UP QUICKLY.
THAT'S WHAT BROTHERS AND SISTERS ARE LIKE, RIGHT?

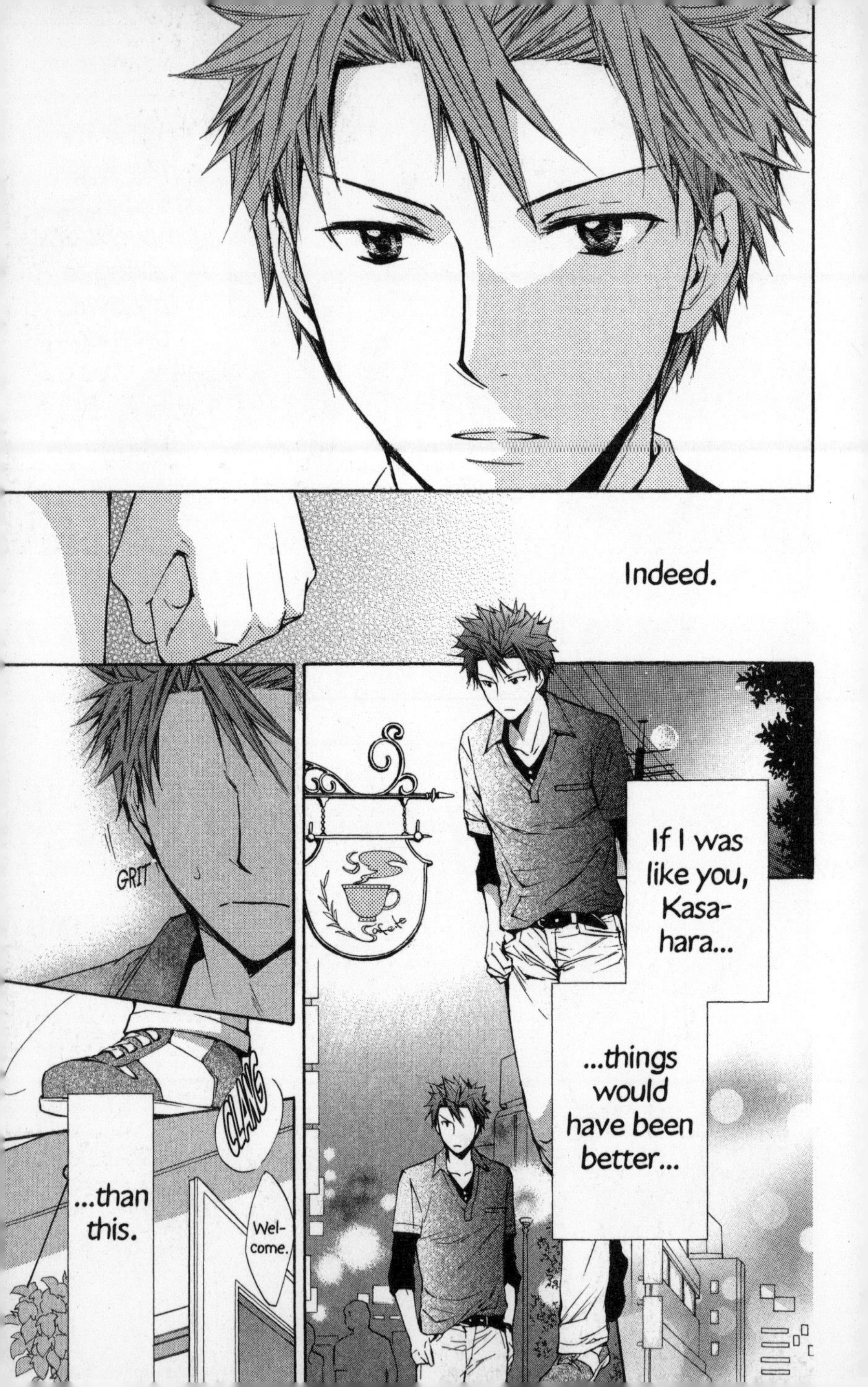
Indeed.
If I was like you, Kasa-hara...
...things would have been better...
GRIT
...than this.
CLANG
Wel-come.

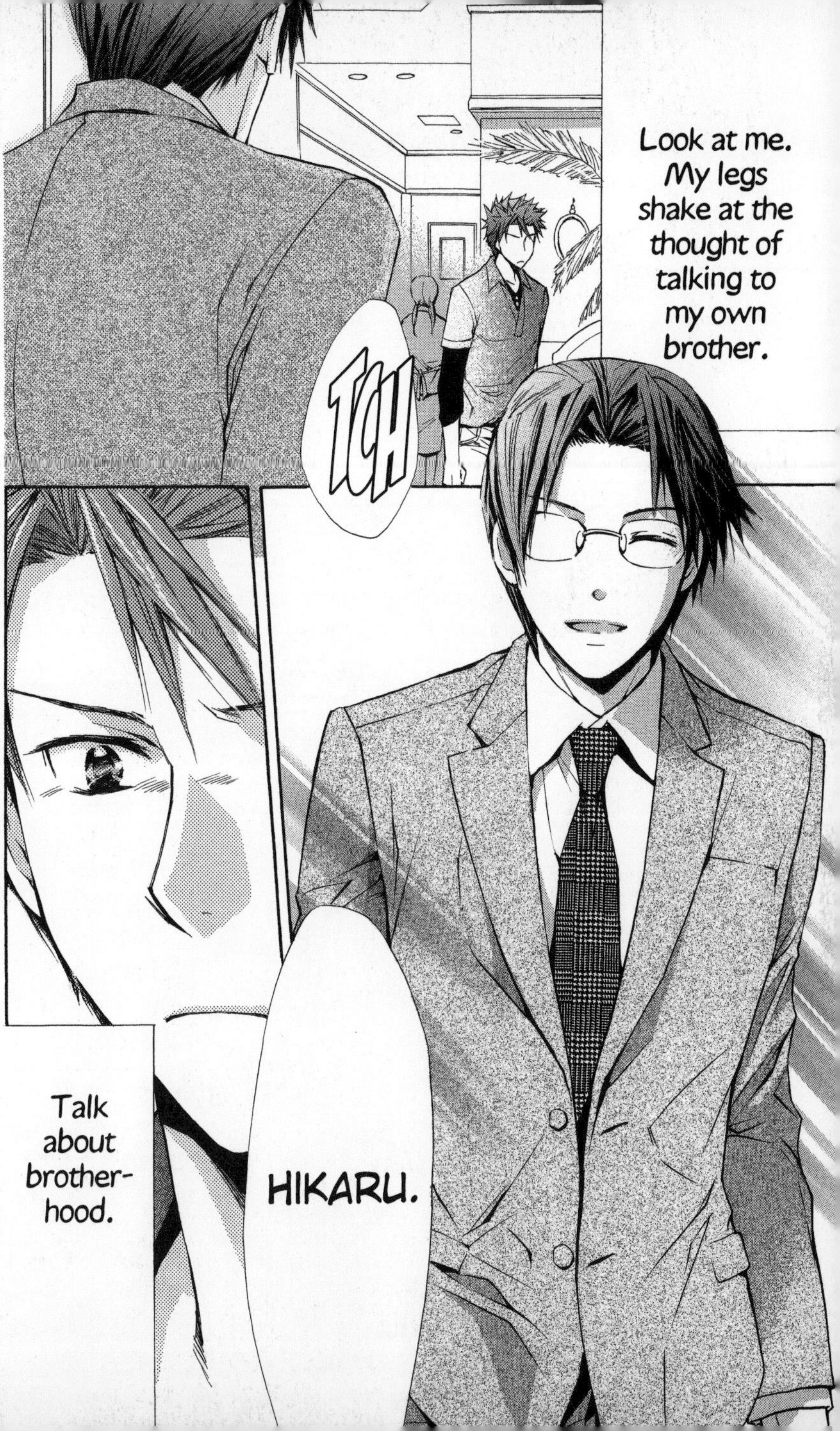
Look at me. My legs shake at the thought of talking to my own brother.
TCH
HIKARU.
Talk about brother-hood.

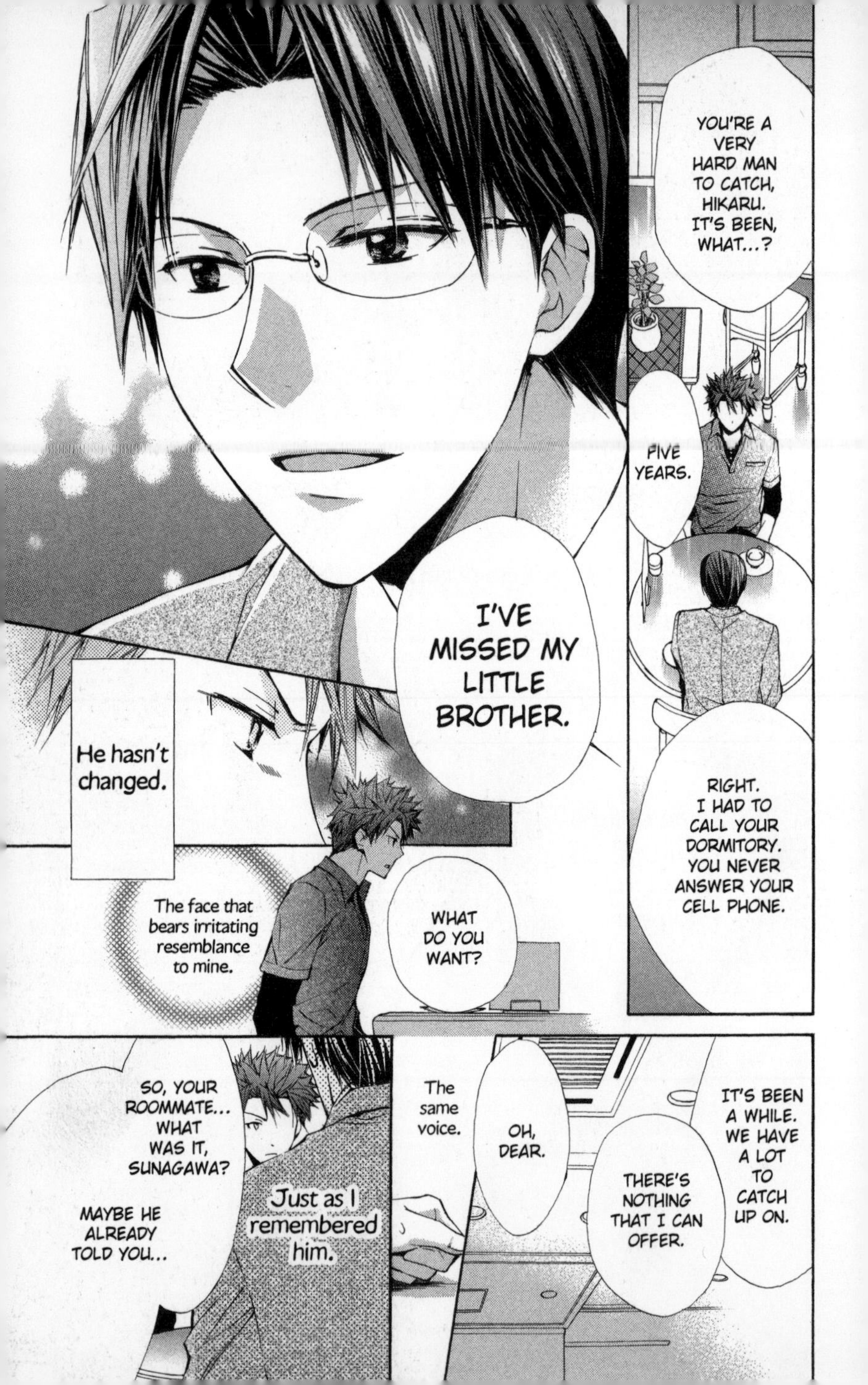

YOU'RE A VERY HARD MAN TO CATCH, HIKARU. IT'S BEEN, WHAT...?
FIVE YEARS.
RIGHT. I HAD TO CALL YOUR DORMITORY. YOU NEVER ANSWER YOUR CELL PHONE.
I'VE MISSED MY LITTLE BROTHER.
He hasn't changed.
The face that bears irritating resemblance to mine.
WHAT DO YOU WANT?
IT'S BEEN A WHILE. WE HAVE A LOT TO CATCH UP ON.
THERE'S NOTHING THAT I CAN OFFER.
OH, DEAR.
The same voice.
Just as I remembered him.
SO, YOUR ROOMMATE... WHAT WAS IT, SUNAGAWA?
MAYBE HE ALREADY TOLD YOU...

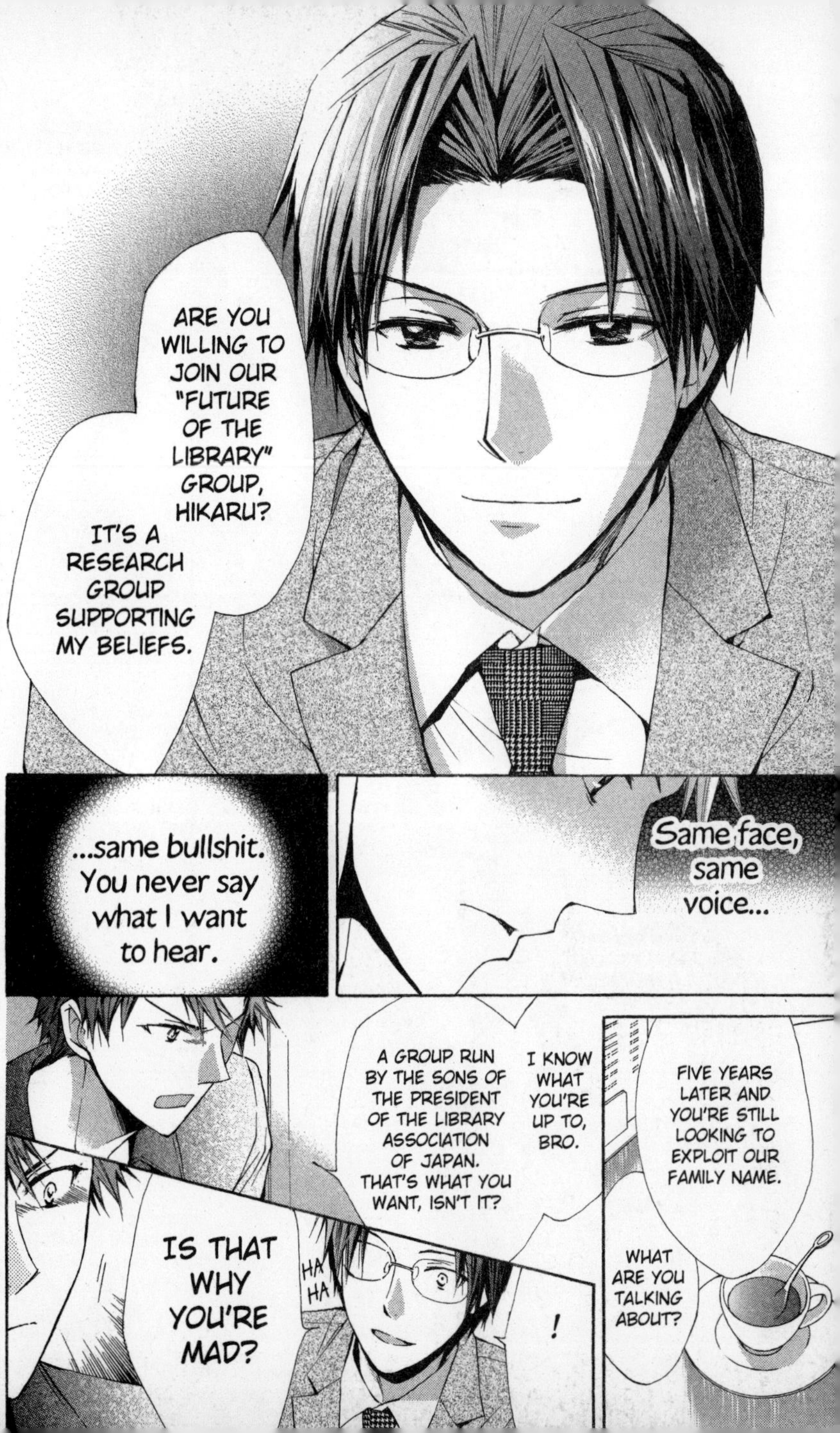
ARE YOU WILLING TO JOIN OUR "FUTURE OF THE LIBRARY" GROUP, HIKARU?
IT'S A RESEARCH GROUP SUPPORTING MY BELIEFS.
Same face, same voice...
...same bullshit. You never say what I want to hear.
FIVE YEARS LATER AND YOU'RE STILL LOOKING TO EXPLOIT OUR FAMILY NAME.
I KNOW WHAT YOU'RE UP TO, BRO.
A GROUP RUN BY THE SONS OF THE PRESIDENT OF THE LIBRARY ASSOCIATION OF JAPAN. THAT'S WHAT YOU WANT, ISN'T IT?
WHAT ARE YOU TALKING ABOUT?
!
HA HA
IS THAT WHY YOU'RE MAD?

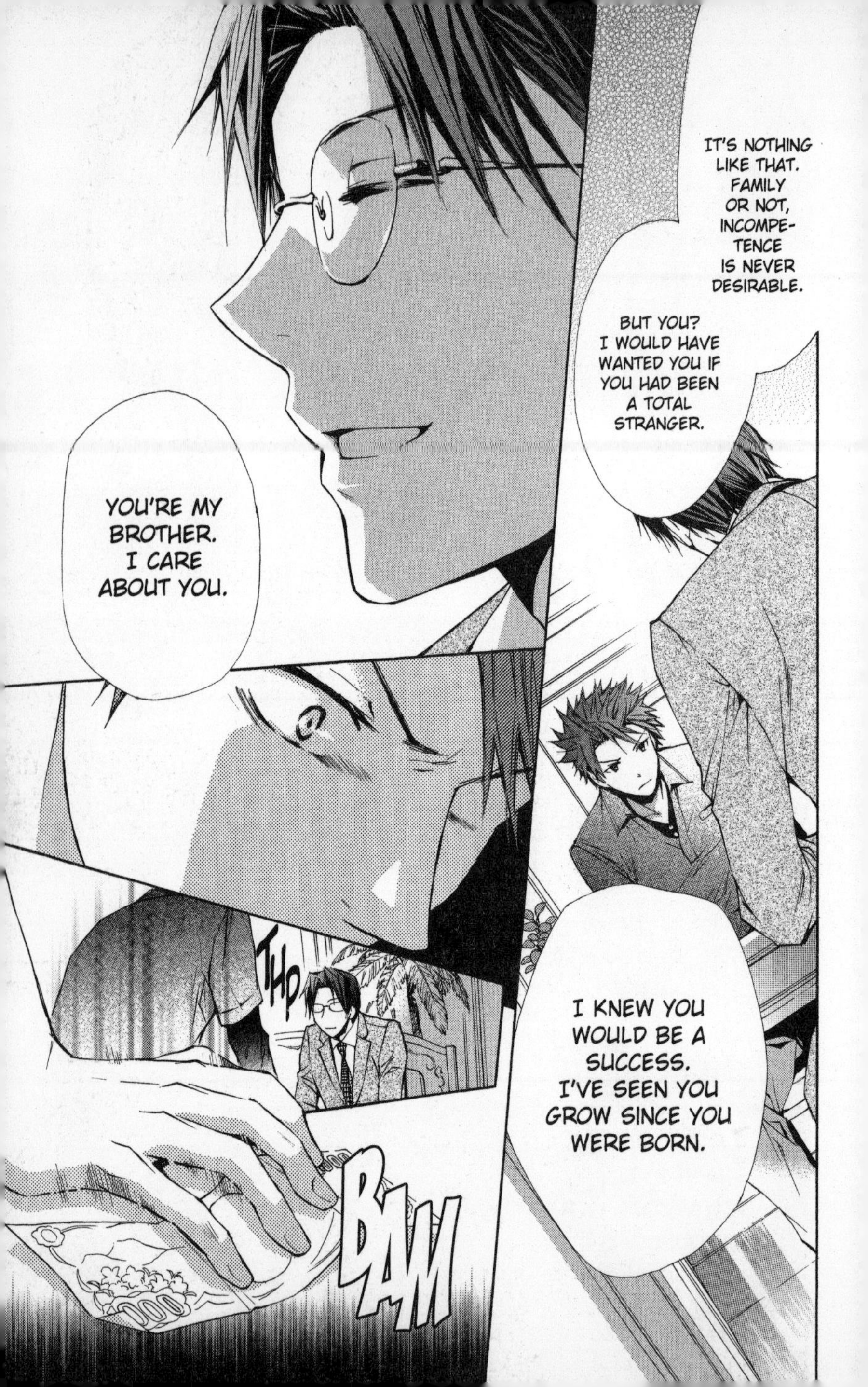
IT'S NOTHING LIKE THAT. FAMILY OR NOT, INCOMPETENCE IS NEVER DESIRABLE.
BUT YOU? I WOULD HAVE WANTED YOU IF YOU HAD BEEN A TOTAL STRANGER.
YOU'RE MY BROTHER. I CARE ABOUT YOU.
I KNEW YOU WOULD BE A SUCCESS. I'VE SEEN YOU GROW SINCE YOU WERE BORN.
THP
BAM

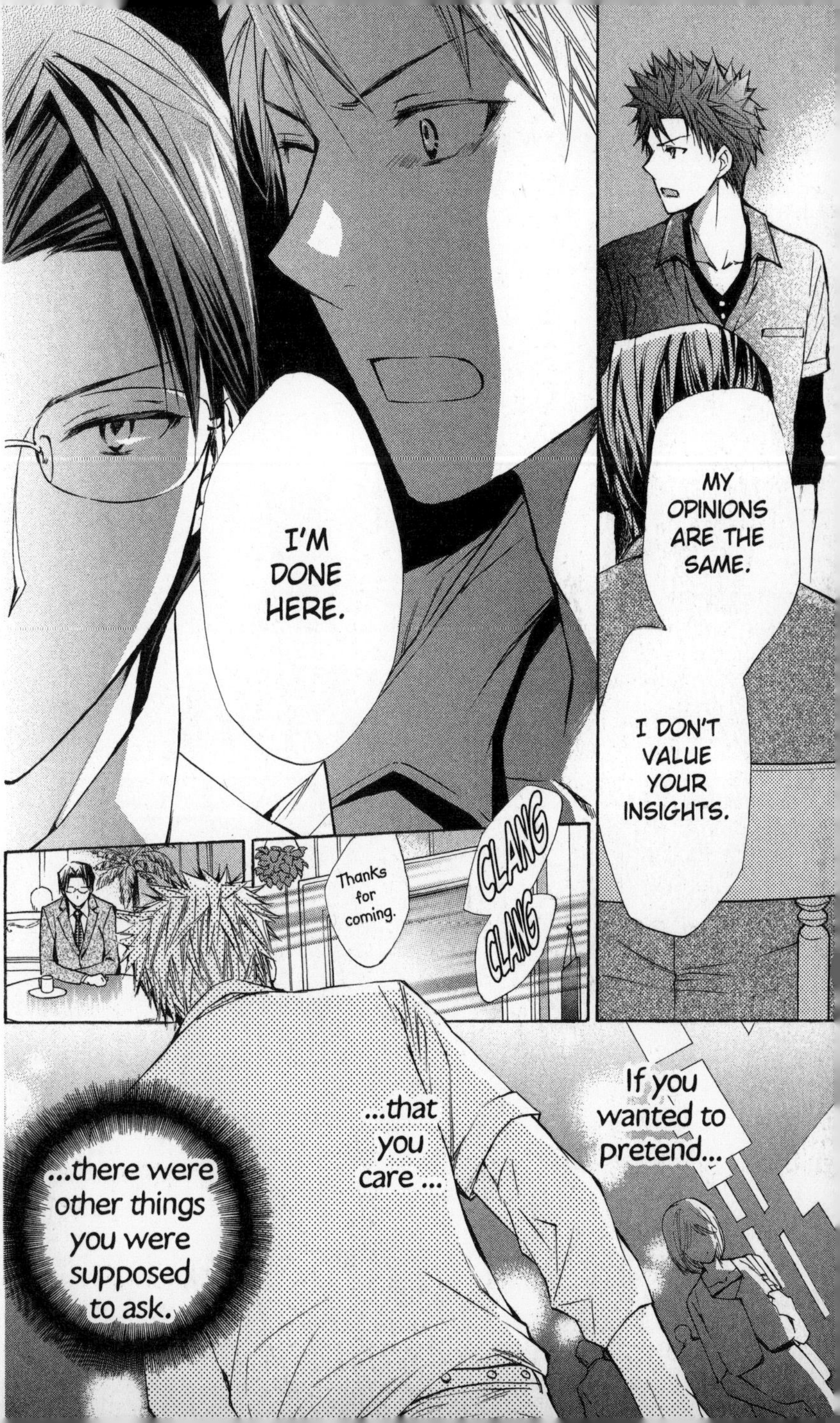
MY OPINIONS ARE THE SAME.
I DON'T VALUE YOUR INSIGHTS.
I'M DONE HERE.
Thanks for coming.
CLANG CLANG
If you wanted to pretend...
...that you care ...
...there were other things you were supposed to ask.

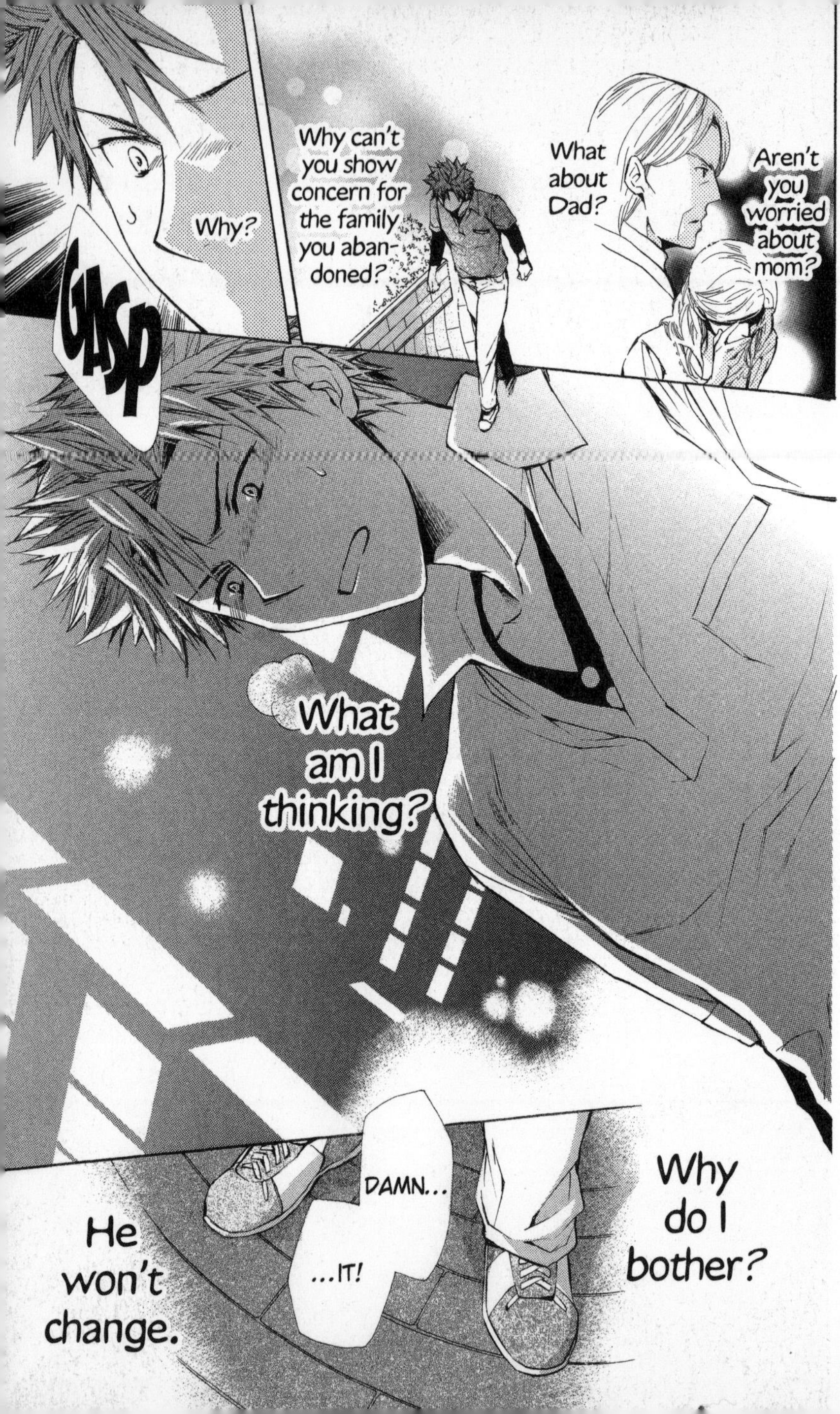
Aren't you worried about mom?
What about Dad?
Why can't you show concern for the family you aban-doned?
Why?
GASP
What am I thinking?
Why do I bother?
DAMN...
...IT!
He won't change.

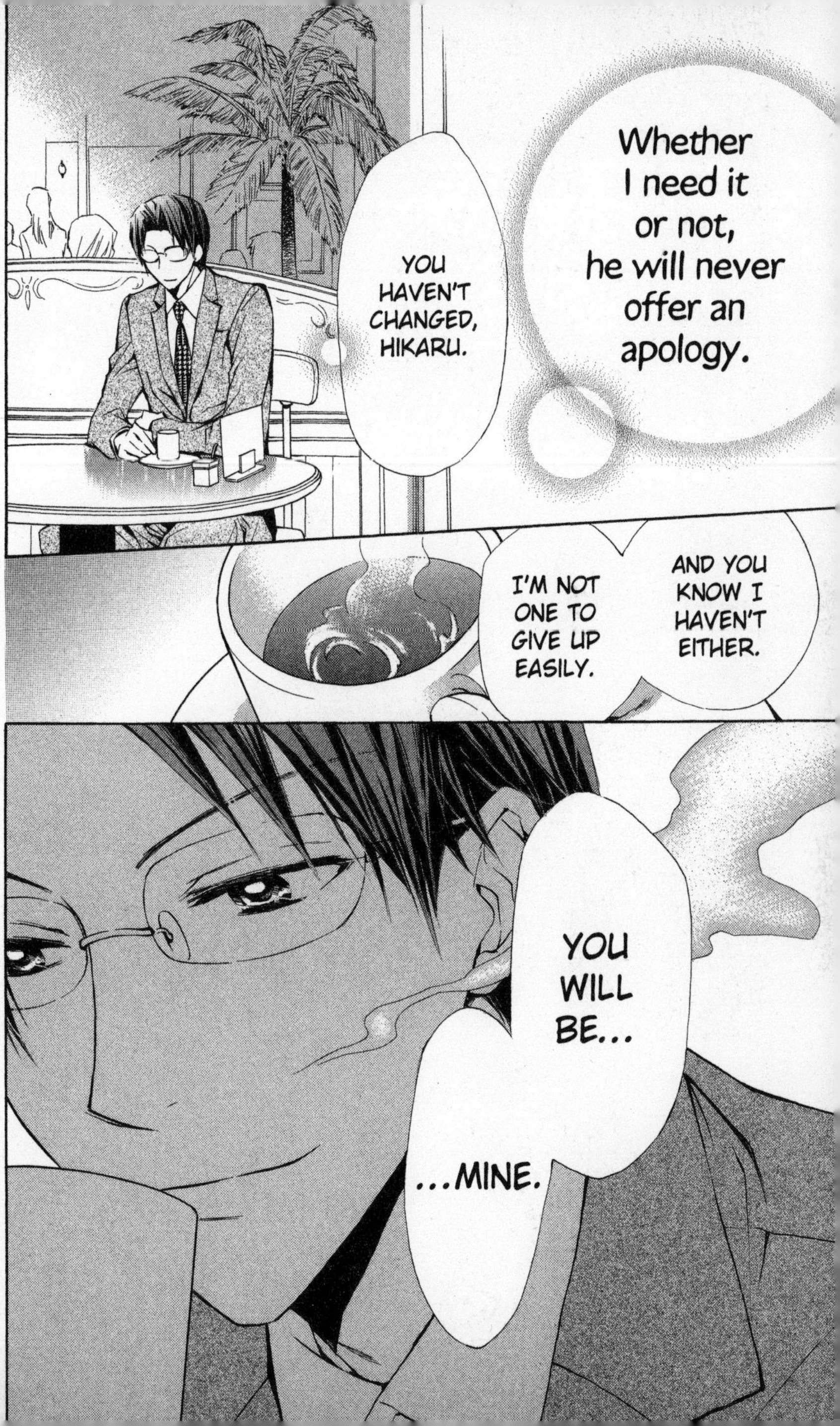
Whether I need it or not, he will never offer an apology.
YOU HAVEN'T CHANGED, HIKARU.
AND YOU KNOW I HAVEN'T EITHER.
I'M NOT ONE TO GIVE UP EASILY.
YOU WILL BE...
...MINE.

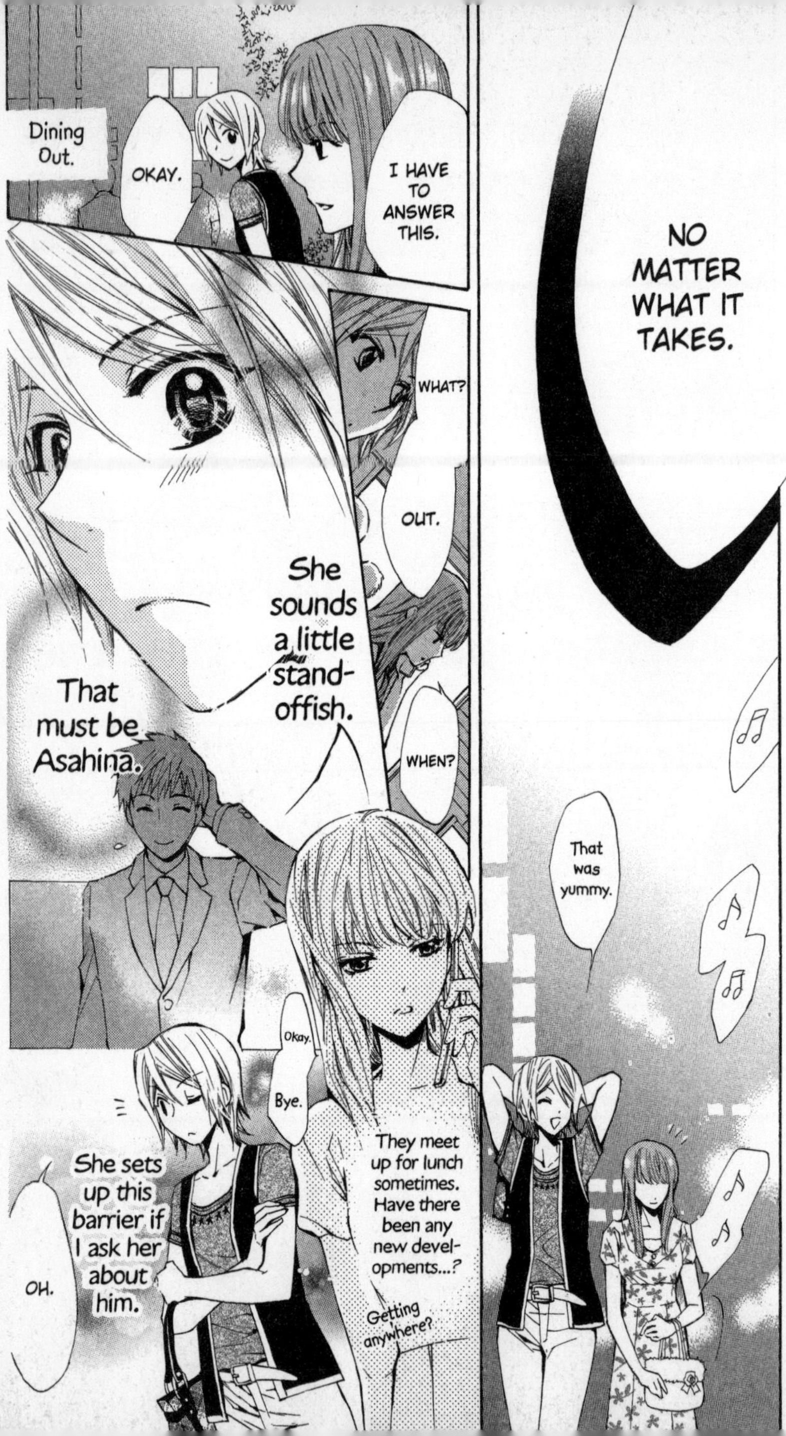
NO MATTER WHAT IT TAKES.
That was yummy.
I HAVE TO ANSWER THIS.
OKAY.
Dining Out.
WHAT?
OUT.
WHEN?
She sounds a little stand-offish.
That must be Asahina.
Okay.
Bye.
They meet up for lunch sometimes. Have there been any new developments...?
Getting anywhere?
She sets up this barrier if I ask her about him.
OH.

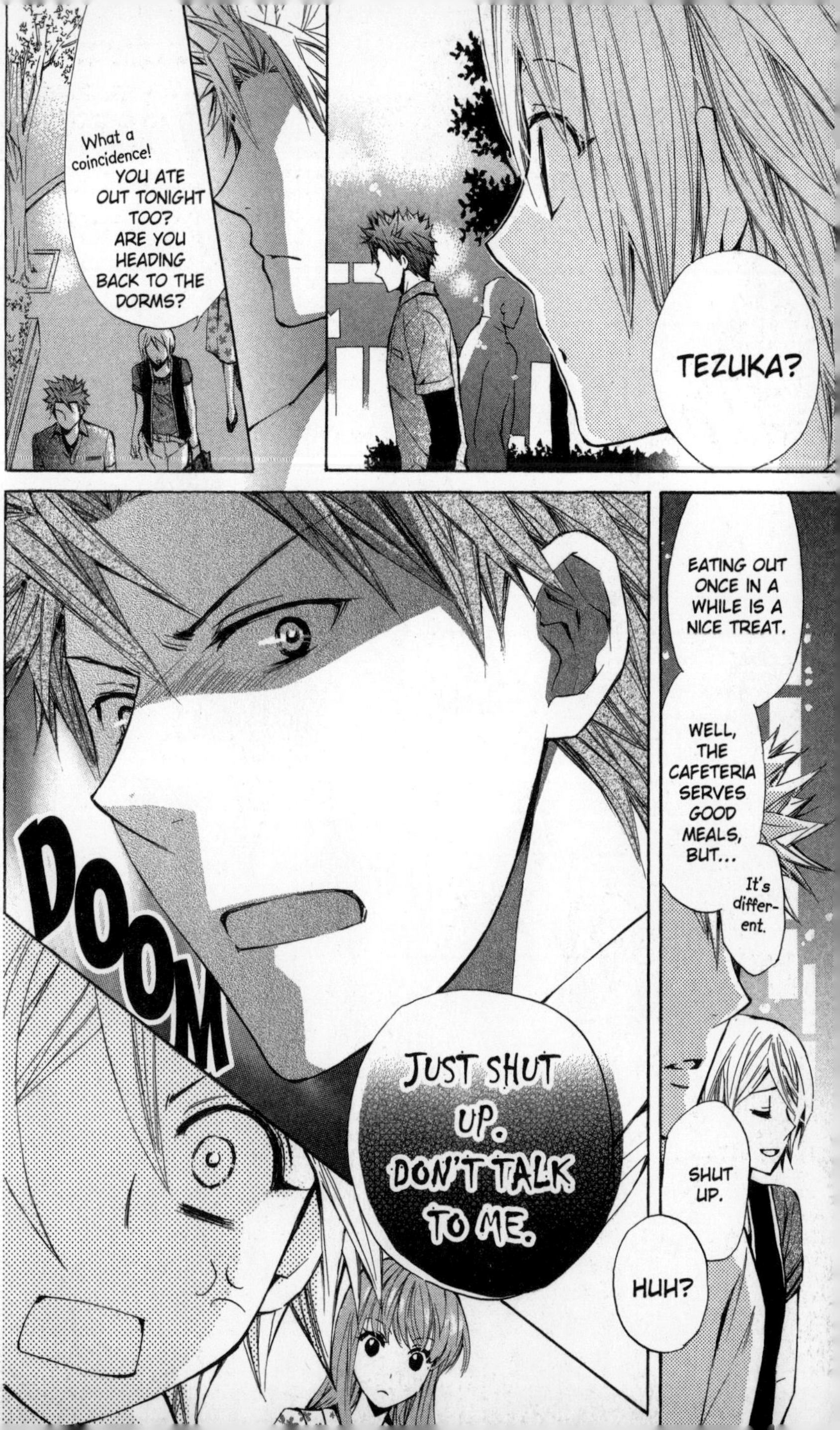
TEZUKA?
What a coincidence!
YOU ATE OUT TONIGHT TOO? ARE YOU HEADING BACK TO THE DORMS?
EATING OUT ONCE IN A WHILE IS A NICE TREAT.
WELL, THE CAFETERIA SERVES GOOD MEALS, BUT...
It's differ-ent.
SHUT UP.
HUH?
DOOM
JUST SHUT UP. DON'T TALK TO ME.

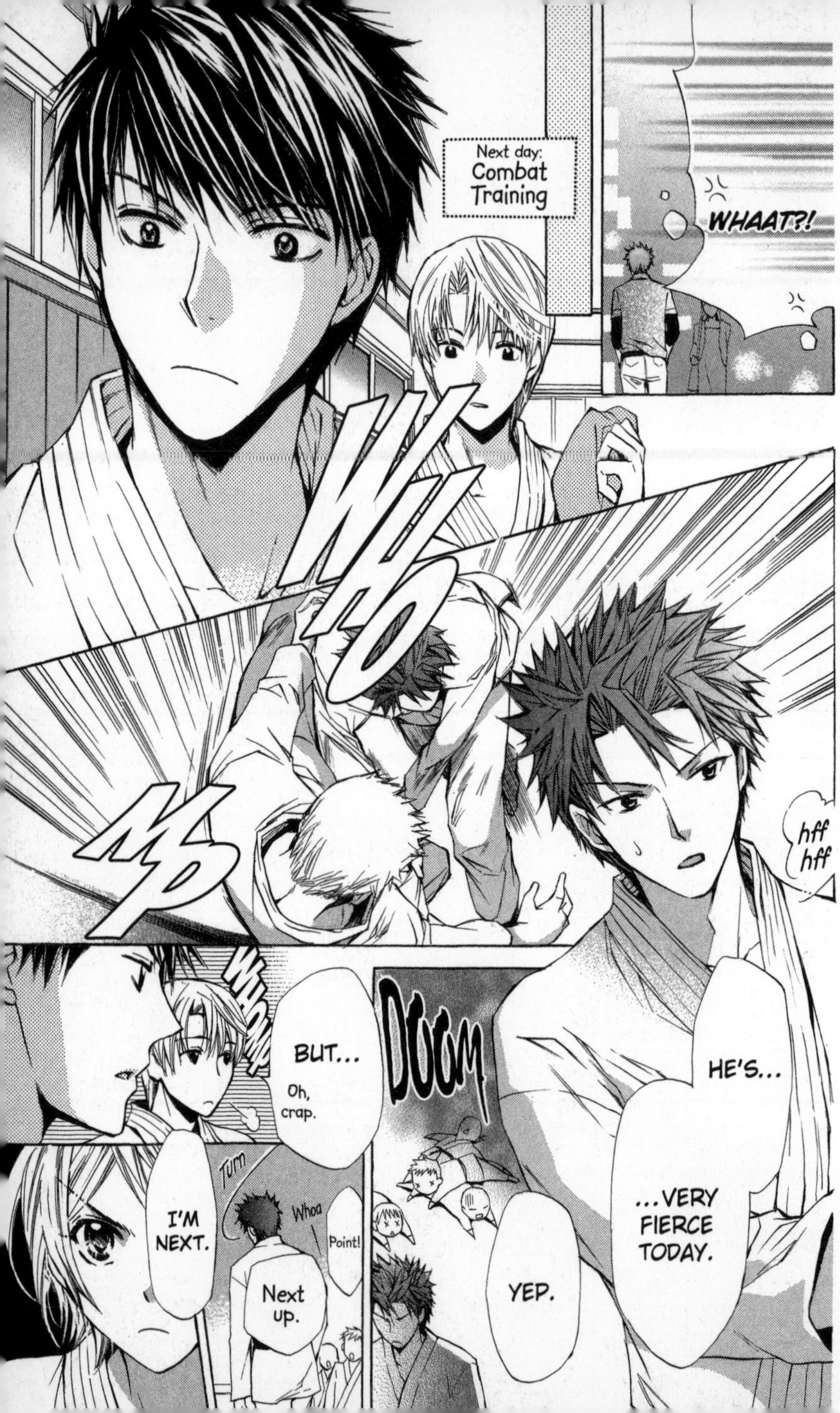
WHAAT?!
Next day: Combat Training
hff hff
WHOMP
HE'S...
...VERY FIERCE TODAY.
DOOM
YEP.
BUT...
Oh, crap.
Turn
Whoa
Point!
Next up.
I'M NEXT.

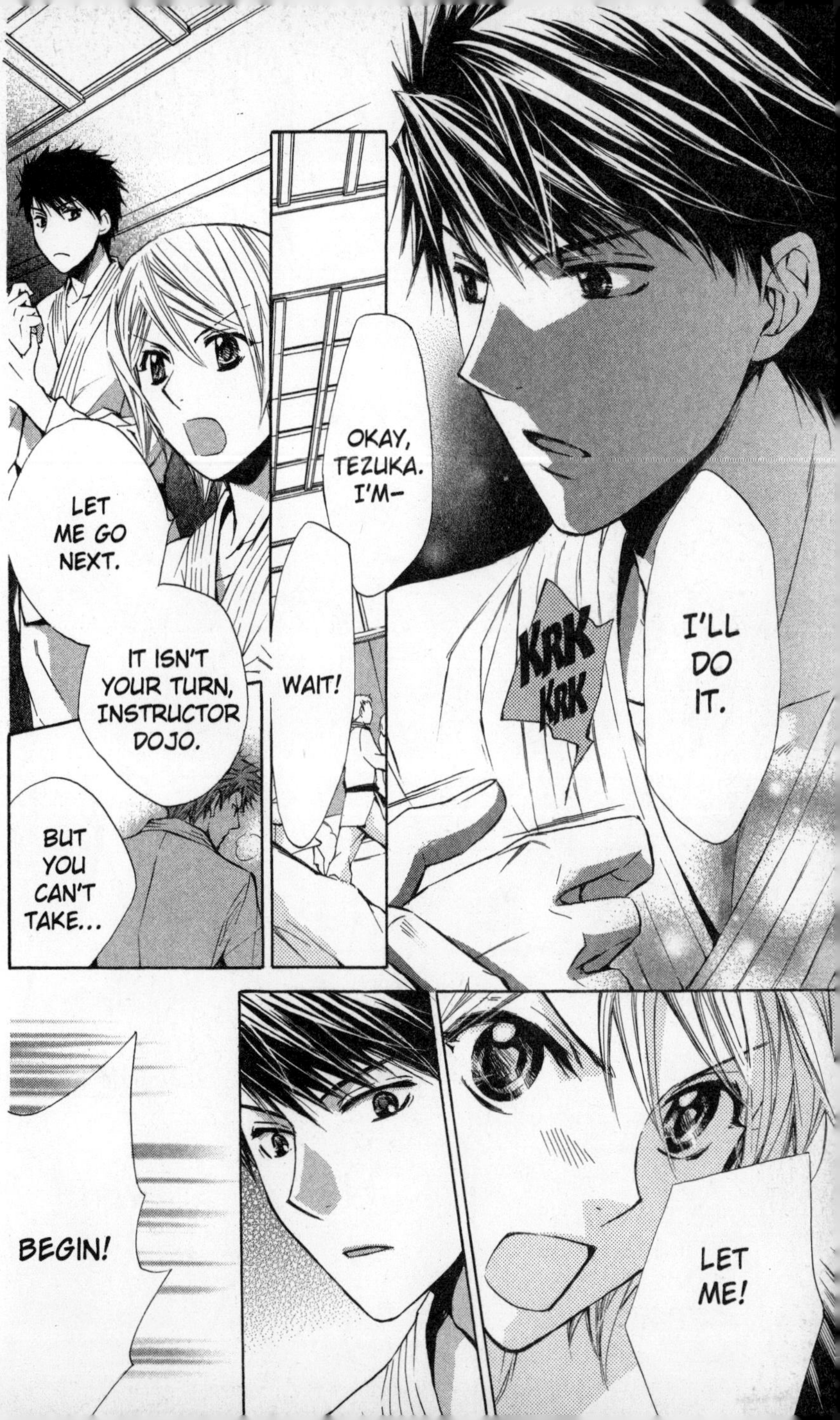
I'LL DO IT.
KRK KRK
OKAY, TEZUKA. I'M-
WAIT!
LET ME GO NEXT.
IT ISN'T YOUR TURN, INSTRUCTOR DOJO.
BUT YOU CAN'T TAKE...
LET ME!
BEGIN!

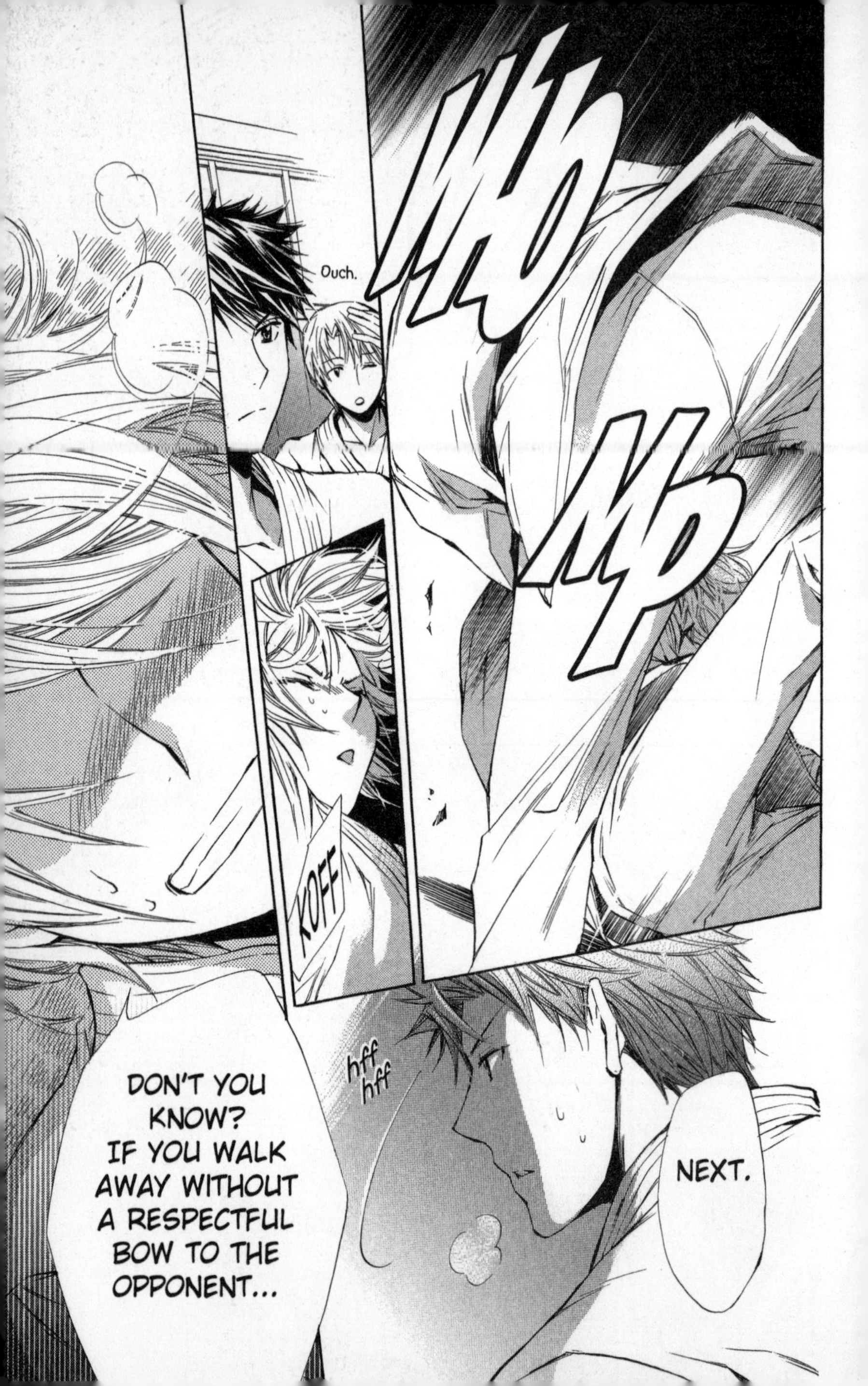
WHOMP
Ouch.
KOFF
NEXT.
hff hff
DON'T YOU KNOW? IF YOU WALK AWAY WITHOUT A RESPECTFUL BOW TO THE OPPONENT...

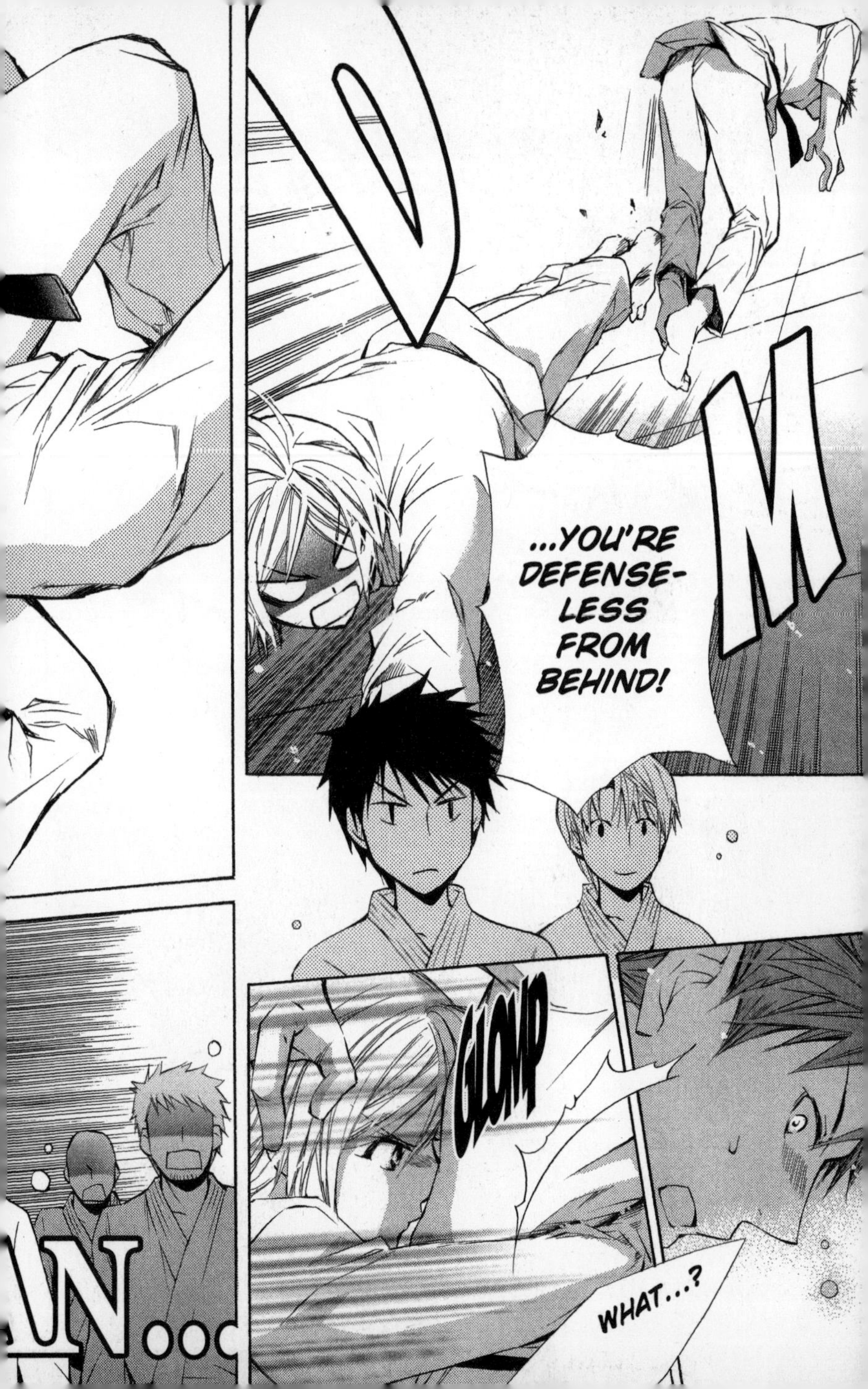

M
...YOU'RE DEFENSE-LESS FROM BEHIND!
WHAT...?
GLOMP
AN...

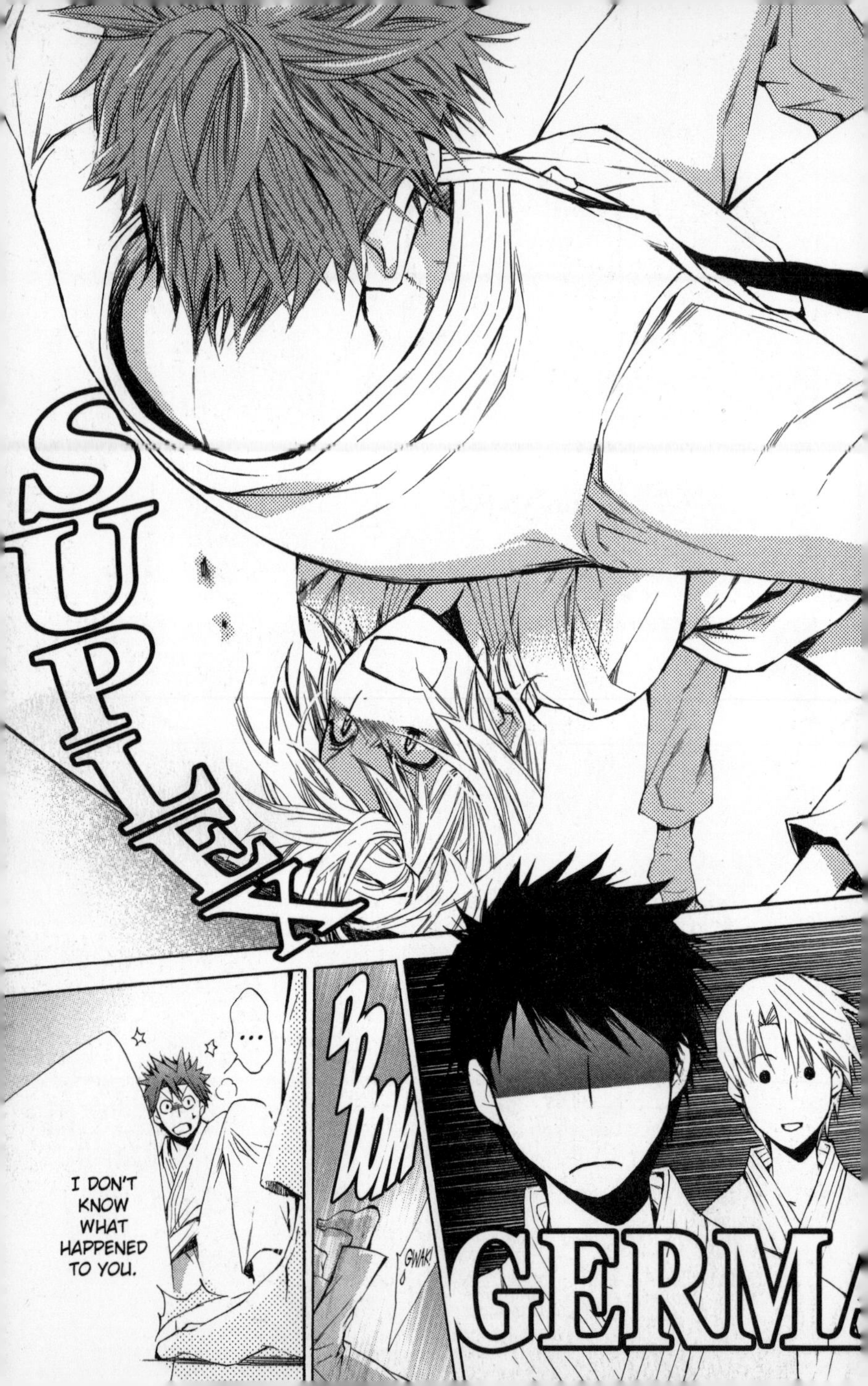
SUPLEX
GERMA
GWAK!
...
I DON'T KNOW WHAT HAPPENED TO YOU.

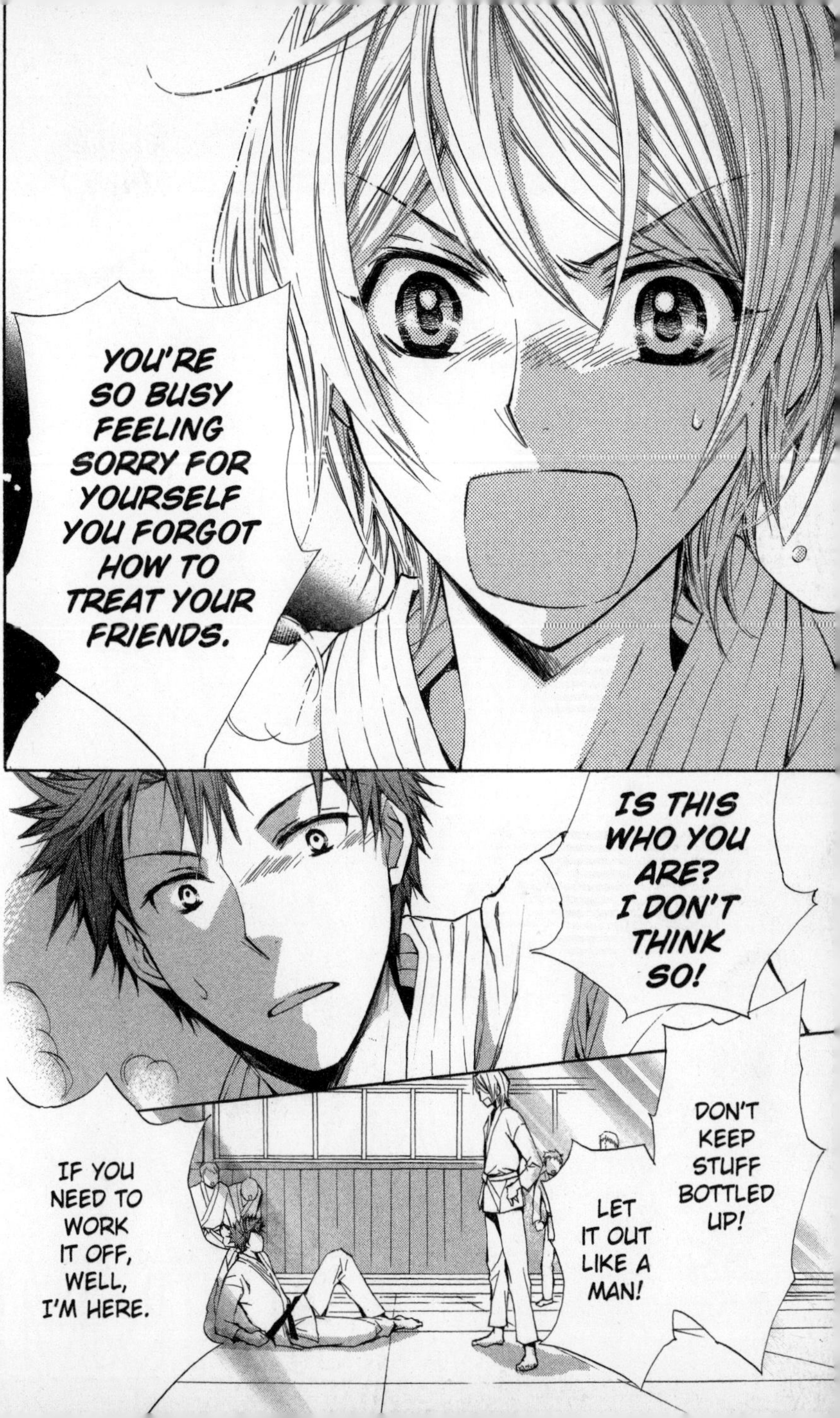
YOU'RE SO BUSY FEELING SORRY FOR YOURSELF YOU FORGOT HOW TO TREAT YOUR FRIENDS.
IS THIS WHO YOU ARE? I DON'T THINK SO!
DON'T KEEP STUFF BOTTLED UP!
LET IT OUT LIKE A MAN!
IF YOU NEED TO WORK IT OFF, WELL, I'M HERE.

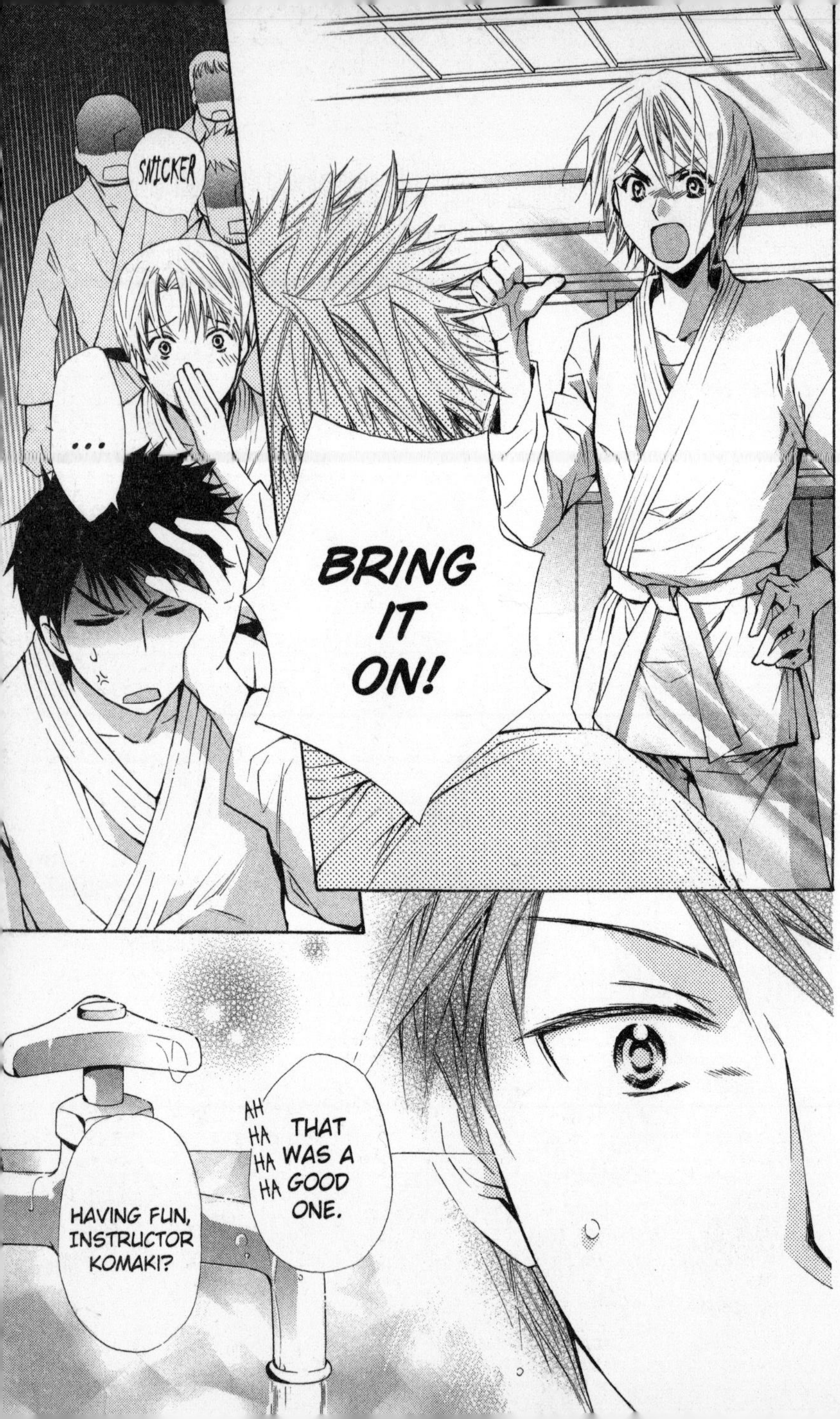
BRING IT ON!
SNICKER
...
AH HA HA HA
THAT WAS A GOOD ONE.
HAVING FUN, INSTRUCTOR KOMAKI?

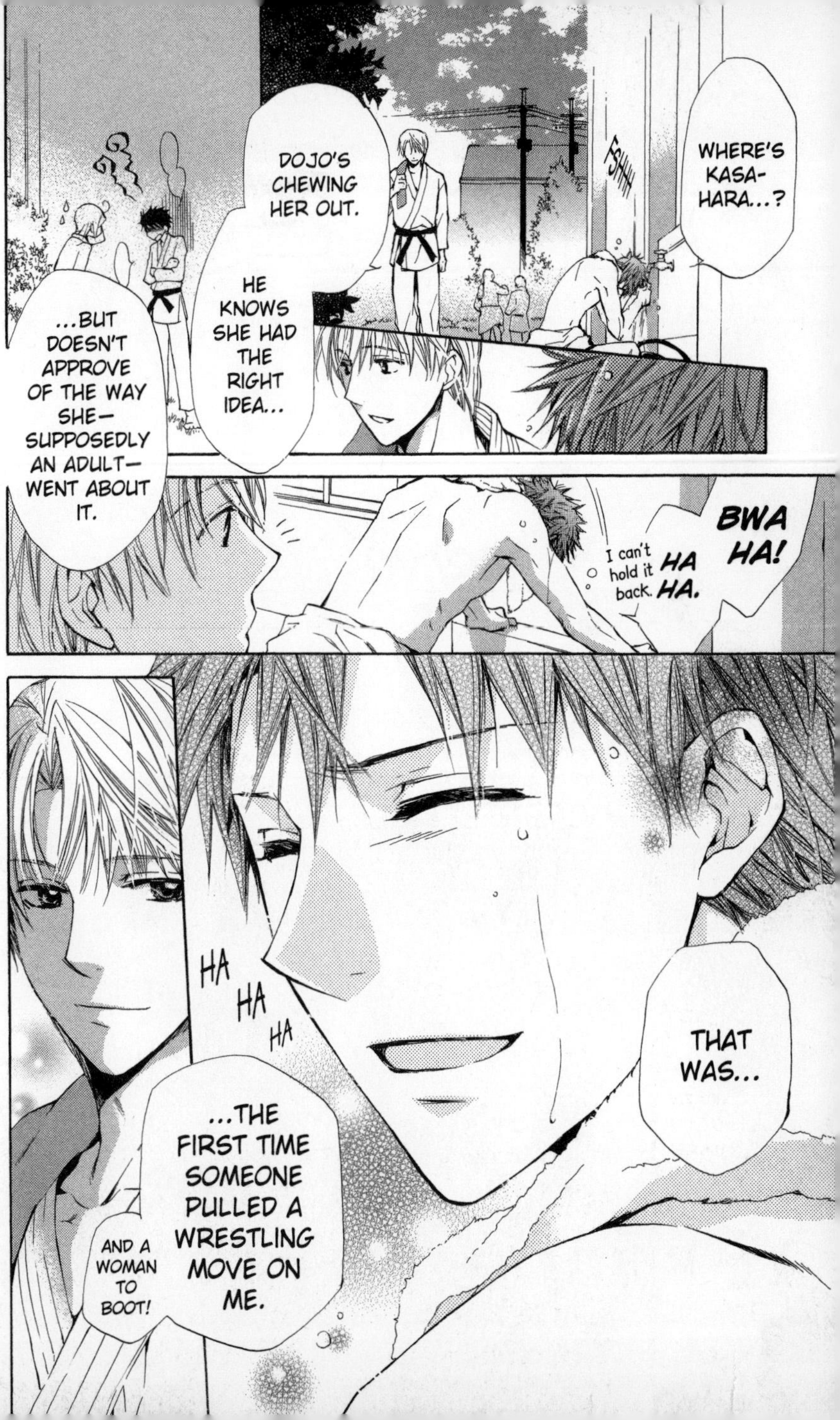
FSHHH
WHERE'S KASA-HARA...?
DOJO'S CHEWING HER OUT.
HE KNOWS SHE HAD THE RIGHT IDEA...
...BUT DOESN'T APPROVE OF THE WAY SHE—SUPPOSEDLY AN ADULT—WENT ABOUT IT.
BWA HA!
HA HA.
I can't hold it back.
THAT WAS...
HA HA HA
...THE FIRST TIME SOMEONE PULLED A WRESTLING MOVE ON ME.
AND A WOMAN TO BOOT!

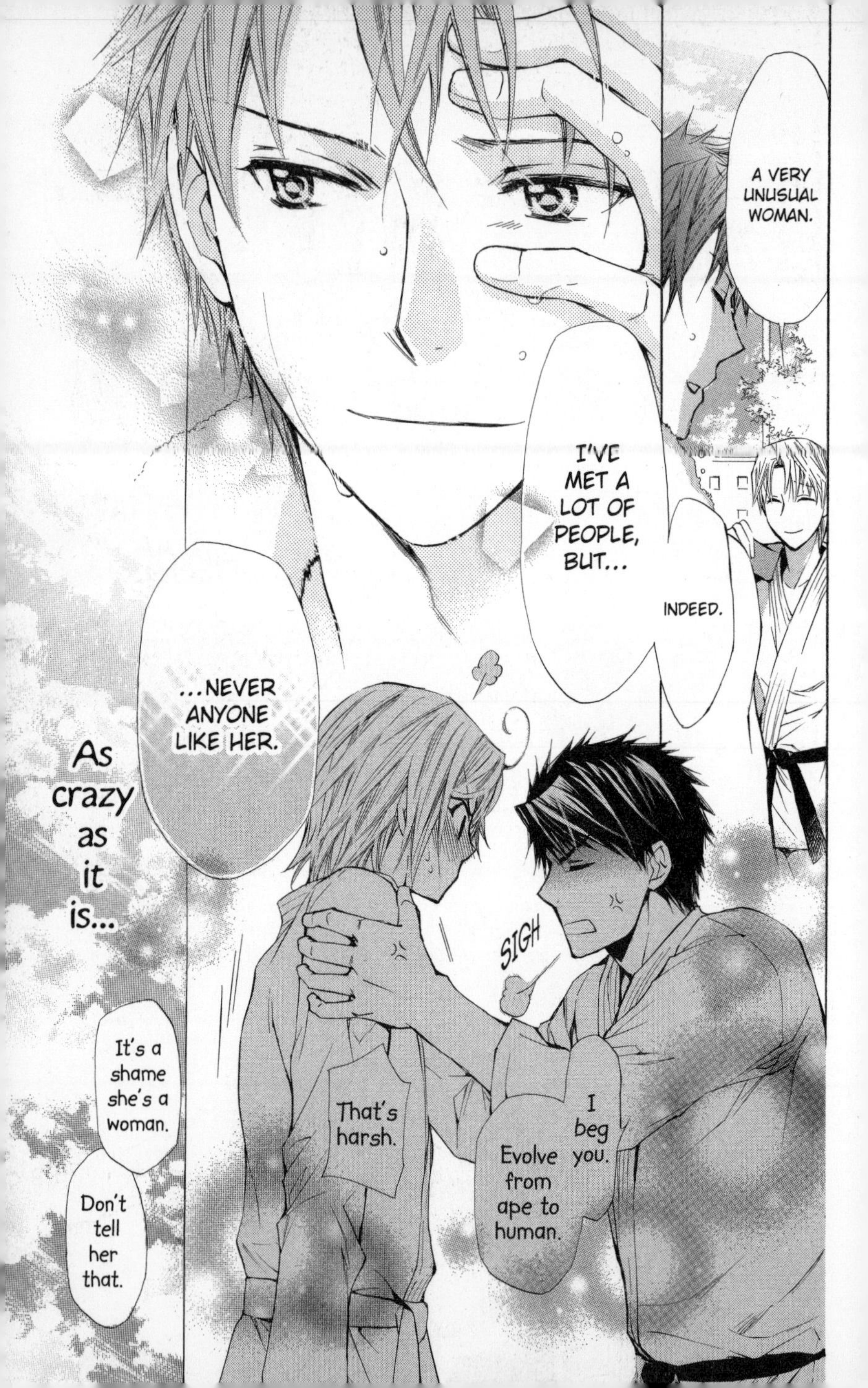
A VERY UNUSUAL WOMAN.
INDEED.
I'VE MET A LOT OF PEOPLE, BUT...
...NEVER ANYONE LIKE HER.
As crazy as it is...
I beg you.
Evolve from ape to human.
SIGH
That's harsh.
It's a shame she's a woman.
Don't tell her that.

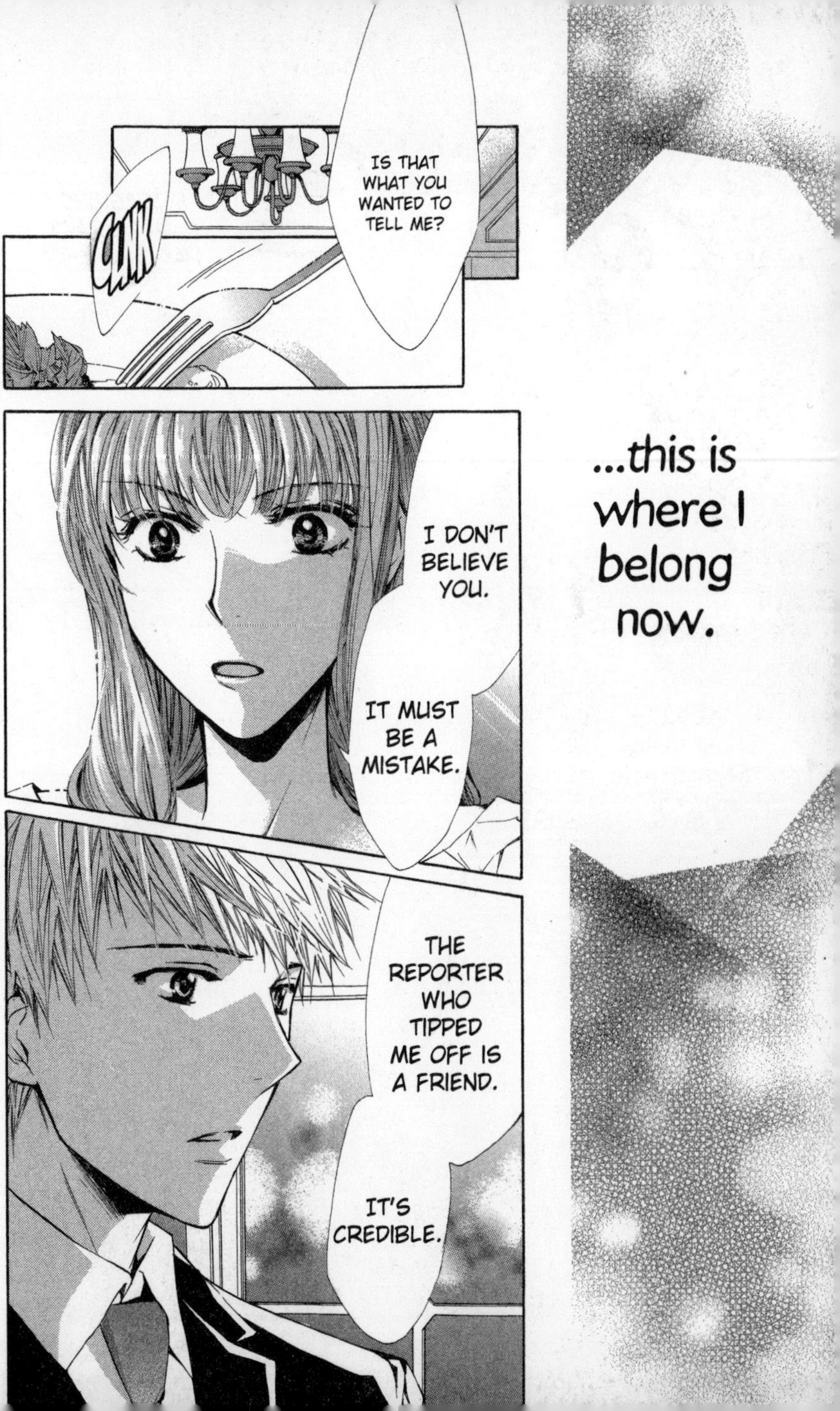
...this is where I belong now.
IS THAT WHAT YOU WANTED TO TELL ME?
CLINK
I DON'T BELIEVE YOU.
IT MUST BE A MISTAKE.
THE REPORTER WHO TIPPED ME OFF IS A FRIEND.
IT'S CREDIBLE.

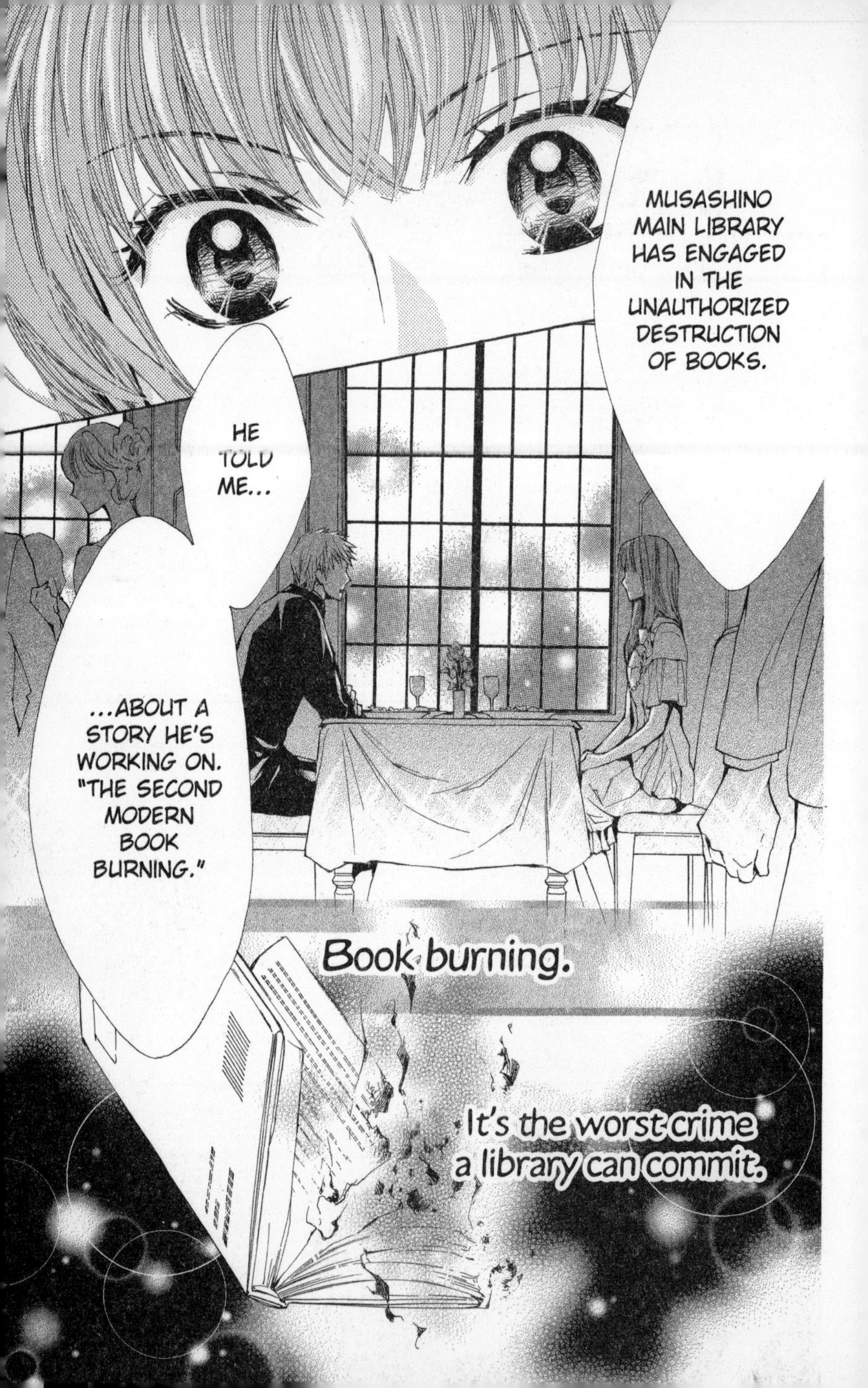
MUSASHINO MAIN LIBRARY HAS ENGAGED IN THE UNAUTHORIZED DESTRUCTION OF BOOKS.
HE TOLD ME...
...ABOUT A STORY HE'S WORKING ON. "THE SECOND MODERN BOOK BURNING."
Book burning.
It's the worst crime a library can commit.

Brother's Angst

After five years apart, I'm going to see my older brother today.
Five years... that's a long time. Is he the same as he was when he abandoned us?
GASP
What if he's changed so much I can't recognize him? How should I react if he's gained a lot of weight or gone bald...?
Laugh at him! That's one way to settle the score. Laugh out loud!
Hikaru.
PHEW
?
Why am I relieved?

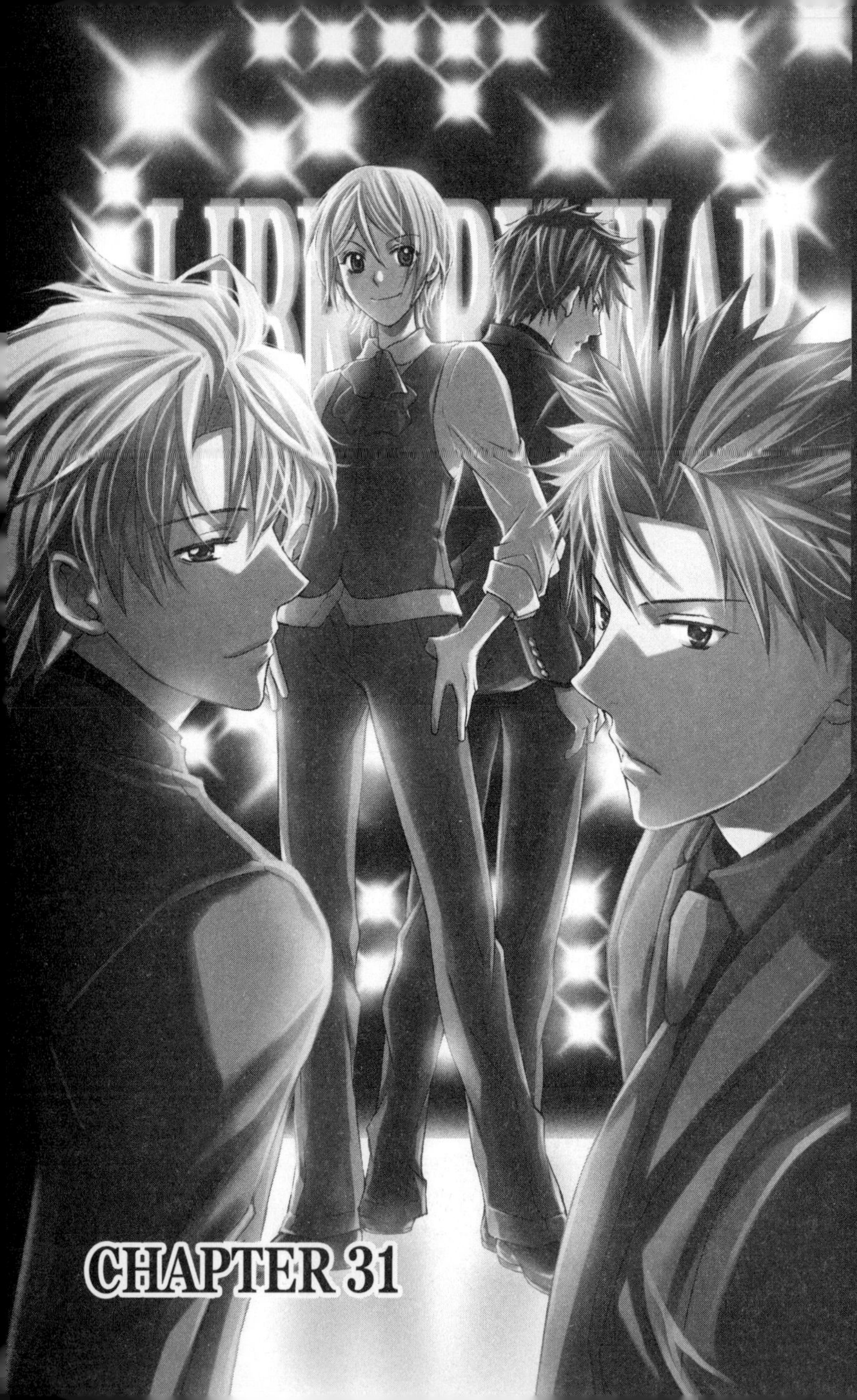
CHAPTER 31

Secret Admirer part 6

PREVIOUSLY
Moburo Agohige has a crush on Iku Kasahara, but it's not working out for him.
Will his love ever bloom? Will Iku at least notice him someday? Good luck to you, Moburo! Hang in there!
MOBURO AGOHIGE
Our first combat training in a while! Freestyle! Sparring with Kasahara!!
CLENCH
No, no, no. I'm not being naughty. I genuinely want to help.
I'm next!
IKU
GLARE
PANT
PANT
Right after the suplex.
Sparring Time: 0.5 seconds

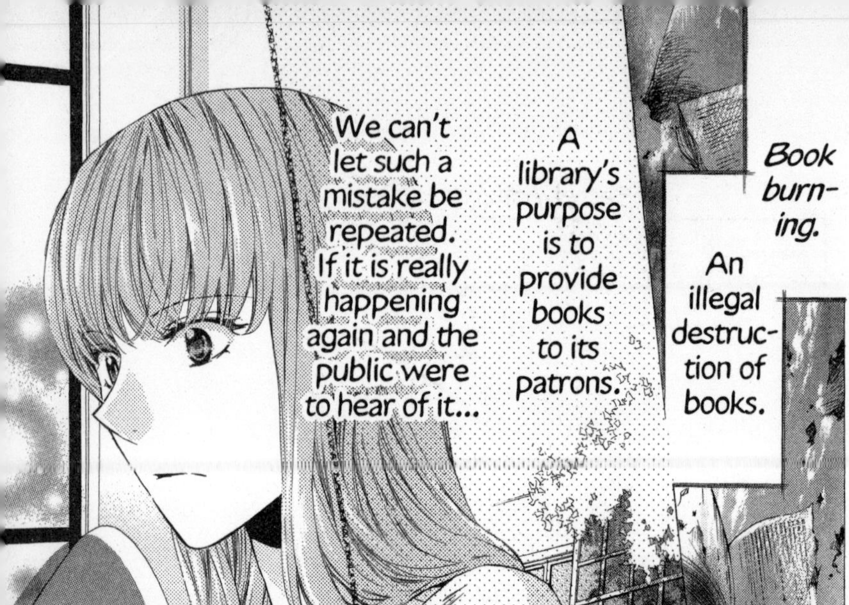
Book burning.
An illegal destruction of books.
A library's purpose is to provide books to its patrons.
We can't let such a mistake be repeated. If it is really happening again and the public were to hear of it...
...support for the library would fall apart.
THE MUSASHINO MAIN LIBRARY.

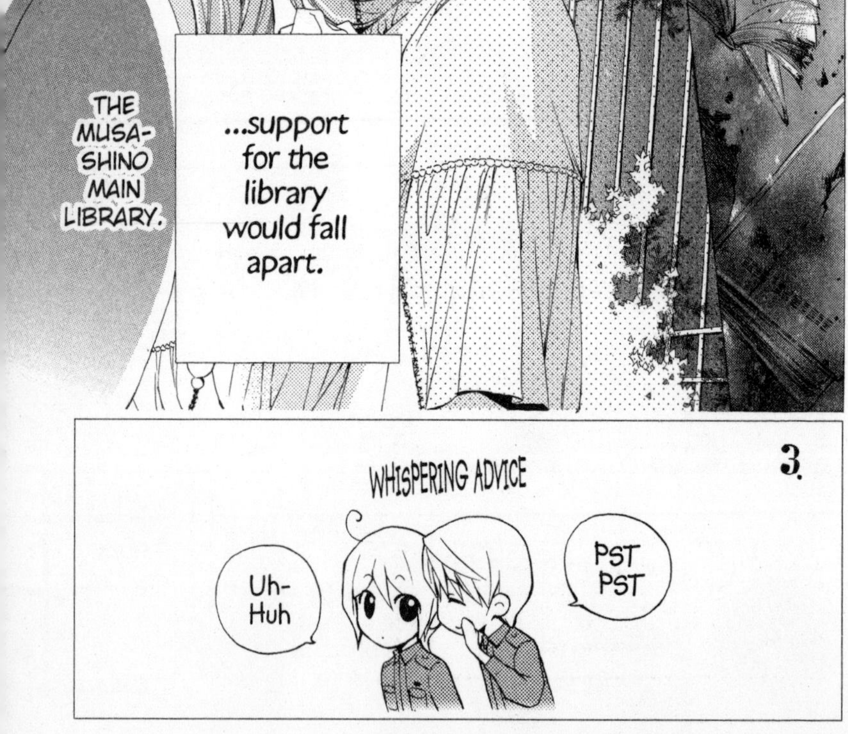
3.
WHISPERING ADVICE
PST PST
Uh-Huh

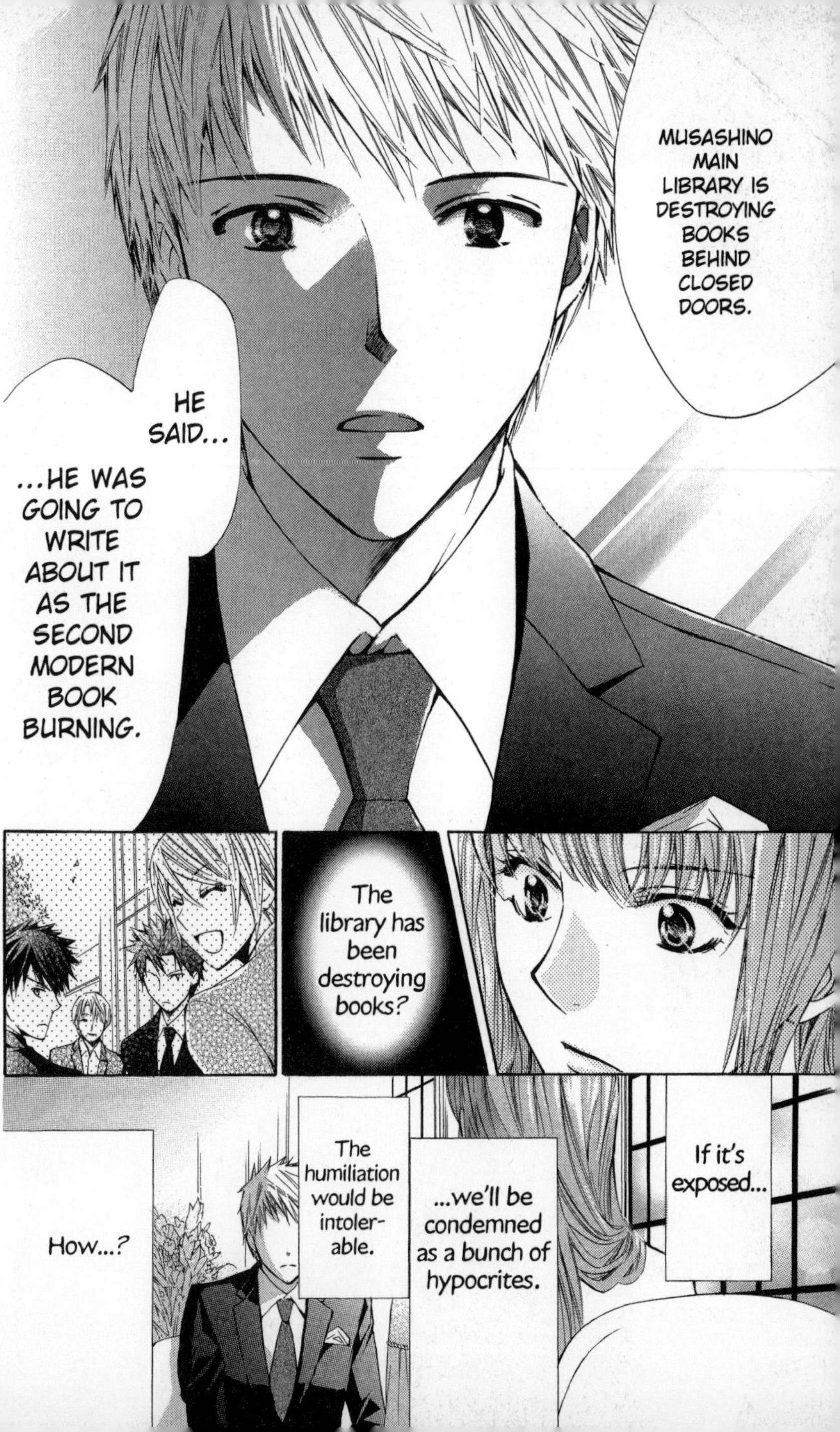
MUSASHINO MAIN LIBRARY IS DESTROYING BOOKS BEHIND CLOSED DOORS.
HE SAID...
...HE WAS GOING TO WRITE ABOUT IT AS THE SECOND MODERN BOOK BURNING.
The library has been destroying books?
If it's exposed...
...we'll be condemned as a bunch of hypocrites.
The humiliation would be intoler-able.
How...?

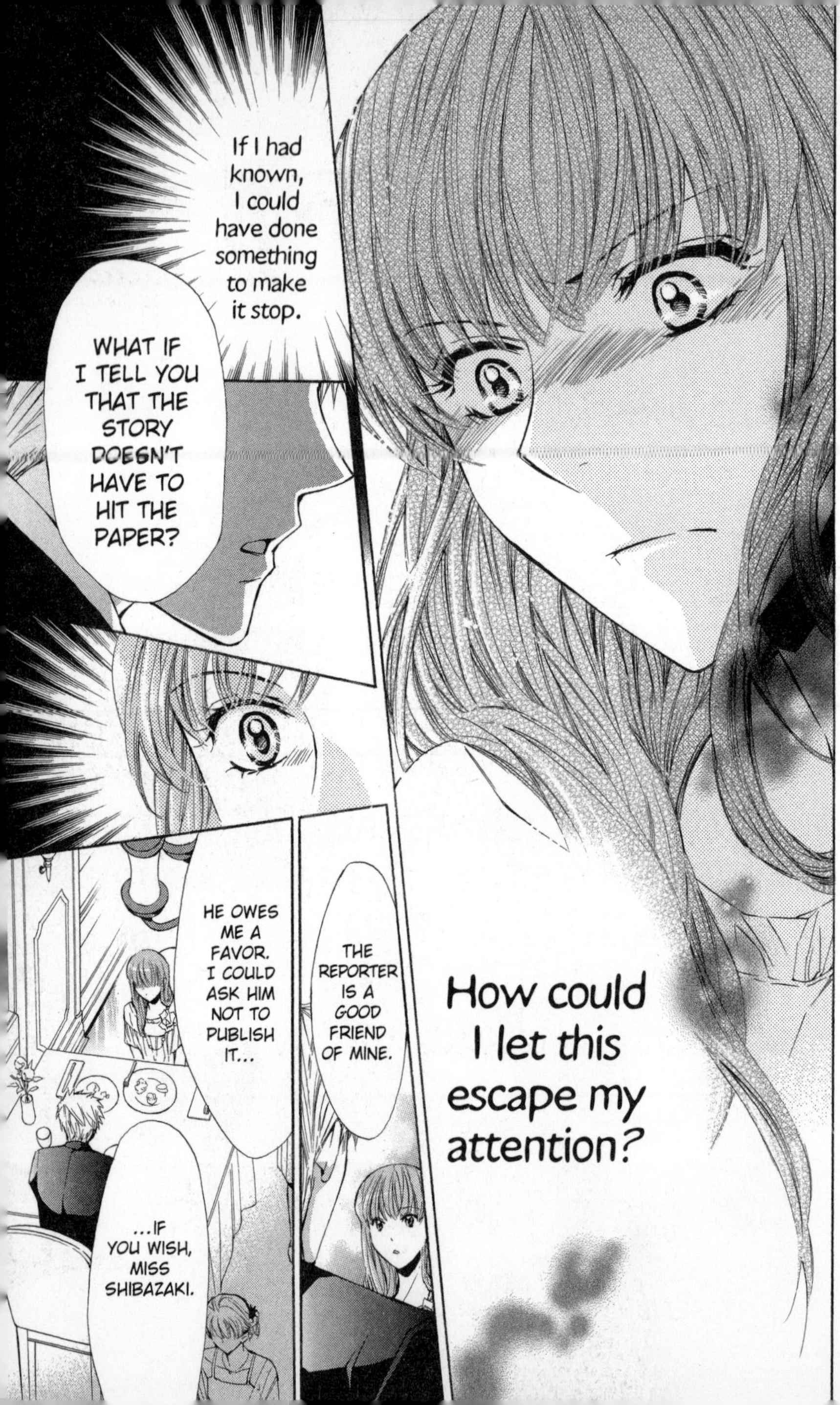
How could I let this escape my attention?
If I had known, I could have done something to make it stop.
WHAT IF I TELL YOU THAT THE STORY DOESN'T HAVE TO HIT THE PAPER?
THE REPORTER IS A GOOD FRIEND OF MINE.
HE OWES ME A FAVOR. I COULD ASK HIM NOT TO PUBLISH IT...
...IF YOU WISH, MISS SHIBAZAKI.

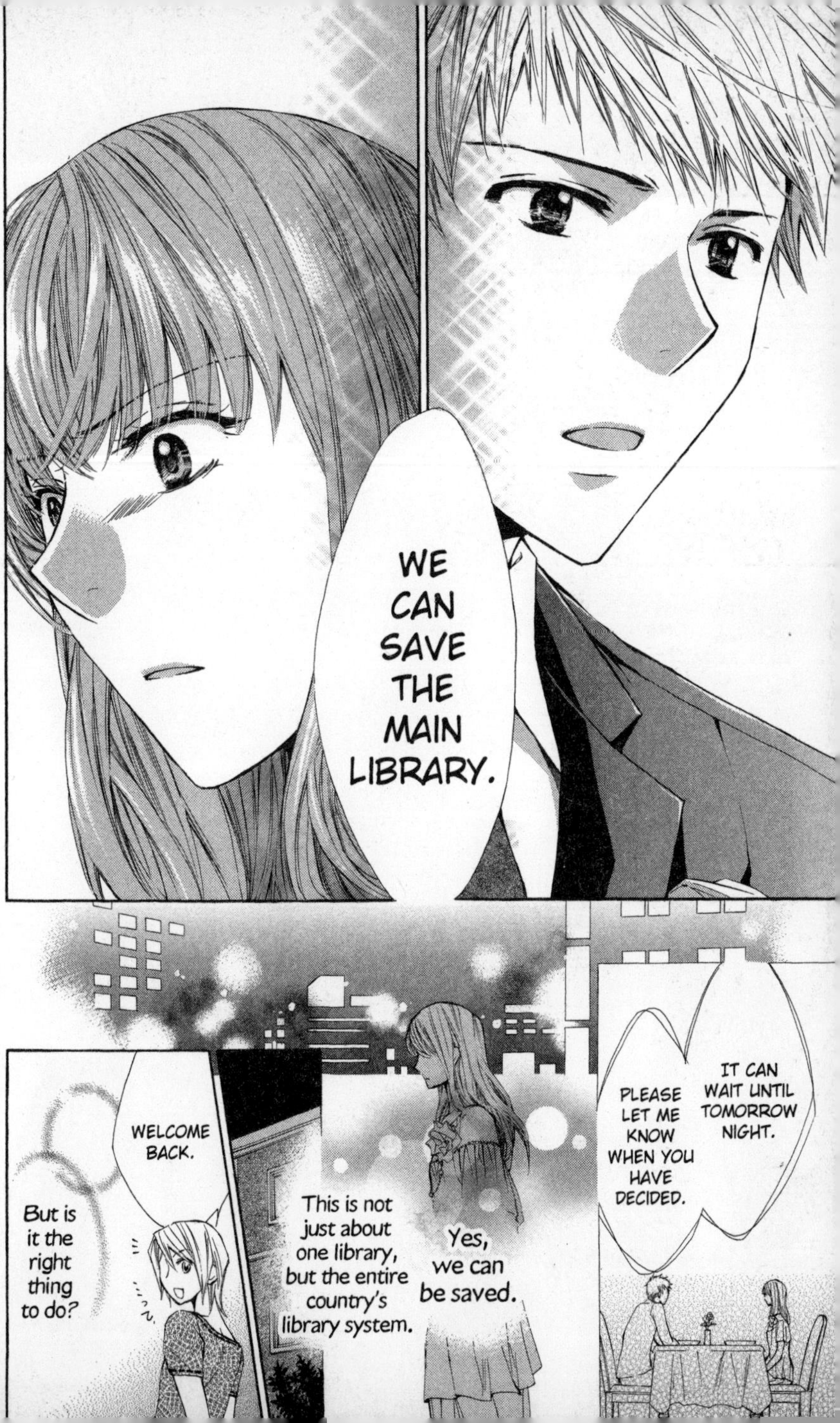
WE CAN SAVE THE MAIN LIBRARY.
IT CAN WAIT UNTIL TOMORROW NIGHT.
PLEASE LET ME KNOW WHEN YOU HAVE DECIDED.
Yes, we can be saved.
This is not just about one library, but the entire country's library system.
WELCOME BACK.
But is it the right thing to do?

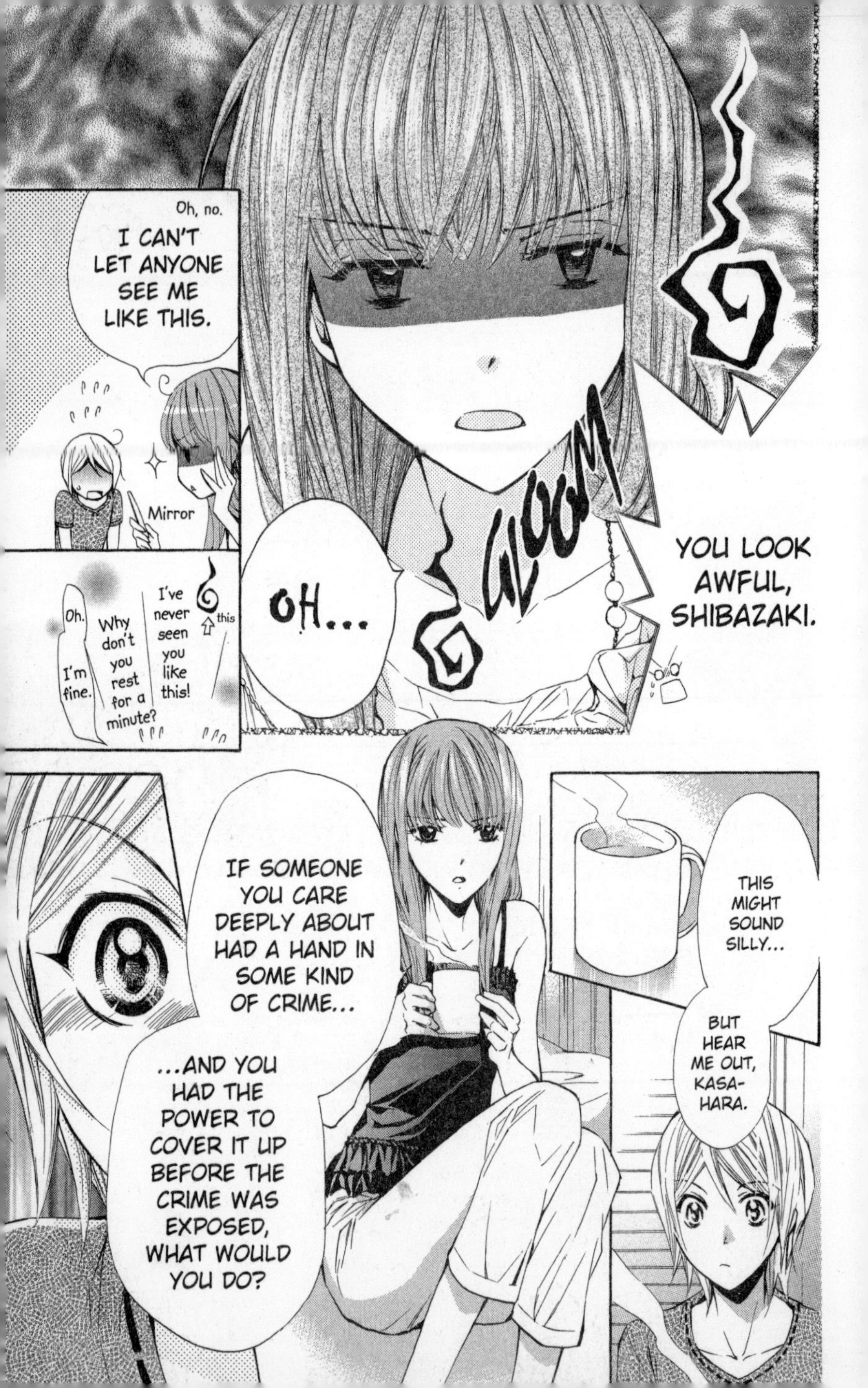
YOU LOOK AWFUL, SHIBAZAKI.
GLOOM
OH...
Oh, no.
I CAN'T LET ANYONE SEE ME LIKE THIS.
Mirror
I've never seen you like this!
this
Why don't you rest for a minute?
Oh.
I'm fine.
THIS MIGHT SOUND SILLY...
BUT HEAR ME OUT, KASA-HARA.
IF SOMEONE YOU CARE DEEPLY ABOUT HAD A HAND IN SOME KIND OF CRIME...
...AND YOU HAD THE POWER TO COVER IT UP BEFORE THE CRIME WAS EXPOSED, WHAT WOULD YOU DO?

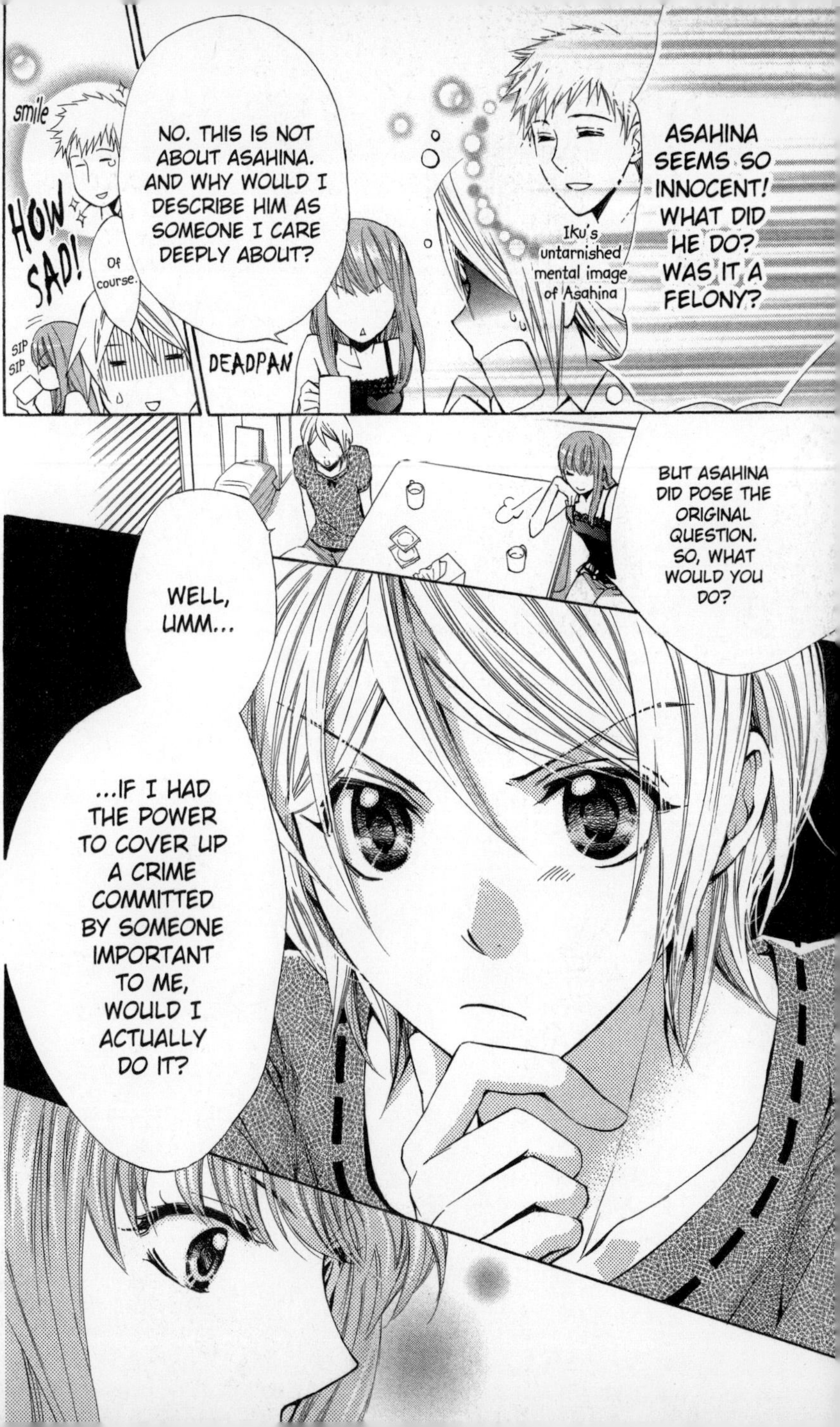
ASAHINA SEEMS SO INNOCENT! WHAT DID HE DO? WAS IT A FELONY?
Iku's untarnished mental image of Asahina
NO. THIS IS NOT ABOUT ASAHINA. AND WHY WOULD I DESCRIBE HIM AS SOMEONE I CARE DEEPLY ABOUT?
DEADPAN
smile
HOW SAD!
Of course.
SIP SIP
BUT ASAHINA DID POSE THE ORIGINAL QUESTION. SO, WHAT WOULD YOU DO?
WELL, UMM...
...IF I HAD THE POWER TO COVER UP A CRIME COMMITTED BY SOMEONE IMPORTANT TO ME, WOULD I ACTUALLY DO IT?

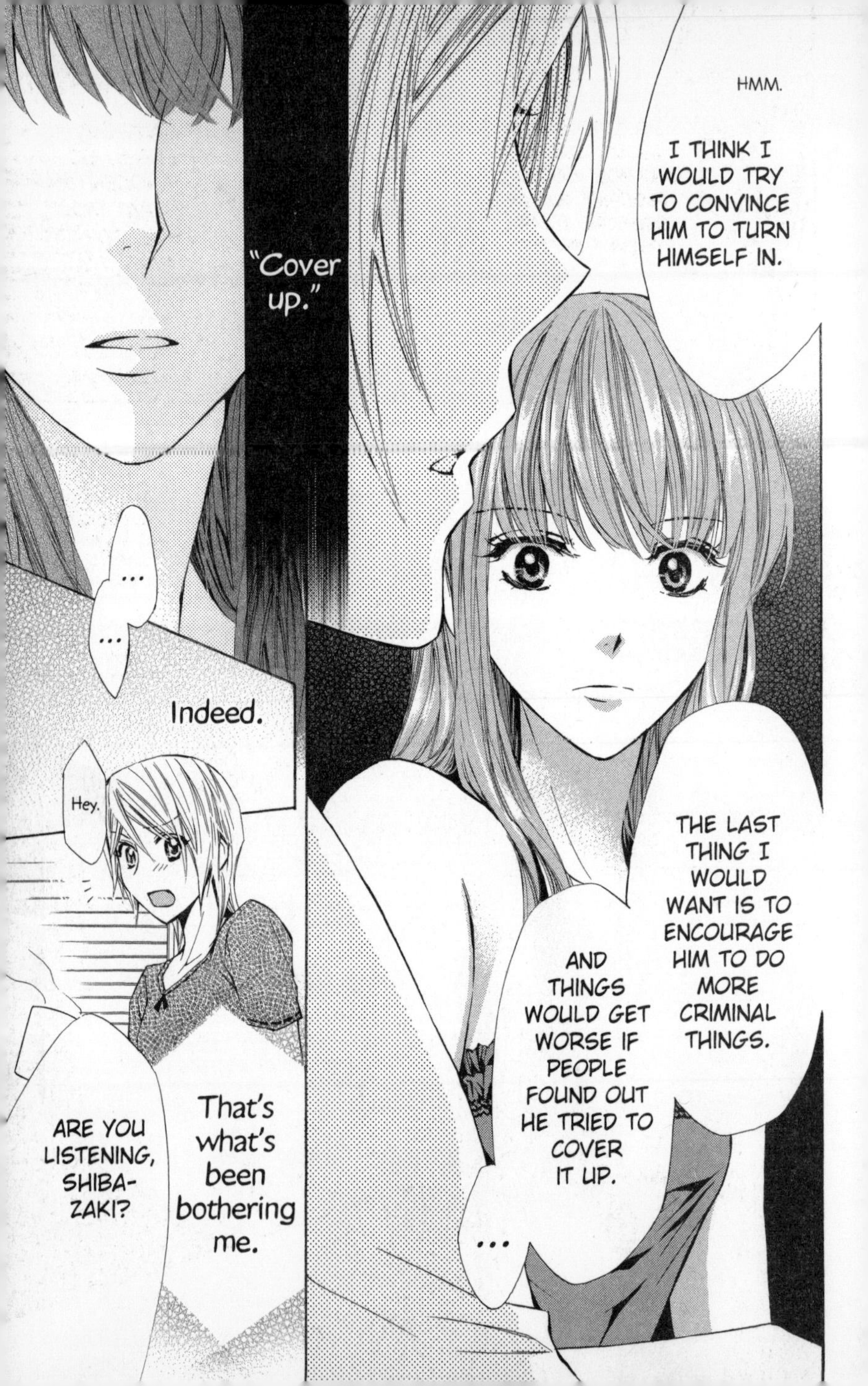
HMM.
I THINK I WOULD TRY TO CONVINCE HIM TO TURN HIMSELF IN.
THE LAST THING I WOULD WANT IS TO ENCOURAGE HIM TO DO MORE CRIMINAL THINGS.
AND THINGS WOULD GET WORSE IF PEOPLE FOUND OUT HE TRIED TO COVER IT UP.
...
"Cover up."
...
...
Indeed.
Hey.
That's what's been bothering me.
ARE YOU LISTENING, SHIBA-ZAKI?

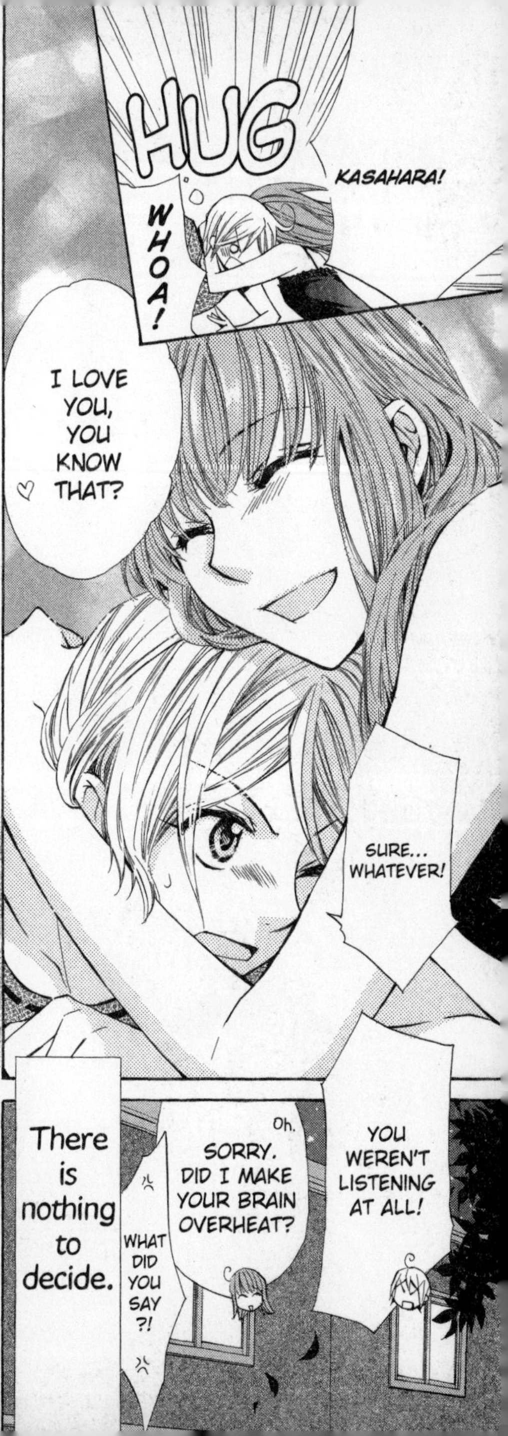
HUG
KASAHARA!
WHOA!
I LOVE YOU, YOU KNOW THAT? ♡
SURE... WHATEVER!
YOU WEREN'T LISTENING AT ALL!
Oh.
SORRY. DID I MAKE YOUR BRAIN OVERHEAT?
WHAT DID YOU SAY?!
There is nothing to decide.

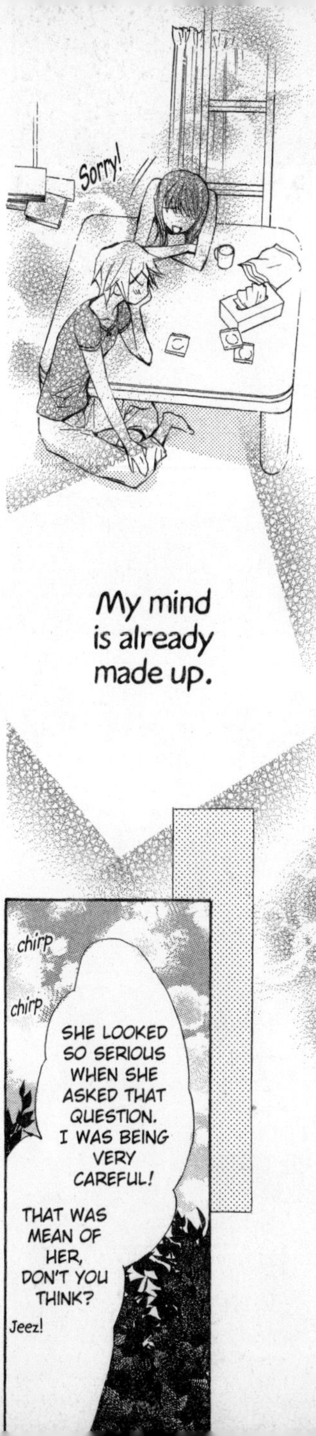
Sorry!
My mind is already made up.
chirp
chirp
SHE LOOKED SO SERIOUS WHEN SHE ASKED THAT QUESTION. I WAS BEING VERY CAREFUL!
THAT WAS MEAN OF HER, DON'T YOU THINK?
Jeez!

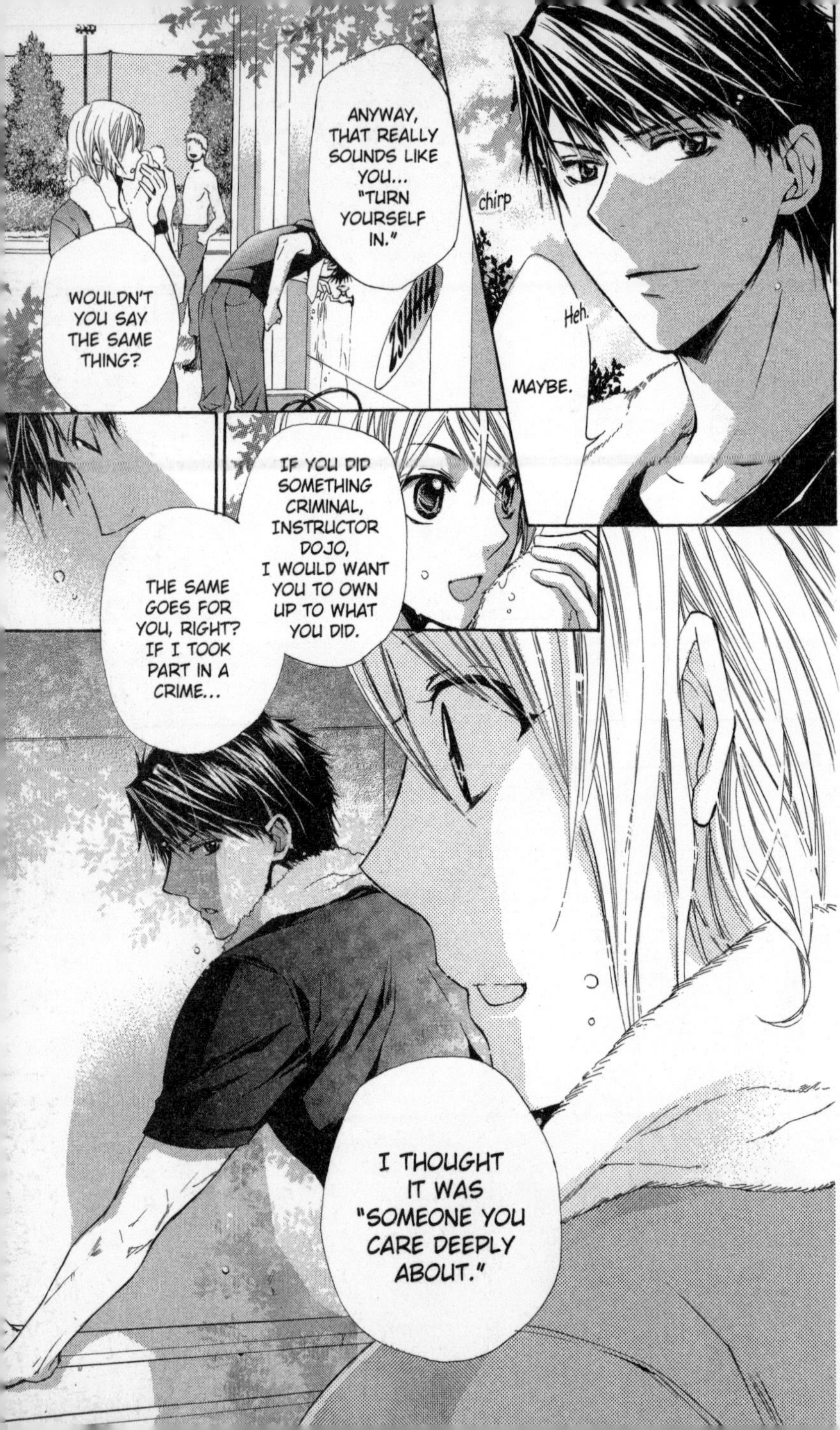

chirp
Heh.
MAYBE.
ANYWAY, THAT REALLY SOUNDS LIKE YOU... "TURN YOURSELF IN."
ZSHHH
WOULDN'T YOU SAY THE SAME THING?
IF YOU DID SOMETHING CRIMINAL, INSTRUCTOR DOJO, I WOULD WANT YOU TO OWN UP TO WHAT YOU DID.
THE SAME GOES FOR YOU, RIGHT? IF I TOOK PART IN A CRIME...
I THOUGHT IT WAS "SOMEONE YOU CARE DEEPLY ABOUT."

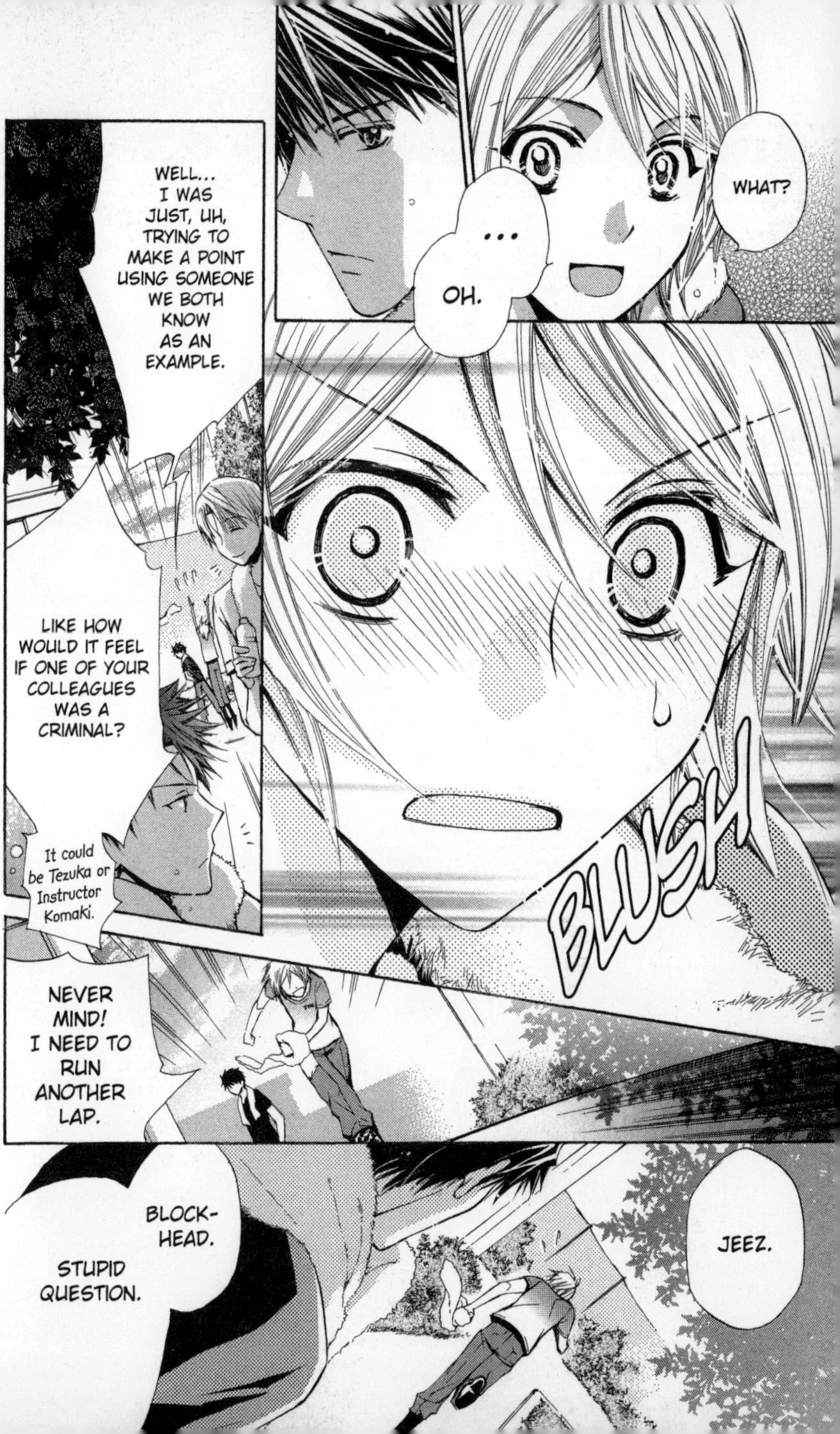
WHAT?
... OH.
BLUSH
WELL... I WAS JUST, UH, TRYING TO MAKE A POINT USING SOMEONE WE BOTH KNOW AS AN EXAMPLE.
LIKE HOW WOULD IT FEEL IF ONE OF YOUR COLLEAGUES WAS A CRIMINAL?
It could be Tezuka or Instructor Komaki.
NEVER MIND! I NEED TO RUN ANOTHER LAP.
JEEZ.
BLOCK-HEAD.
STUPID QUESTION.

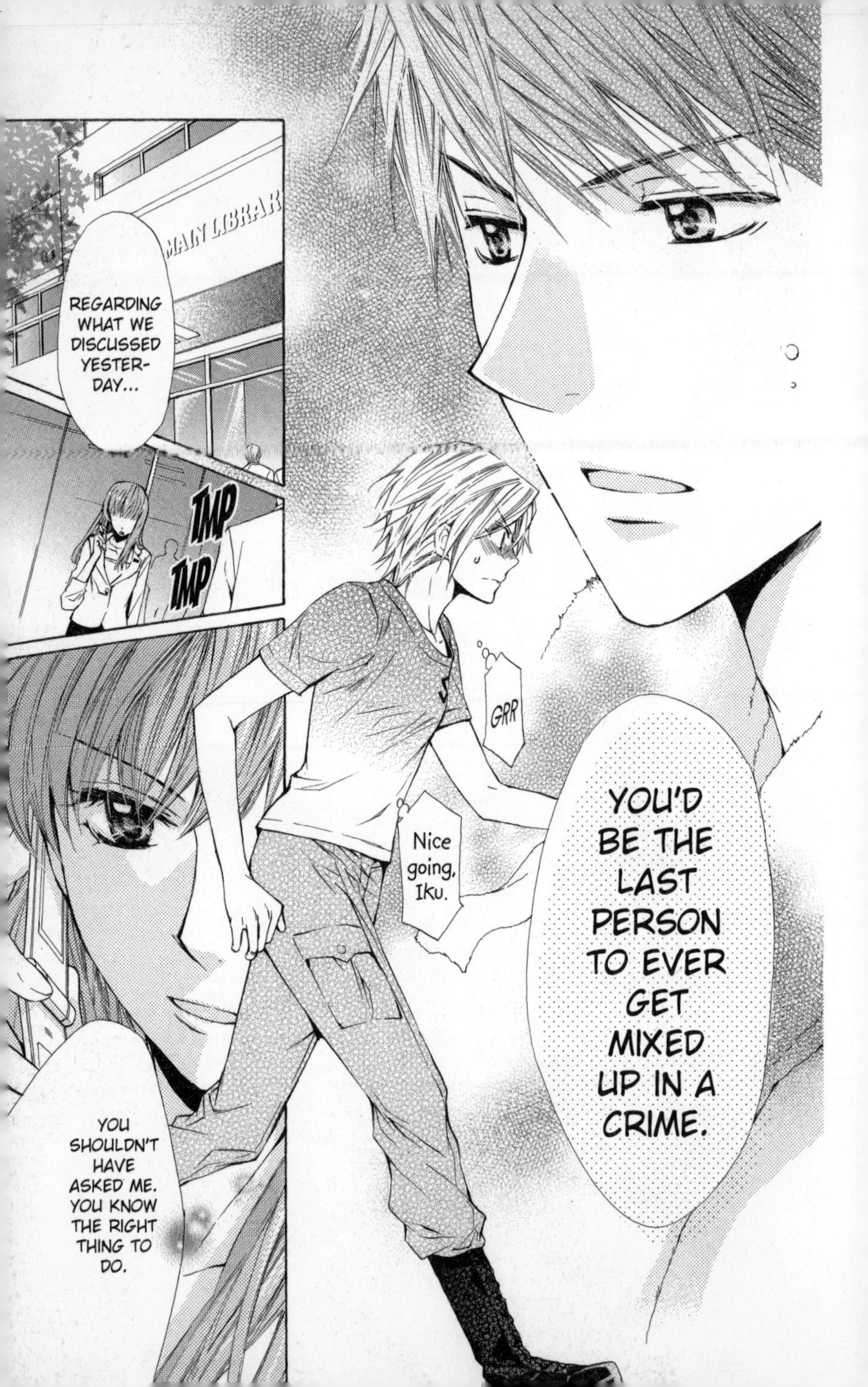
YOU'D BE THE LAST PERSON TO EVER GET MIXED UP IN A CRIME.
GRR
Nice going, Iku.
MAIN LIBRAR
REGARDING WHAT WE DISCUSSED YESTER-DAY...
TMP
TMP
YOU SHOULDN'T HAVE ASKED ME. YOU KNOW THE RIGHT THING TO DO.

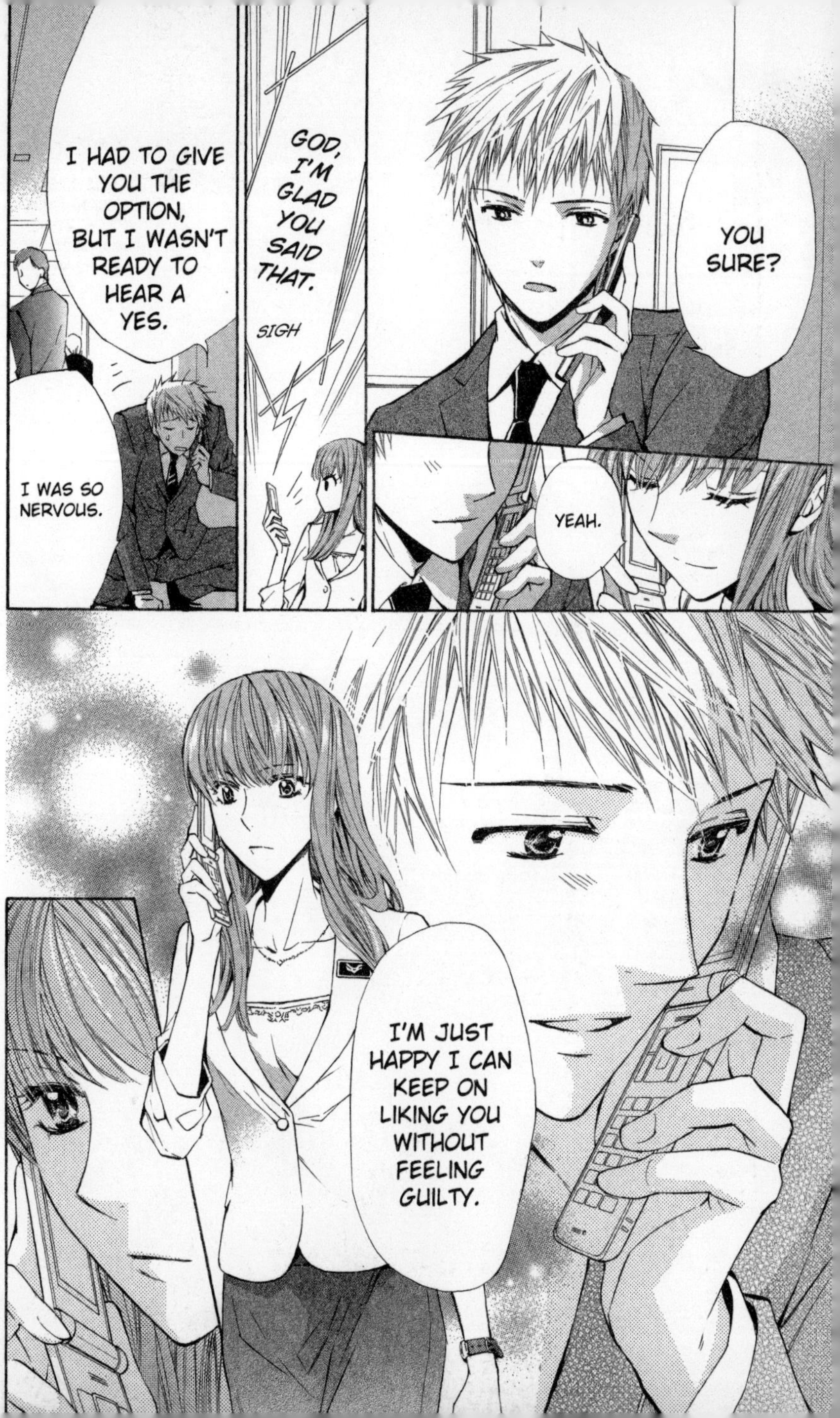
YOU SURE?
YEAH.
GOD, I'M GLAD YOU SAID THAT.
SIGH
I HAD TO GIVE YOU THE OPTION, BUT I WASN'T READY TO HEAR A YES.
I WAS SO NERVOUS.
I'M JUST HAPPY I CAN KEEP ON LIKING YOU WITHOUT FEELING GUILTY.

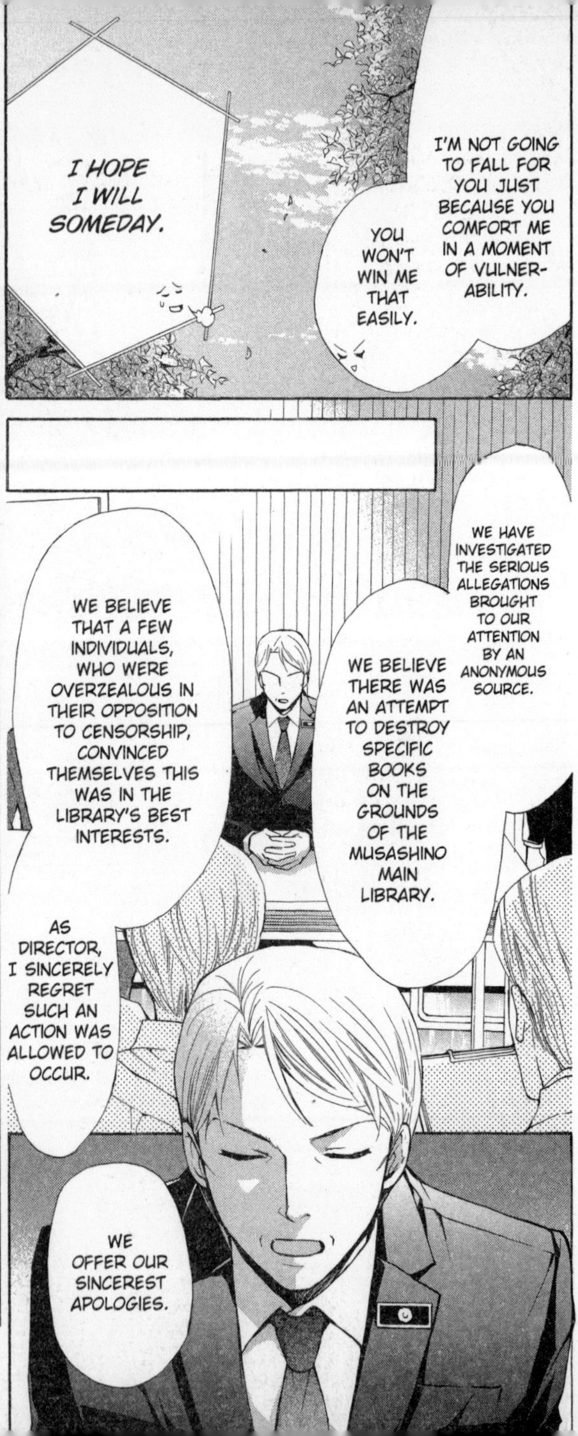
I'M NOT GOING TO FALL FOR YOU JUST BECAUSE YOU COMFORT ME IN A MOMENT OF VULNER-ABILITY.
YOU WON'T WIN ME THAT EASILY.
I HOPE I WILL SOMEDAY.
WE HAVE INVESTIGATED THE SERIOUS ALLEGATIONS BROUGHT TO OUR ATTENTION BY AN ANONYMOUS SOURCE.
WE BELIEVE THERE WAS AN ATTEMPT TO DESTROY SPECIFIC BOOKS ON THE GROUNDS OF THE MUSASHINO MAIN LIBRARY.
WE BELIEVE THAT A FEW INDIVIDUALS, WHO WERE OVERZEALOUS IN THEIR OPPOSITION TO CENSORSHIP, CONVINCED THEMSELVES THIS WAS IN THE LIBRARY'S BEST INTERESTS.
AS DIRECTOR, I SINCERELY REGRET SUCH AN ACTION WAS ALLOWED TO OCCUR.
WE OFFER OUR SINCEREST APOLOGIES.

3

*

Recently—actually, for a long time—I've had a habit of making too many typos and misspellings and flubs when I speak. I'm very disappointed with myself... especially with the flubs.

I used to be a smooth talker. I was better at making people laugh. So when I come across a charismatic talker on TV or friends who are good conversationalists, I'm easily impressed.

I suck at so many things, don't I?

But life is good!

*

*

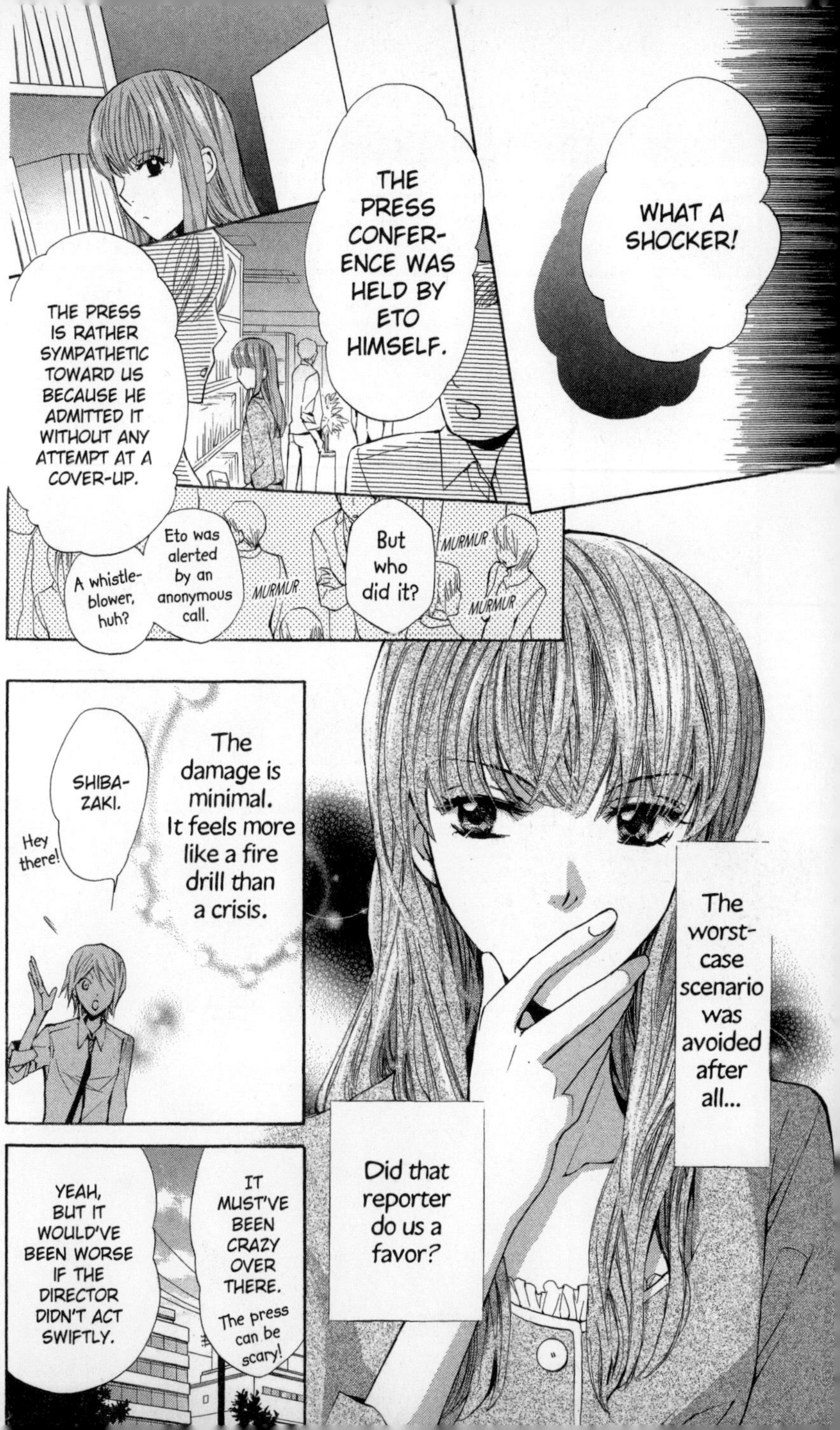
WHAT A SHOCKER!
THE PRESS CONFERENCE WAS HELD BY ETO HIMSELF.
THE PRESS IS RATHER SYMPATHETIC TOWARD US BECAUSE HE ADMITTED IT WITHOUT ANY ATTEMPT AT A COVER-UP.
MURMUR
MURMUR
But who did it?
MURMUR
Eto was alerted by an anonymous call.
A whistle-blower, huh?
The worst-case scenario was avoided after all...
Did that reporter do us a favor?
The damage is minimal. It feels more like a fire drill than a crisis.
SHIBAZAKI.
Hey there!
IT MUST'VE BEEN CRAZY OVER THERE.
The press can be scary!
YEAH, BUT IT WOULD'VE BEEN WORSE IF THE DIRECTOR DIDN'T ACT SWIFTLY.

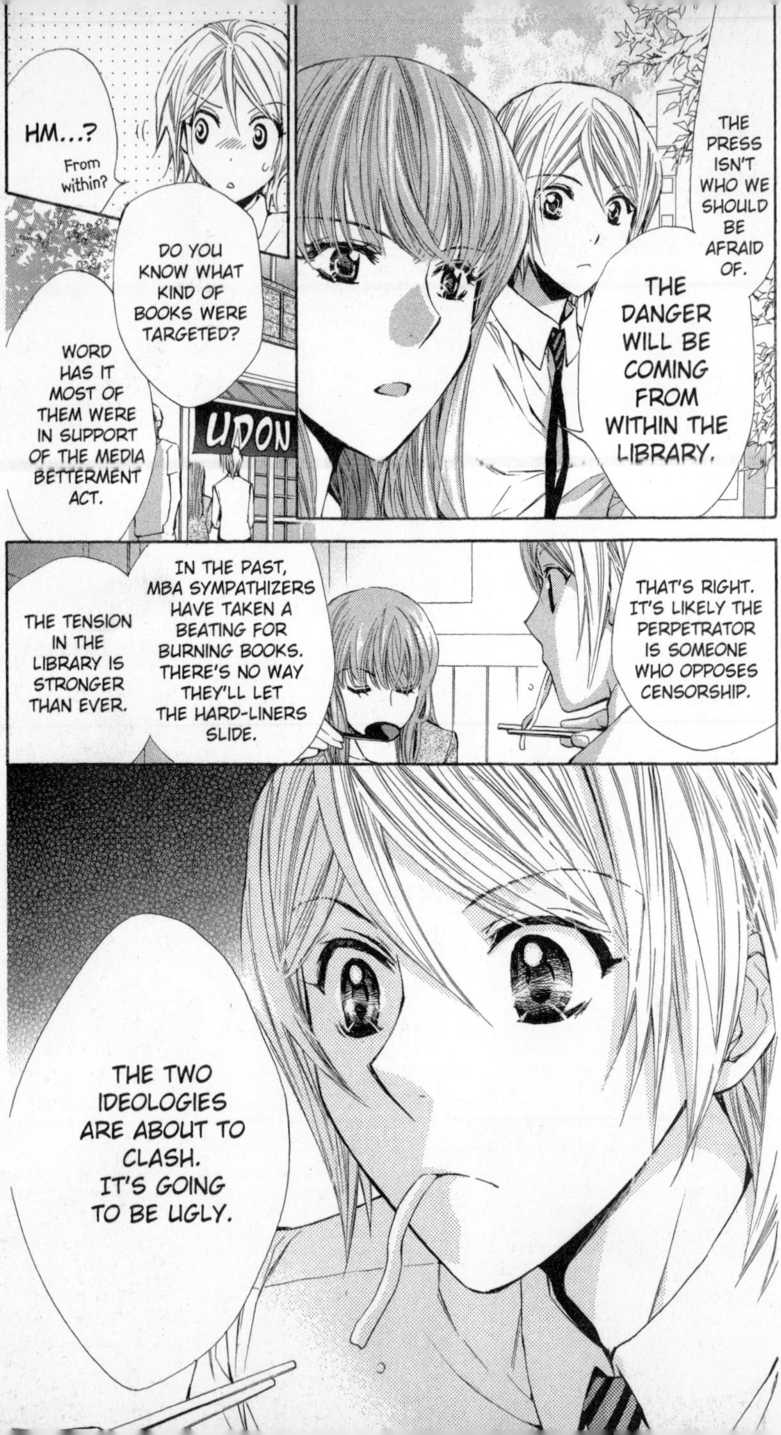
THE PRESS ISN'T WHO WE SHOULD BE AFRAID OF.
THE DANGER WILL BE COMING FROM WITHIN THE LIBRARY.
HM...?
From within?
DO YOU KNOW WHAT KIND OF BOOKS WERE TARGETED?
WORD HAS IT MOST OF THEM WERE IN SUPPORT OF THE MEDIA BETTERMENT ACT.
UDON
THAT'S RIGHT. IT'S LIKELY THE PERPETRATOR IS SOMEONE WHO OPPOSES CENSORSHIP.
IN THE PAST, MBA SYMPATHIZERS HAVE TAKEN A BEATING FOR BURNING BOOKS. THERE'S NO WAY THEY'LL LET THE HARD-LINERS SLIDE.
THE TENSION IN THE LIBRARY IS STRONGER THAN EVER.
THE TWO IDEOLOGIES ARE ABOUT TO CLASH. IT'S GOING TO BE UGLY.

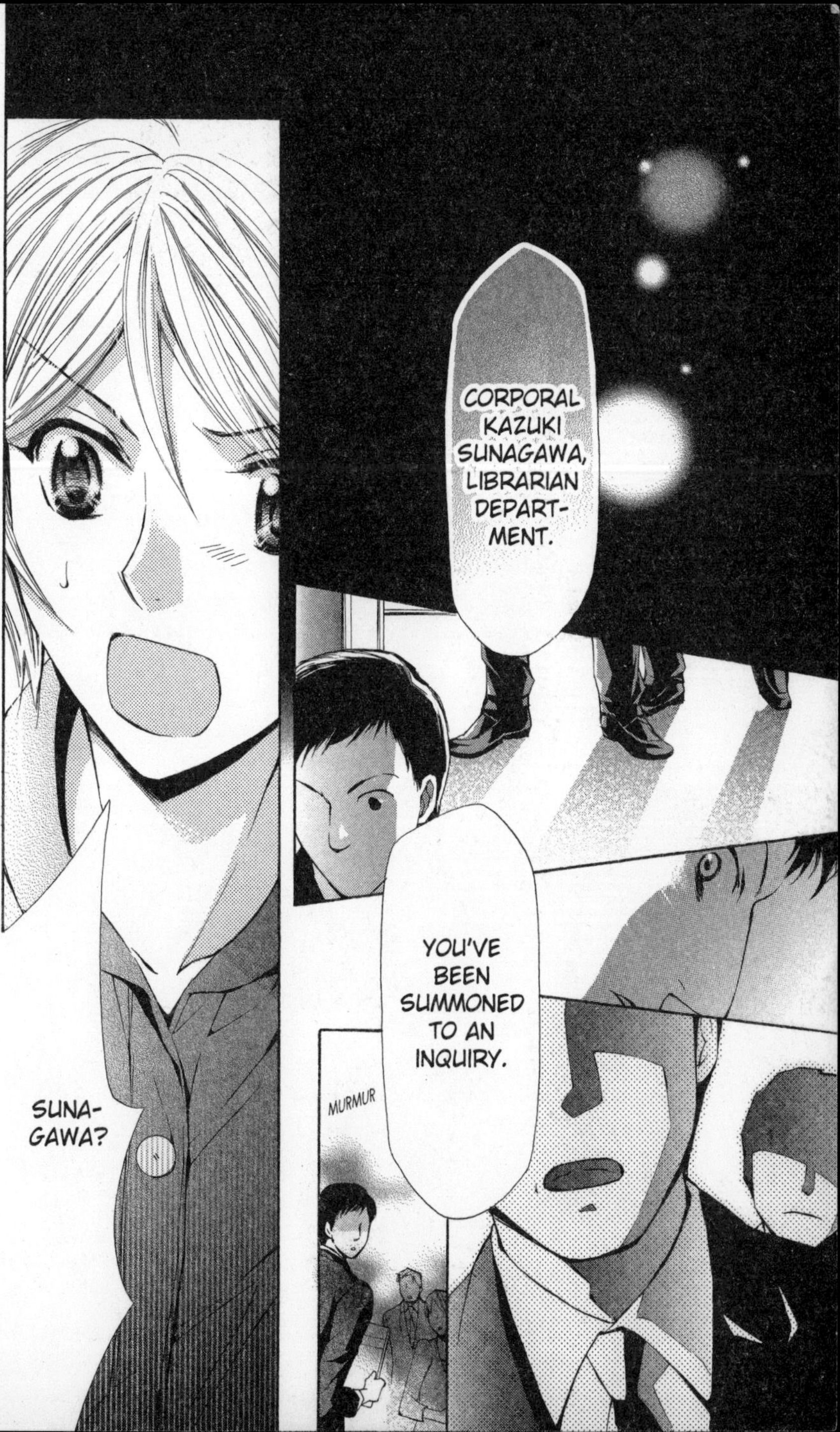
CORPORAL KAZUKI SUNAGAWA, LIBRARIAN DEPART-MENT.
YOU'VE BEEN SUMMONED TO AN INQUIRY.
MURMUR
SUNA-GAWA?

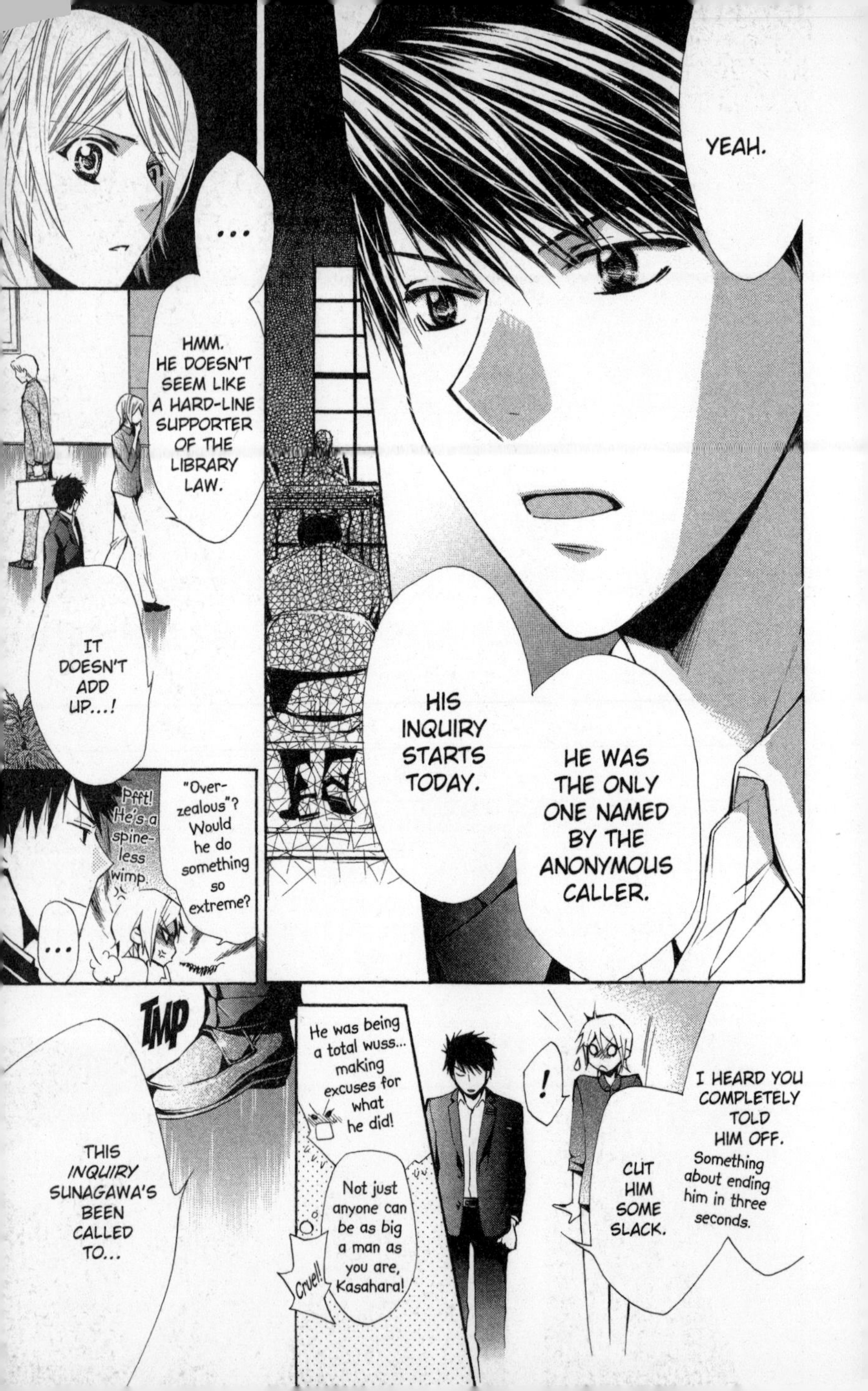
YEAH.
HE WAS THE ONLY ONE NAMED BY THE ANONYMOUS CALLER.
HIS INQUIRY STARTS TODAY.
...
HMM. HE DOESN'T SEEM LIKE A HARD-LINE SUPPORTER OF THE LIBRARY LAW.
IT DOESN'T ADD UP...!
"Over-zealous"? Would he do something so extreme?
Pfft! He's a spine-less wimp.
...
I HEARD YOU COMPLETELY TOLD HIM OFF.
Something about ending him in three seconds.
CUT HIM SOME SLACK.
!
He was being a total wuss... making excuses for what he did!
Not just anyone can be as big a man as you are, Kasahara!
Cruel!
TMP
THIS *INQUIRY* SUNAGAWA'S BEEN CALLED TO...

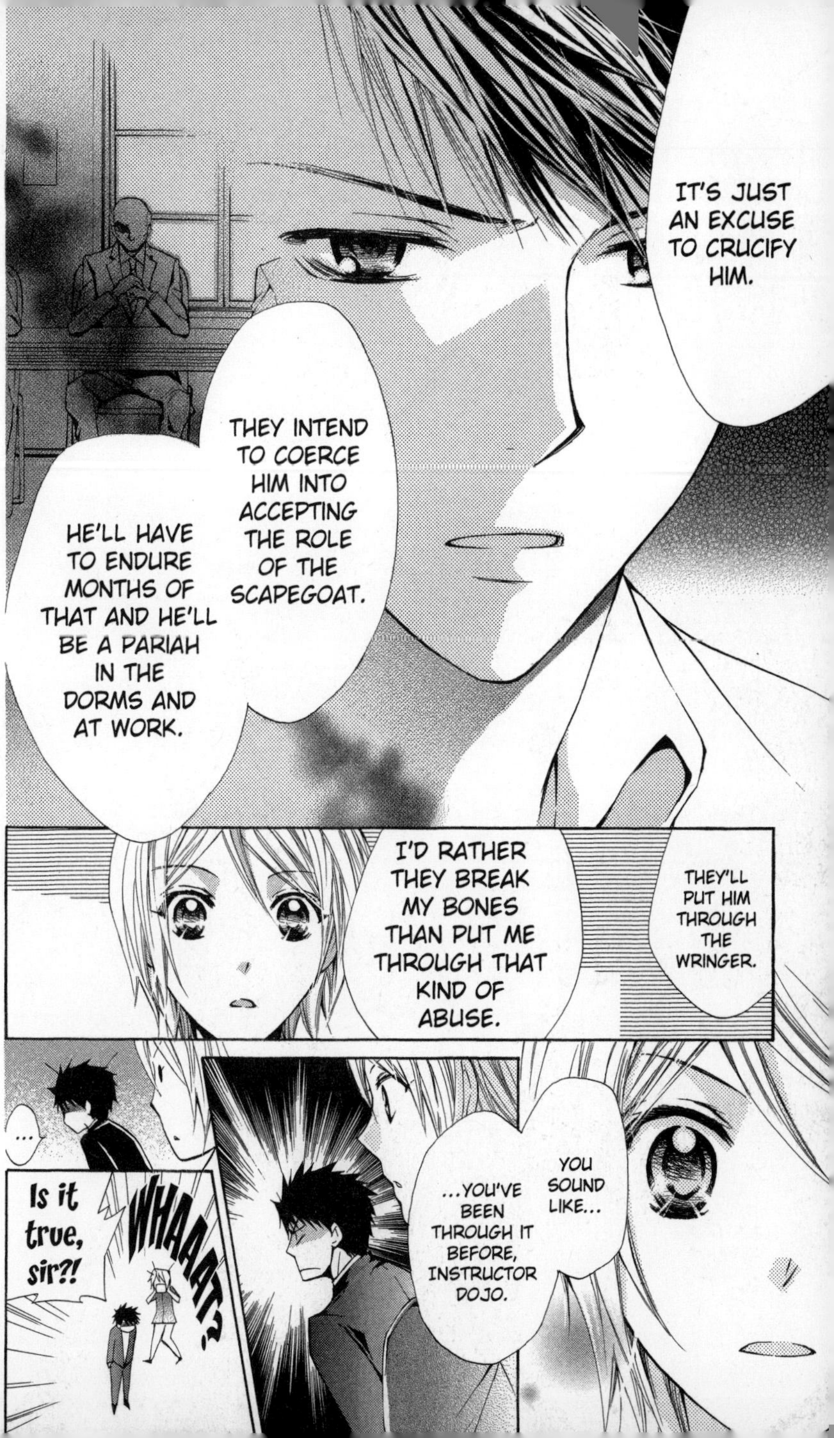
IT'S JUST AN EXCUSE TO CRUCIFY HIM.
THEY INTEND TO COERCE HIM INTO ACCEPTING THE ROLE OF THE SCAPEGOAT.
HE'LL HAVE TO ENDURE MONTHS OF THAT AND HE'LL BE A PARIAH IN THE DORMS AND AT WORK.
THEY'LL PUT HIM THROUGH THE WRINGER.
I'D RATHER THEY BREAK MY BONES THAN PUT ME THROUGH THAT KIND OF ABUSE.
YOU SOUND LIKE...
...YOU'VE BEEN THROUGH IT BEFORE, INSTRUCTOR DOJO.
...
WHAAAT?
Is it true, sir?!

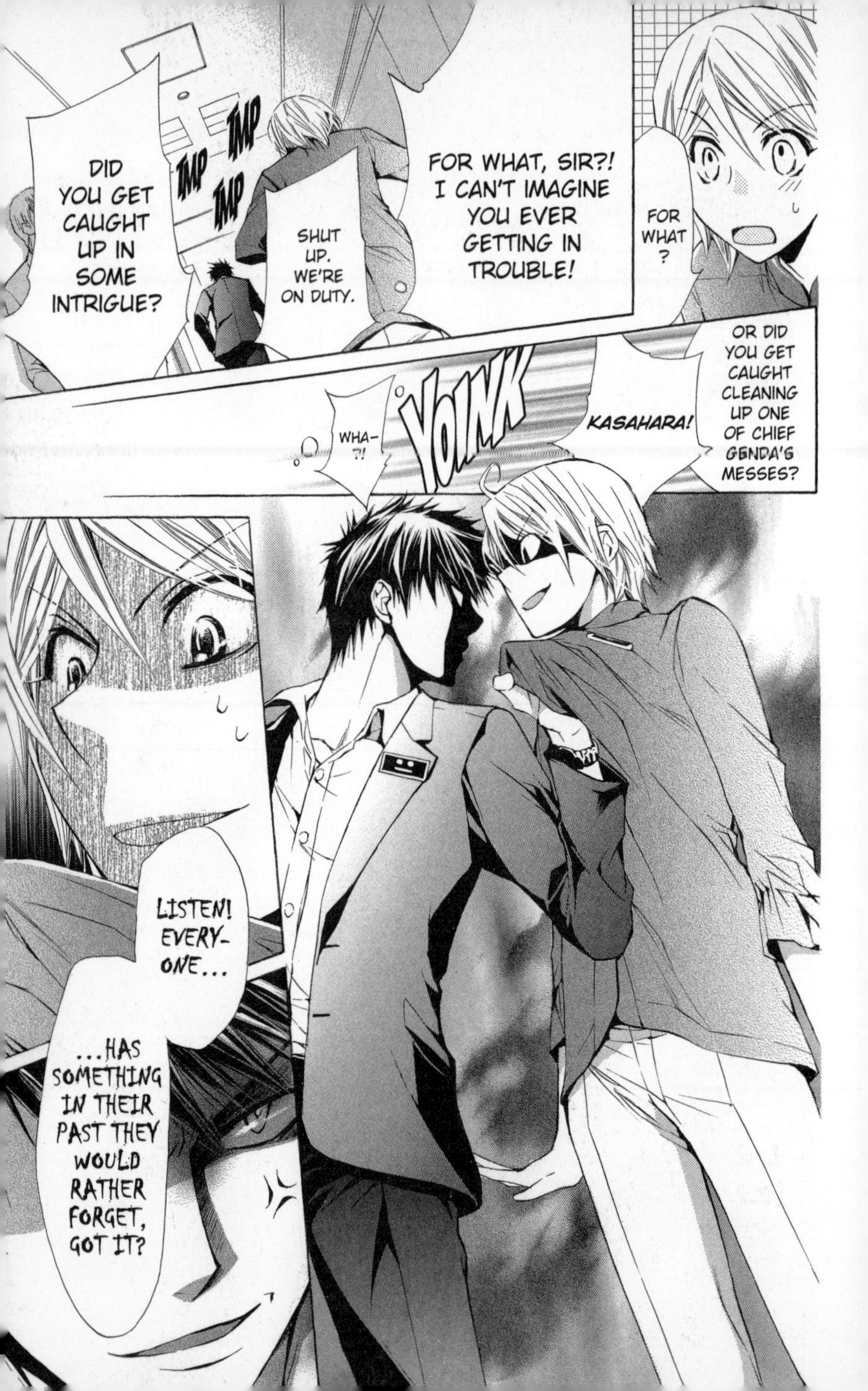
FOR WHAT?
FOR WHAT, SIR?! I CAN'T IMAGINE YOU EVER GETTING IN TROUBLE!
TMP TMP TMP
SHUT UP. WE'RE ON DUTY.
DID YOU GET CAUGHT UP IN SOME INTRIGUE?
OR DID YOU GET CAUGHT CLEANING UP ONE OF CHIEF GENDA'S MESSES?
KASAHARA!
VOINK
WHA-?!
LISTEN! EVERY-ONE...
...HAS SOMETHING IN THEIR PAST THEY WOULD RATHER FORGET, GOT IT?

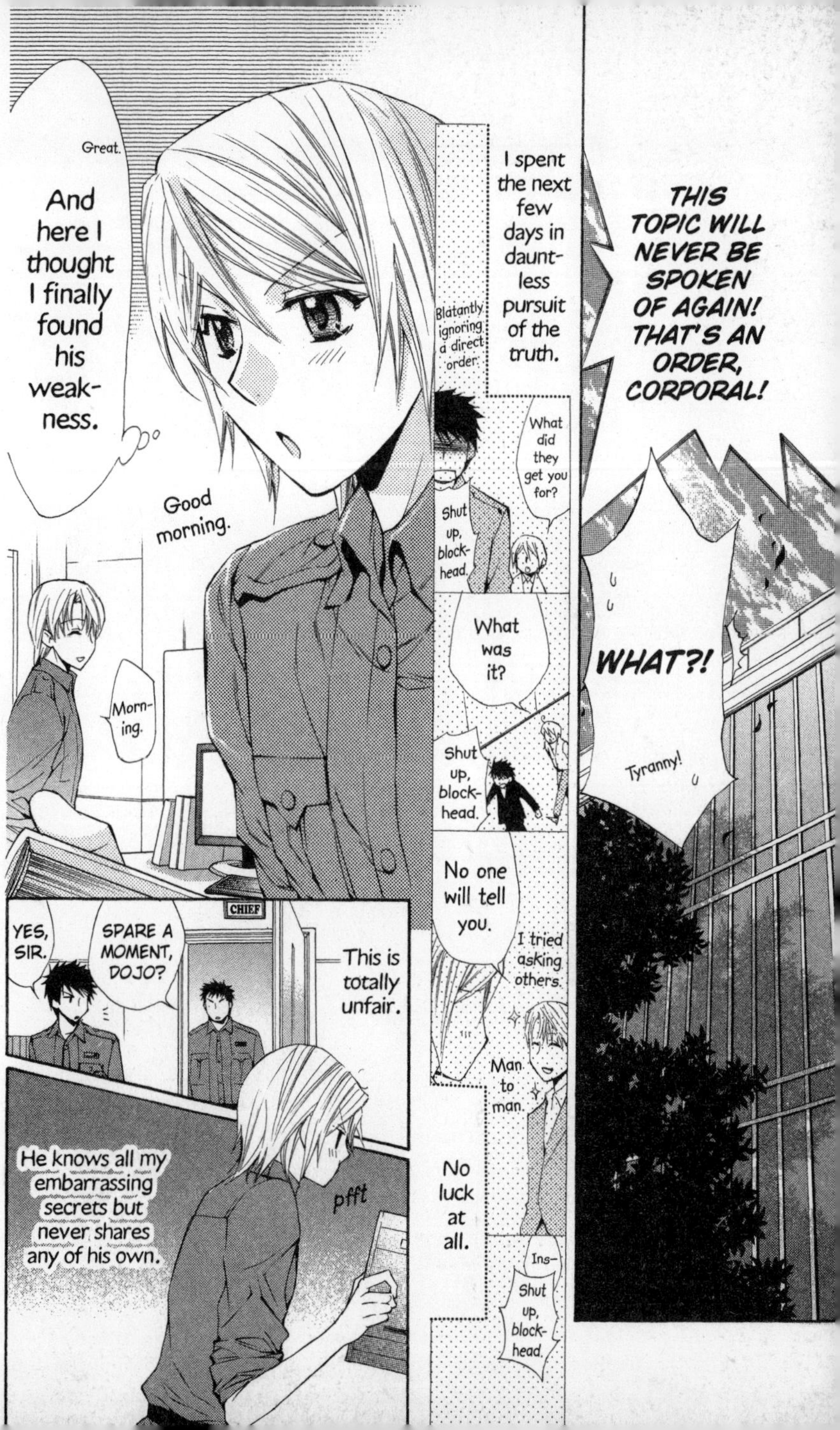
THIS TOPIC WILL NEVER BE SPOKEN OF AGAIN! THAT'S AN ORDER, CORPORAL!
WHAT?!
Tyranny!
I spent the next few days in dauntless pursuit of the truth.
Blatantly ignoring a direct order.
What did they get you for?
Shut up, blockhead.
What was it?
Shut up, blockhead.
No one will tell you.
I tried asking others.
Man to man.
No luck at all.
Ins-
Shut up, blockhead.
Great.
And here I thought I finally found his weakness.
Good morning.
Morning.
CHIEF
This is totally unfair.
SPARE A MOMENT, DOJO?
YES, SIR.
He knows all my embarrassing secrets but never shares any of his own.
pfft

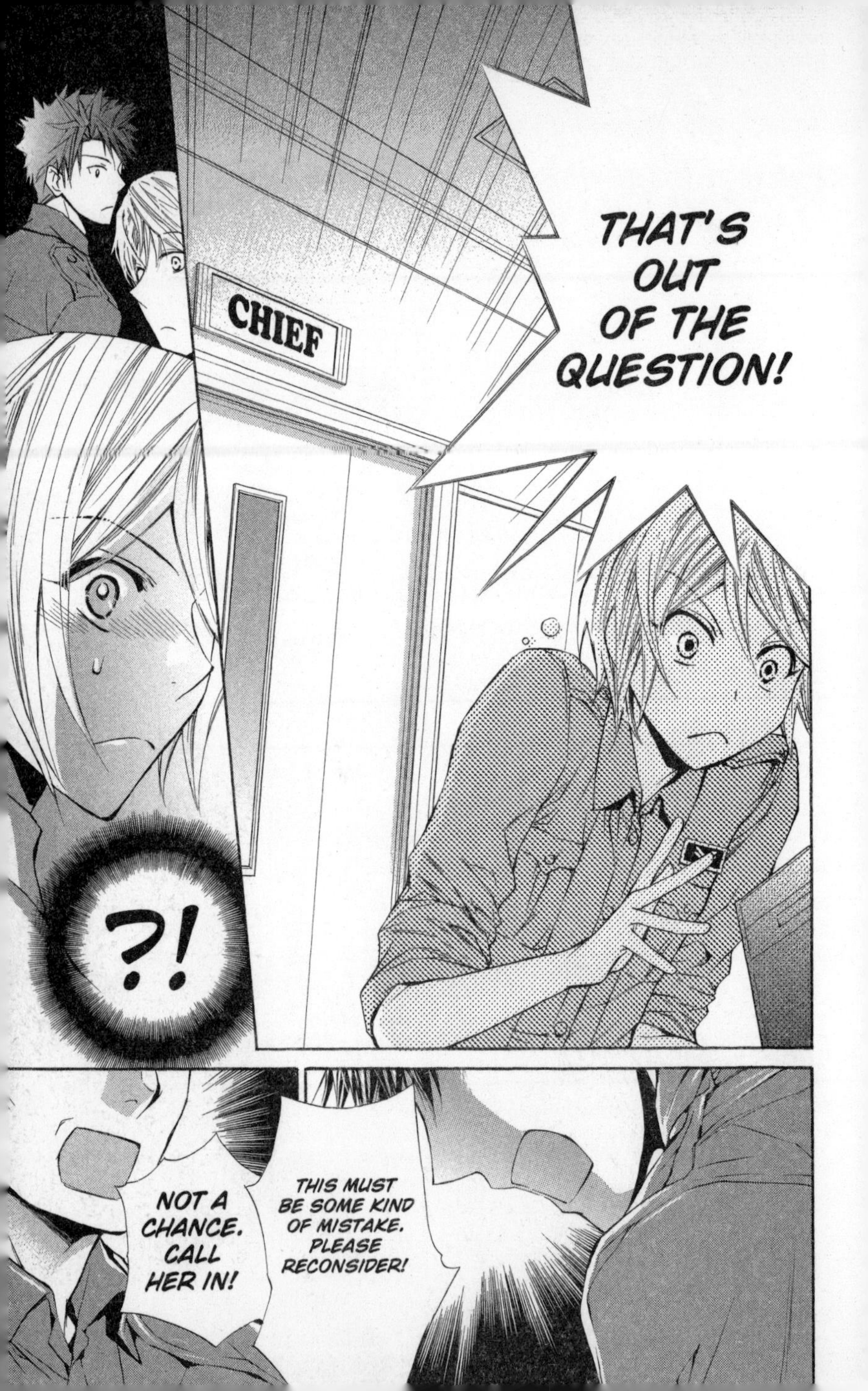
THAT'S OUT OF THE QUESTION!
CHIEF
?!
THIS MUST BE SOME KIND OF MISTAKE. PLEASE RECONSIDER!
NOT A CHANCE. CALL HER IN!

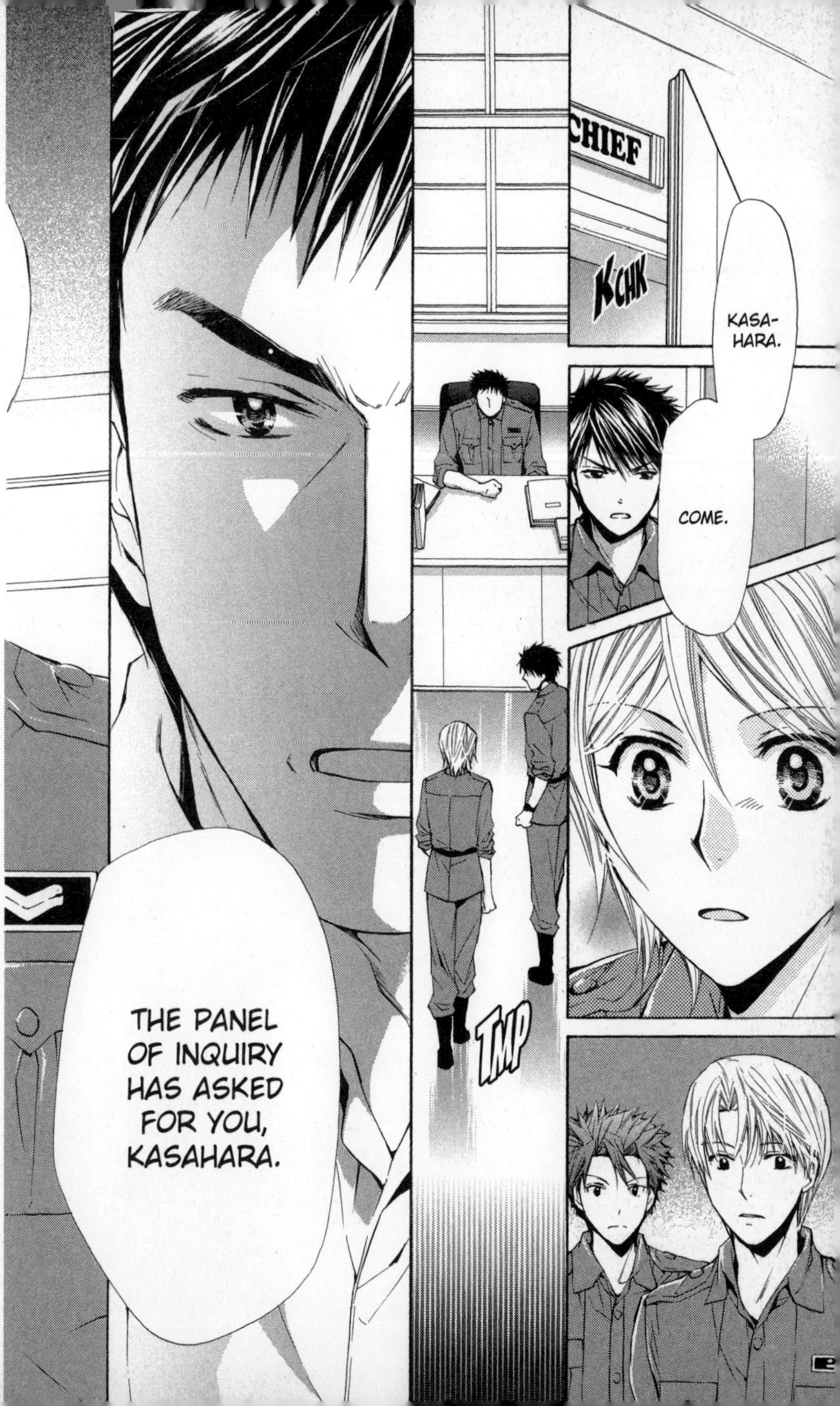
CHIEF
K'CHK
KASA-HARA.
COME.
TMP
THE PANEL OF INQUIRY HAS ASKED FOR YOU, KASAHARA.

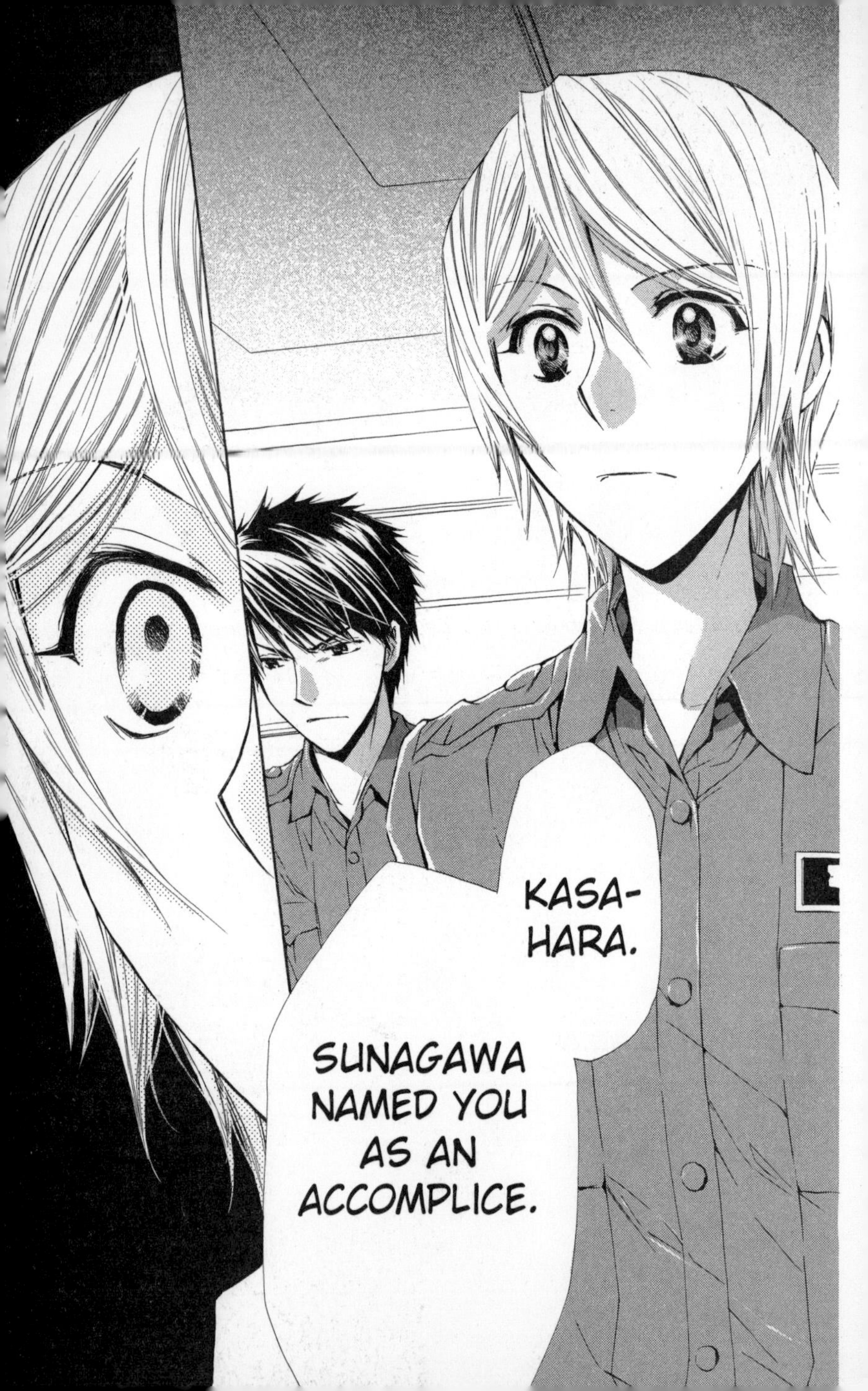
KASA-HARA.
SUNAGAWA NAMED YOU AS AN ACCOMPLICE.

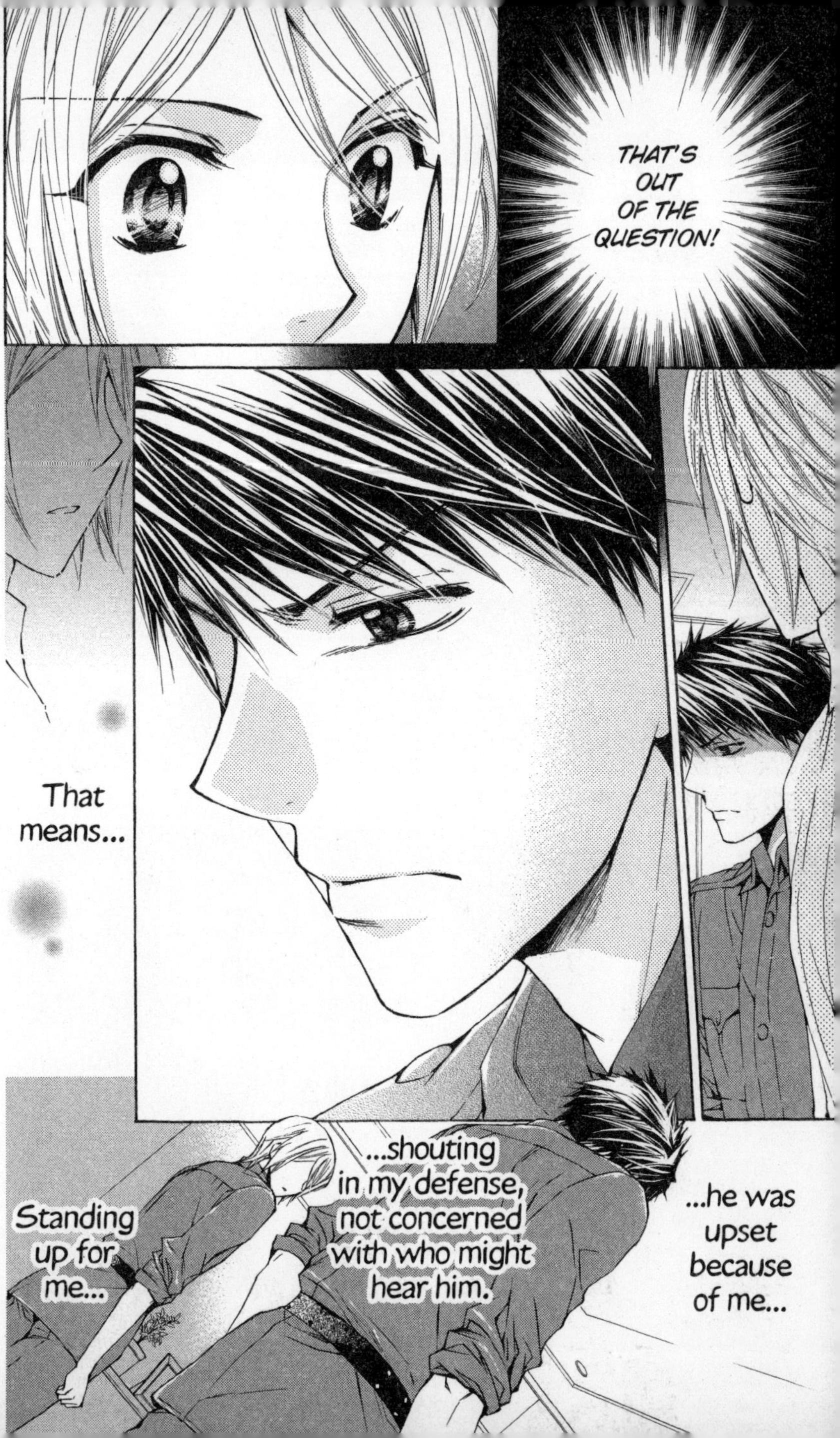
THAT'S OUT OF THE QUESTION!
That means...
...he was upset because of me...
...shouting in my defense, not concerned with who might hear him.
Standing up for me...

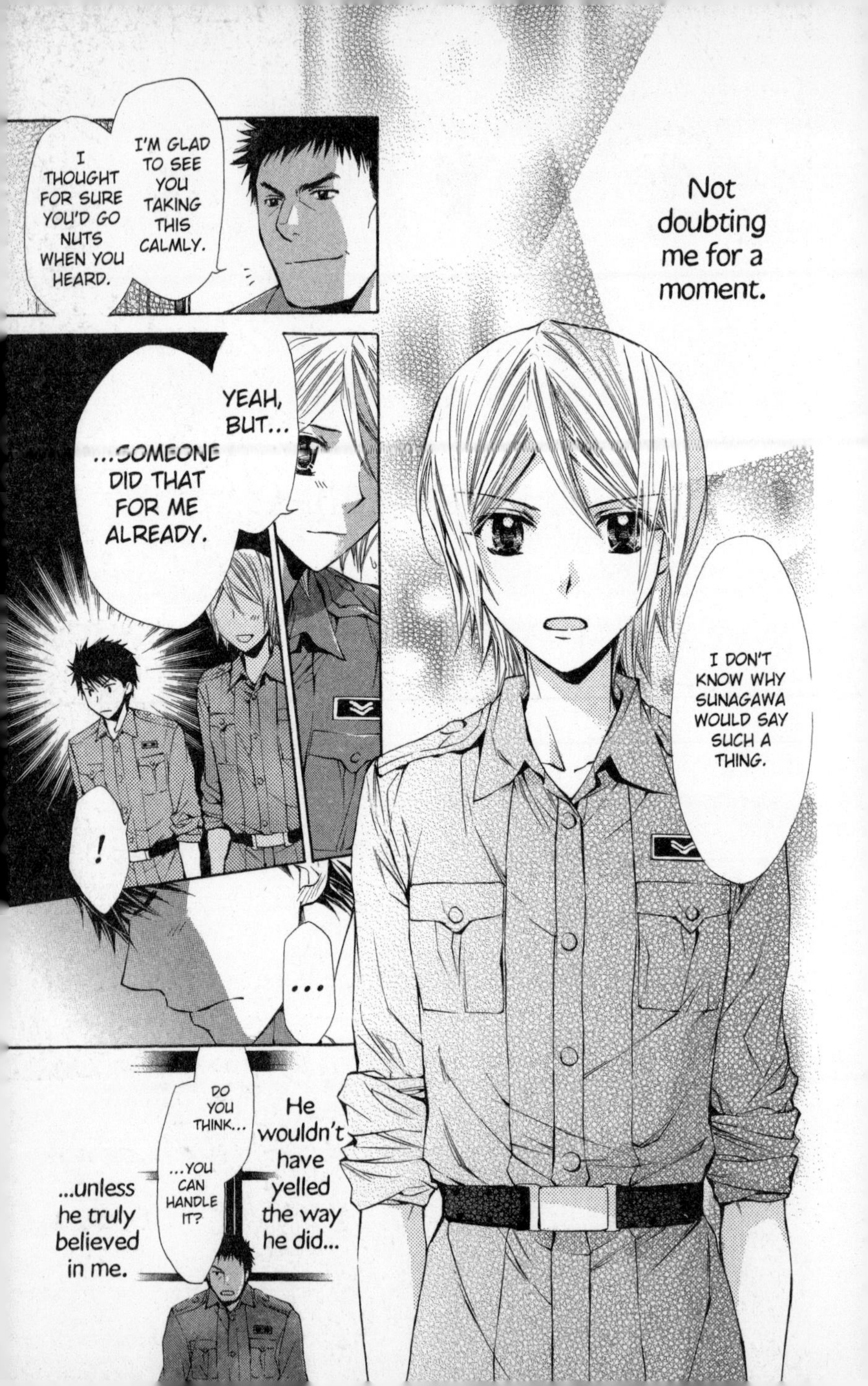
Not doubting me for a moment.
I DON'T KNOW WHY SUNAGAWA WOULD SAY SUCH A THING.
I'M GLAD TO SEE YOU TAKING THIS CALMLY.
I THOUGHT FOR SURE YOU'D GO NUTS WHEN YOU HEARD.
YEAH, BUT...
...SOMEONE DID THAT FOR ME ALREADY.
!
...
He wouldn't have yelled the way he did...
DO YOU THINK...
...YOU CAN HANDLE IT?
...unless he truly believed in me.

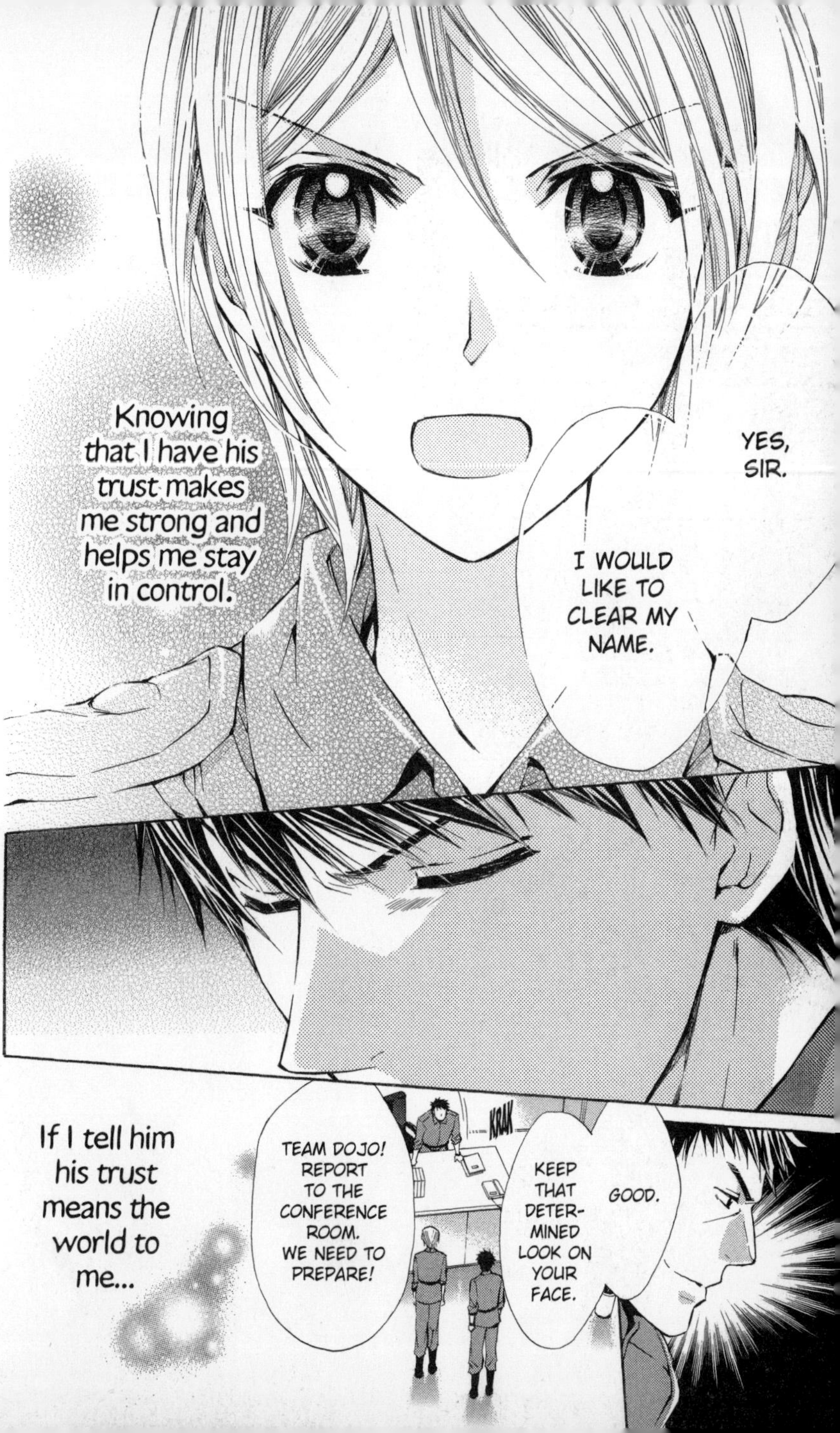
YES, SIR.
I WOULD LIKE TO CLEAR MY NAME.
Knowing that I have his trust makes me strong and helps me stay in control.
GOOD.
KEEP THAT DETERMINED LOOK ON YOUR FACE.
KRAK
TEAM DOJO! REPORT TO THE CONFERENCE ROOM. WE NEED TO PREPARE!
If I tell him his trust means the world to me...

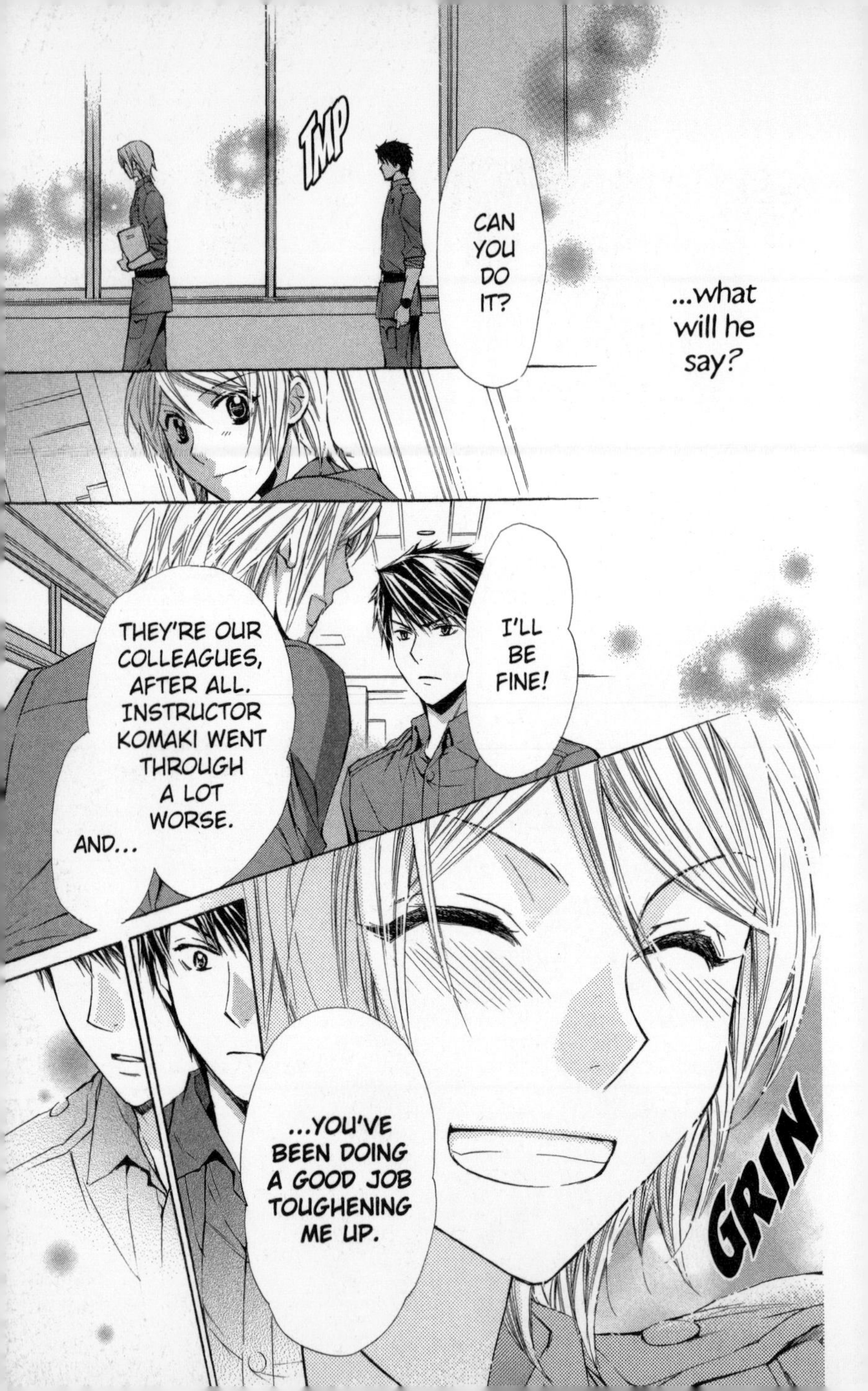
TMP
CAN YOU DO IT?
...what will he say?
I'LL BE FINE!
THEY'RE OUR COLLEAGUES, AFTER ALL. INSTRUCTOR KOMAKI WENT THROUGH A LOT WORSE.
AND...
...YOU'VE BEEN DOING A GOOD JOB TOUGHENING ME UP.
GRIN

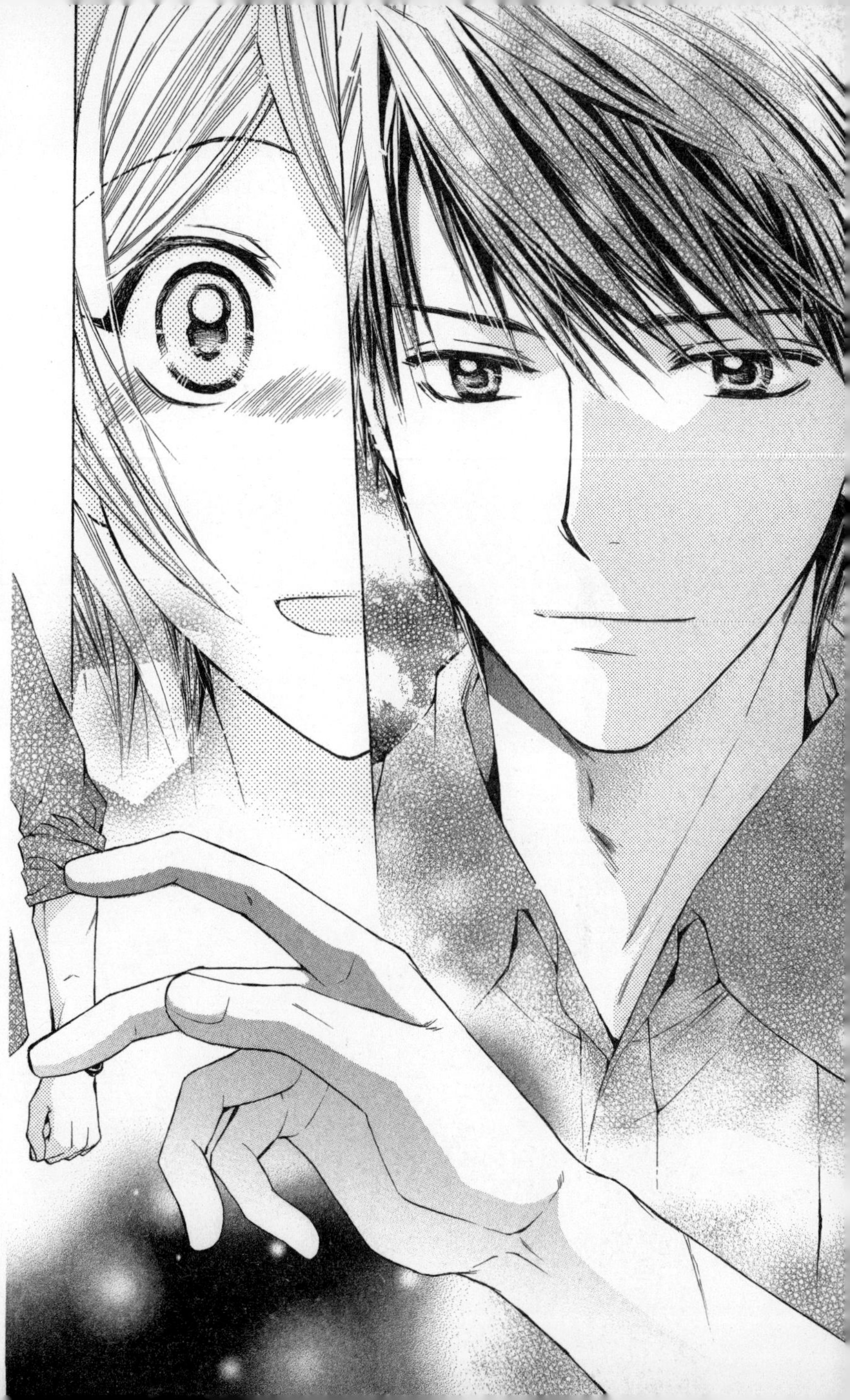

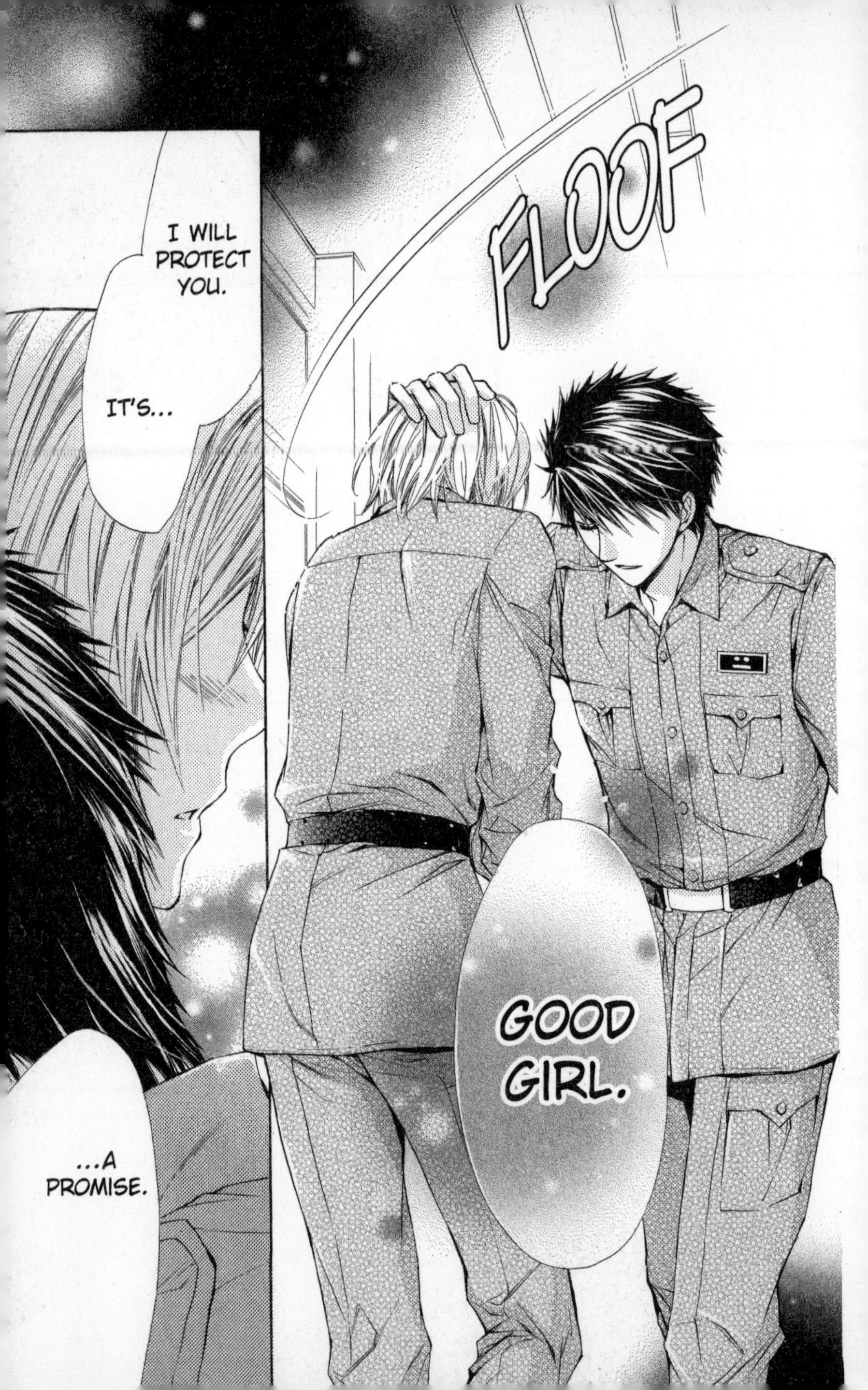
FLOOF
GOOD GIRL.
I WILL PROTECT YOU.
IT'S...
...A PROMISE.

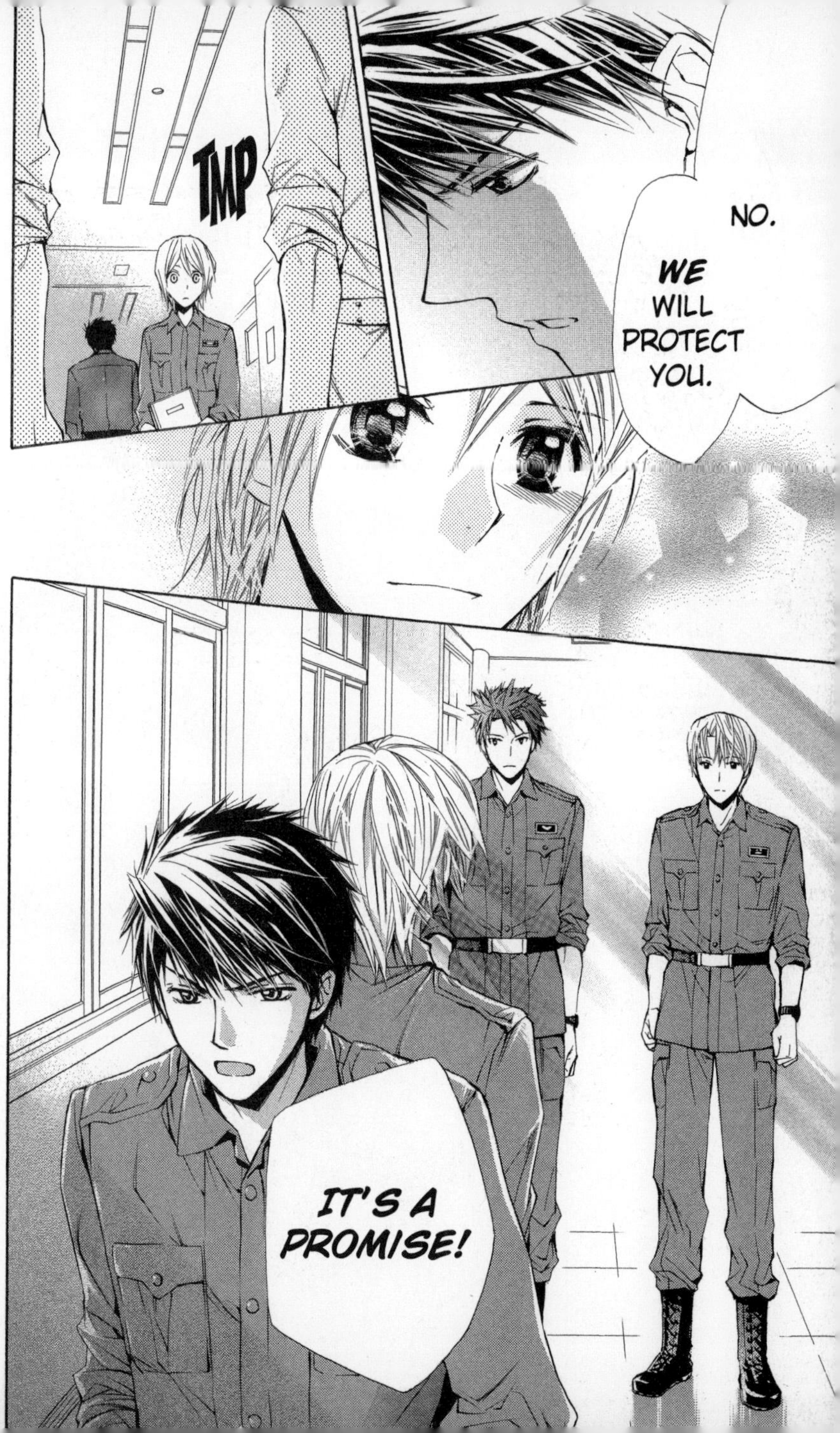
NO.
WE WILL PROTECT YOU.
TMP
IT'S A PROMISE!

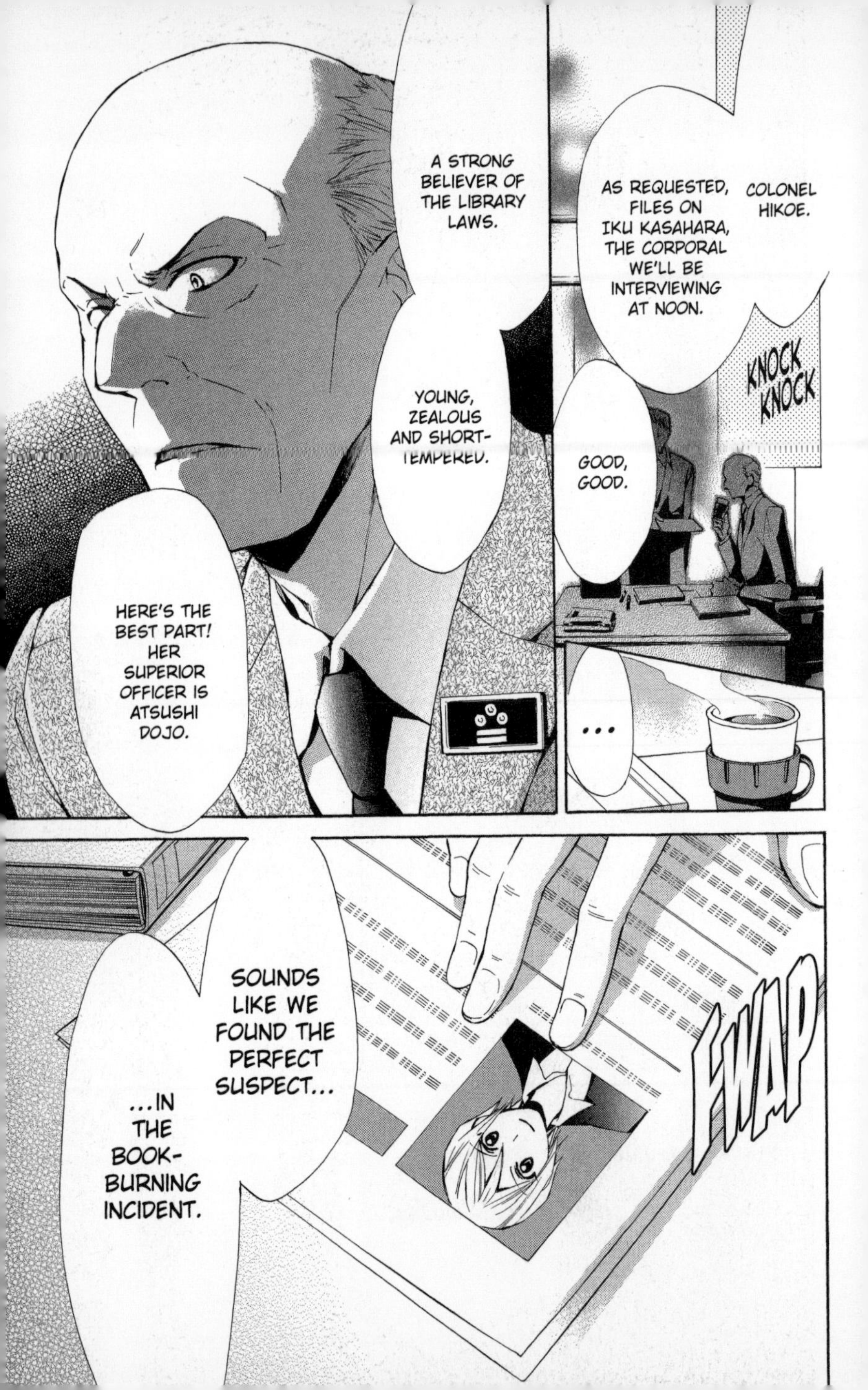
COLONEL HIKOE.
AS REQUESTED, FILES ON IKU KASAHARA, THE CORPORAL WE'LL BE INTERVIEWING AT NOON.
KNOCK KNOCK
GOOD, GOOD.
...
A STRONG BELIEVER OF THE LIBRARY LAWS.
YOUNG, ZEALOUS AND SHORT-TEMPERED.
HERE'S THE BEST PART! HER SUPERIOR OFFICER IS ATSUSHI DOJO.
SOUNDS LIKE WE FOUND THE PERFECT SUSPECT...
...IN THE BOOK-BURNING INCIDENT.
FWAP

Run, Iku, run!

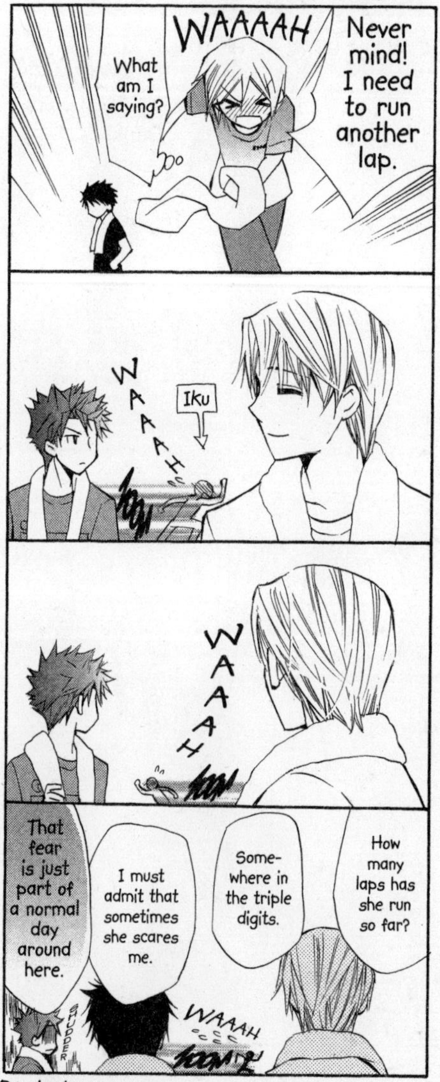
Never mind! I need to run another lap.
WAAAAH
What am I saying?
Iku
WAAAH
WAAAH
How many laps has she run so far?
Some-where in the triple digits.
I must admit that sometimes she scares me.
That fear is just part of a normal day around here.
WAAAH
SHUDDER

Dawning terror...

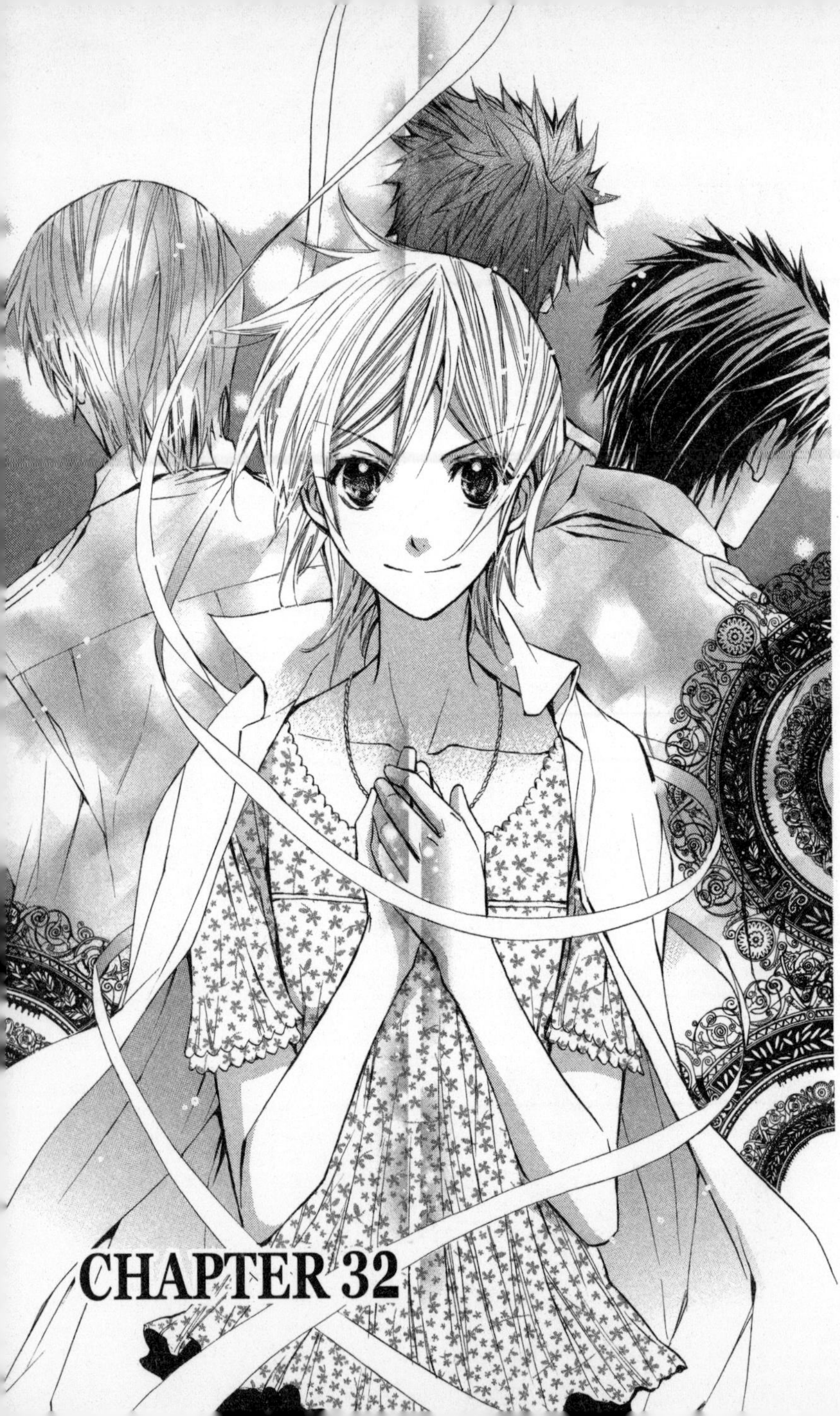
CHAPTER 32

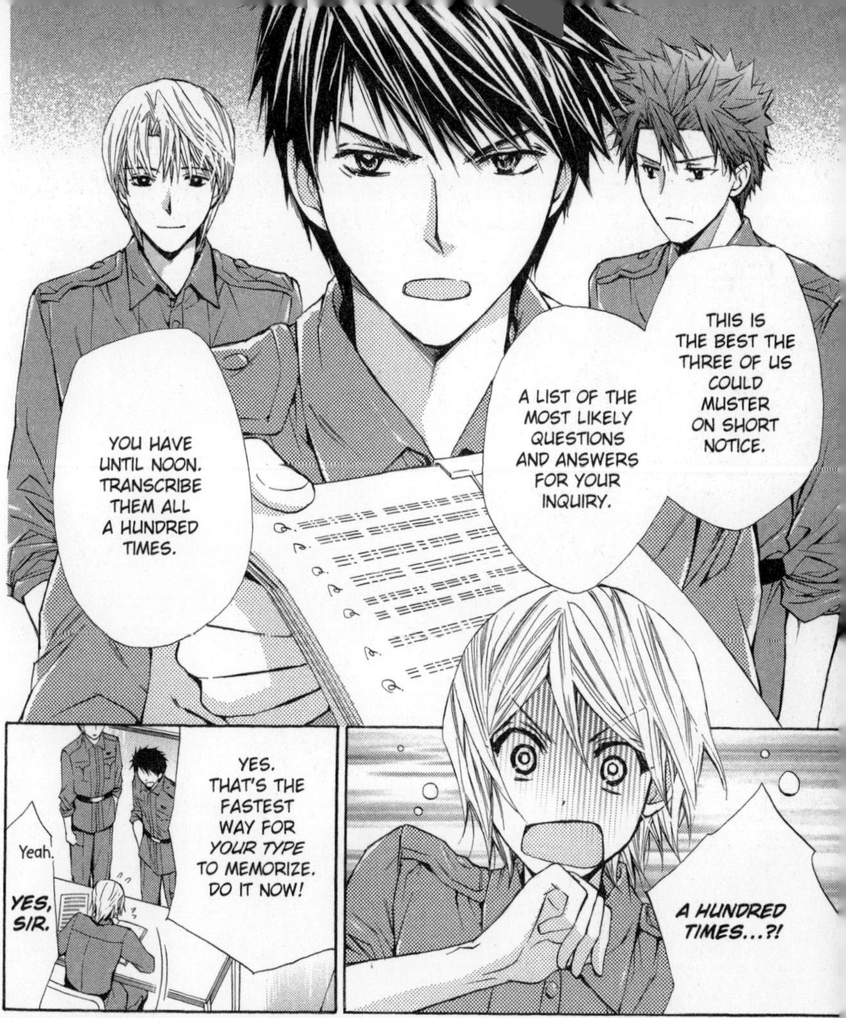
THIS IS THE BEST THE THREE OF US COULD MUSTER ON SHORT NOTICE.
A LIST OF THE MOST LIKELY QUESTIONS AND ANSWERS FOR YOUR INQUIRY.
YOU HAVE UNTIL NOON. TRANSCRIBE THEM ALL A HUNDRED TIMES.
A HUNDRED TIMES...?!
YES. THAT'S THE FASTEST WAY FOR *YOUR TYPE* TO MEMORIZE. DO IT NOW!
Yeah.
YES, SIR.

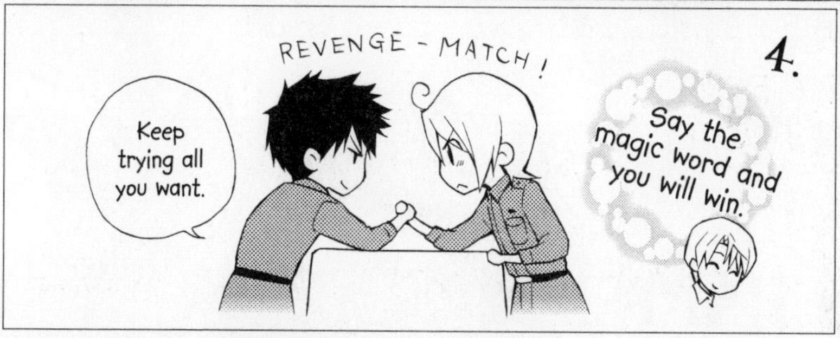
4.
REVENGE - MATCH!
Say the magic word and you will win.
Keep trying all you want.

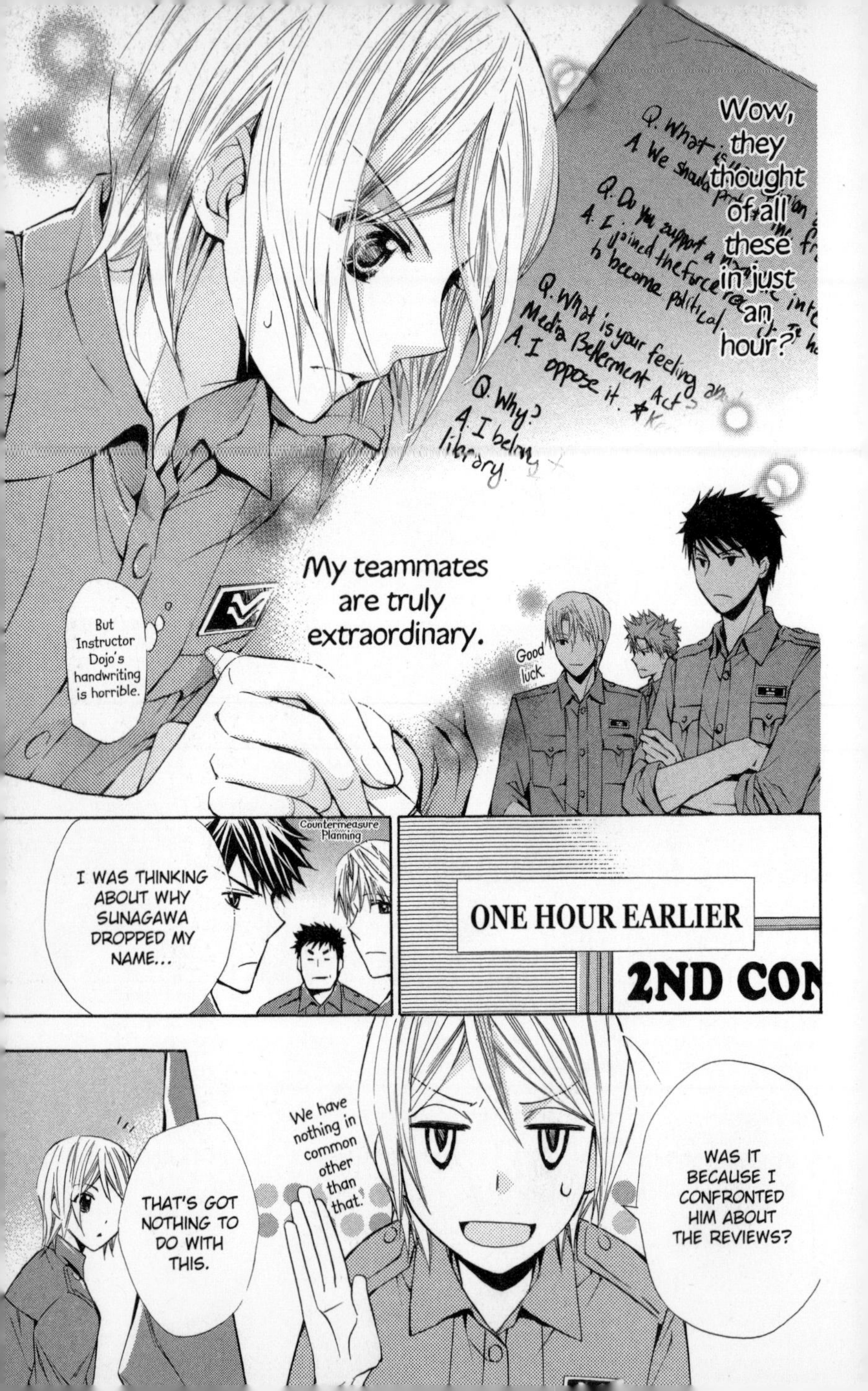
Wow, they thought of all these in just an hour?
My teammates are truly extraordinary.
Good luck.
But Instructor Dojo's handwriting is horrible.
ONE HOUR EARLIER
2ND CON
Countermeasure Planning
I WAS THINKING ABOUT WHY SUNAGAWA DROPPED MY NAME...
WAS IT BECAUSE I CONFRONTED HIM ABOUT THE REVIEWS?
We have nothing in common other than that.
THAT'S GOT NOTHING TO DO WITH THIS.

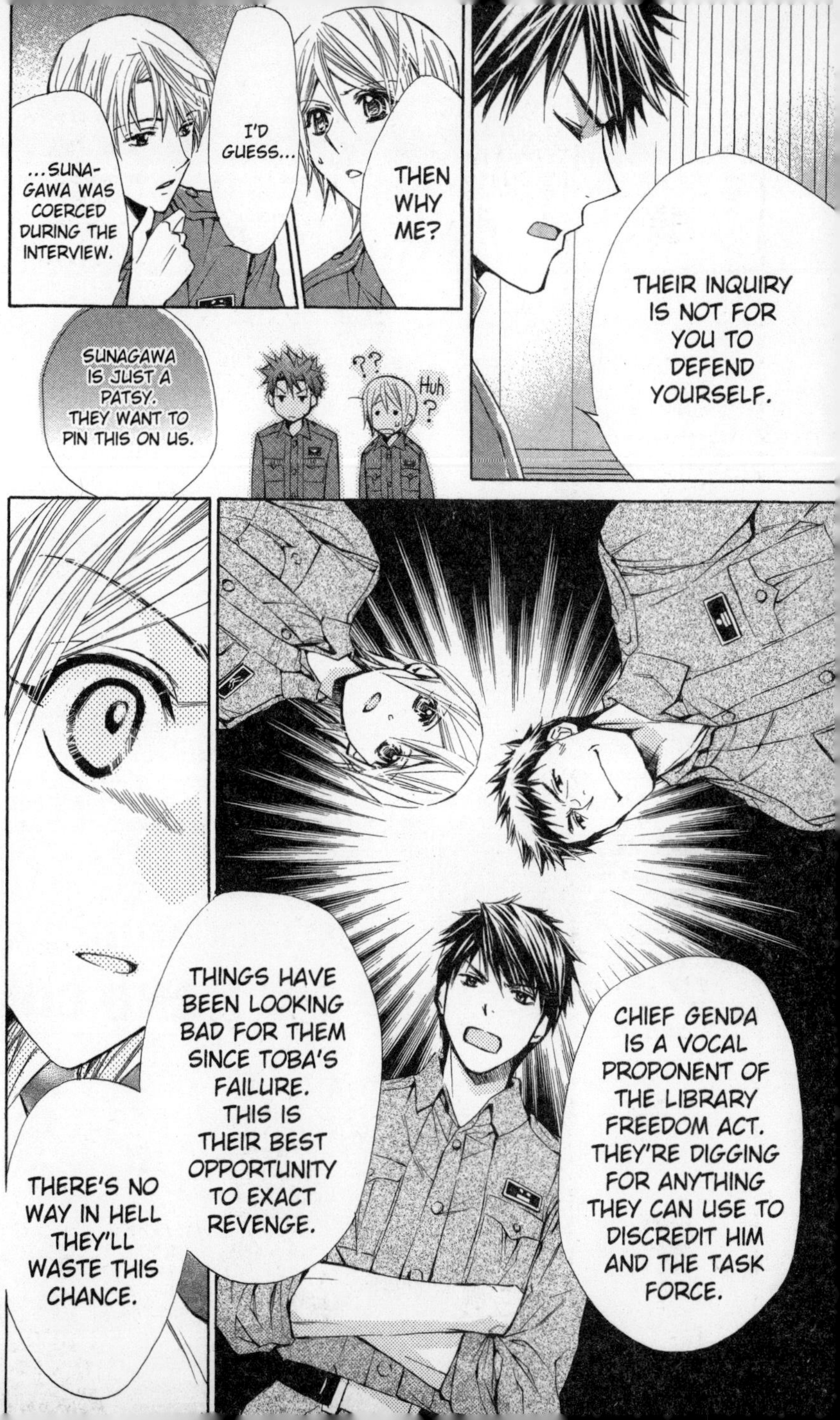

THEIR INQUIRY IS NOT FOR YOU TO DEFEND YOURSELF.
THEN WHY ME?
I'D GUESS...
...SUNAGAWA WAS COERCED DURING THE INTERVIEW.
??
Huh ?
SUNAGAWA IS JUST A PATSY. THEY WANT TO PIN THIS ON US.
CHIEF GENDA IS A VOCAL PROPONENT OF THE LIBRARY FREEDOM ACT. THEY'RE DIGGING FOR ANYTHING THEY CAN USE TO DISCREDIT HIM AND THE TASK FORCE.
THINGS HAVE BEEN LOOKING BAD FOR THEM SINCE TOBA'S FAILURE. THIS IS THEIR BEST OPPORTUNITY TO EXACT REVENGE.
THERE'S NO WAY IN HELL THEY'LL WASTE THIS CHANCE.

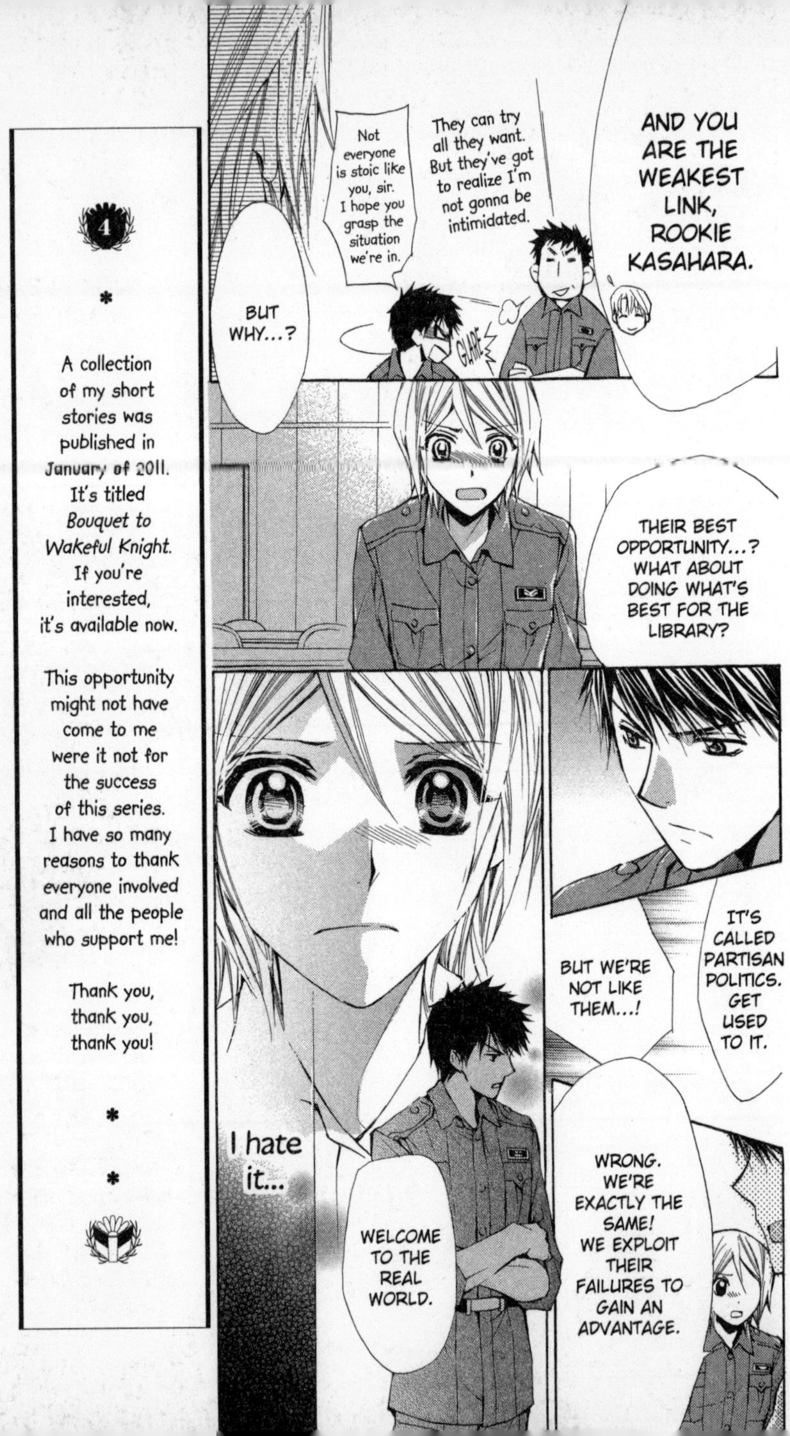
AND YOU ARE THE WEAKEST LINK, ROOKIE KASAHARA.
They can try all they want. But they've got to realize I'm not gonna be intimidated.
Not everyone is stoic like you, sir. I hope you grasp the situation we're in.
GLARE
BUT WHY...?
THEIR BEST OPPORTUNITY...? WHAT ABOUT DOING WHAT'S BEST FOR THE LIBRARY?
IT'S CALLED PARTISAN POLITICS. GET USED TO IT.
BUT WE'RE NOT LIKE THEM...!
WRONG. WE'RE EXACTLY THE SAME! WE EXPLOIT THEIR FAILURES TO GAIN AN ADVANTAGE.
I hate it...
WELCOME TO THE REAL WORLD.

4

*

A collection of my short stories was published in January of 2011. It's titled *Bouquet to Wakeful Knight.* If you're interested, it's available now.

This opportunity might not have come to me were it not for the success of this series. I have so many reasons to thank everyone involved and all the people who support me!

Thank you, thank you, thank you!

*

*

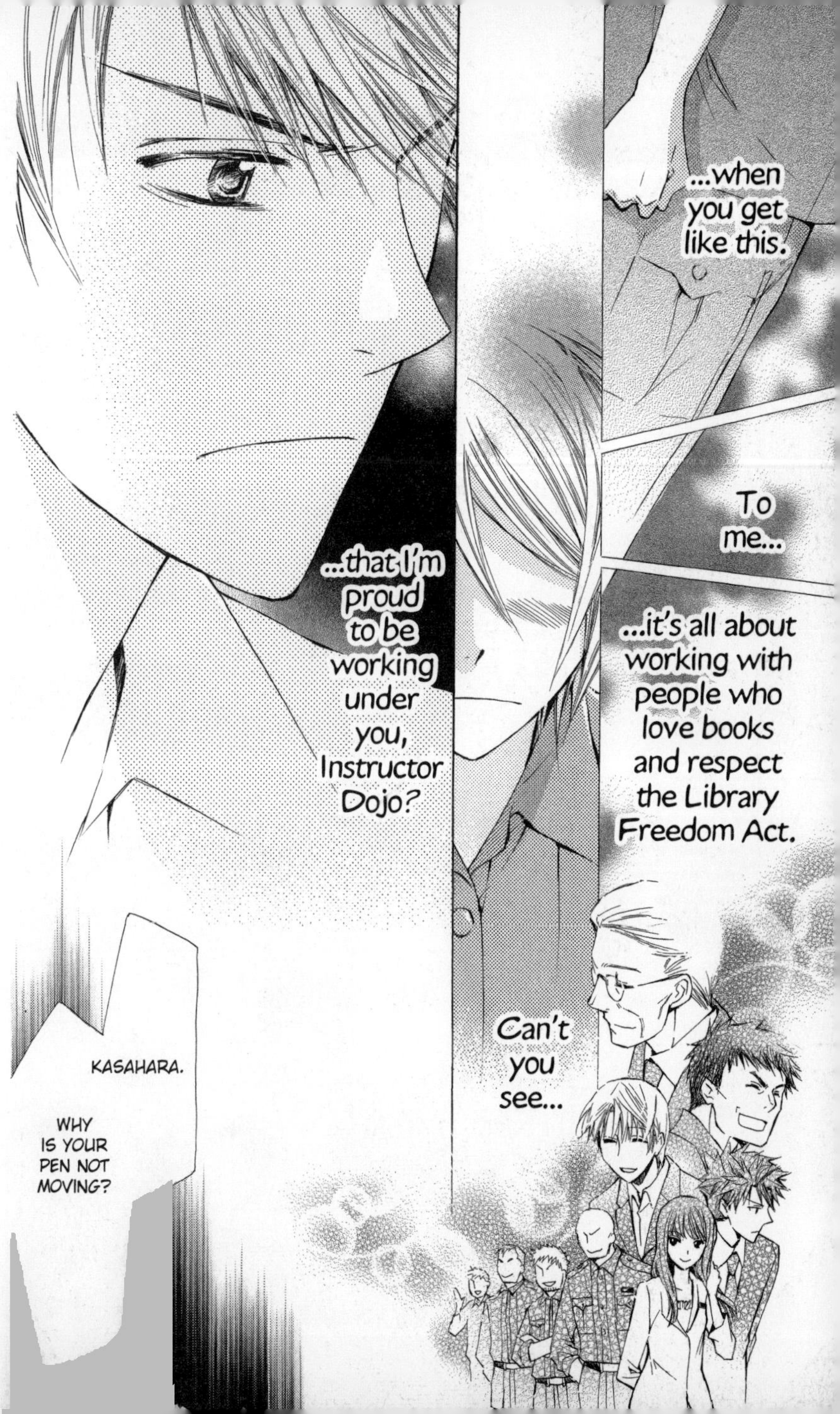
...when you get like this.
To me...
...it's all about working with people who love books and respect the Library Freedom Act.
Can't you see...
...that I'm proud to be working under you, Instructor Dojo?
KASAHARA.
WHY IS YOUR PEN NOT MOVING?

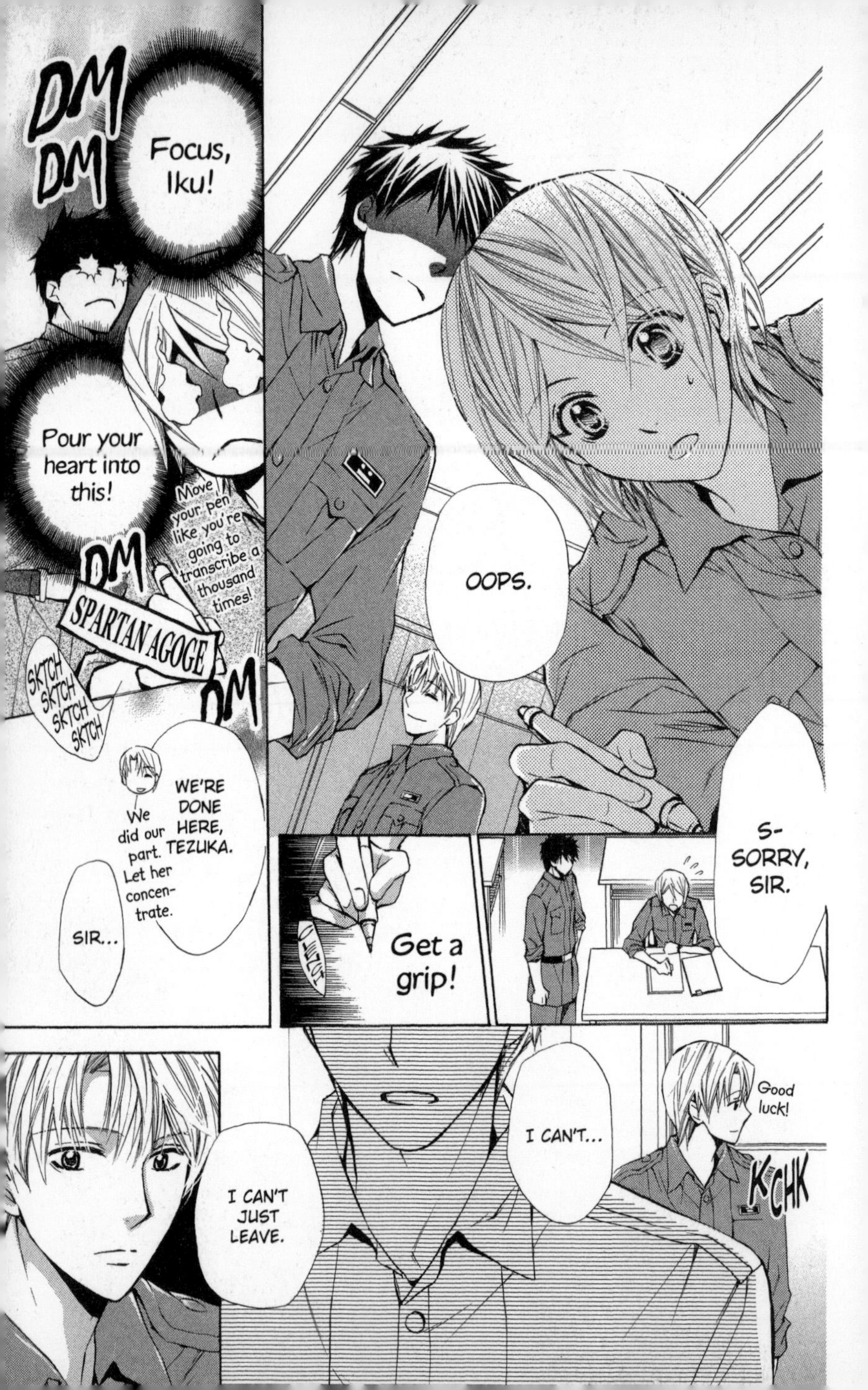
OOPS.
S-SORRY, SIR.
Get a grip!
ZOT
DM DM
Focus, Iku!
Pour your heart into this!
Move your pen like you're going to transcribe a thousand times!
DM
SPARTAN AGOGE
DM
SKTCH SKTCH SKTCH SKTCH
WE'RE DONE HERE, TEZUKA.
We did our part. Let her concentrate.
SIR...
Good luck!
KCHK
I CAN'T...
I CAN'T JUST LEAVE.

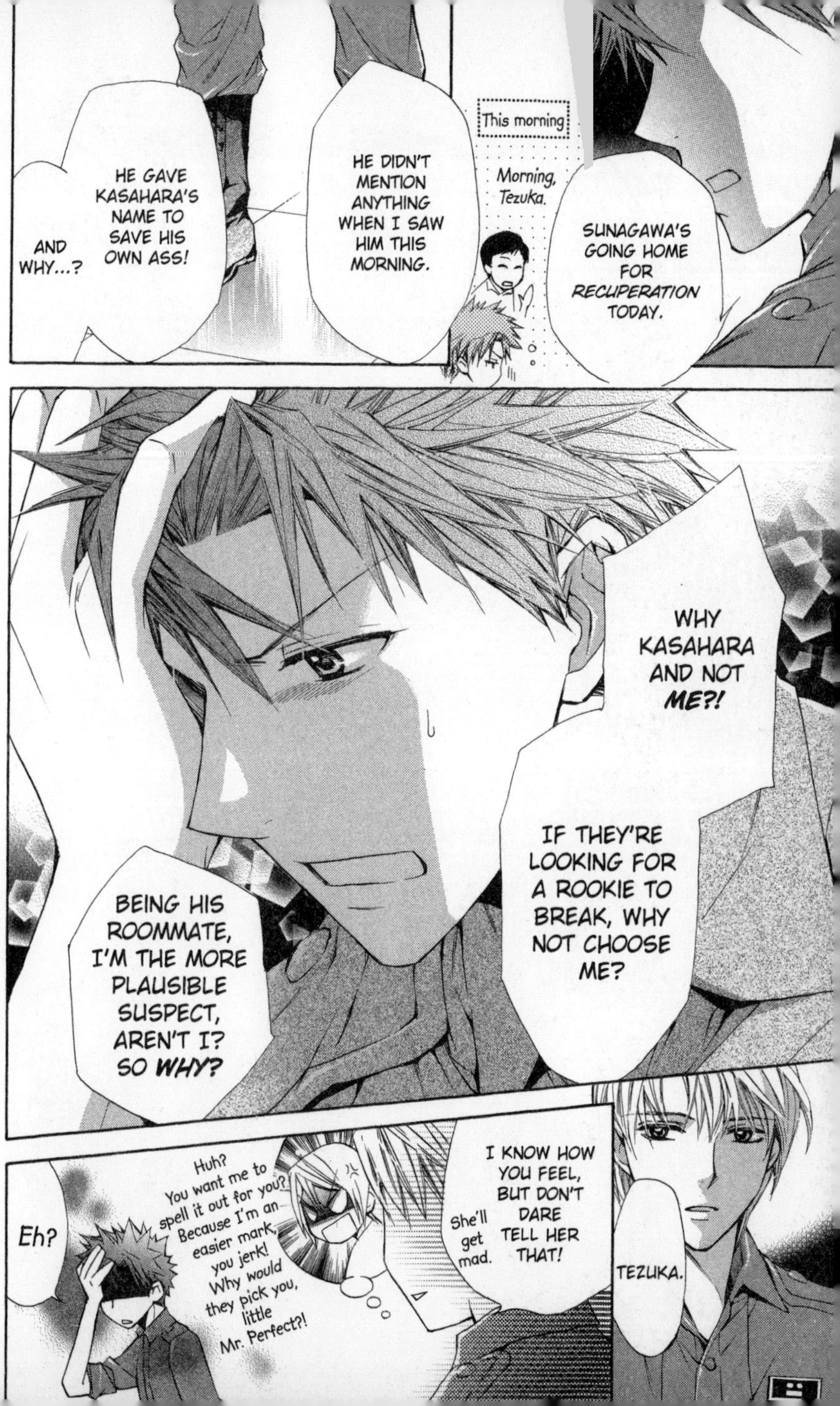
SUNAGAWA'S GOING HOME FOR *RECUPERATION* TODAY.
This morning
Morning, Tezuka.
HE DIDN'T MENTION ANYTHING WHEN I SAW HIM THIS MORNING.
HE GAVE KASAHARA'S NAME TO SAVE HIS OWN ASS!
AND WHY...?
WHY KASAHARA AND NOT ***ME?!***
IF THEY'RE LOOKING FOR A ROOKIE TO BREAK, WHY NOT CHOOSE ME?
BEING HIS ROOMMATE, I'M THE MORE PLAUSIBLE SUSPECT, AREN'T I? SO ***WHY?***
TEZUKA.
I KNOW HOW YOU FEEL, BUT DON'T DARE TELL HER THAT!
She'll get mad.
Huh? You want me to spell it out for you? Because I'm an easier mark, you jerk! Why would they pick you, little Mr. Perfect?!
Eh?

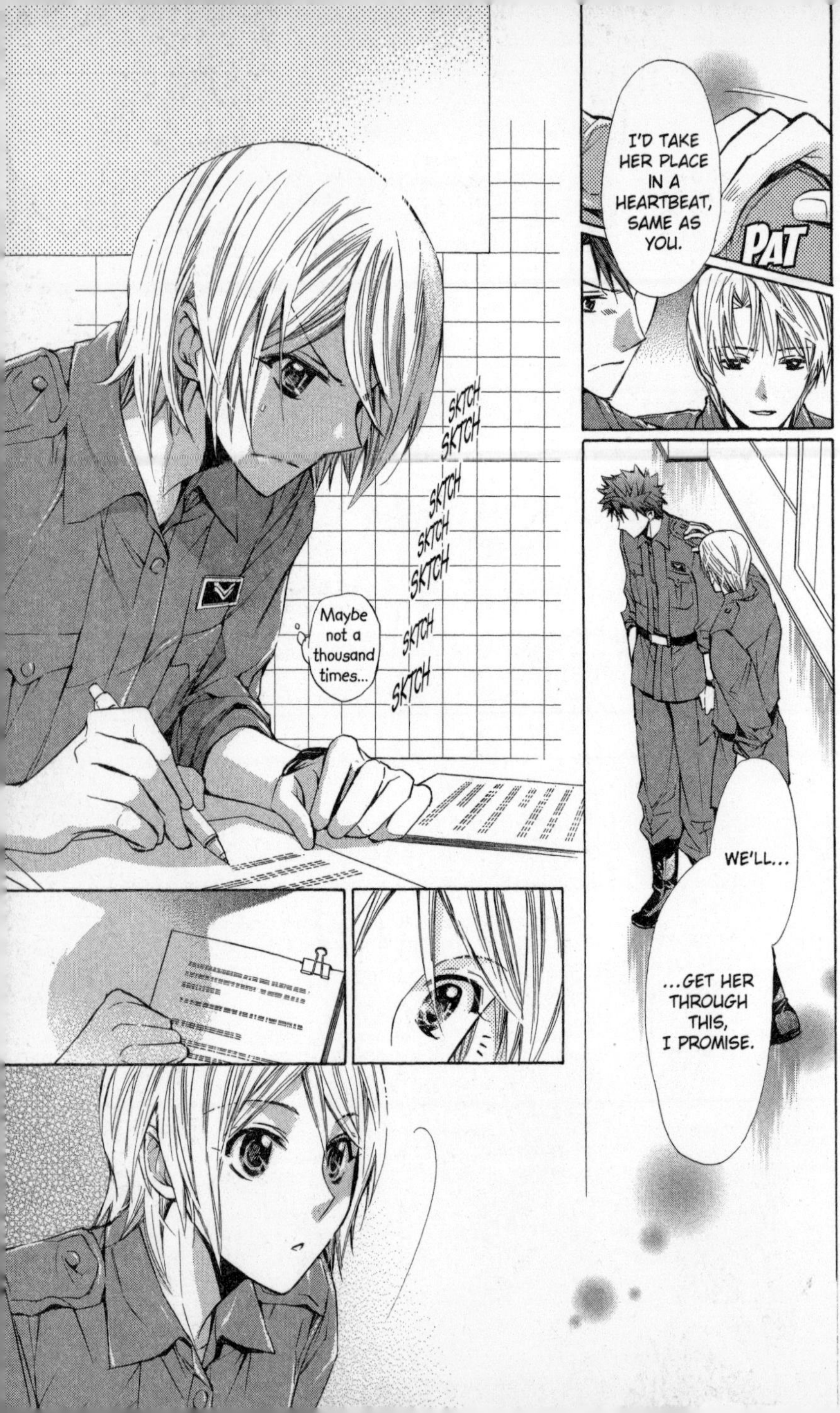
I'D TAKE HER PLACE IN A HEARTBEAT, SAME AS YOU.
PAT
WE'LL...
...GET HER THROUGH THIS, I PROMISE.
SKTCH SKTCH SKTCH SKTCH SKTCH SKTCH SKTCH
Maybe not a thousand times...

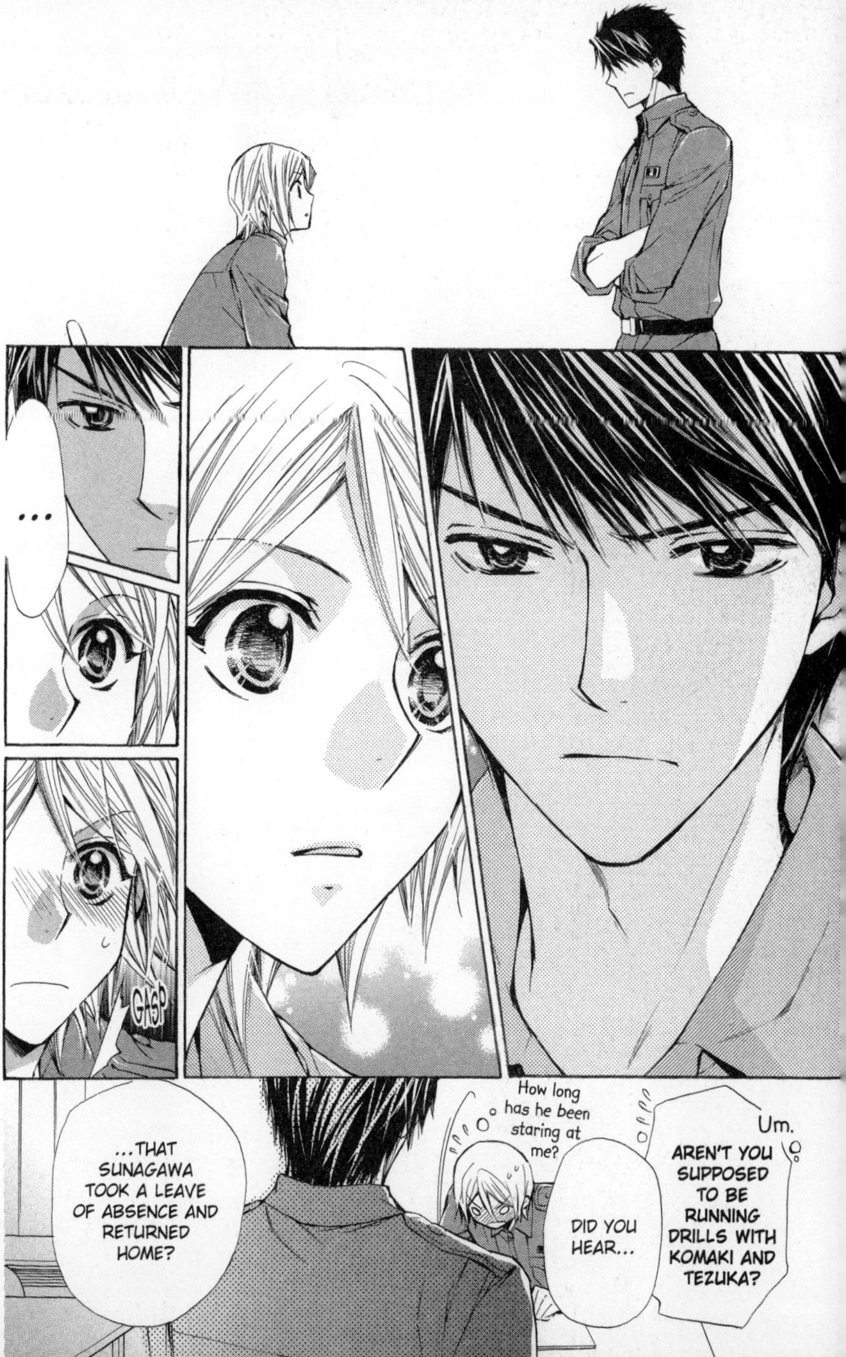
...
GASP
Um.
AREN'T YOU SUPPOSED TO BE RUNNING DRILLS WITH KOMAKI AND TEZUKA?
How long has he been staring at me?
DID YOU HEAR...
...THAT SUNAGAWA TOOK A LEAVE OF ABSENCE AND RETURNED HOME?

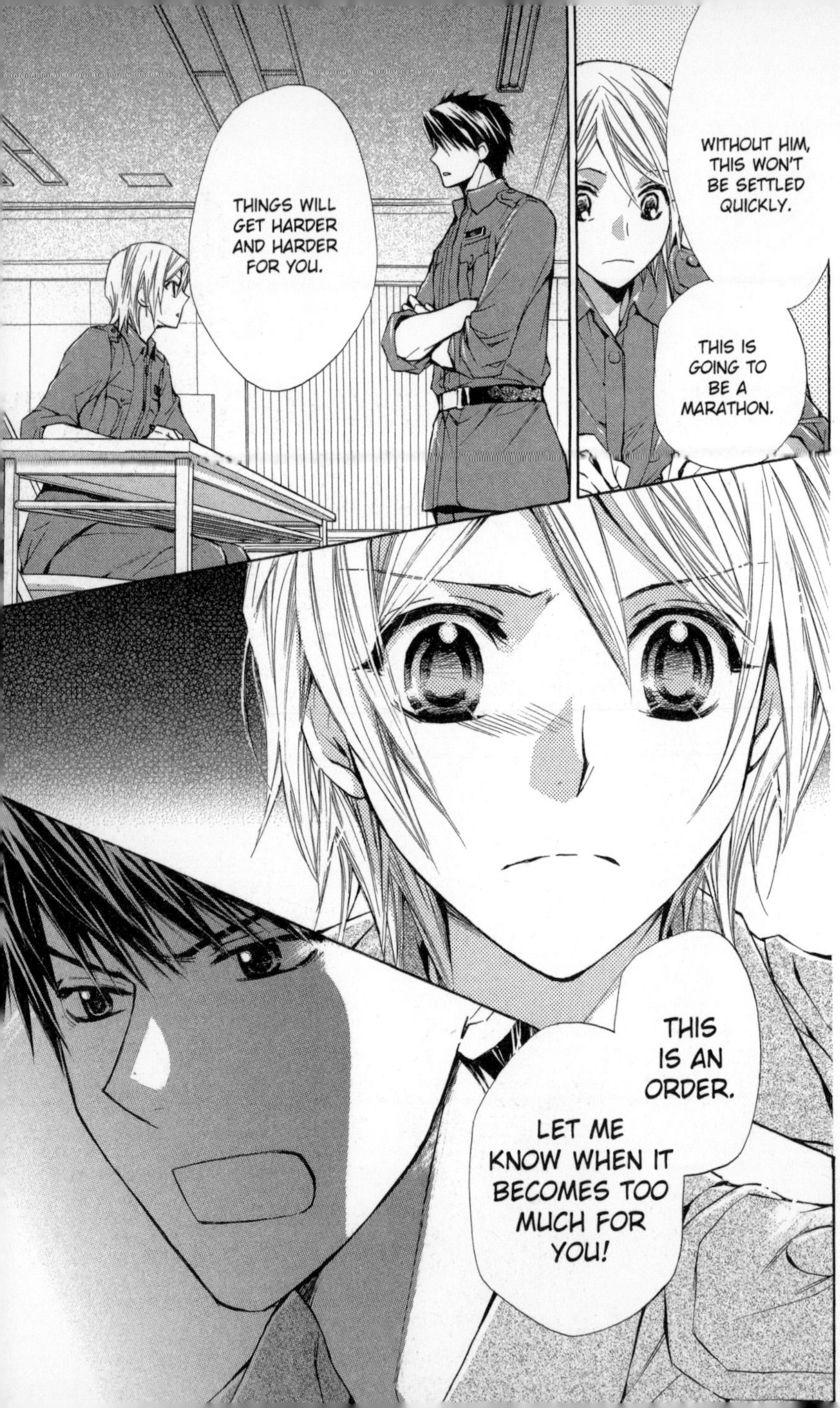
WITHOUT HIM, THIS WON'T BE SETTLED QUICKLY.
THIS IS GOING TO BE A MARATHON.
THINGS WILL GET HARDER AND HARDER FOR YOU.
THIS IS AN ORDER.
LET ME KNOW WHEN IT BECOMES TOO MUCH FOR YOU!

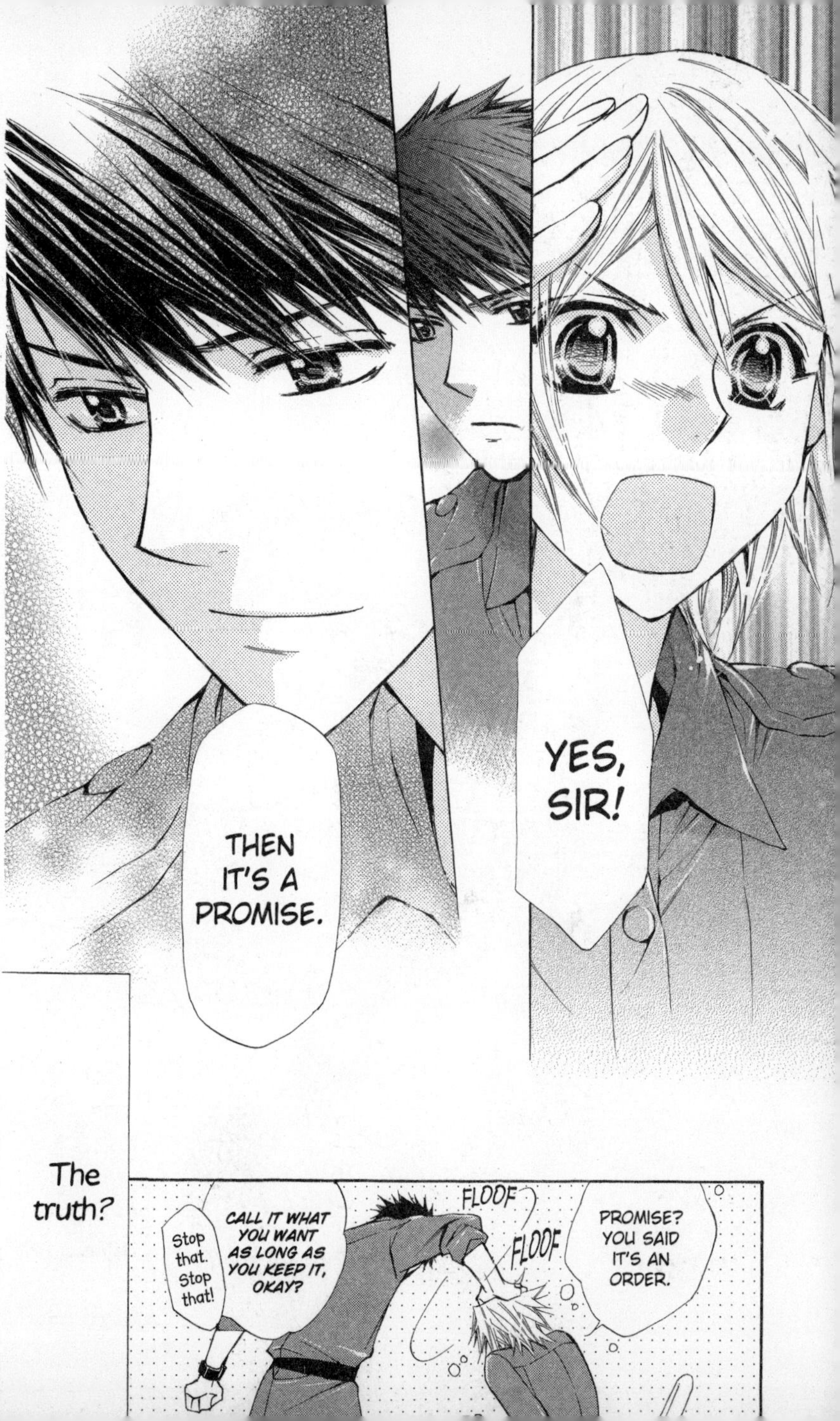
YES, SIR!
THEN IT'S A PROMISE.
PROMISE? YOU SAID IT'S AN ORDER.
FLOOF
FLOOF
CALL IT WHAT YOU WANT AS LONG AS YOU KEEP IT, OKAY?
Stop that. Stop that!
The truth?

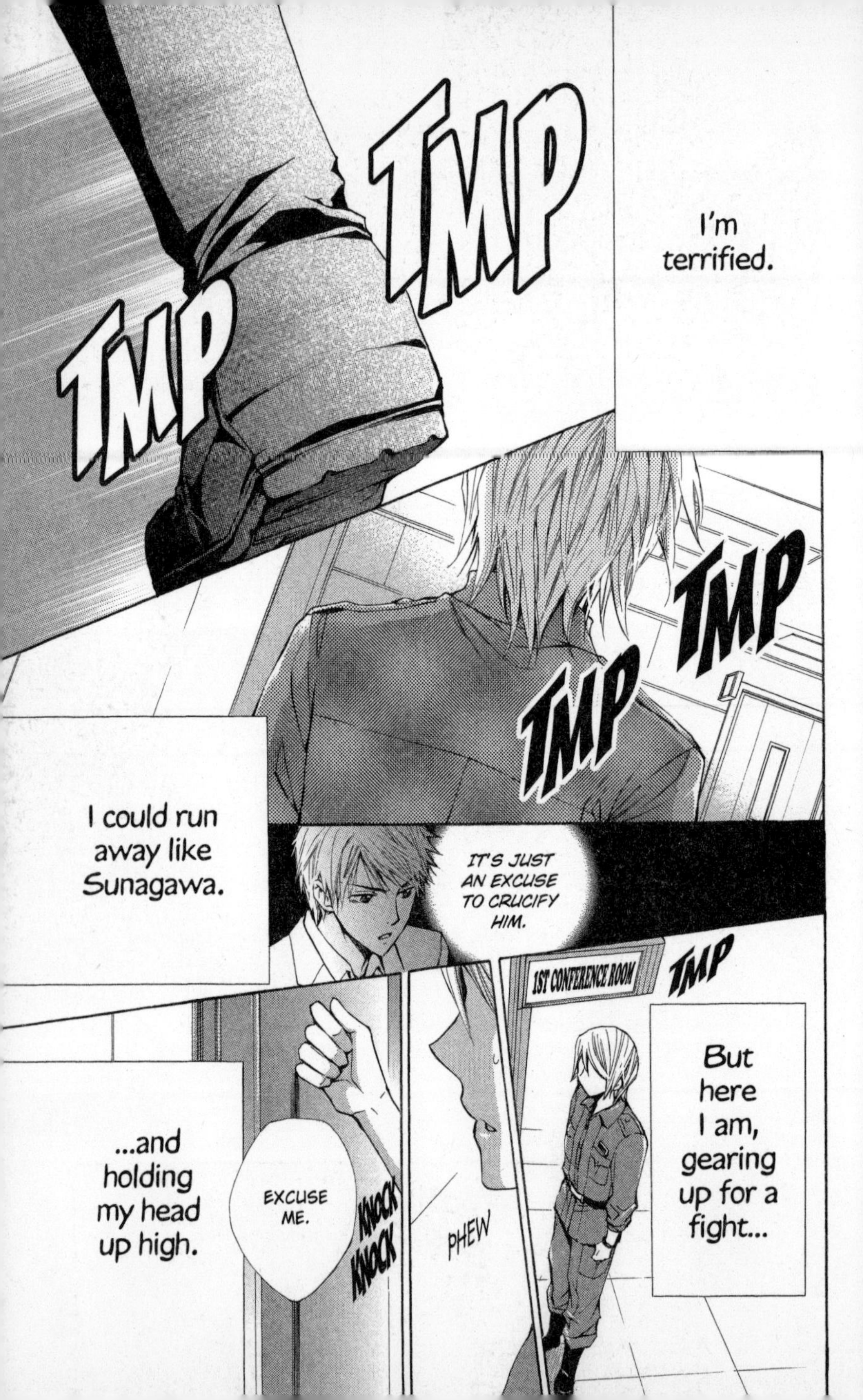
I'm terrified.
TMP
TMP
TMP
TMP
I could run away like Sunagawa.
IT'S JUST AN EXCUSE TO CRUCIFY HIM.
1ST CONFERENCE ROOM
TMP
But here I am, gearing up for a fight...
PHEW
KNOCK KNOCK
EXCUSE ME.
...and holding my head up high.

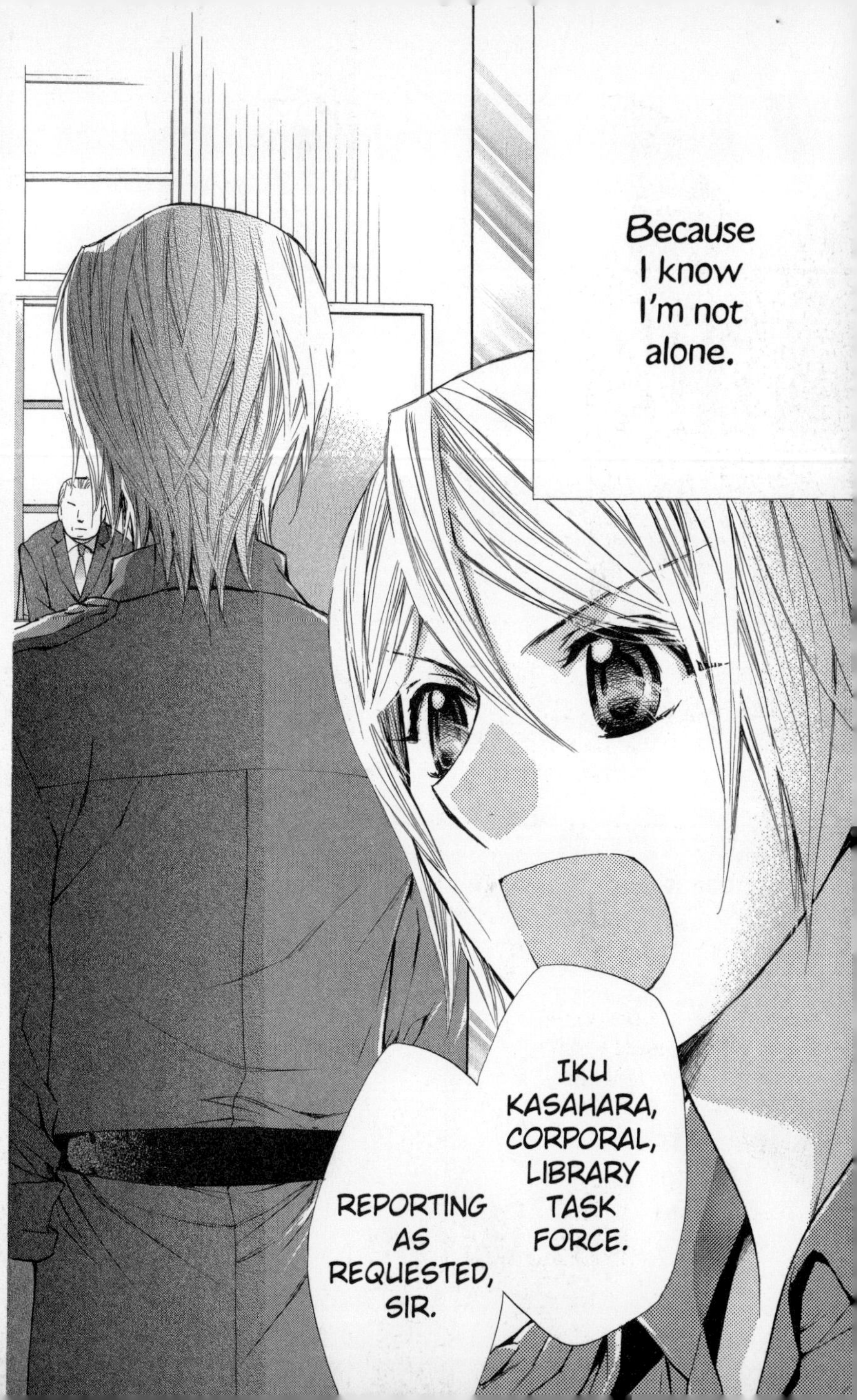
Because I know I'm not alone.
IKU KASAHARA, CORPORAL, LIBRARY TASK FORCE.
REPORTING AS REQUESTED, SIR.

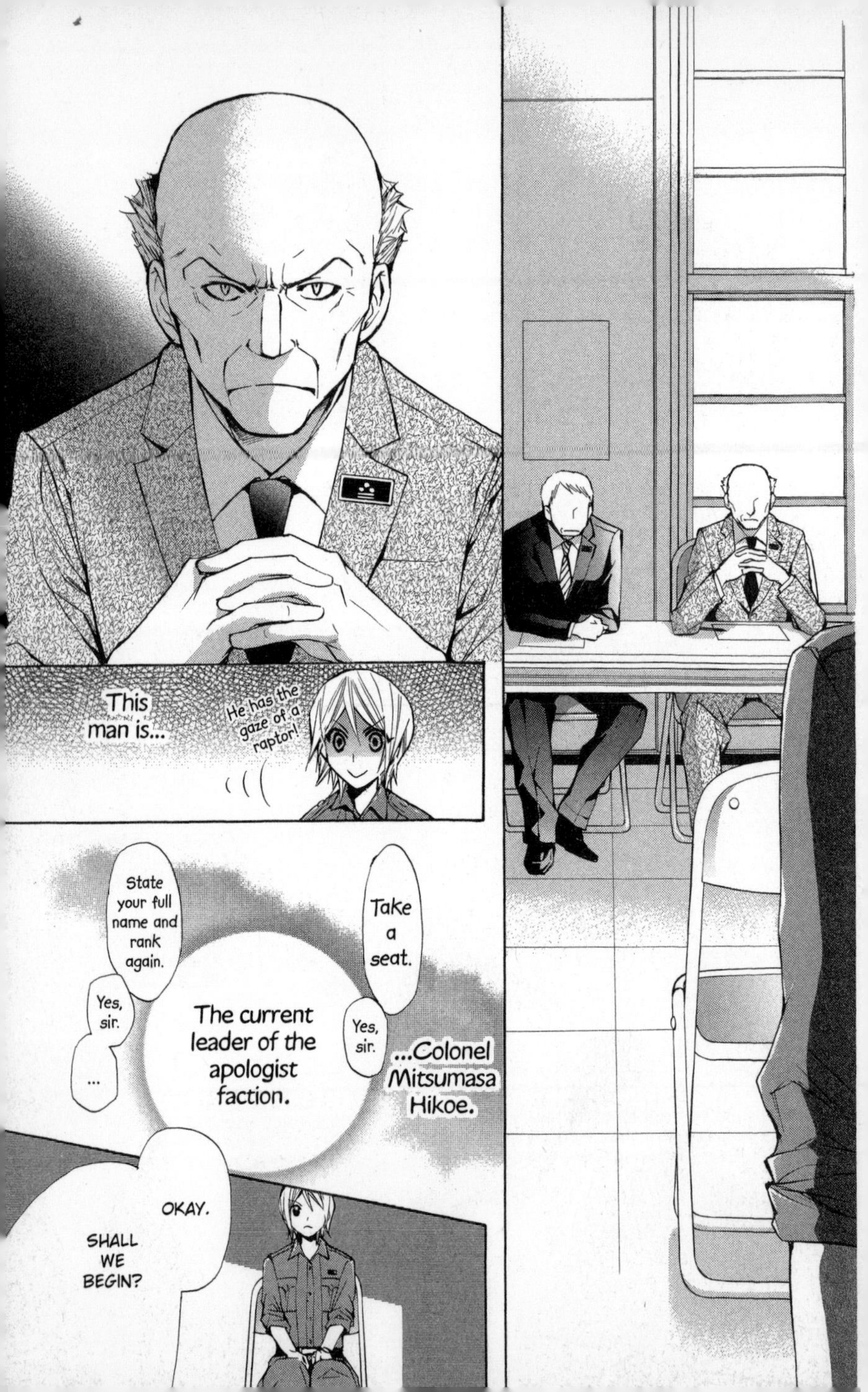
He has the gaze of a raptor!
This man is...
Take a seat.
Yes, sir.
State your full name and rank again.
Yes, sir.
...
The current leader of the apologist faction.
...Colonel Mitsumasa Hikoe.
OKAY.
SHALL WE BEGIN?

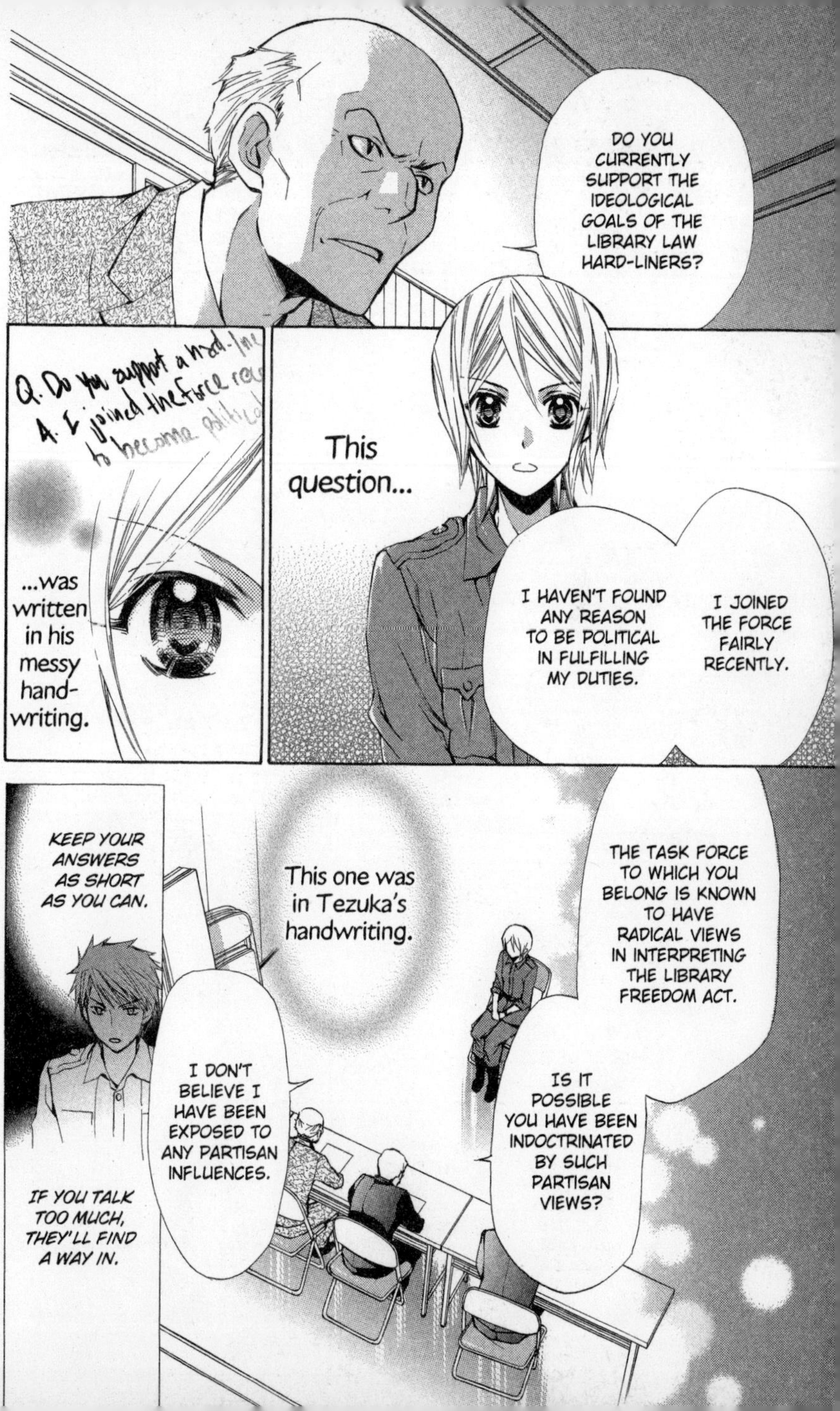
DO YOU CURRENTLY SUPPORT THE IDEOLOGICAL GOALS OF THE LIBRARY LAW HARD-LINERS?
This question...
I JOINED THE FORCE FAIRLY RECENTLY.
I HAVEN'T FOUND ANY REASON TO BE POLITICAL IN FULFILLING MY DUTIES.
Q. Do you support a
A. I joined the force
to become
...was written in his messy hand-writing.
THE TASK FORCE TO WHICH YOU BELONG IS KNOWN TO HAVE RADICAL VIEWS IN INTERPRETING THE LIBRARY FREEDOM ACT.
IS IT POSSIBLE YOU HAVE BEEN INDOCTRINATED BY SUCH PARTISAN VIEWS?
This one was in Tezuka's handwriting.
I DON'T BELIEVE I HAVE BEEN EXPOSED TO ANY PARTISAN INFLUENCES.
KEEP YOUR ANSWERS AS SHORT AS YOU CAN.
IF YOU TALK TOO MUCH, THEY'LL FIND A WAY IN.

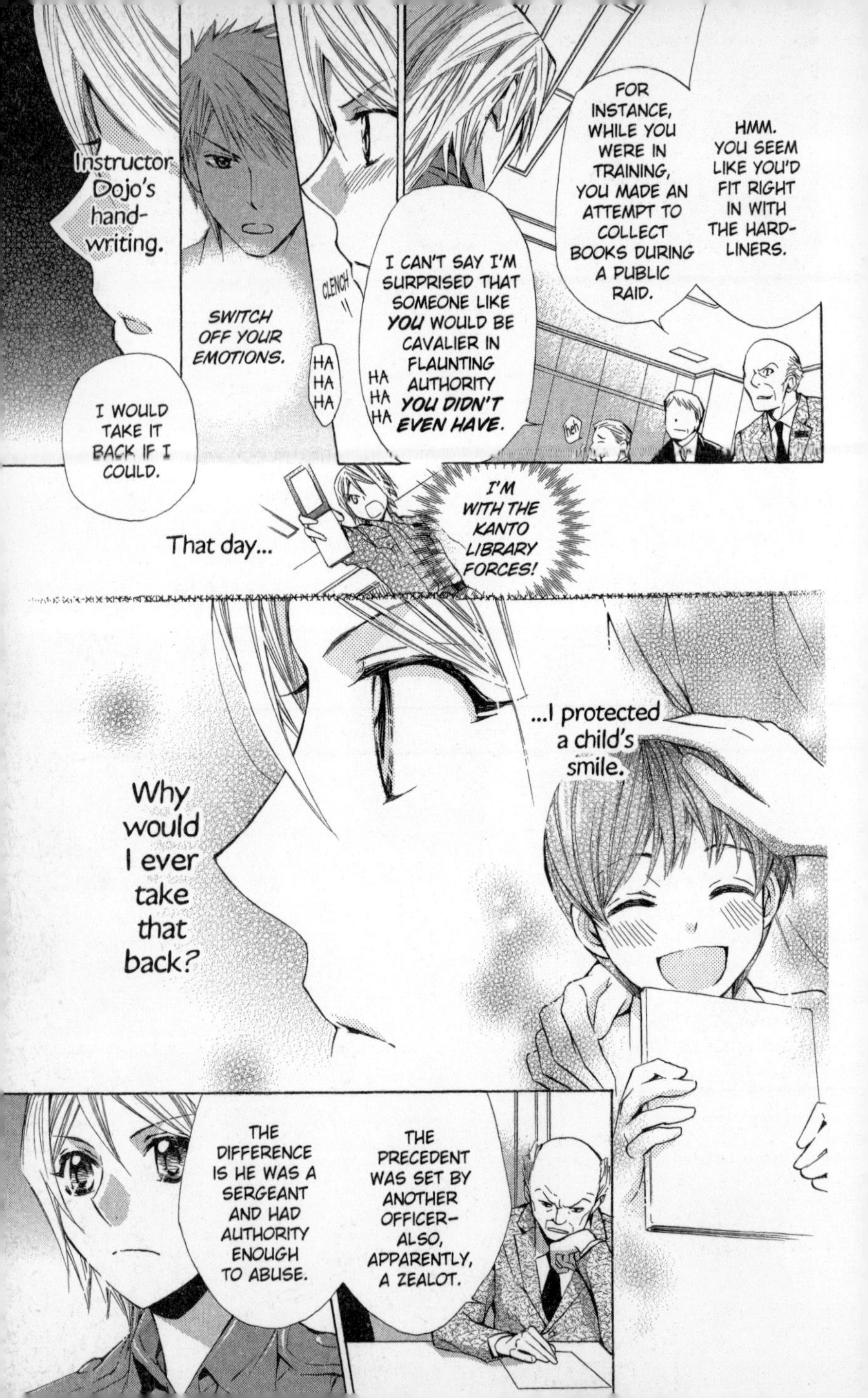
HMM. YOU SEEM LIKE YOU'D FIT RIGHT IN WITH THE HARD-LINERS.
FOR INSTANCE, WHILE YOU WERE IN TRAINING, YOU MADE AN ATTEMPT TO COLLECT BOOKS DURING A PUBLIC RAID.
heh
I CAN'T SAY I'M SURPRISED THAT SOMEONE LIKE *YOU* WOULD BE CAVALIER IN FLAUNTING AUTHORITY *YOU DIDN'T EVEN HAVE*.
HA HA HA
CLENCH
HA HA HA
SWITCH OFF YOUR EMOTIONS.
Instructor Dojo's hand-writing.
I WOULD TAKE IT BACK IF I COULD.
I'M WITH THE KANTO LIBRARY FORCES!
That day...
...I protected a child's smile.
Why would I ever take that back?
THE PRECEDENT WAS SET BY ANOTHER OFFICER—ALSO, APPARENTLY, A ZEALOT.
THE DIFFERENCE IS HE WAS A SERGEANT AND HAD AUTHORITY ENOUGH TO ABUSE.

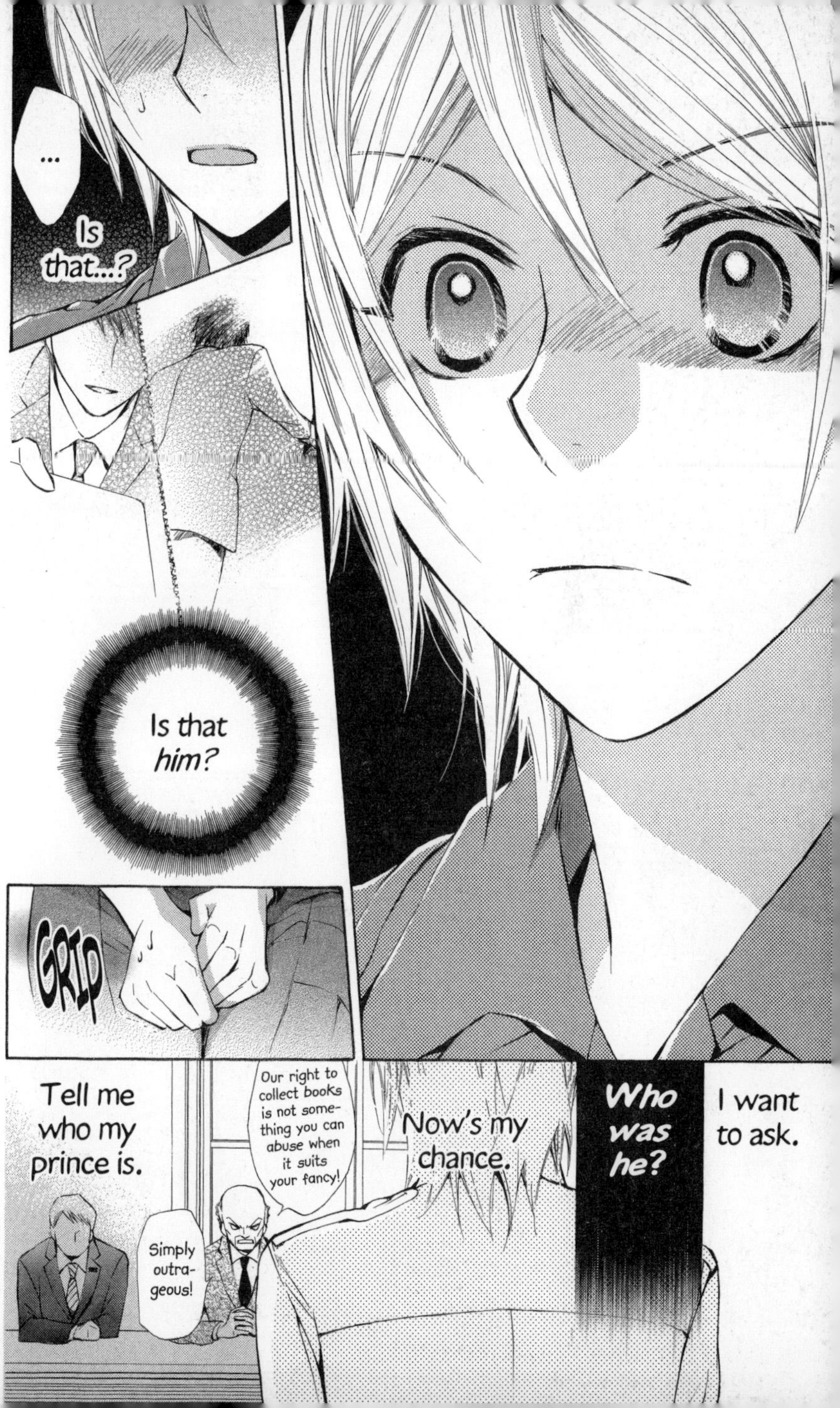

...
Is that...?
Is that *him?*
GRIP
I want to ask.
Who was he?
Now's my chance.
Our right to collect books is not something you can abuse when it suits your fancy!
Simply outrageous!
Tell me who my prince is.

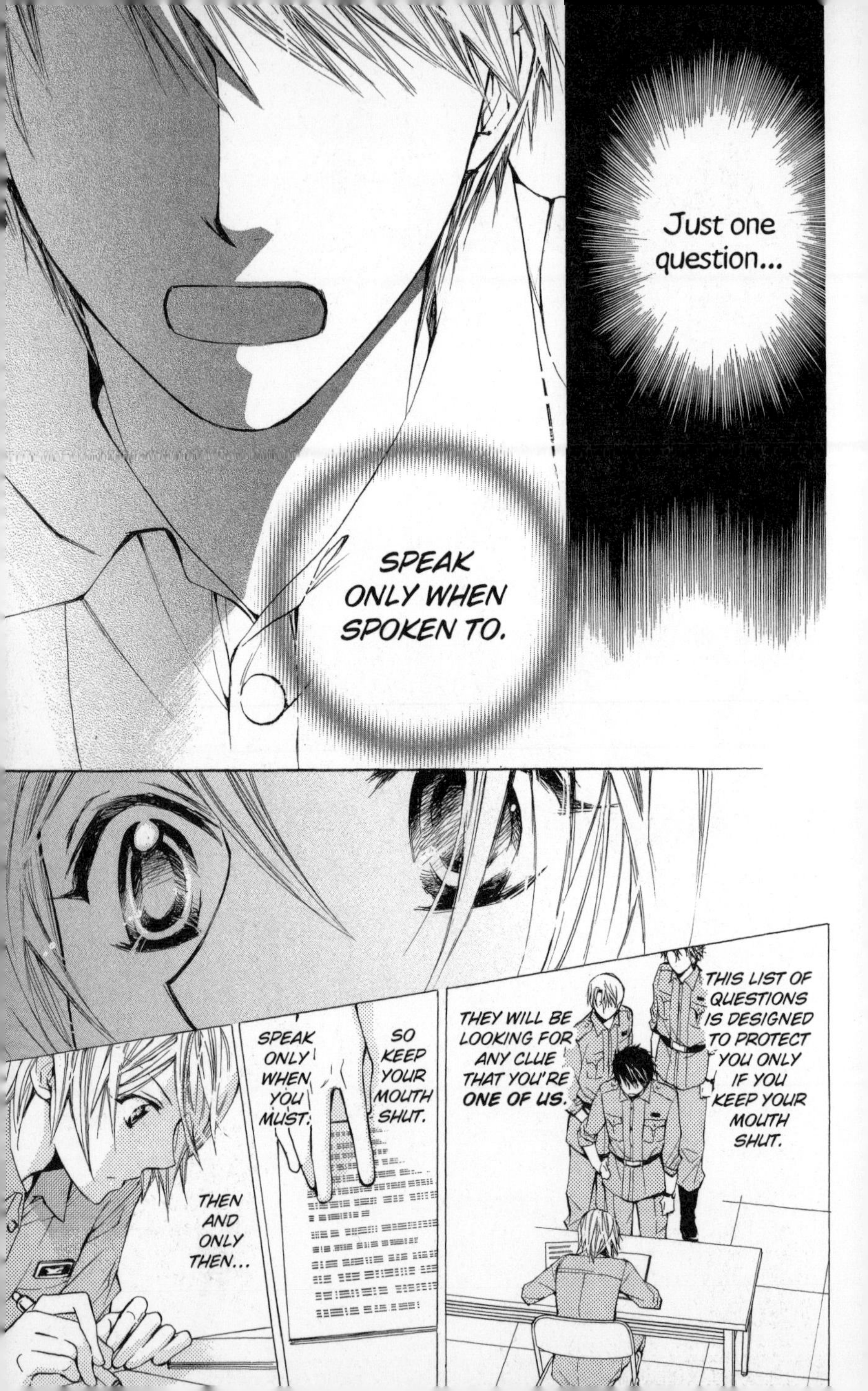
Just one question...
SPEAK ONLY WHEN SPOKEN TO.
THIS LIST OF QUESTIONS IS DESIGNED TO PROTECT YOU ONLY IF YOU KEEP YOUR MOUTH SHUT.
THEY WILL BE LOOKING FOR ANY CLUE THAT YOU'RE ONE OF US.
SO KEEP YOUR MOUTH SHUT.
SPEAK ONLY WHEN YOU MUST.
THEN AND ONLY THEN...

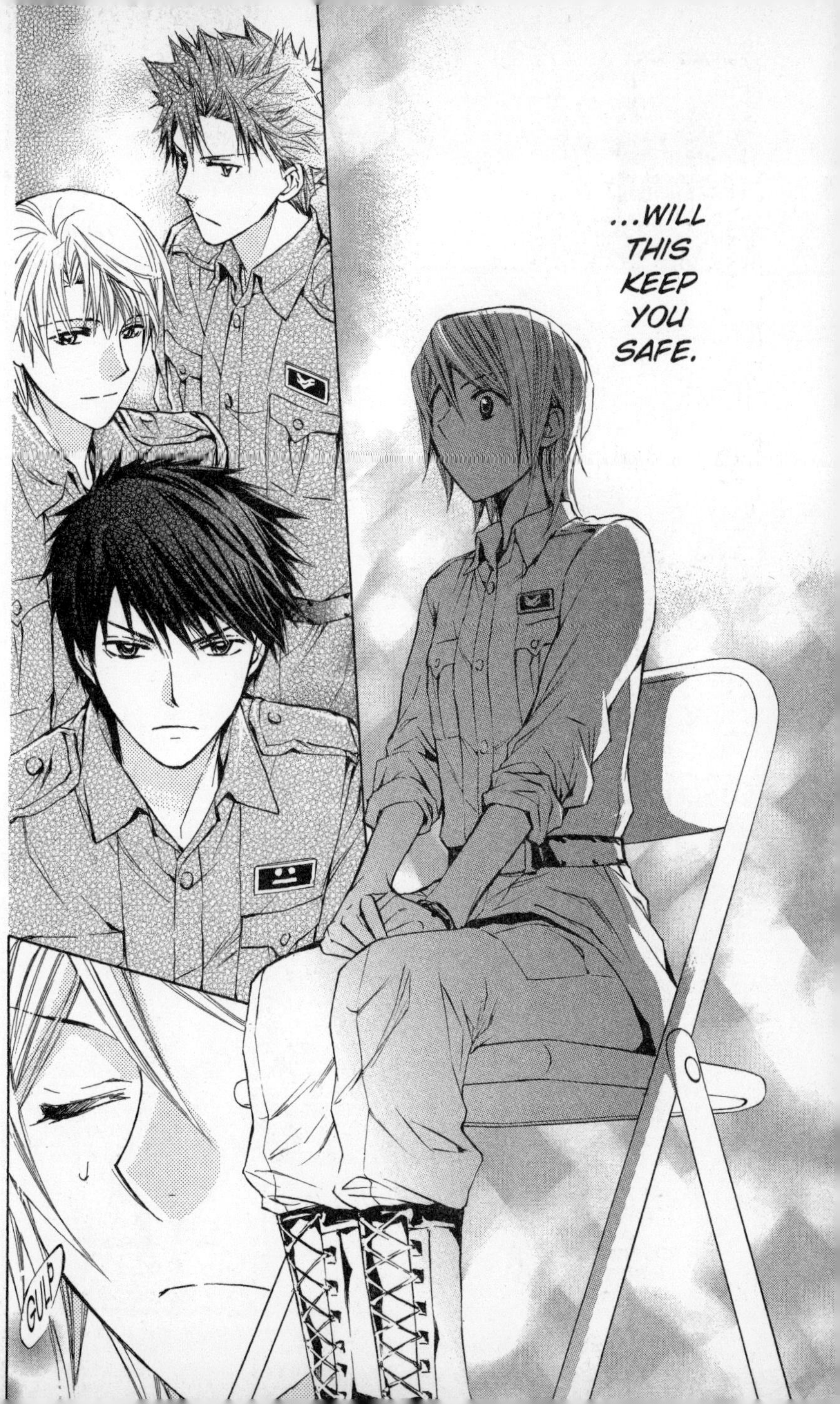
...WILL THIS KEEP YOU SAFE.
GULP

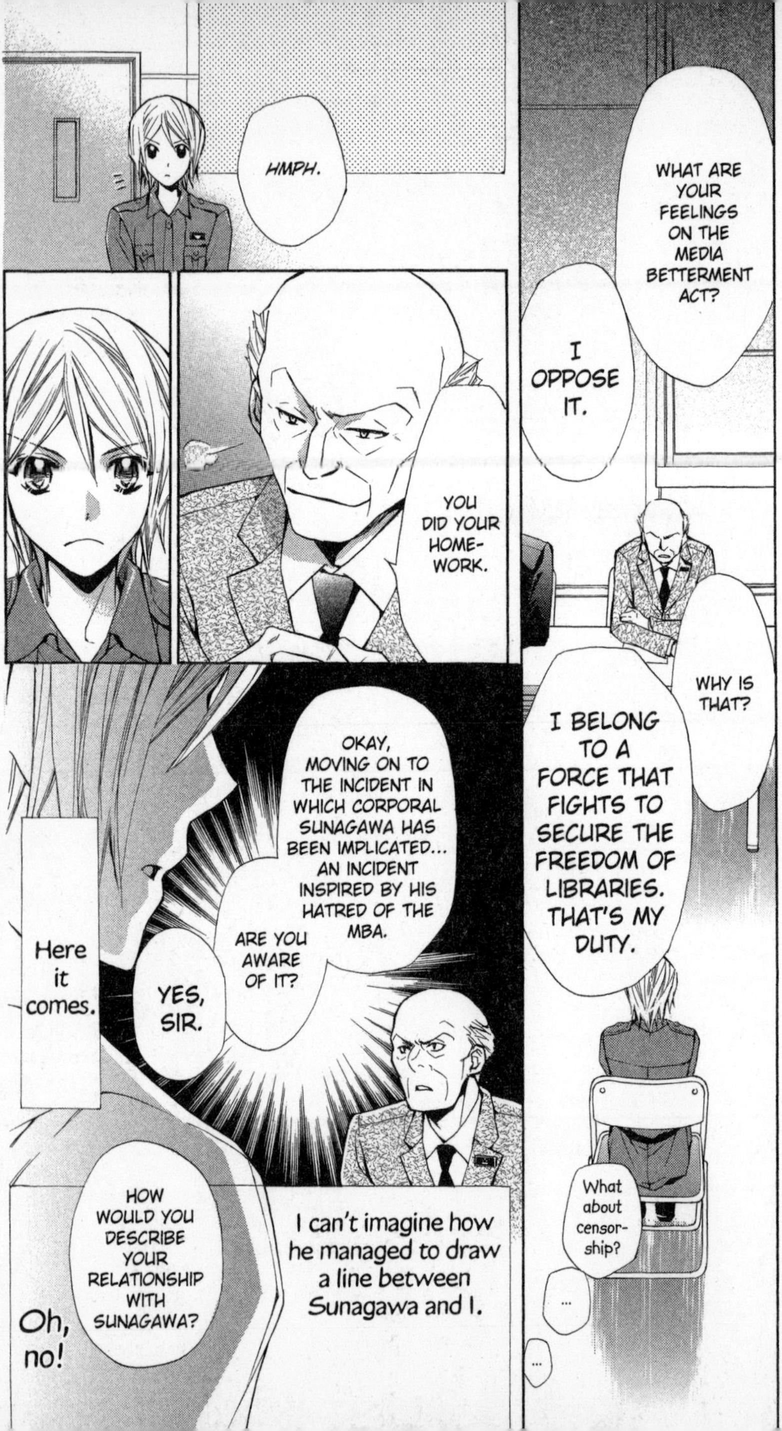
WHAT ARE YOUR FEELINGS ON THE MEDIA BETTERMENT ACT?
I OPPOSE IT.
WHY IS THAT?
I BELONG TO A FORCE THAT FIGHTS TO SECURE THE FREEDOM OF LIBRARIES. THAT'S MY DUTY.
What about censorship?
...
...
HMPH.
YOU DID YOUR HOMEWORK.
OKAY, MOVING ON TO THE INCIDENT IN WHICH CORPORAL SUNAGAWA HAS BEEN IMPLICATED... AN INCIDENT INSPIRED BY HIS HATRED OF THE MBA.
ARE YOU AWARE OF IT?
YES, SIR.
Here it comes.
I can't imagine how he managed to draw a line between Sunagawa and I.
HOW WOULD YOU DESCRIBE YOUR RELATIONSHIP WITH SUNAGAWA?
Oh, no!

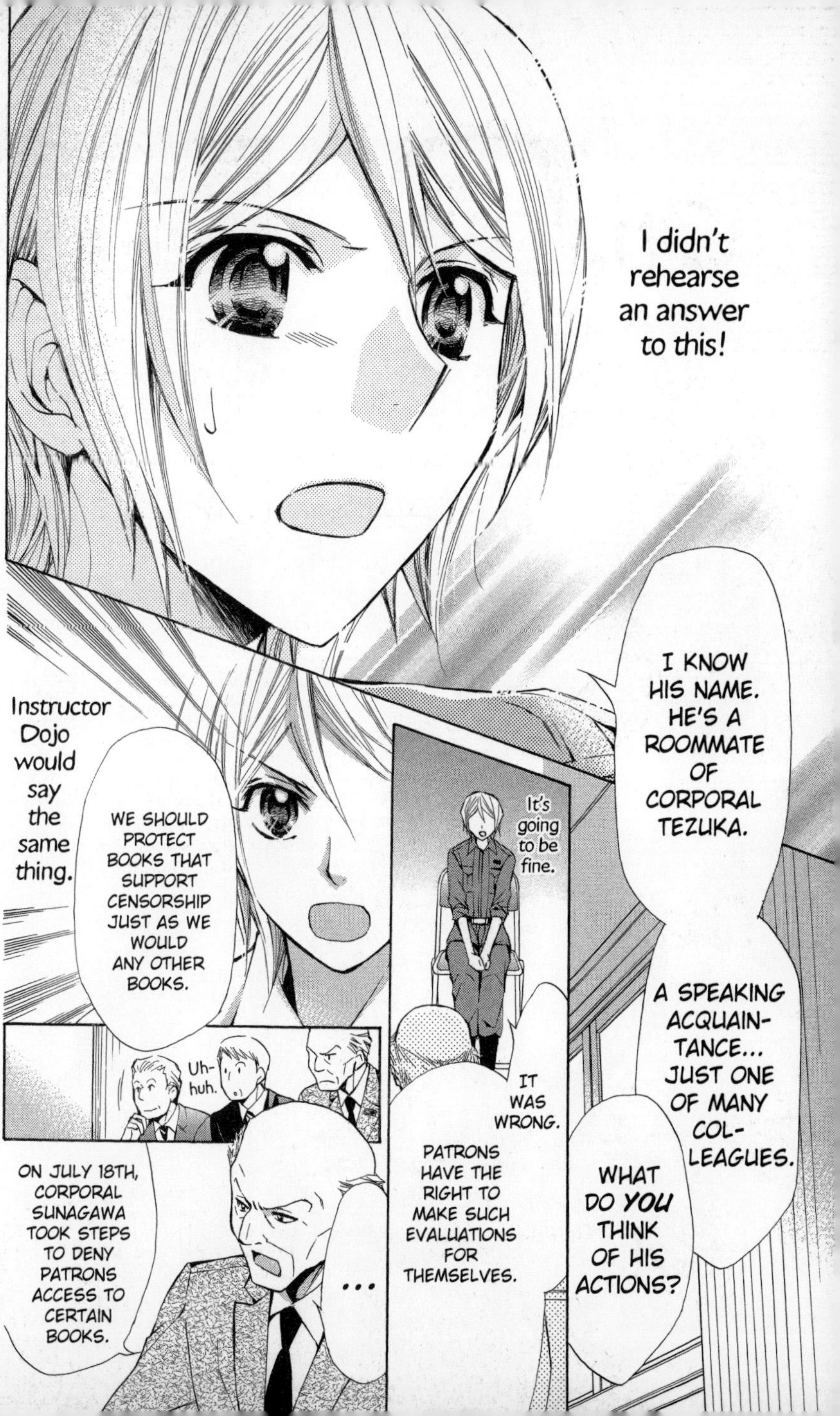

I didn't rehearse an answer to this!
I KNOW HIS NAME. HE'S A ROOMMATE OF CORPORAL TEZUKA.
A SPEAKING ACQUAIN-TANCE... JUST ONE OF MANY COL-LEAGUES.
WHAT DO *YOU* THINK OF HIS ACTIONS?
It's going to be fine.
IT WAS WRONG.
PATRONS HAVE THE RIGHT TO MAKE SUCH EVALUATIONS FOR THEMSELVES.
...
ON JULY 18TH, CORPORAL SUNAGAWA TOOK STEPS TO DENY PATRONS ACCESS TO CERTAIN BOOKS.
WE SHOULD PROTECT BOOKS THAT SUPPORT CENSORSHIP JUST AS WE WOULD ANY OTHER BOOKS.
Instructor Dojo would say the same thing.
Uh-huh.

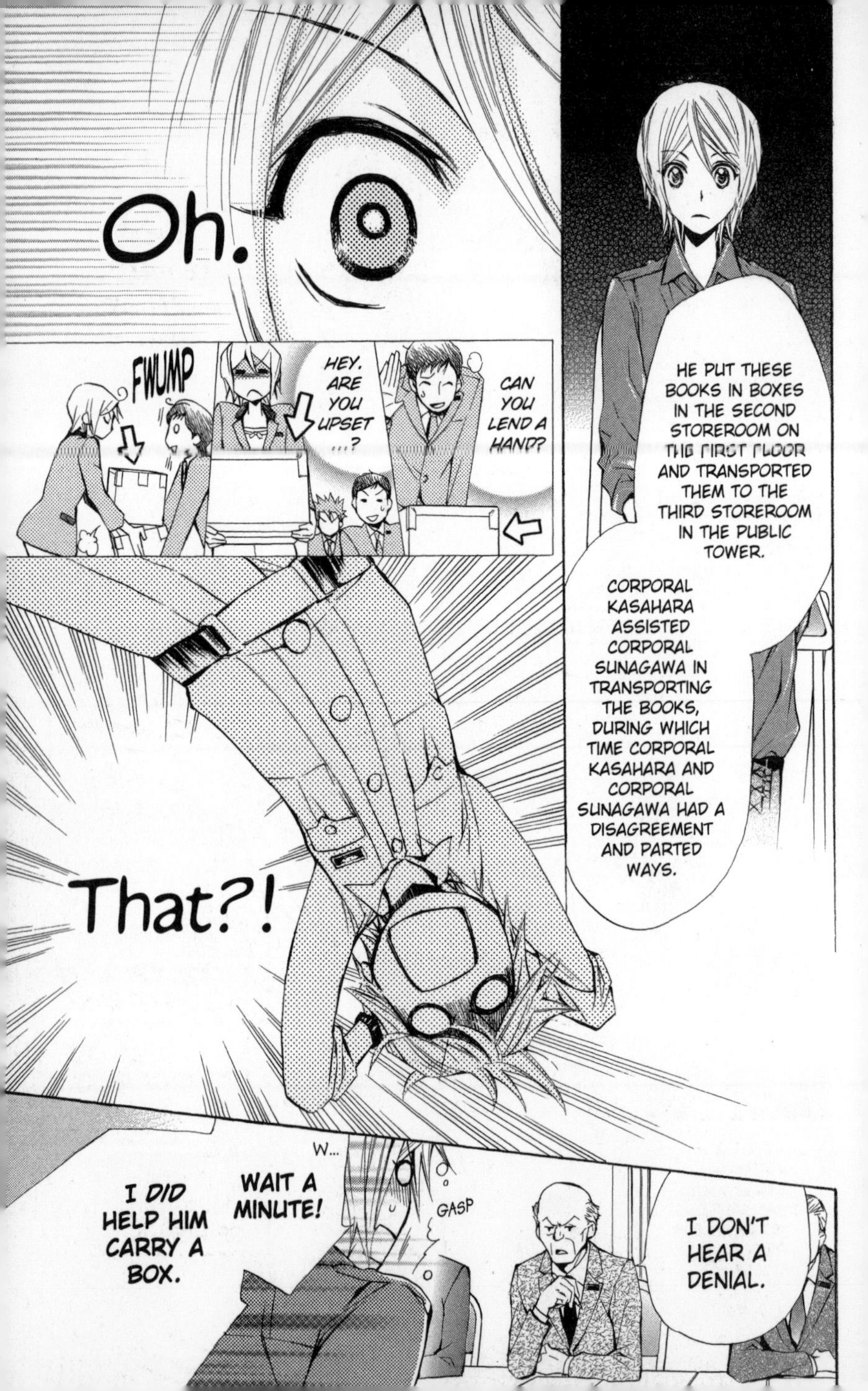

HE PUT THESE BOOKS IN BOXES IN THE SECOND STOREROOM ON THE FIRST FLOOR AND TRANSPORTED THEM TO THE THIRD STOREROOM IN THE PUBLIC TOWER.
CORPORAL KASAHARA ASSISTED CORPORAL SUNAGAWA IN TRANSPORTING THE BOOKS, DURING WHICH TIME CORPORAL KASAHARA AND CORPORAL SUNAGAWA HAD A DISAGREEMENT AND PARTED WAYS.
Oh.
CAN YOU LEND A HAND?
HEY. ARE YOU UPSET ...?
FWUMP
That?!
I DON'T HEAR A DENIAL.
GASP
W...
WAIT A MINUTE!
I DID HELP HIM CARRY A BOX.

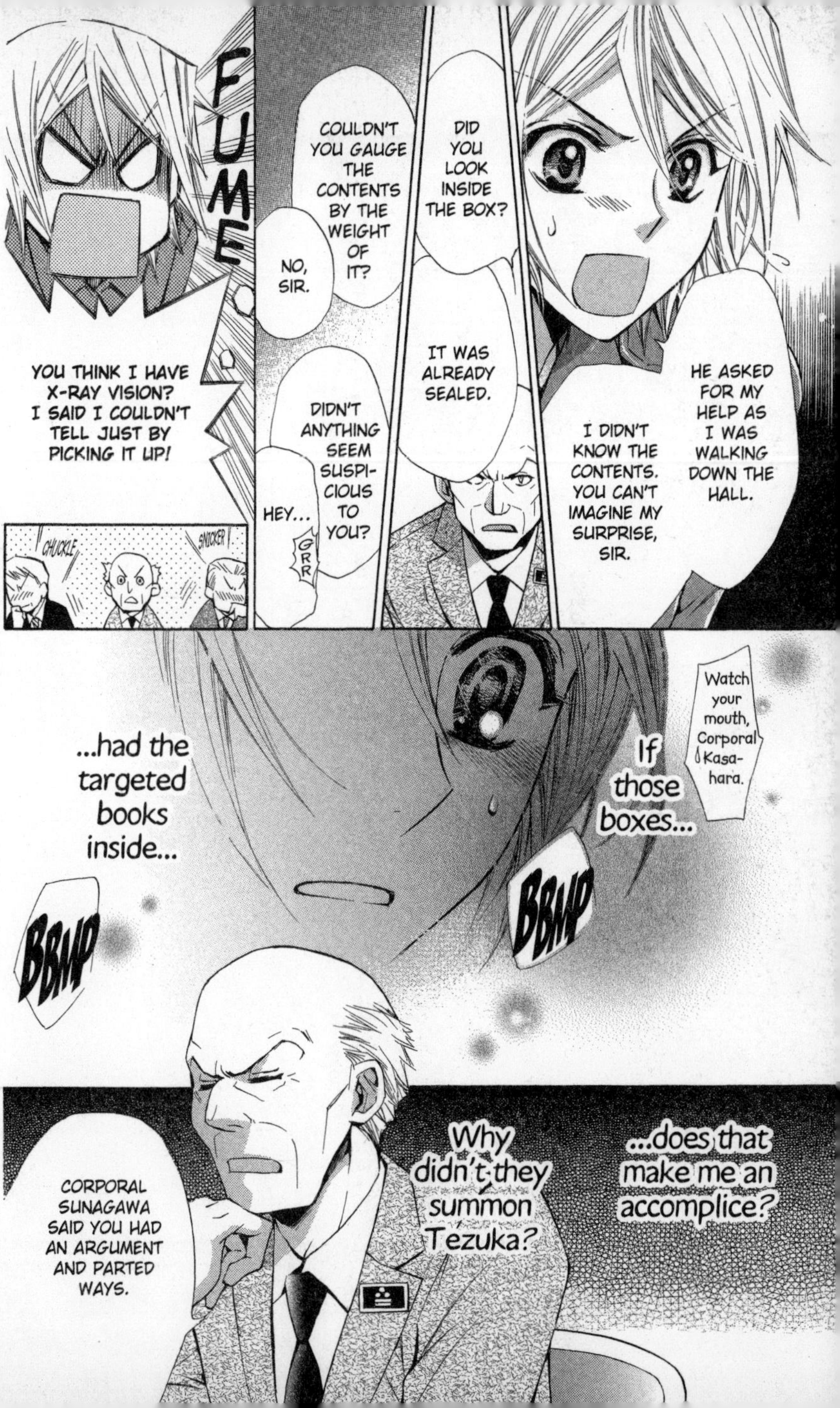
HE ASKED FOR MY HELP AS I WAS WALKING DOWN THE HALL.
I DIDN'T KNOW THE CONTENTS. YOU CAN'T IMAGINE MY SURPRISE, SIR.
DID YOU LOOK INSIDE THE BOX?
IT WAS ALREADY SEALED.
COULDN'T YOU GAUGE THE CONTENTS BY THE WEIGHT OF IT?
NO, SIR.
DIDN'T ANYTHING SEEM SUSPICIOUS TO YOU?
HEY...
GRR
FUME
YOU THINK I HAVE X-RAY VISION? I SAID I COULDN'T TELL JUST BY PICKING IT UP!
SNICKER
CHUCKLE
Watch your mouth, Corporal Kasahara.
If those boxes...
...had the targeted books inside...
BBMP
BBMP
...does that make me an accomplice?
Why didn't they summon Tezuka?
CORPORAL SUNAGAWA SAID YOU HAD AN ARGUMENT AND PARTED WAYS.

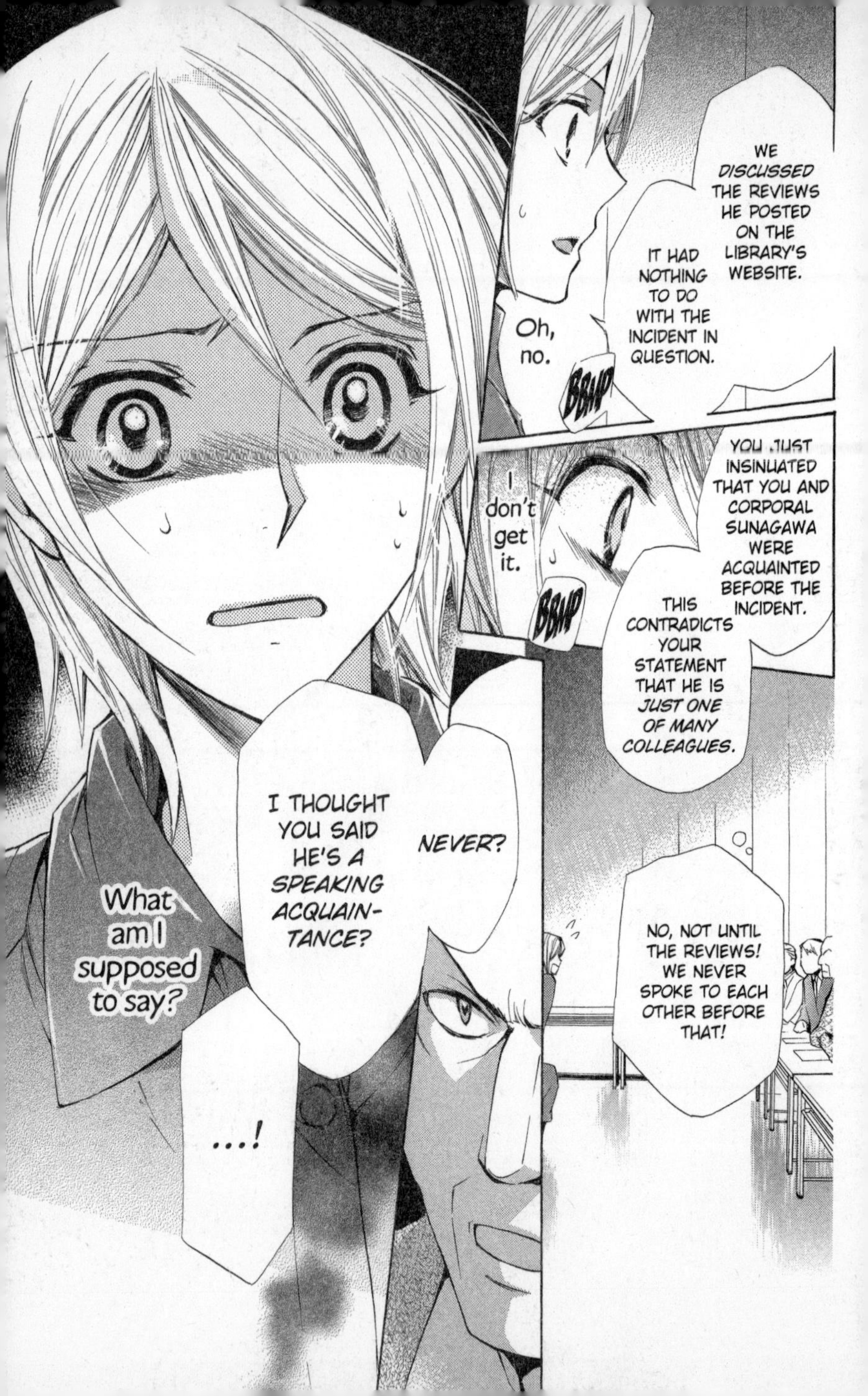

WE DISCUSSED THE REVIEWS HE POSTED ON THE LIBRARY'S WEBSITE.
IT HAD NOTHING TO DO WITH THE INCIDENT IN QUESTION.
Oh, no.
BBMP
YOU JUST INSINUATED THAT YOU AND CORPORAL SUNAGAWA WERE ACQUAINTED BEFORE THE INCIDENT.
THIS CONTRADICTS YOUR STATEMENT THAT HE IS JUST ONE OF MANY COLLEAGUES.
I don't get it.
BBMP
NO, NOT UNTIL THE REVIEWS! WE NEVER SPOKE TO EACH OTHER BEFORE THAT!
NEVER?
I THOUGHT YOU SAID HE'S A SPEAKING ACQUAINTANCE?
What am I supposed to say?
...!

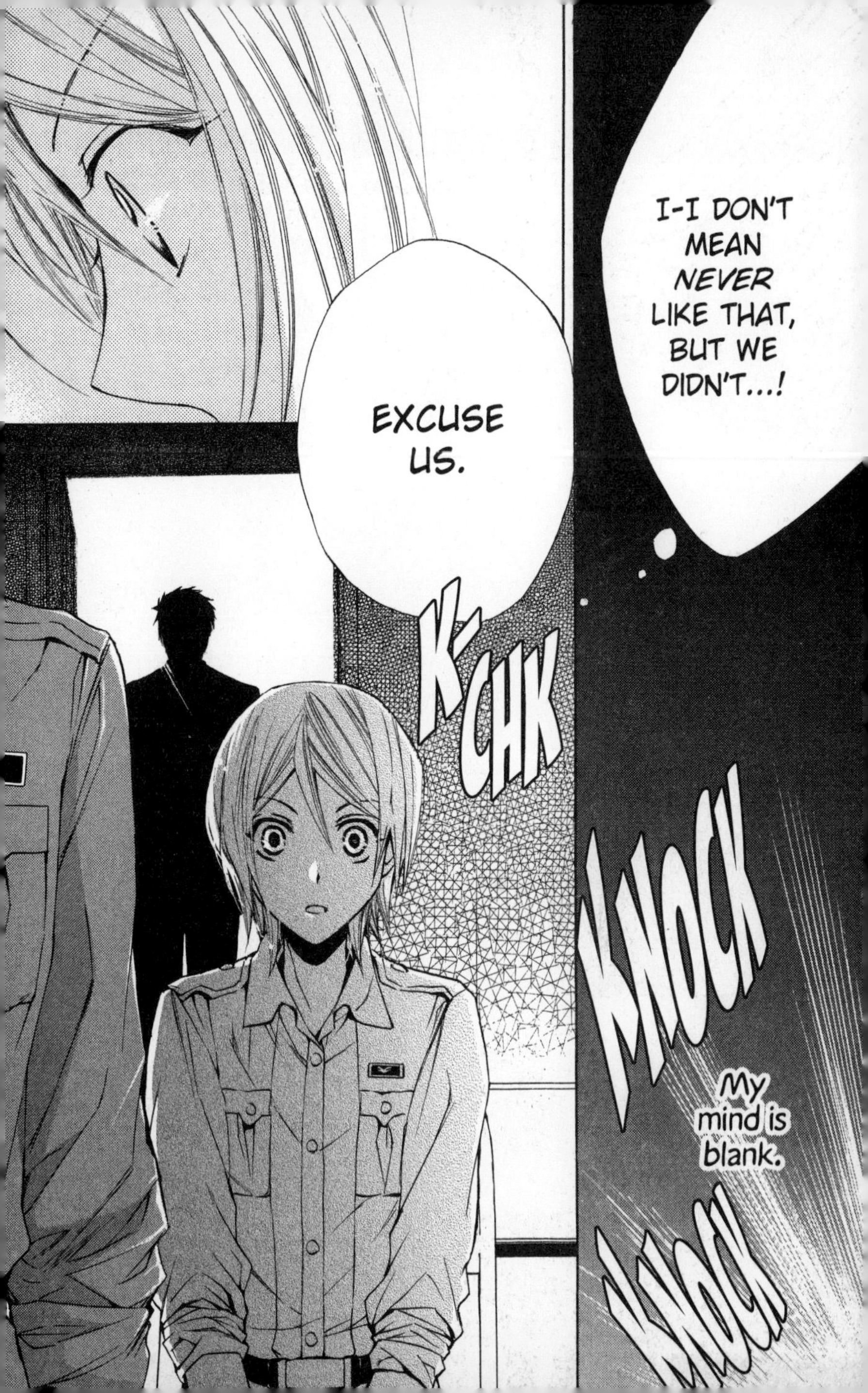
I-I DON'T MEAN *NEVER* LIKE THAT, BUT WE DIDN'T...!
KNOCK
My mind is blank.
KNOCK
EXCUSE US.
K-CHK

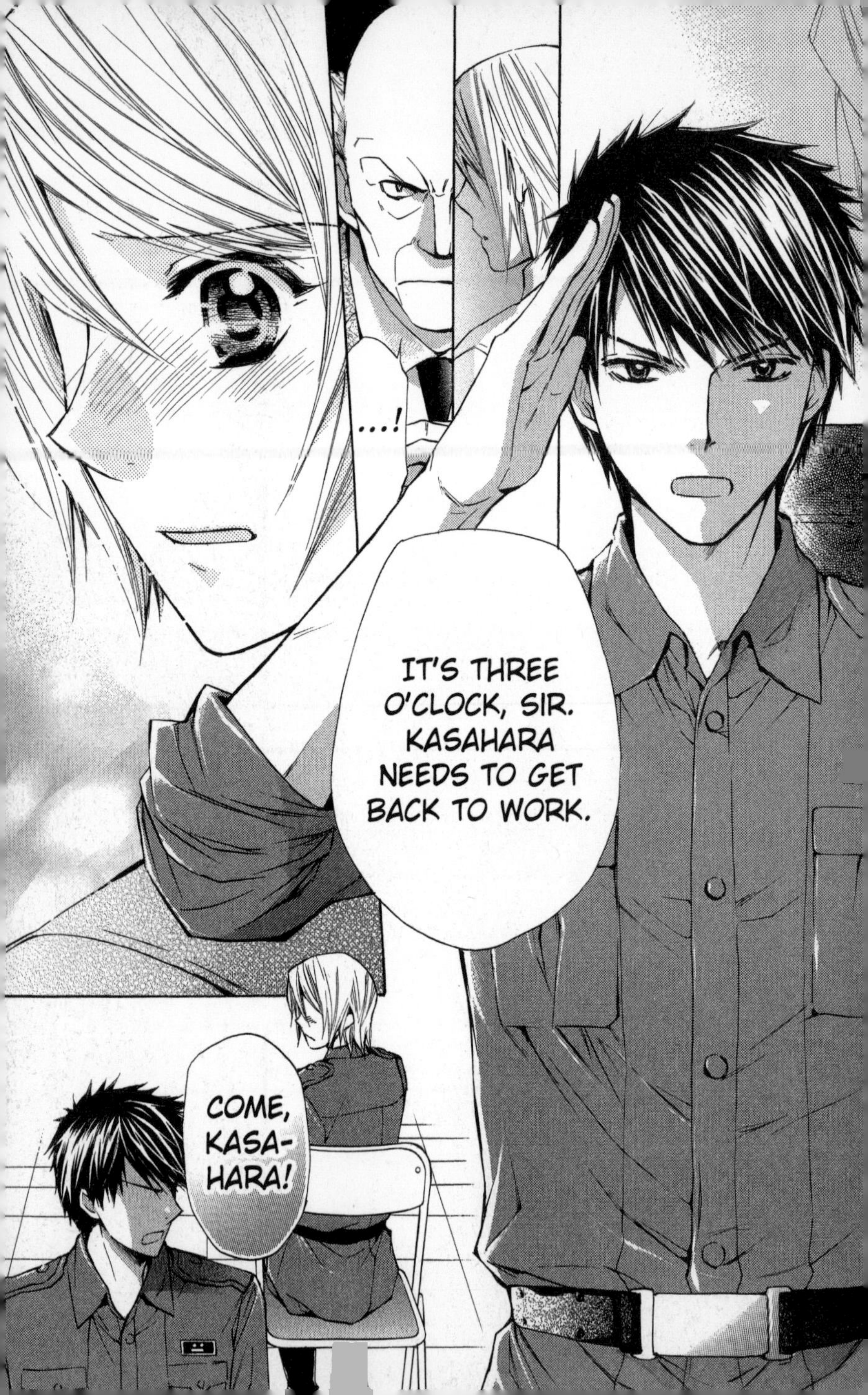
...!
IT'S THREE O'CLOCK, SIR. KASAHARA NEEDS TO GET BACK TO WORK.
COME, KASA-HARA!

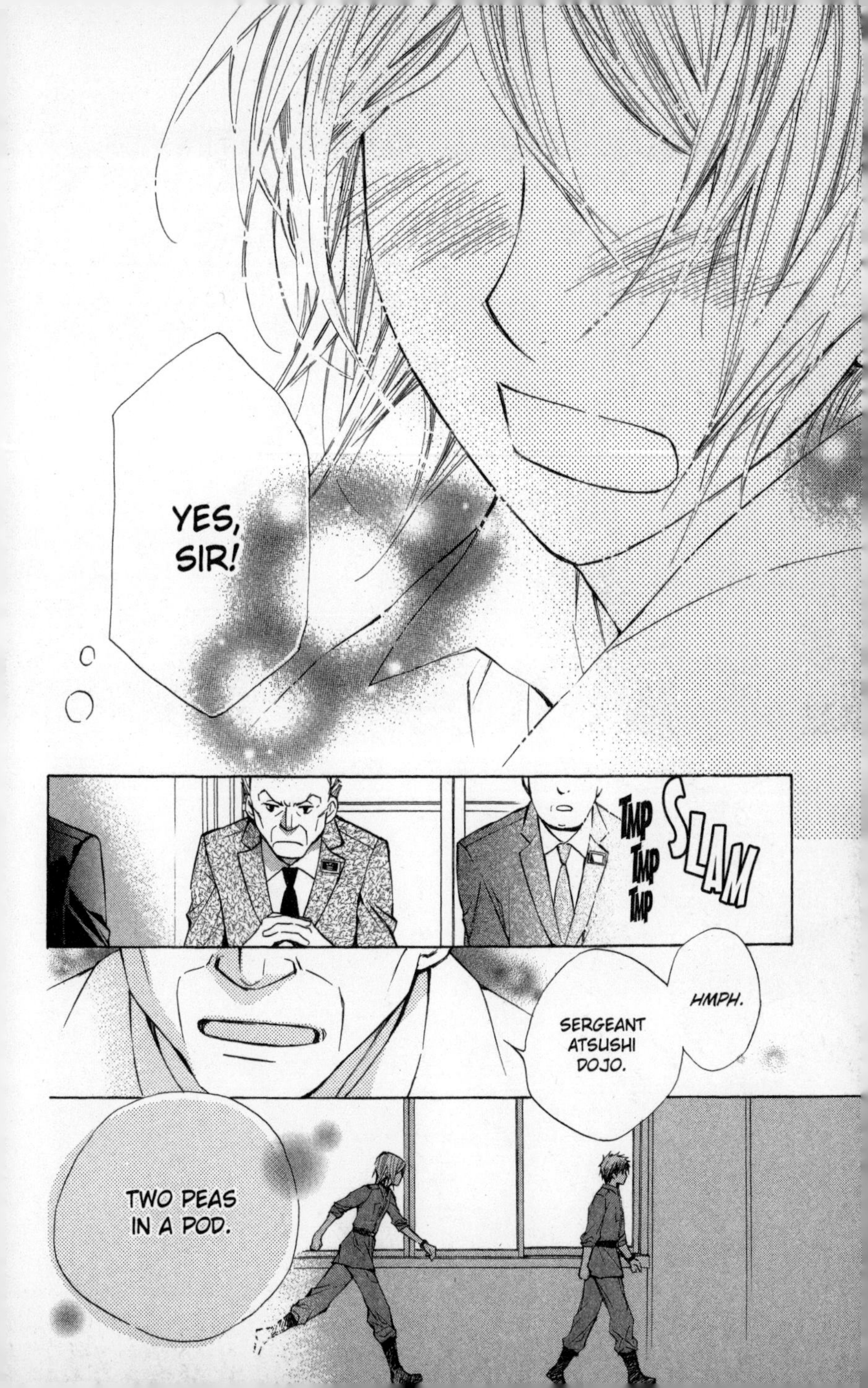
YES, SIR!
SLAM
TMP TMP TMP
HMPH.
SERGEANT ATSUSHI DOJO.
TWO PEAS IN A POD.

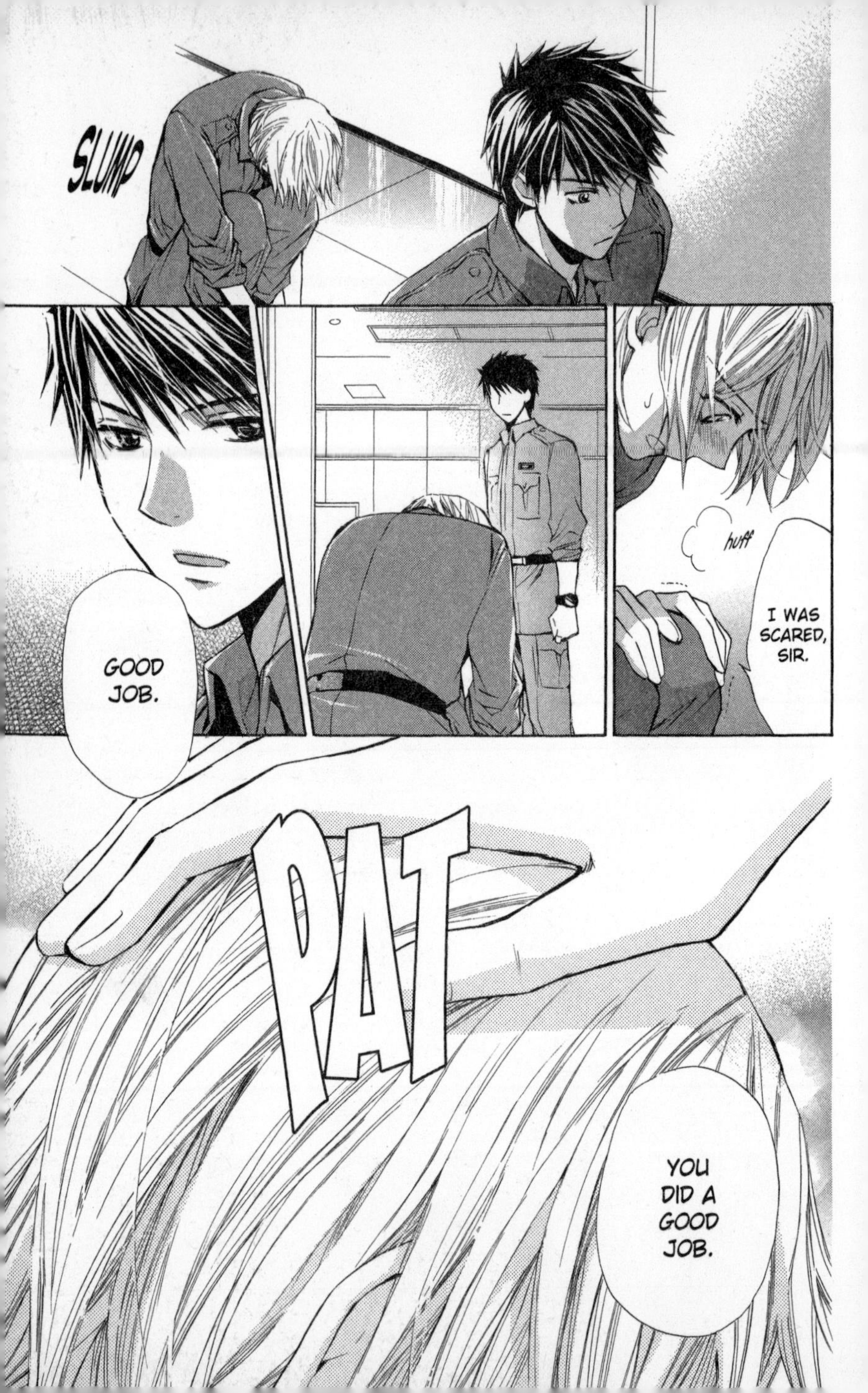
SLUMP
huff
I WAS SCARED, SIR.
GOOD JOB.
PAT
YOU DID A GOOD JOB.

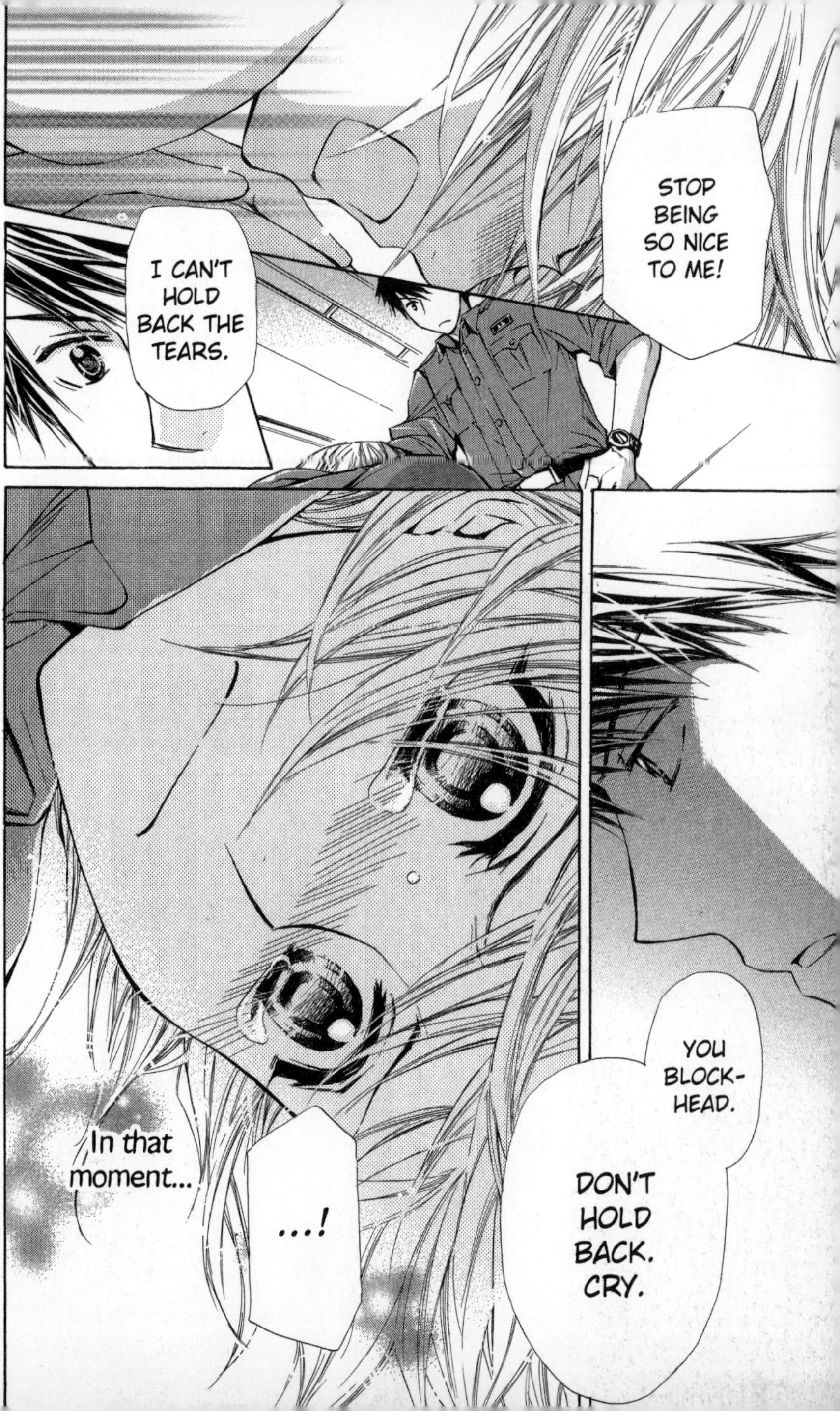
STOP BEING SO NICE TO ME!
I CAN'T HOLD BACK THE TEARS.
YOU BLOCK-HEAD.
DON'T HOLD BACK. CRY.
...!
In that moment...

...I was vulnerable.
And...
...his consoling hand felt wonderful on my head.
It felt like he rescued me from the gallows.
If I cry, it's like giving in to them.
Look... this isn't a game.
I didn't realize the hardest part was yet to come.

Treat With Care!

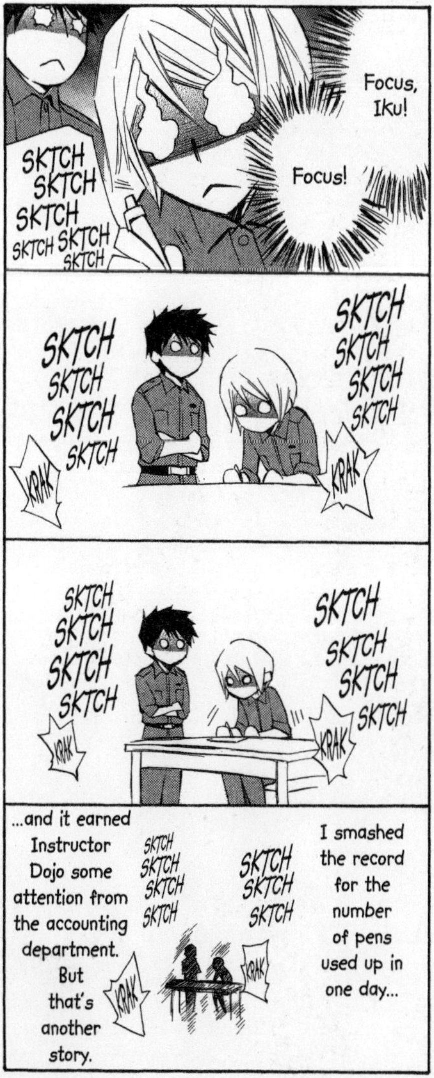

Focus, Iku!
Focus!
SKTCH SKTCH SKTCH SKTCH SKTCH SKTCH
SKTCH SKTCH SKTCH SKTCH
KRAK
SKTCH SKTCH SKTCH SKTCH
KRAK
SKTCH SKTCH SKTCH SKTCH
KRAK
SKTCH SKTCH SKTCH SKTCH
KRAK
I smashed the record for the number of pens used up in one day...
SKTCH SKTCH SKTCH
KRAK
SKTCH SKTCH SKTCH SKTCH
KRAK
...and it earned Instructor Dojo some attention from the accounting department. But that's another story.

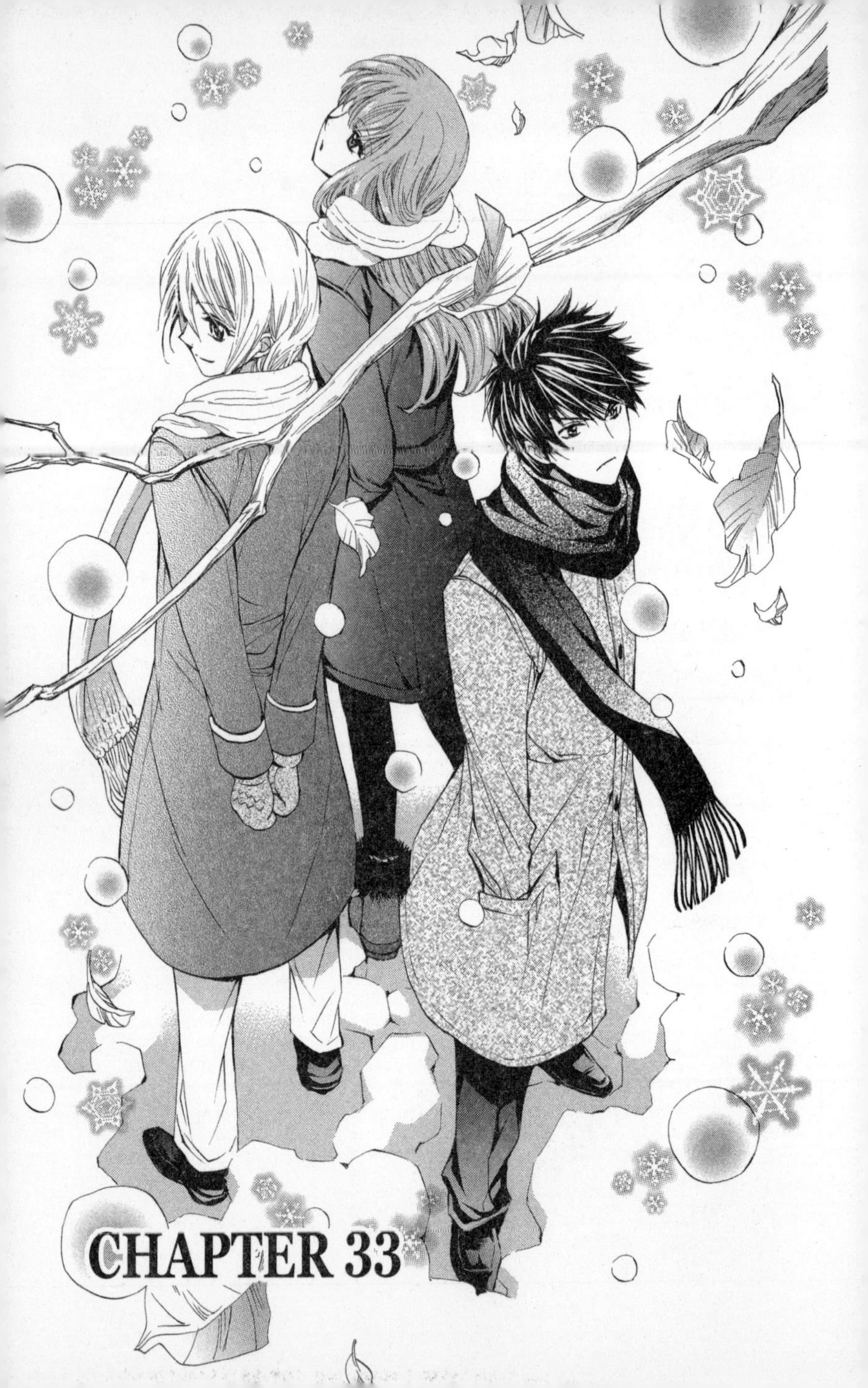
CHAPTER 33

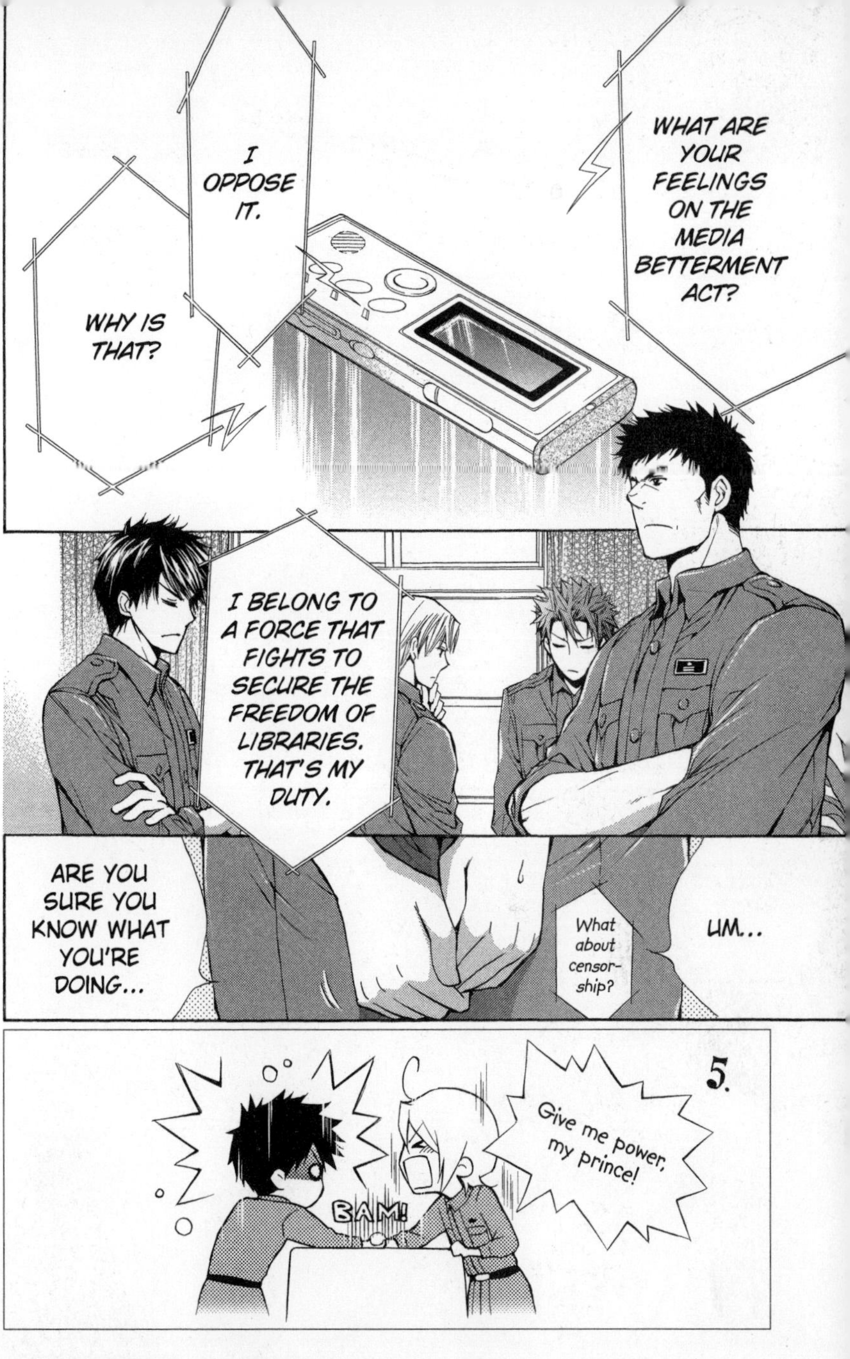
WHAT ARE YOUR FEELINGS ON THE MEDIA BETTERMENT ACT?
I OPPOSE IT.
WHY IS THAT?
I BELONG TO A FORCE THAT FIGHTS TO SECURE THE FREEDOM OF LIBRARIES. THAT'S MY DUTY.
UM...
What about censorship?
ARE YOU SURE YOU KNOW WHAT YOU'RE DOING...
5.
Give me power, my prince!
BAM!

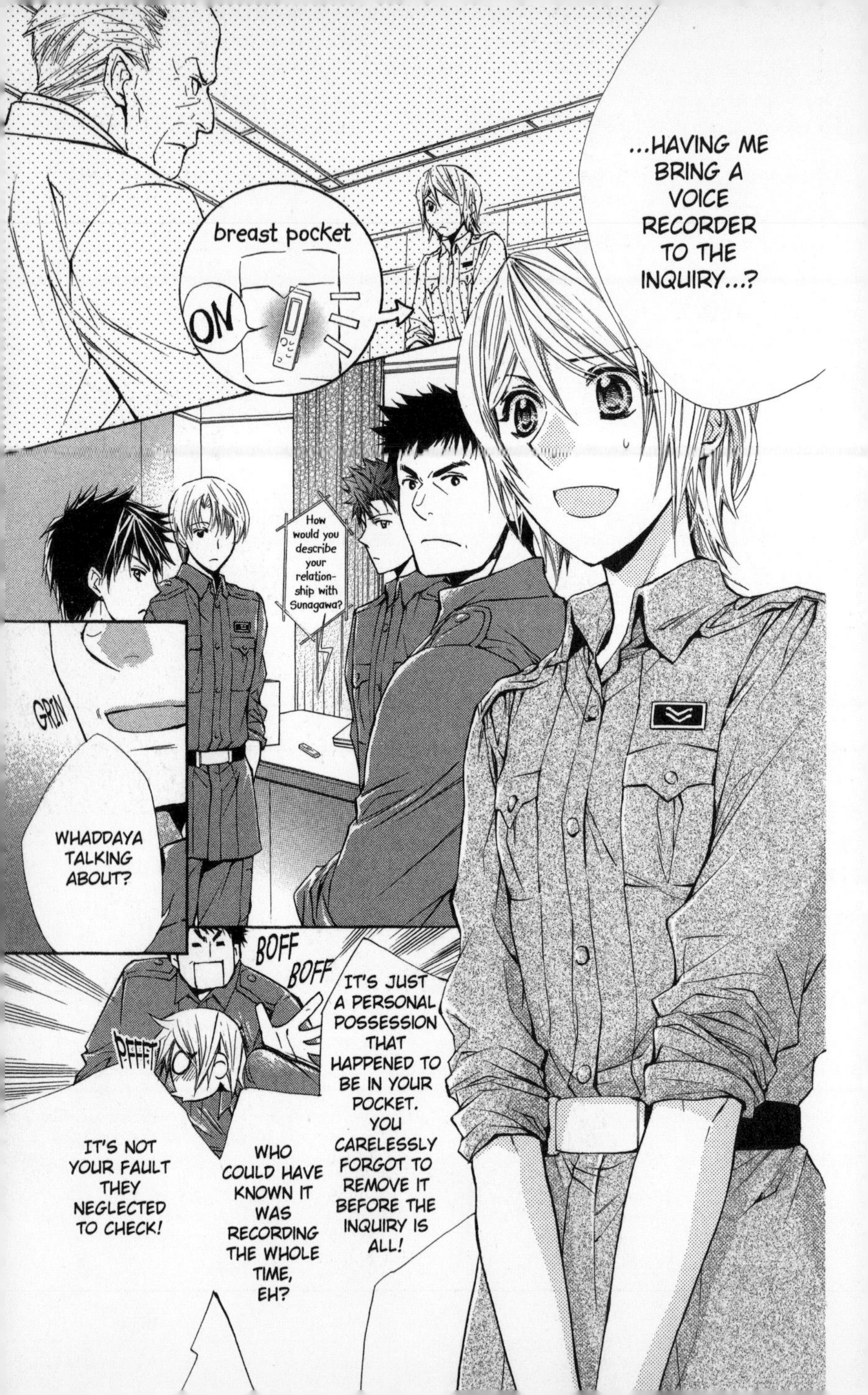
...HAVING ME BRING A VOICE RECORDER TO THE INQUIRY...?
breast pocket
ON
How would you describe your relationship with Sunagawa?
GRIN
WHADDAYA TALKING ABOUT?
IT'S JUST A PERSONAL POSSESSION THAT HAPPENED TO BE IN YOUR POCKET. YOU CARELESSLY FORGOT TO REMOVE IT BEFORE THE INQUIRY IS ALL!
BOFF BOFF
PFFFT
WHO COULD HAVE KNOWN IT WAS RECORDING THE WHOLE TIME, EH?
IT'S NOT YOUR FAULT THEY NEGLECTED TO CHECK!

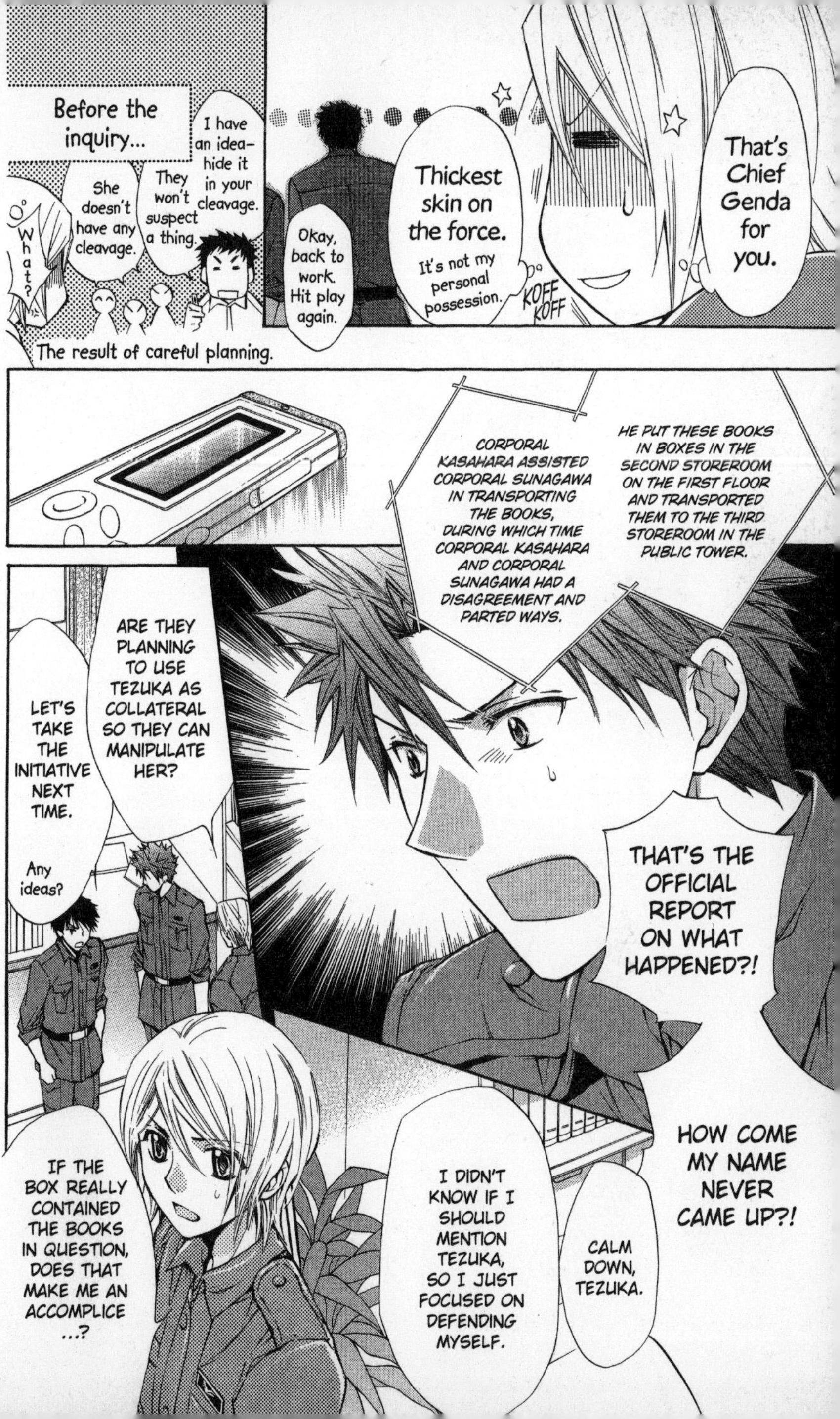

That's Chief Genda for you.
Thickest skin on the force.
It's not my personal possession.
KOFF KOFF
Okay, back to work. Hit play again.
Before the inquiry...
I have an idea—hide it in your cleavage.
They won't suspect a thing.
She doesn't have any cleavage.
What?
The result of careful planning.
HE PUT THESE BOOKS IN BOXES IN THE SECOND STOREROOM ON THE FIRST FLOOR AND TRANSPORTED THEM TO THE THIRD STOREROOM IN THE PUBLIC TOWER.
CORPORAL KASAHARA ASSISTED CORPORAL SUNAGAWA IN TRANSPORTING THE BOOKS, DURING WHICH TIME CORPORAL KASAHARA AND CORPORAL SUNAGAWA HAD A DISAGREEMENT AND PARTED WAYS.
THAT'S THE OFFICIAL REPORT ON WHAT HAPPENED?!
ARE THEY PLANNING TO USE TEZUKA AS COLLATERAL SO THEY CAN MANIPULATE HER?
LET'S TAKE THE INITIATIVE NEXT TIME.
Any ideas?
HOW COME MY NAME NEVER CAME UP?!
CALM DOWN, TEZUKA.
I DIDN'T KNOW IF I SHOULD MENTION TEZUKA, SO I JUST FOCUSED ON DEFENDING MYSELF.
IF THE BOX REALLY CONTAINED THE BOOKS IN QUESTION, DOES THAT MAKE ME AN ACCOMPLICE ...?

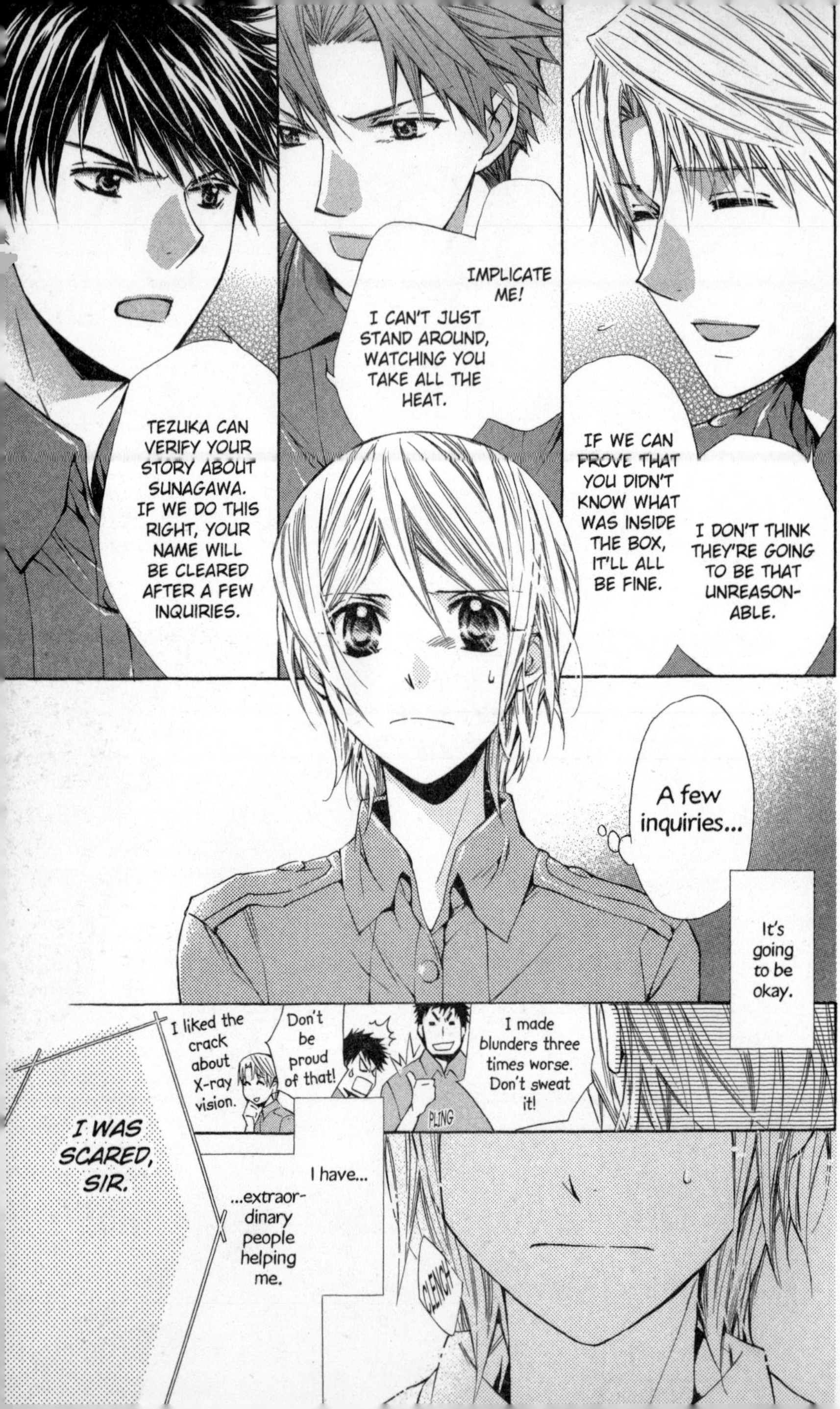
I DON'T THINK THEY'RE GOING TO BE THAT UNREASON-ABLE.
IF WE CAN PROVE THAT YOU DIDN'T KNOW WHAT WAS INSIDE THE BOX, IT'LL ALL BE FINE.
IMPLICATE ME!
I CAN'T JUST STAND AROUND, WATCHING YOU TAKE ALL THE HEAT.
TEZUKA CAN VERIFY YOUR STORY ABOUT SUNAGAWA. IF WE DO THIS RIGHT, YOUR NAME WILL BE CLEARED AFTER A FEW INQUIRIES.
A few inquiries...
It's going to be okay.
I made blunders three times worse. Don't sweat it!
PLING
Don't be proud of that!
I liked the crack about X-ray vision.
I have...
...extraor-dinary people helping me.
CLENCH
I WAS SCARED, SIR.

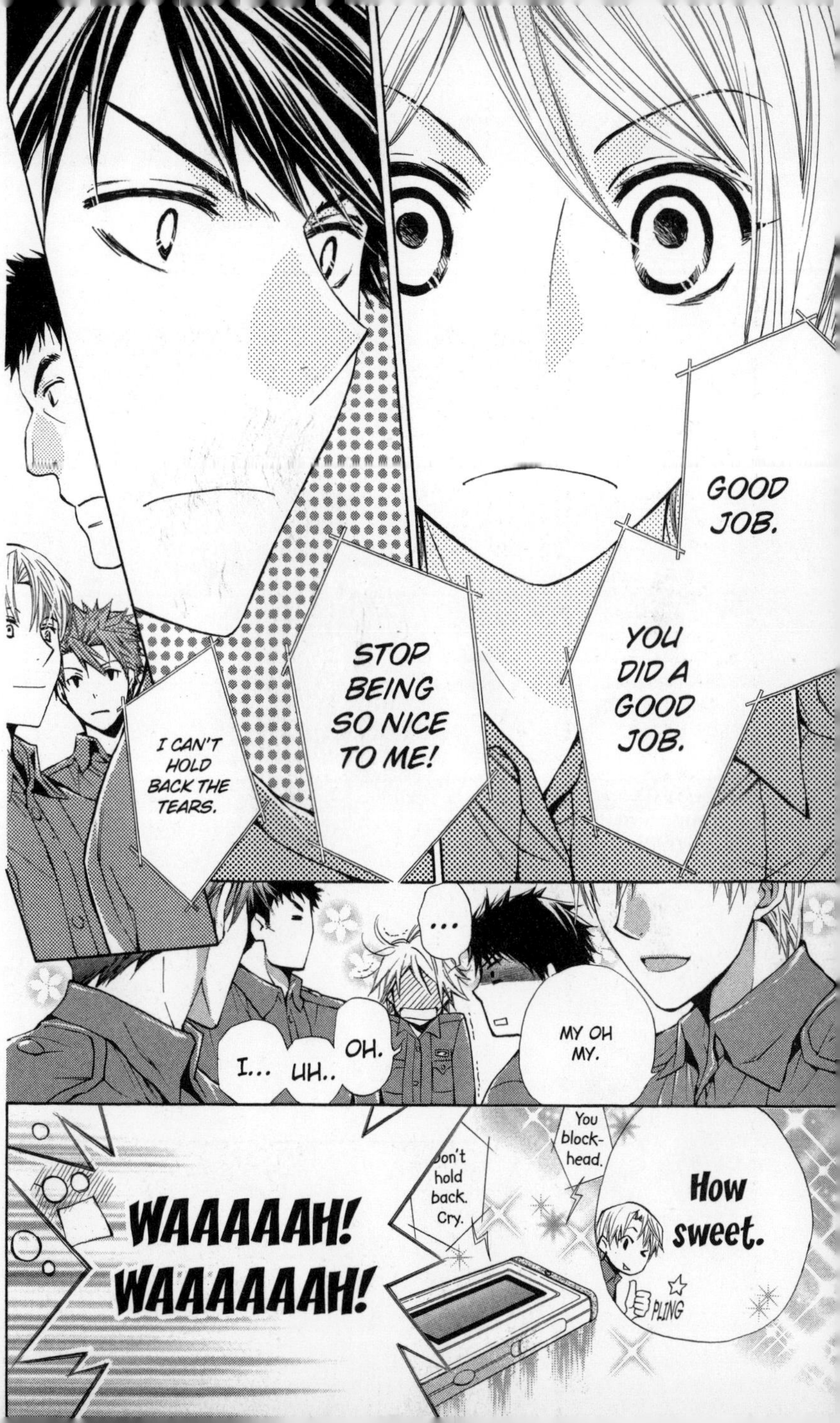
GOOD JOB.
YOU DID A GOOD JOB.
STOP BEING SO NICE TO ME!
I CAN'T HOLD BACK THE TEARS.
MY OH MY.
...
OH.
UH..
I...
How sweet.
PLING
You block-head.
Don't hold back. Cry.
WAAAAAH! WAAAAAAH!

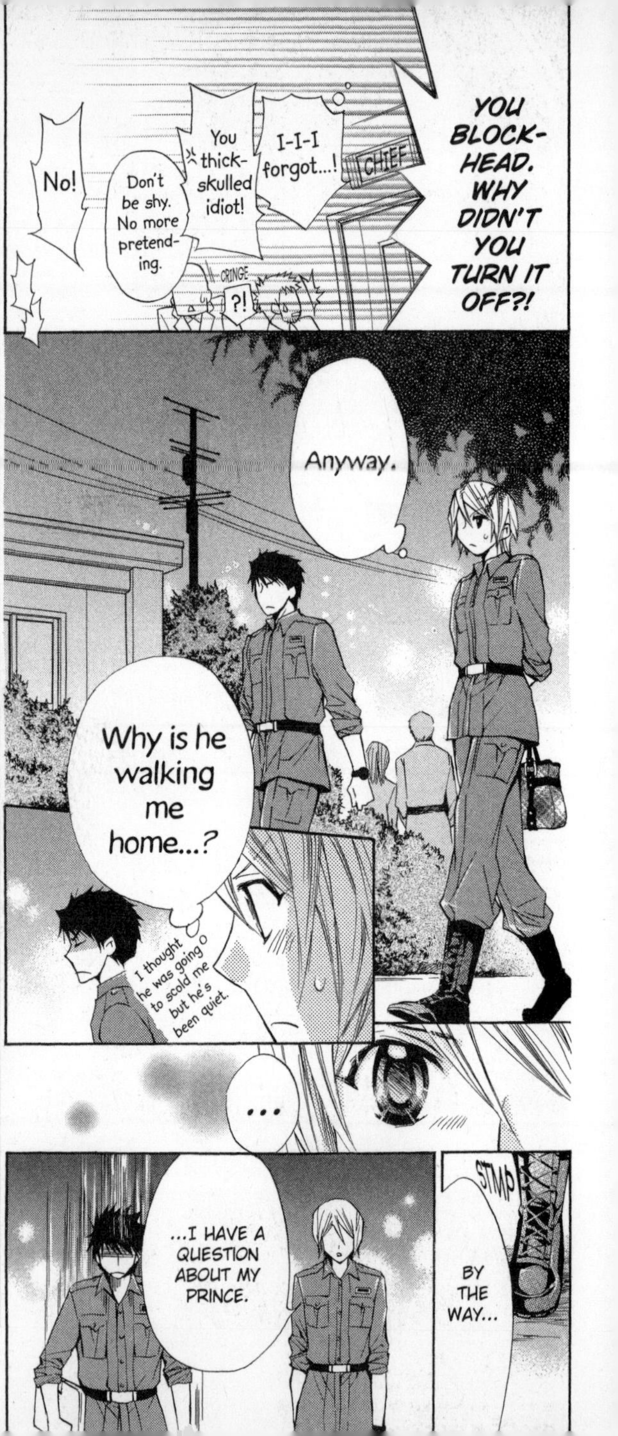
YOU BLOCKHEAD. WHY DIDN'T YOU TURN IT OFF?!
CHIEF
I-I-I forgot...!
You thick-skulled idiot!
Don't be shy. No more pretending.
No!
CRINGE
?!
Anyway.
Why is he walking me home...?
I thought he was going to scold me but he's been quiet.
...
STMP
BY THE WAY...
...I HAVE A QUESTION ABOUT MY PRINCE.

5

*

This is the last sidebar of the volume. Thanks so much for reading all this way. I'm thanking you very often in this volume, aren't I?

You've heard me say this enough times, but I enjoy drawing the characters. This volume is no exception!

If you could sense that by reading this manga, it would make me more than happy.

Bye-bye!

Special Thanks are at the end of the book.

Kiiro Yumi
弓きいろ

*

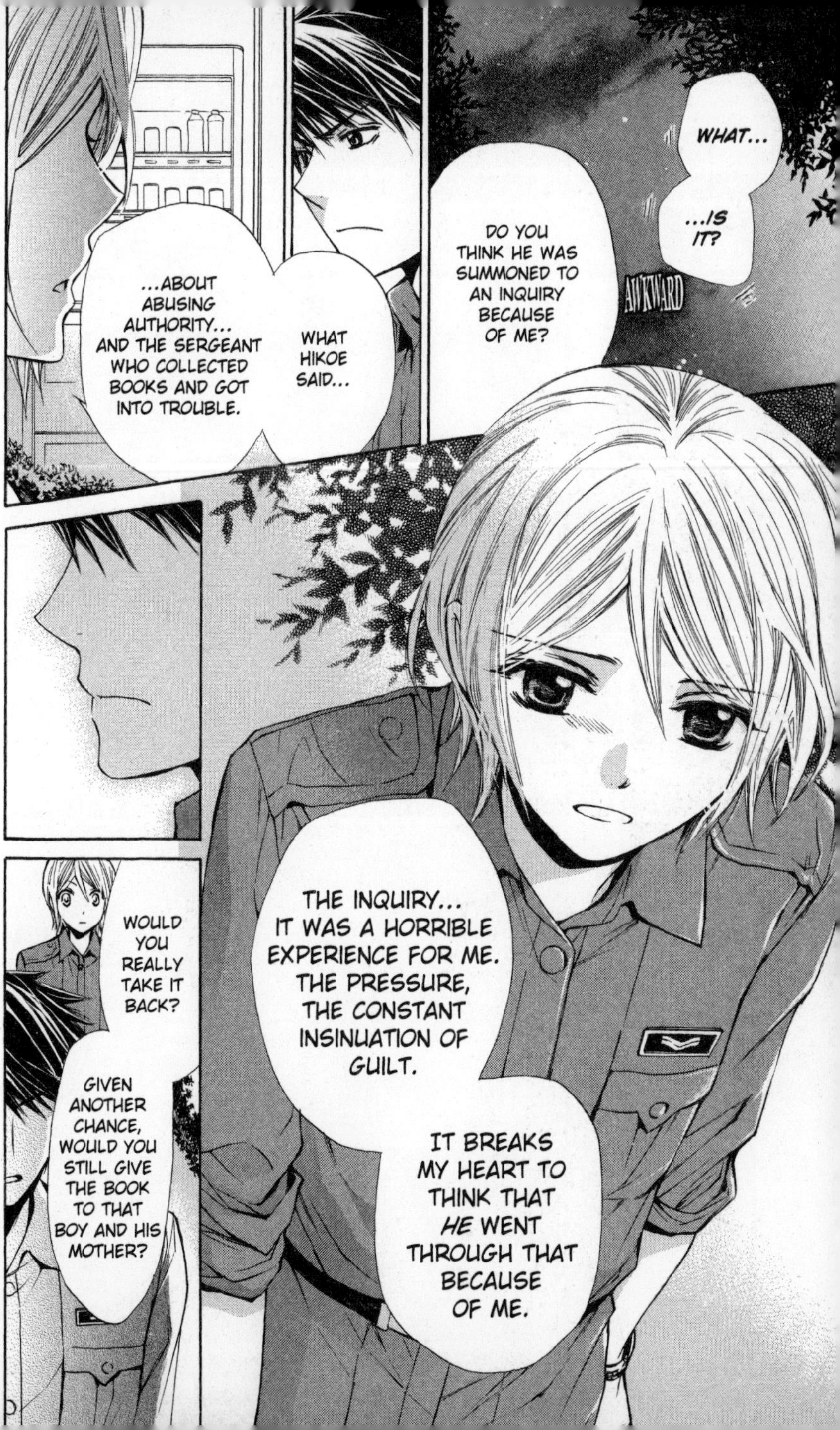
WHAT...
...IS IT?
AWKWARD
DO YOU THINK HE WAS SUMMONED TO AN INQUIRY BECAUSE OF ME?
WHAT HIKOE SAID...
...ABOUT ABUSING AUTHORITY... AND THE SERGEANT WHO COLLECTED BOOKS AND GOT INTO TROUBLE.
THE INQUIRY... IT WAS A HORRIBLE EXPERIENCE FOR ME. THE PRESSURE, THE CONSTANT INSINUATION OF GUILT.
IT BREAKS MY HEART TO THINK THAT *HE* WENT THROUGH THAT BECAUSE OF ME.
WOULD YOU REALLY TAKE IT BACK?
GIVEN ANOTHER CHANCE, WOULD YOU STILL GIVE THE BOOK TO THAT BOY AND HIS MOTHER?

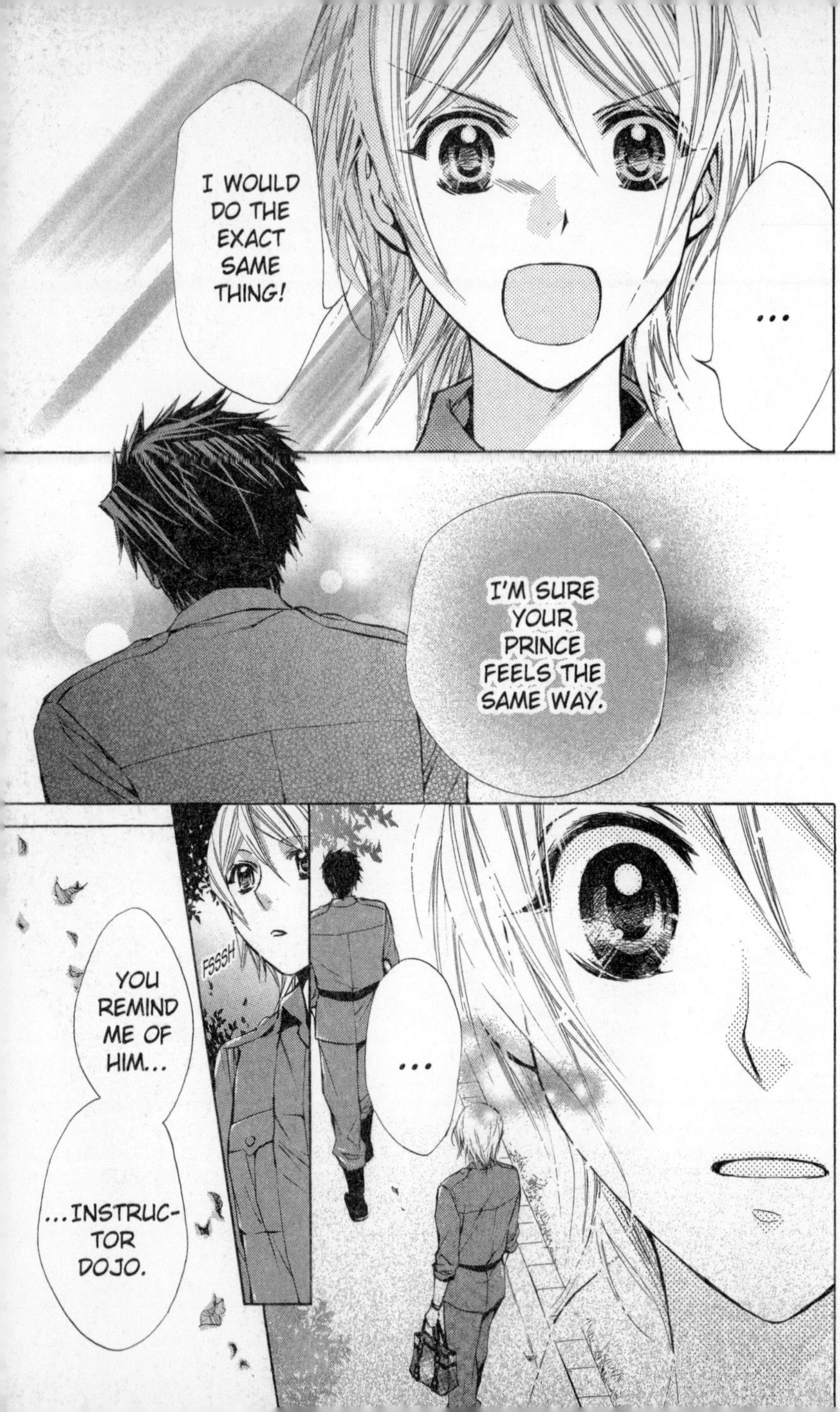
...
I WOULD DO THE EXACT SAME THING!
I'M SURE YOUR PRINCE FEELS THE SAME WAY.
...
FSSSH
YOU REMIND ME OF HIM...
...INSTRUC-TOR DOJO.

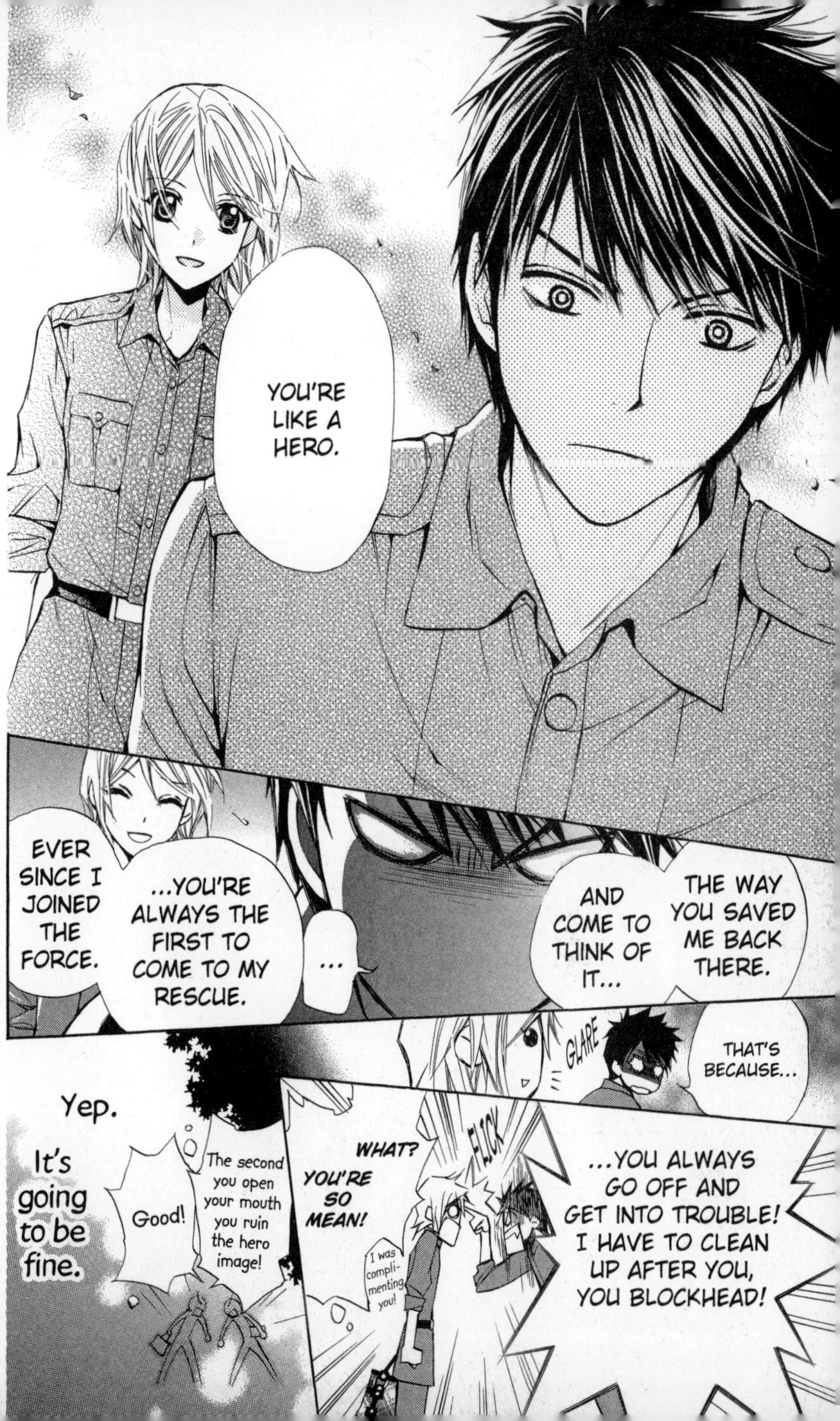
YOU'RE LIKE A HERO.
THE WAY YOU SAVED ME BACK THERE.
AND COME TO THINK OF IT...
...
...YOU'RE ALWAYS THE FIRST TO COME TO MY RESCUE.
EVER SINCE I JOINED THE FORCE.
THAT'S BECAUSE...
GLARE
...YOU ALWAYS GO OFF AND GET INTO TROUBLE! I HAVE TO CLEAN UP AFTER YOU, YOU BLOCKHEAD!
FLICK
WHAT?
YOU'RE SO MEAN!
I was compli-menting you!
The second you open your mouth you ruin the hero image!
Good!
Yep.
It's going to be fine.

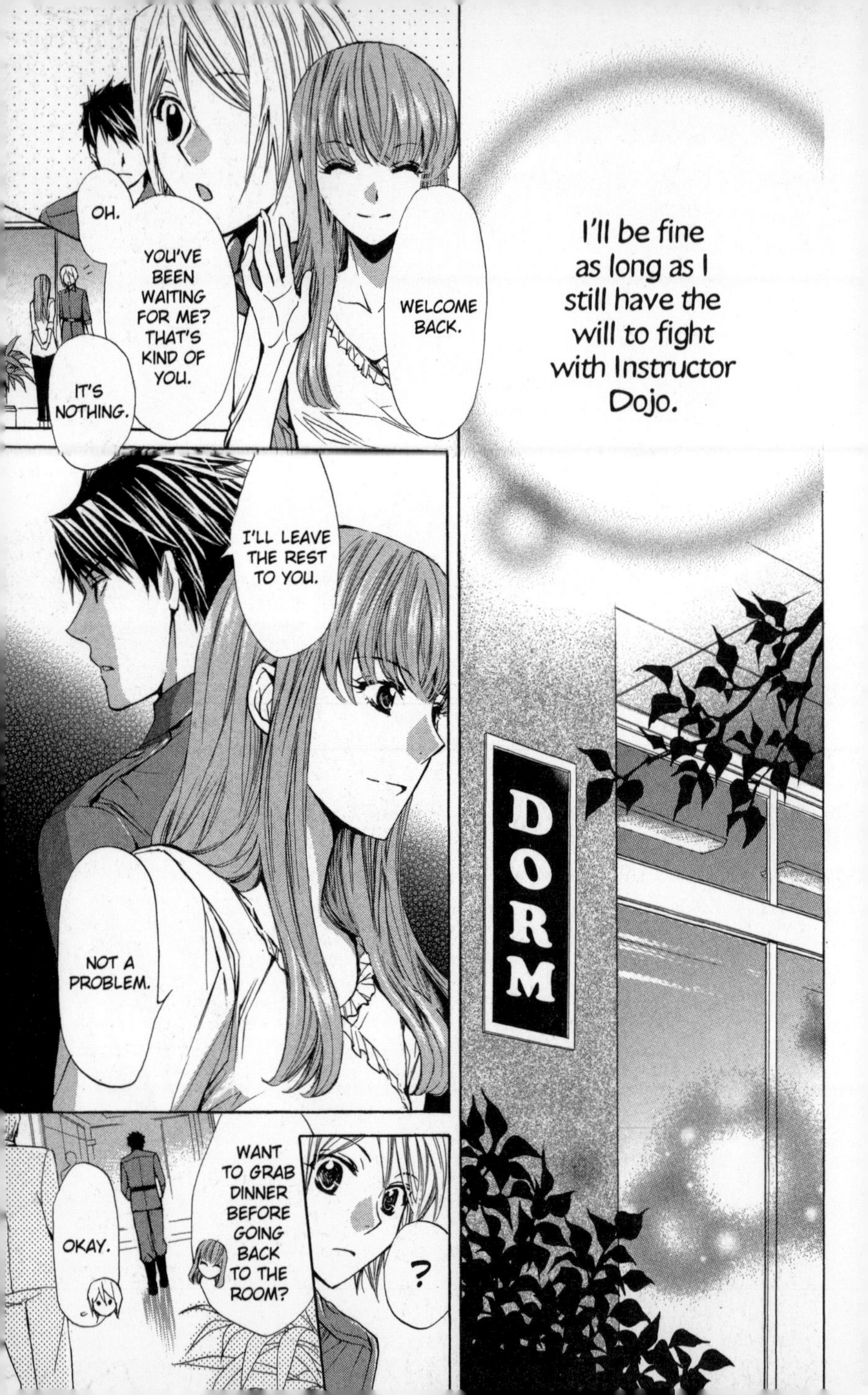
I'll be fine as long as I still have the will to fight with Instructor Dojo.
DORM
WELCOME BACK.
OH.
YOU'VE BEEN WAITING FOR ME? THAT'S KIND OF YOU.
IT'S NOTHING.
I'LL LEAVE THE REST TO YOU.
NOT A PROBLEM.
?
WANT TO GRAB DINNER BEFORE GOING BACK TO THE ROOM?
OKAY.

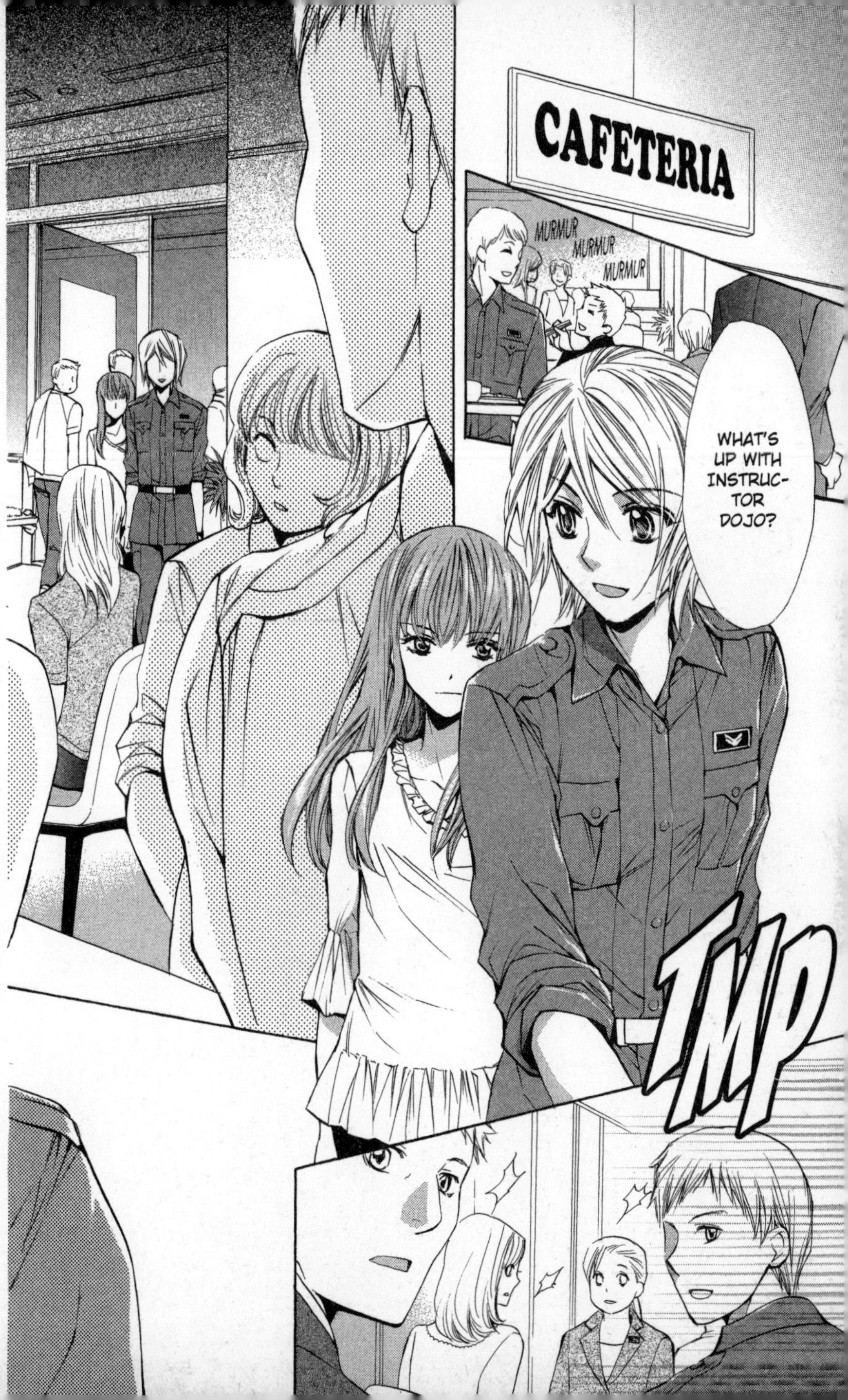
CAFETERIA
MURMUR
MURMUR
MURMUR
WHAT'S UP WITH INSTRUCTOR DOJO?
TMP

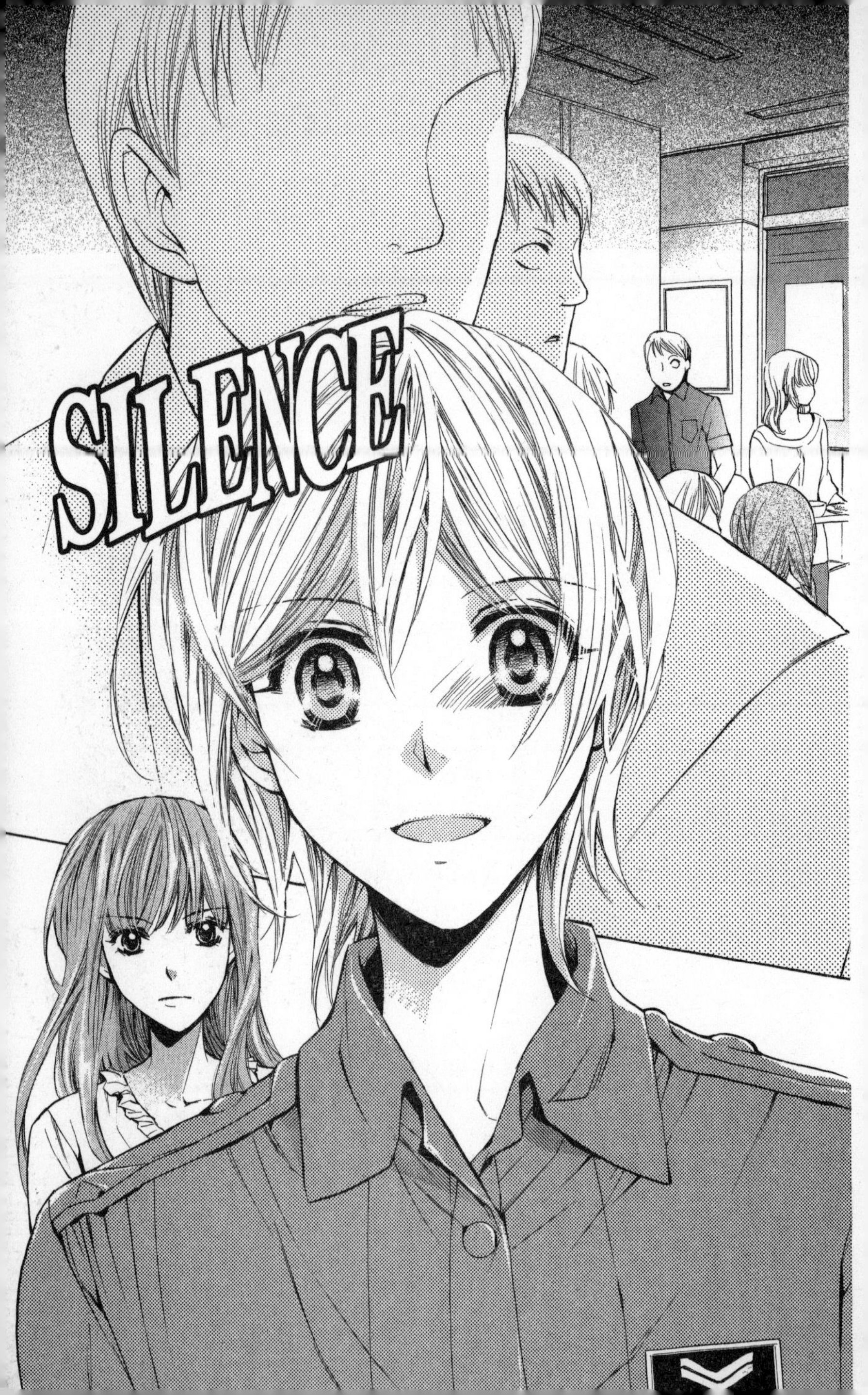
SILENCE

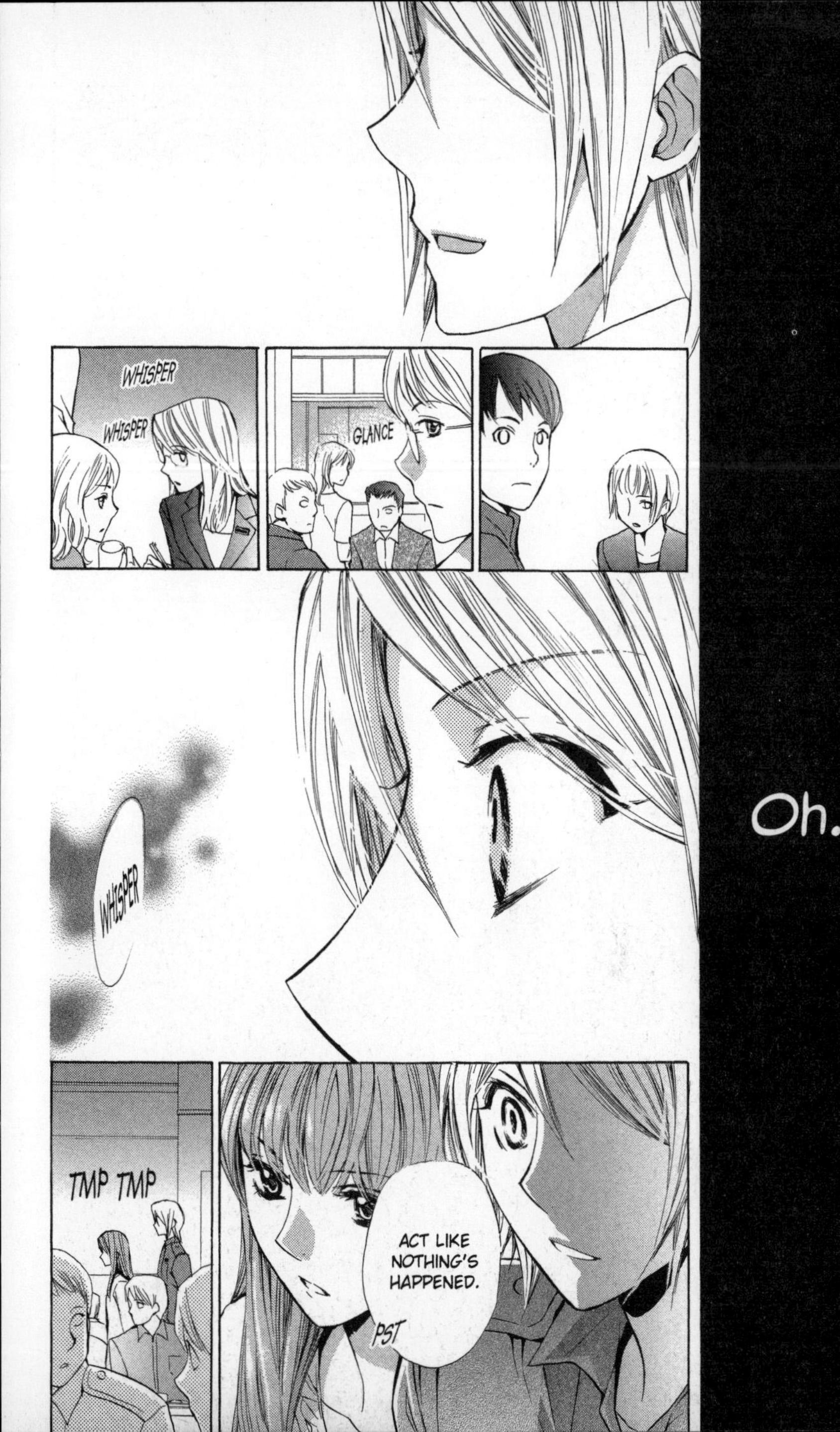
GLANCE
WHISPER
WHISPER
Oh.
WHISPER
ACT LIKE NOTHING'S HAPPENED.
PST
TMP TMP

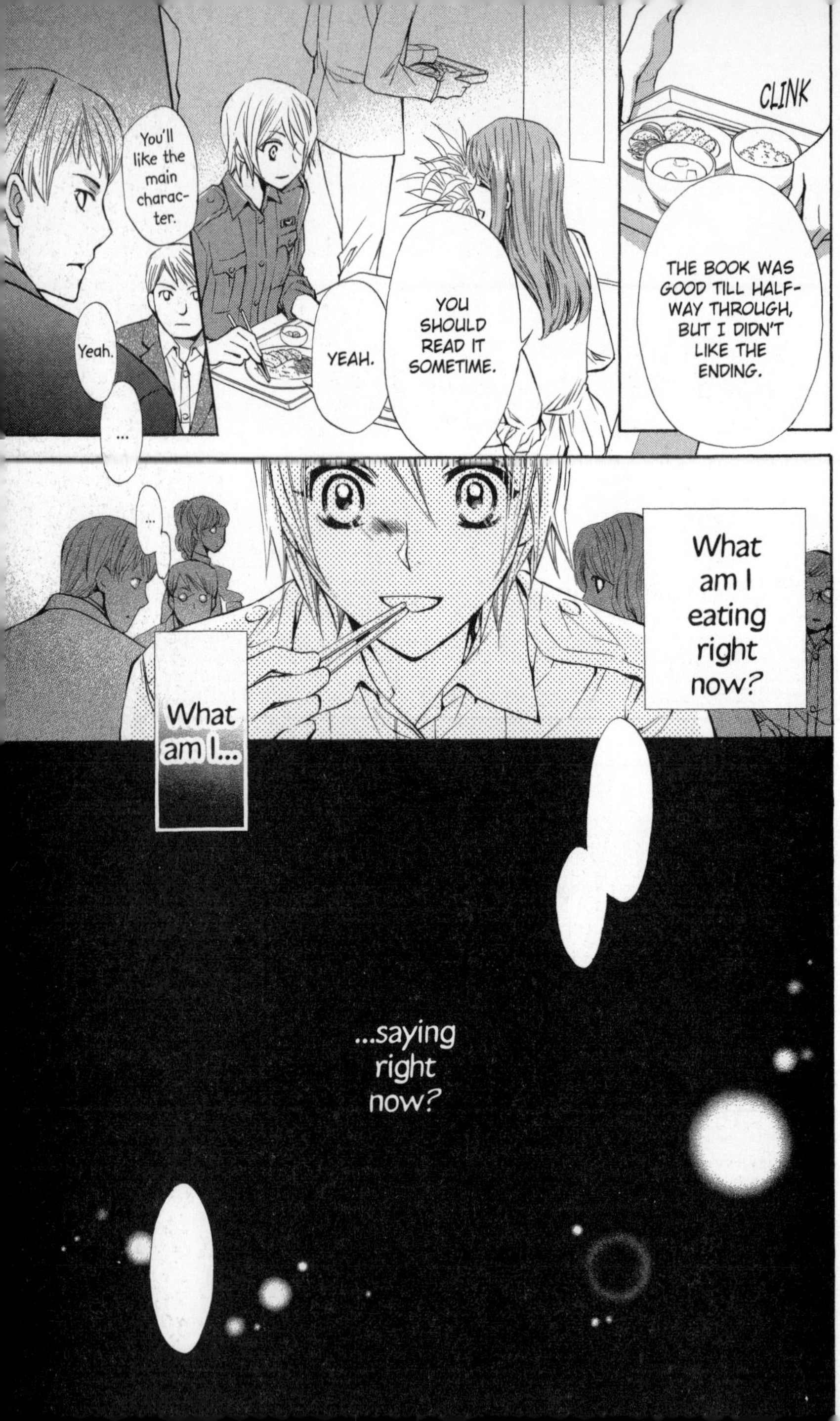
CLINK
THE BOOK WAS GOOD TILL HALF-WAY THROUGH, BUT I DIDN'T LIKE THE ENDING.
YOU SHOULD READ IT SOMETIME.
YEAH.
You'll like the main charac-ter.
Yeah.
...
What am I eating right now?
...
What am I...
...saying right now?

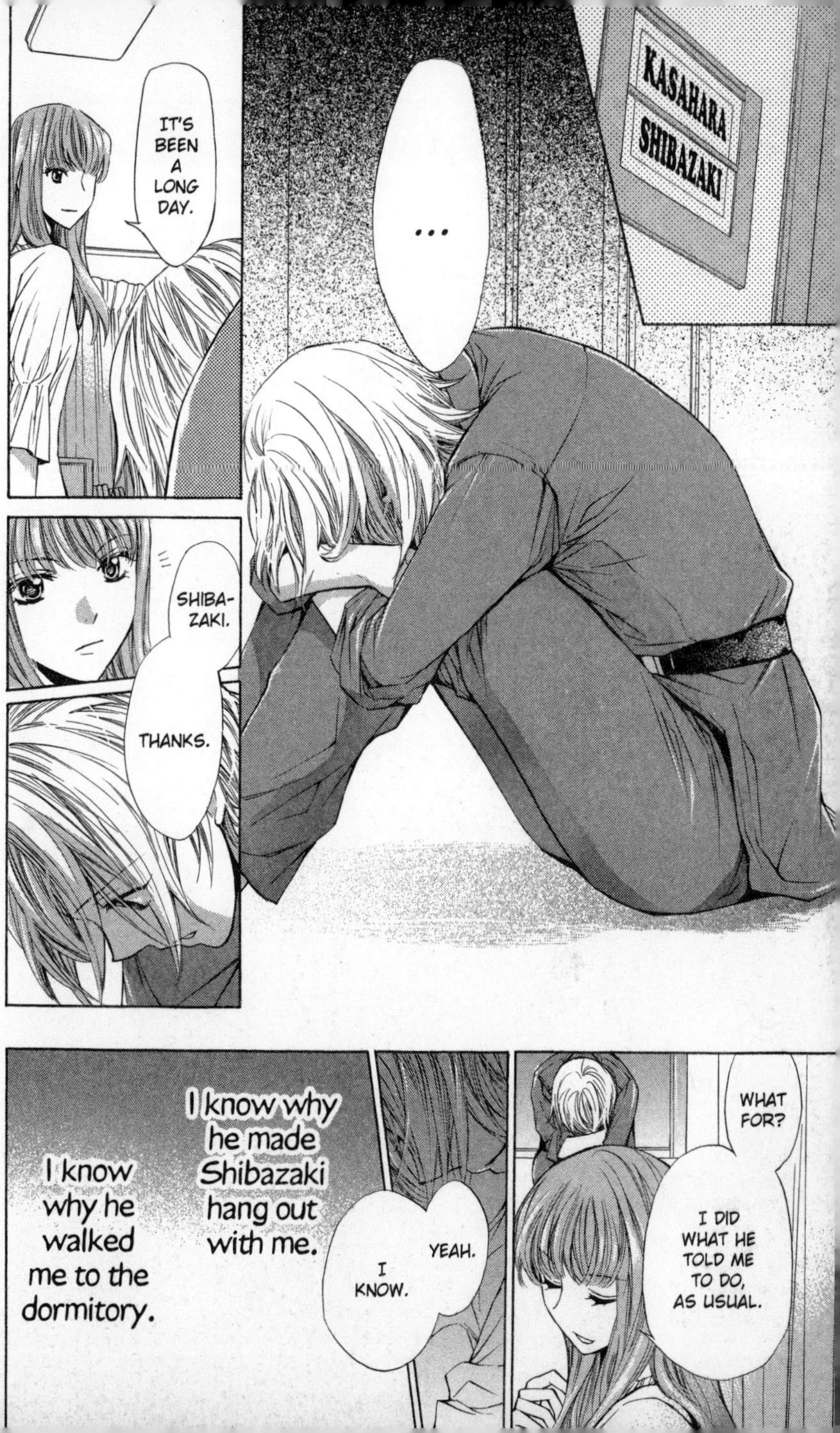
KASAHARA
SHIBAZAKI
...
IT'S BEEN A LONG DAY.
SHIBAZAKI.
THANKS.
WHAT FOR?
I DID WHAT HE TOLD ME TO DO, AS USUAL.
YEAH.
I KNOW.
I know why he made Shibazaki hang out with me.
I know why he walked me to the dormitory.

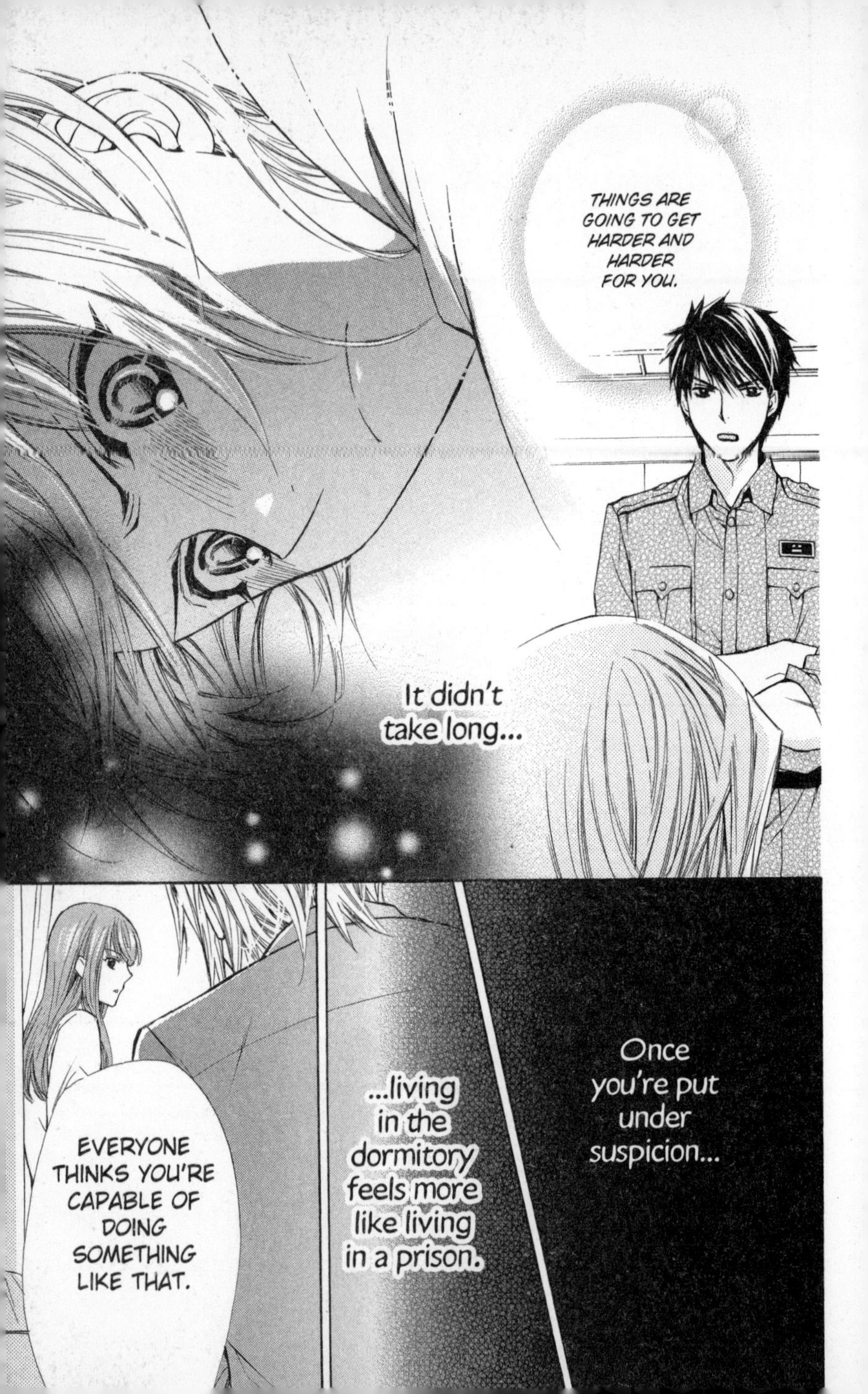
THINGS ARE GOING TO GET HARDER AND HARDER FOR YOU.
It didn't take long...
Once you're put under suspicion...
...living in the dormitory feels more like living in a prison.
EVERYONE THINKS YOU'RE CAPABLE OF DOING SOMETHING LIKE THAT.

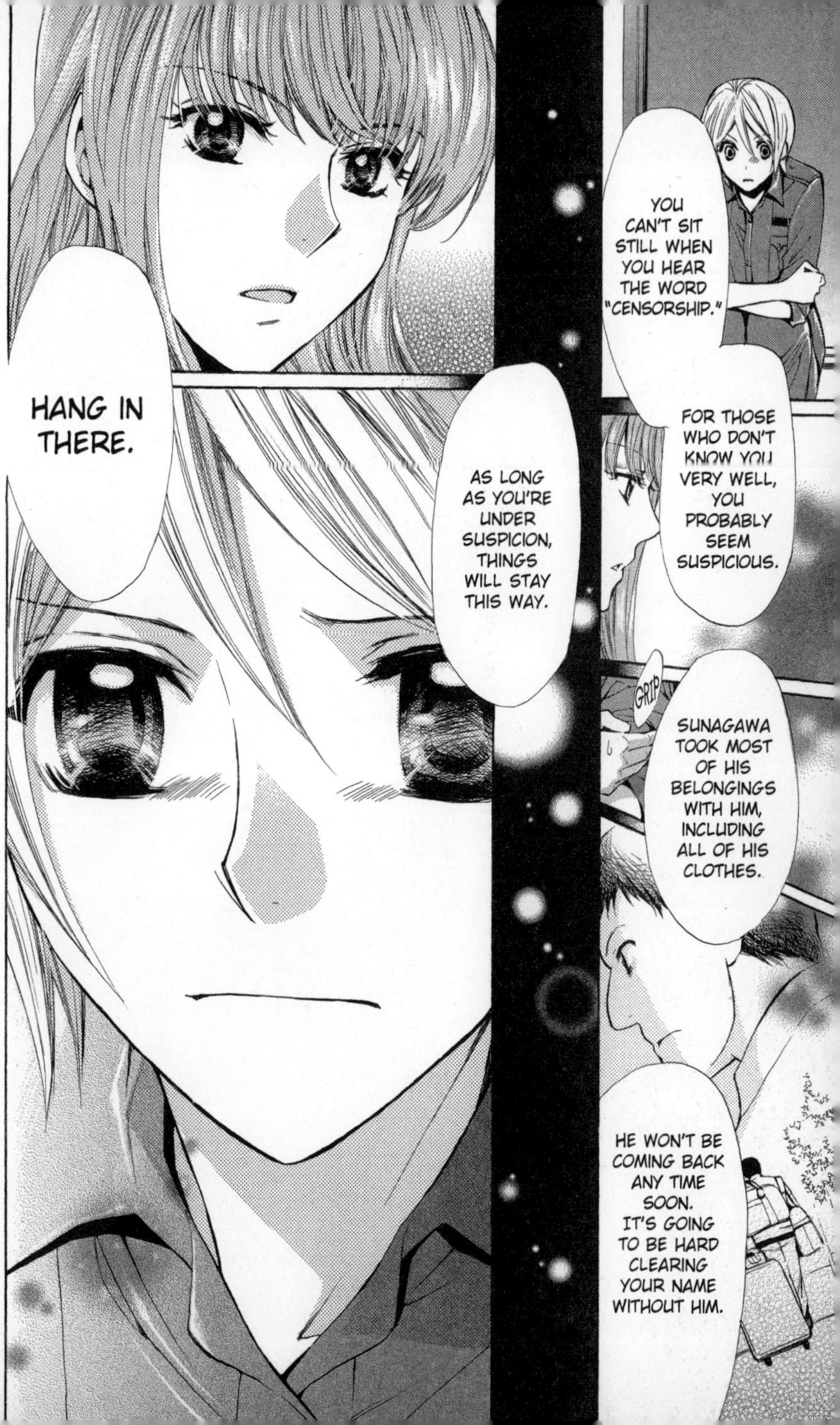
YOU CAN'T SIT STILL WHEN YOU HEAR THE WORD "CENSORSHIP."
FOR THOSE WHO DON'T KNOW YOU VERY WELL, YOU PROBABLY SEEM SUSPICIOUS.
GRIP
SUNAGAWA TOOK MOST OF HIS BELONGINGS WITH HIM, INCLUDING ALL OF HIS CLOTHES.
HE WON'T BE COMING BACK ANY TIME SOON. IT'S GOING TO BE HARD CLEARING YOUR NAME WITHOUT HIM.
AS LONG AS YOU'RE UNDER SUSPICION, THINGS WILL STAY THIS WAY.
HANG IN THERE.

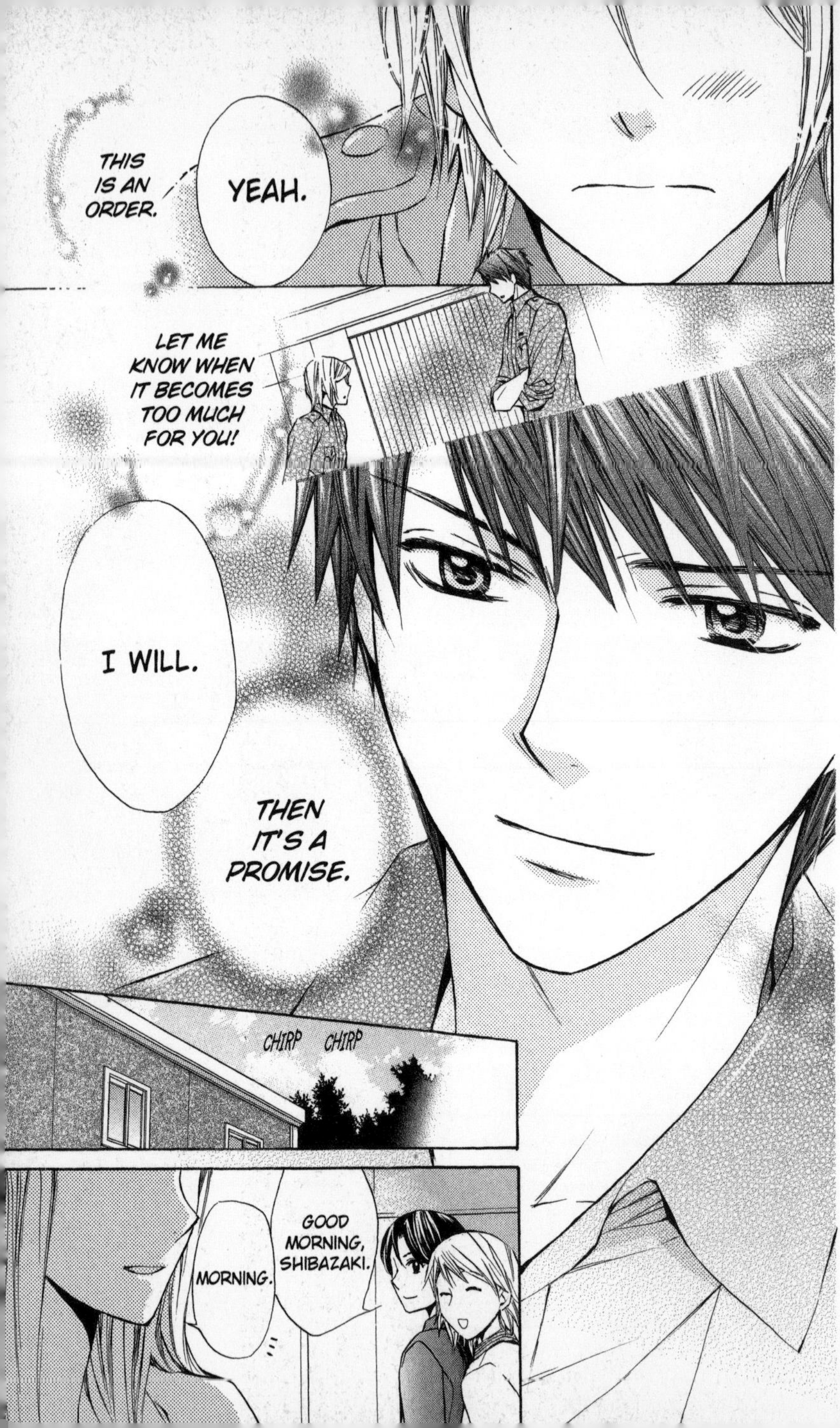
YEAH.
THIS IS AN ORDER.
LET ME KNOW WHEN IT BECOMES TOO MUCH FOR YOU!
I WILL.
THEN IT'S A PROMISE.
CHIRP CHIRP
GOOD MORNING, SHIBAZAKI.
MORNING.

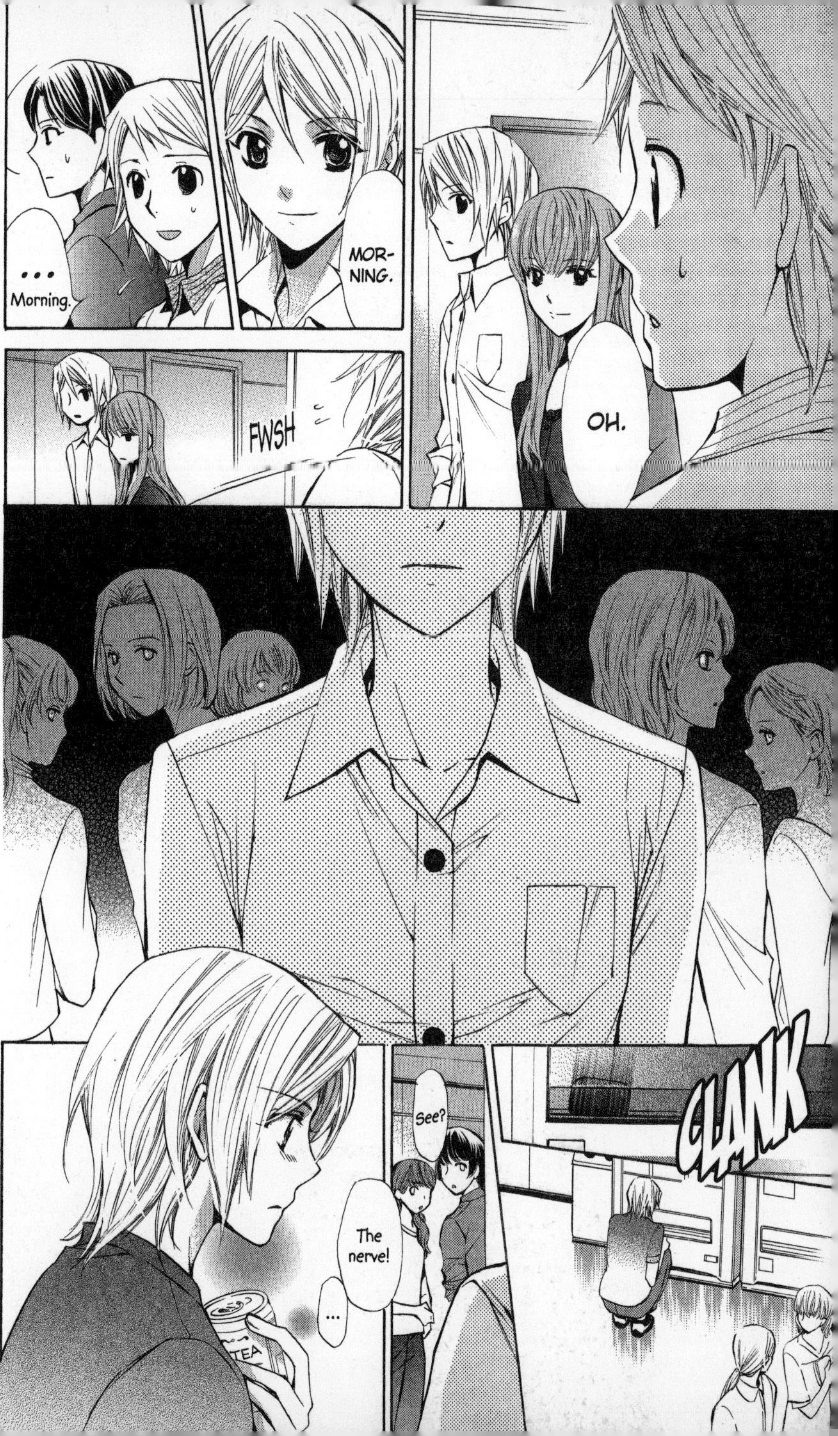
OH.
MOR-
NING.
...
Morning.
FWSH
CLANK
See?
The nerve!
...

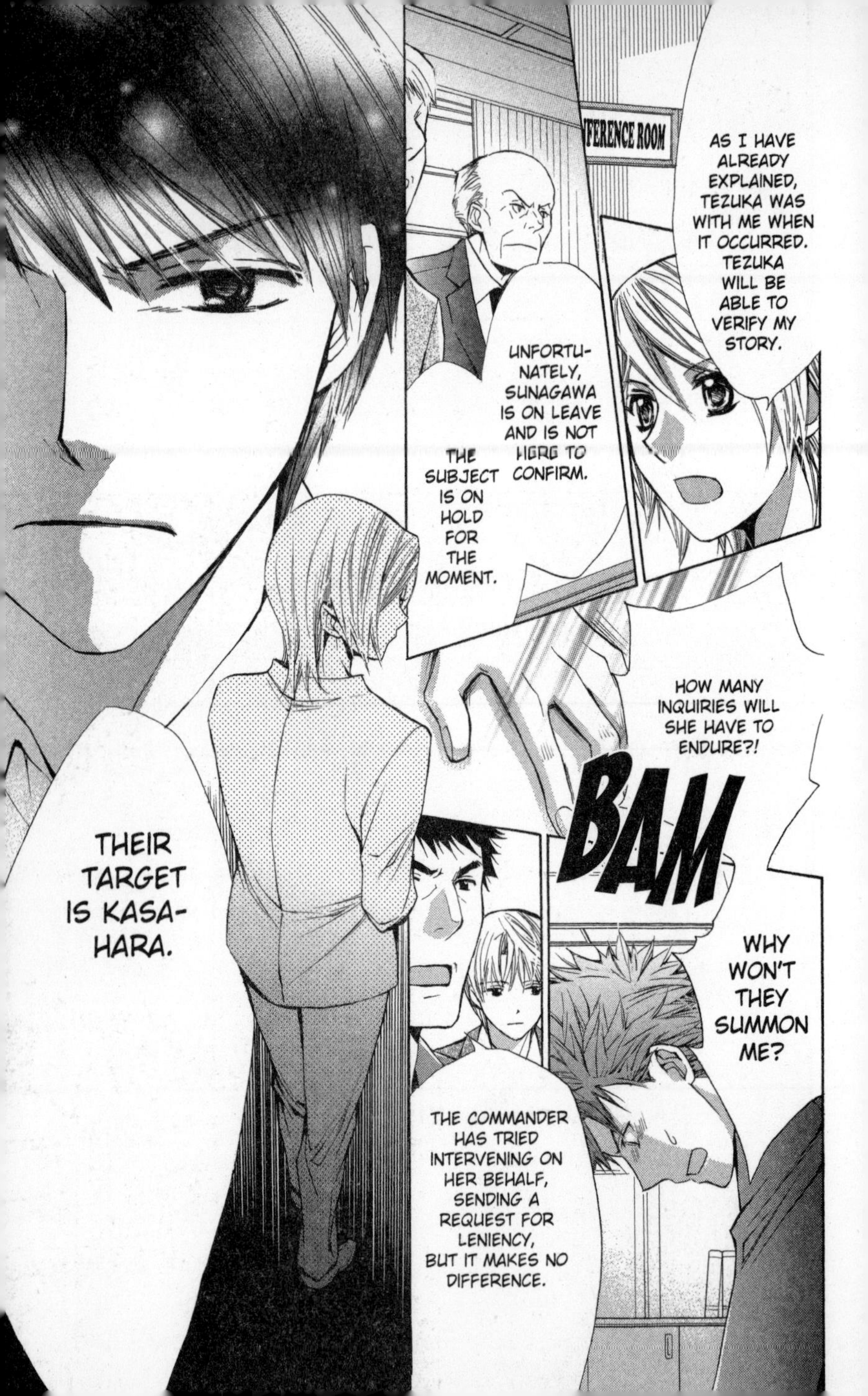
FERENCE ROOM
AS I HAVE ALREADY EXPLAINED, TEZUKA WAS WITH ME WHEN IT OCCURRED. TEZUKA WILL BE ABLE TO VERIFY MY STORY.
UNFORTUNATELY, SUNAGAWA IS ON LEAVE AND IS NOT HERE TO CONFIRM.
THE SUBJECT IS ON HOLD FOR THE MOMENT.
HOW MANY INQUIRIES WILL SHE HAVE TO ENDURE?!
BAM
WHY WON'T THEY SUMMON ME?
THE COMMANDER HAS TRIED INTERVENING ON HER BEHALF, SENDING A REQUEST FOR LENIENCY, BUT IT MAKES NO DIFFERENCE.
THEIR TARGET IS KASAHARA.

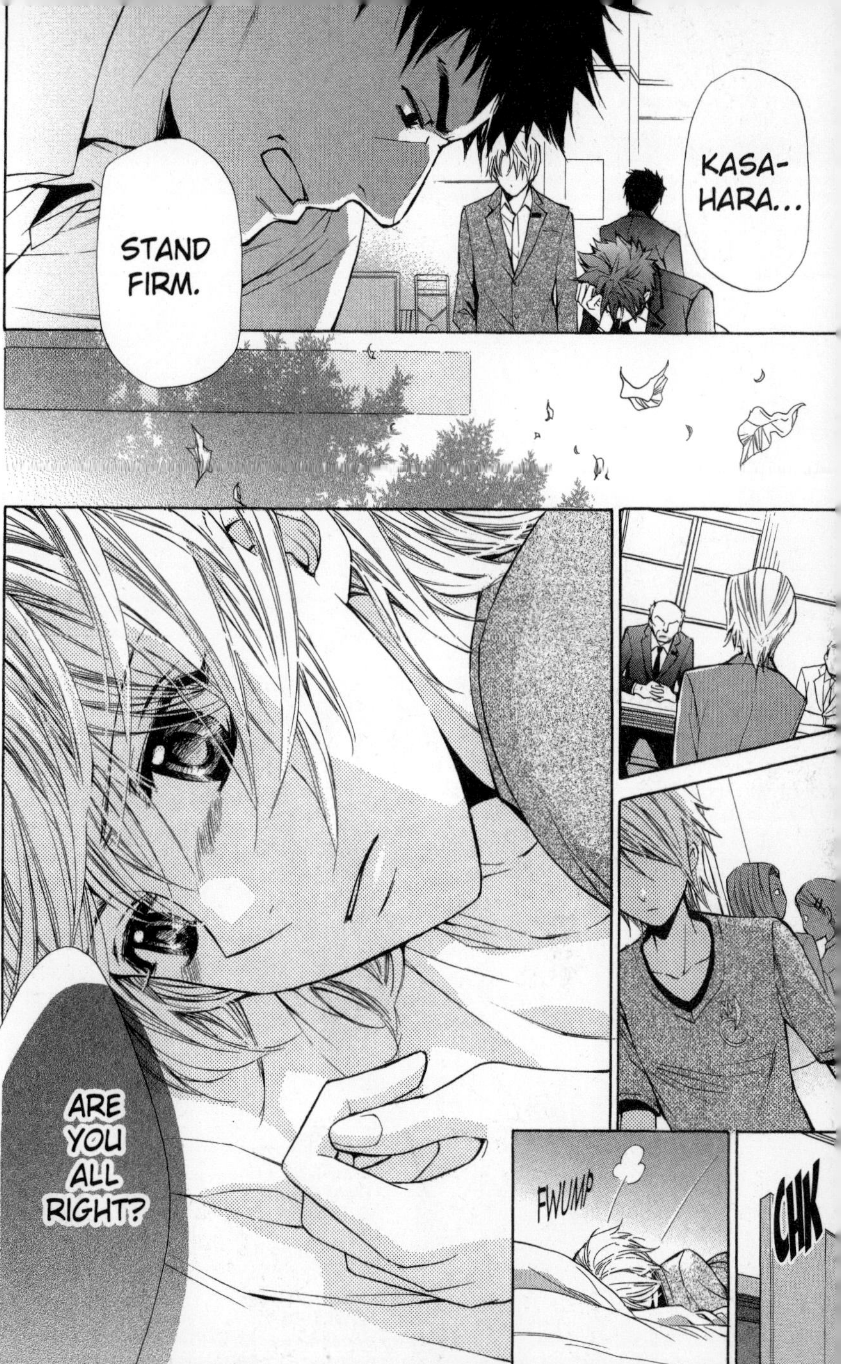
KASA-HARA...
STAND FIRM.
CHK
FWUMP
ARE YOU ALL RIGHT?

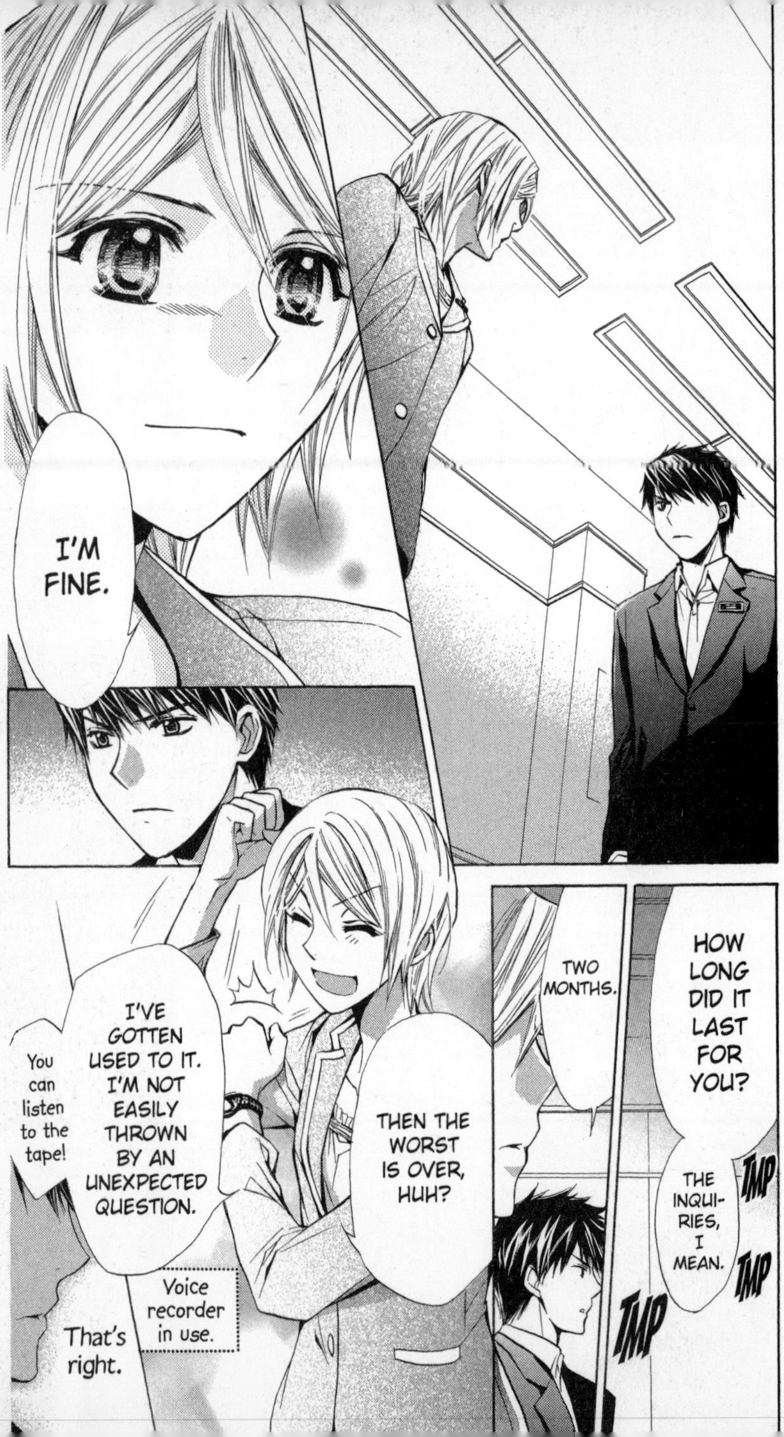
I'M FINE.
HOW LONG DID IT LAST FOR YOU?
THE INQUIRIES, I MEAN.
TWO MONTHS.
TMP
TMP
TMP
THEN THE WORST IS OVER, HUH?
I'VE GOTTEN USED TO IT. I'M NOT EASILY THROWN BY AN UNEXPECTED QUESTION.
You can listen to the tape!
Voice recorder in use.
That's right.

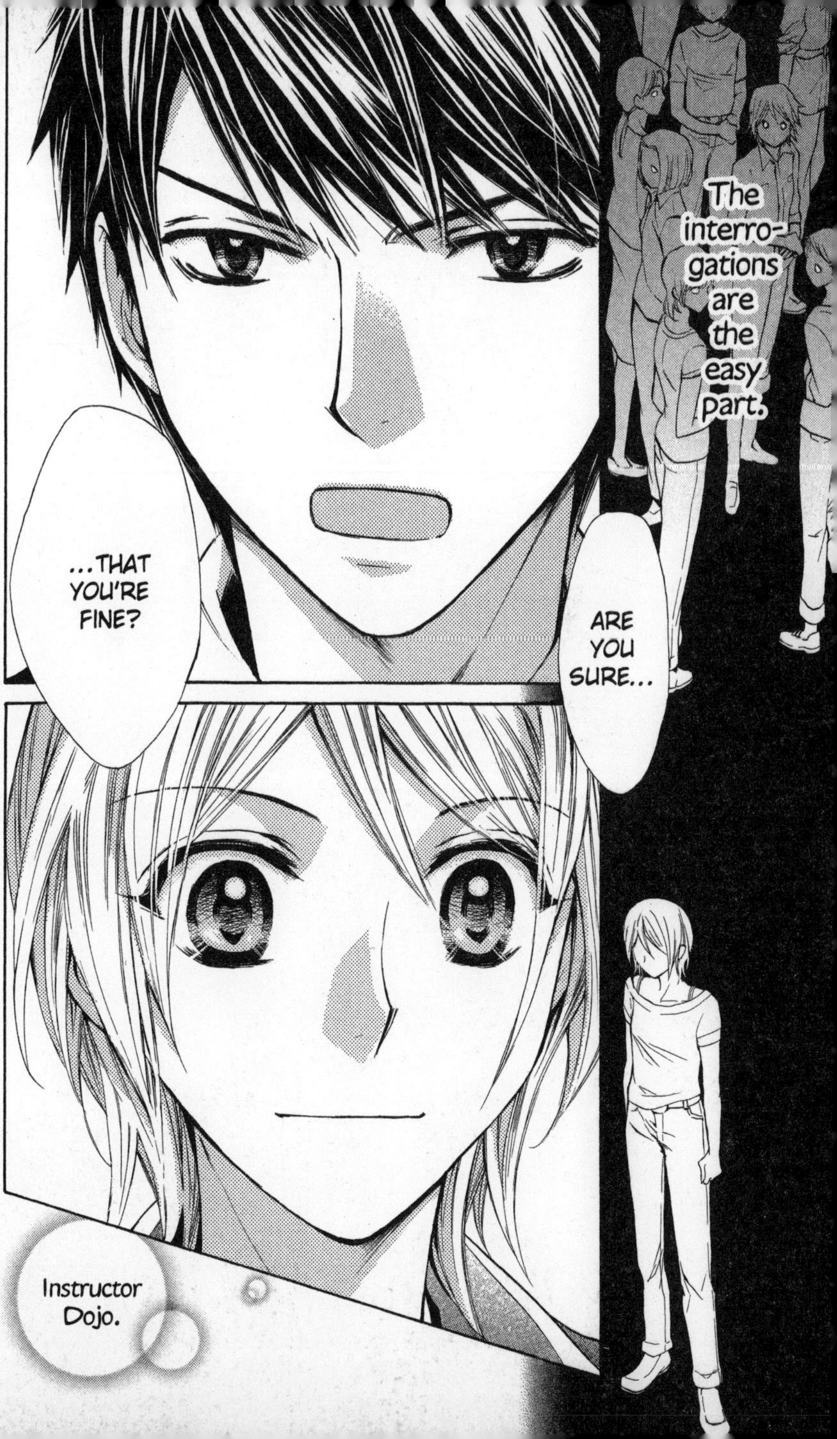
The interrogations are the easy part.
ARE YOU SURE...
...THAT YOU'RE FINE?
Instructor Dojo.

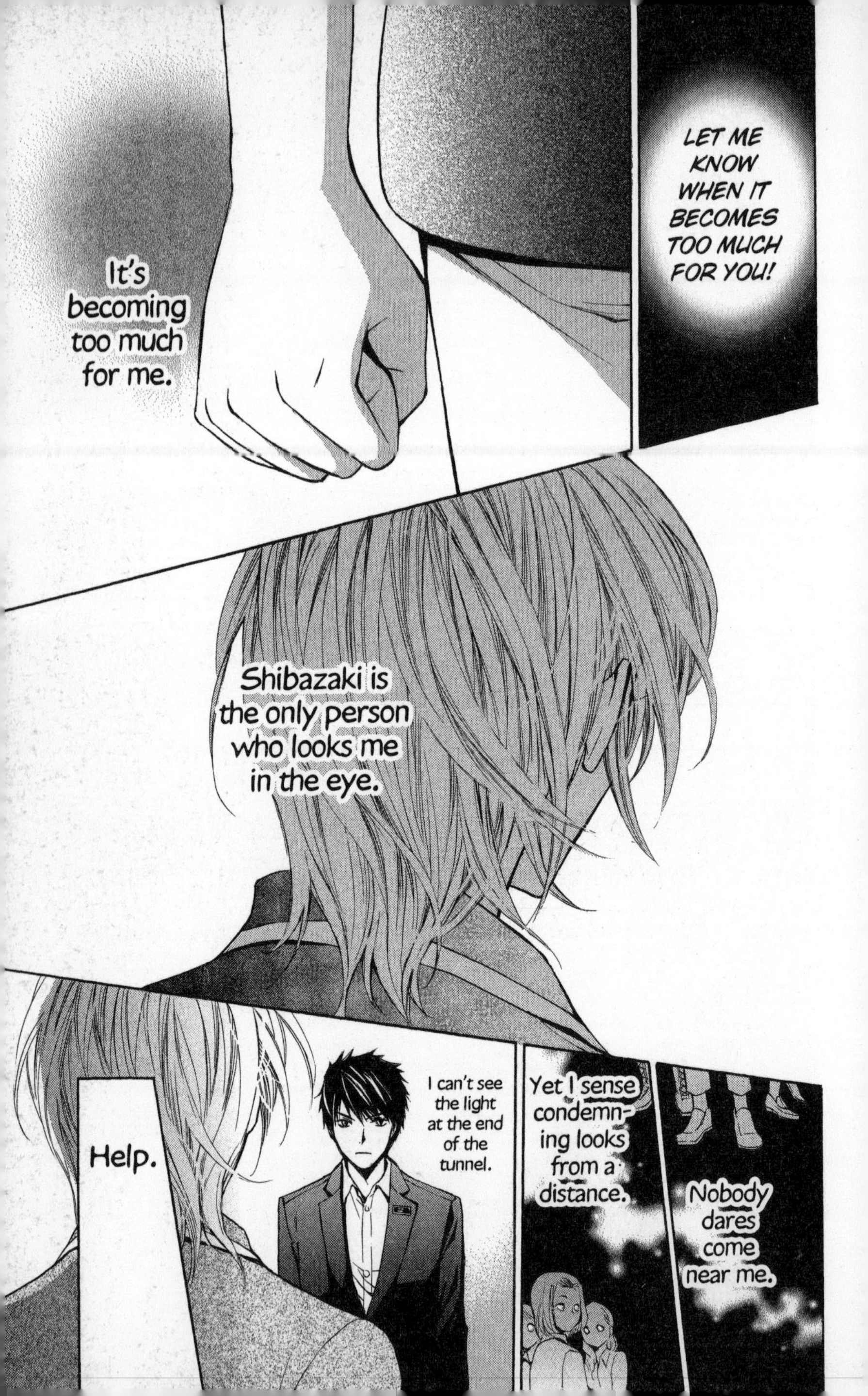
LET ME KNOW WHEN IT BECOMES TOO MUCH FOR YOU!
It's becoming too much for me.
Shibazaki is the only person who looks me in the eye.
Nobody dares come near me.
Yet I sense condemning looks from a distance.
I can't see the light at the end of the tunnel.
Help.

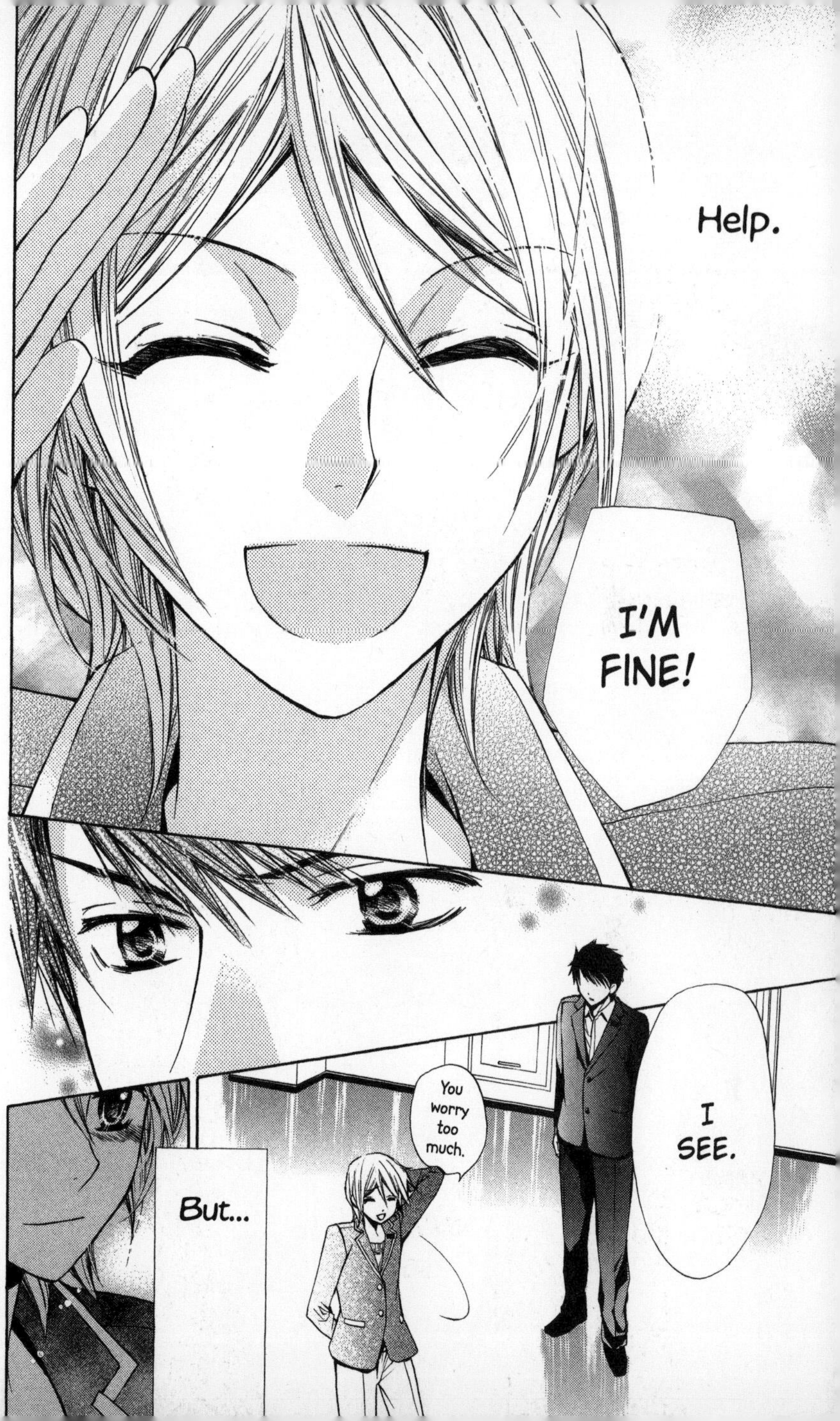
Help.
I'M FINE!
I SEE.
You worry too much.
But...

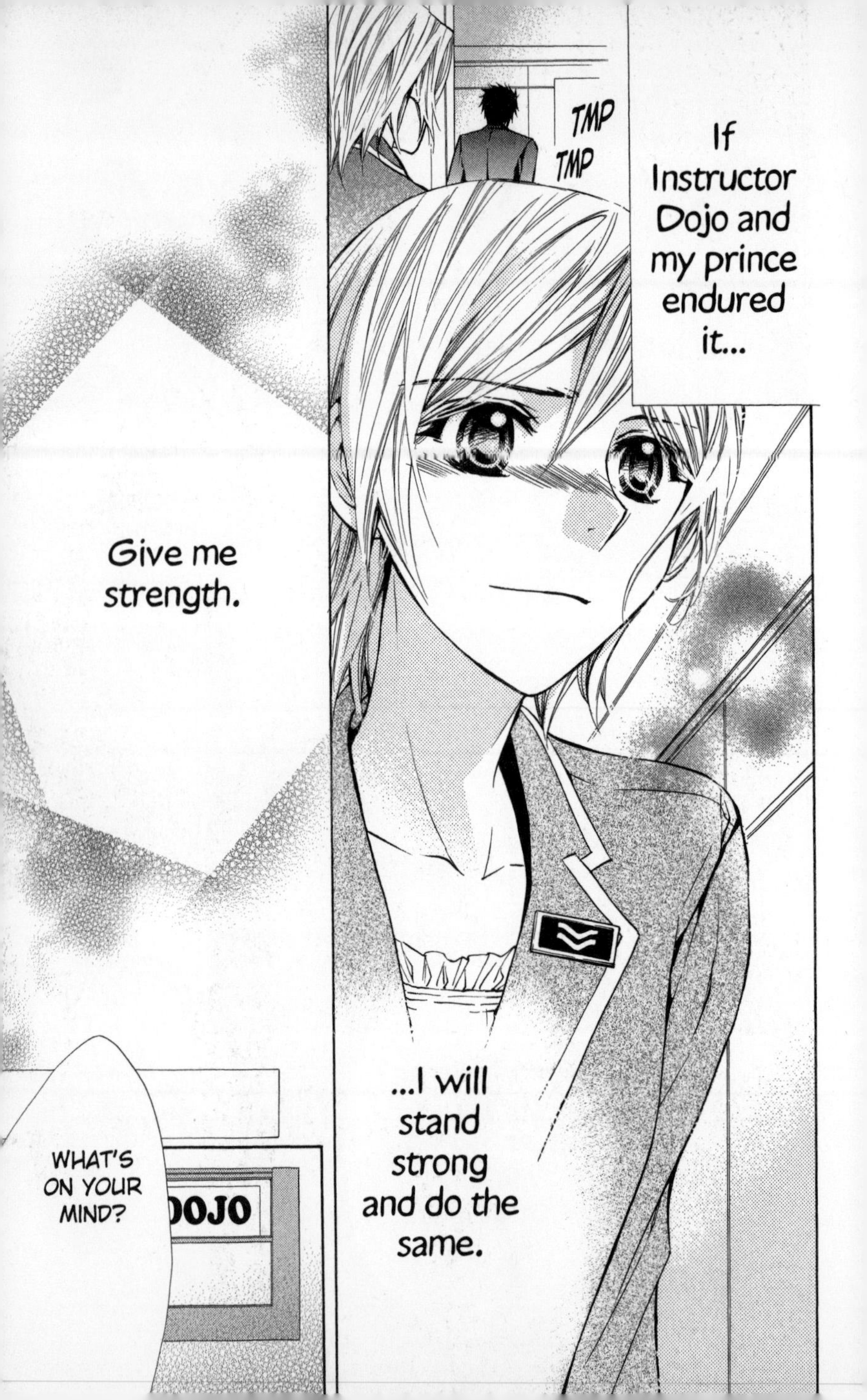
TMP
TMP
If Instructor Dojo and my prince endured it...
...I will stand strong and do the same.
Give me strength.
WHAT'S ON YOUR MIND?
DOJO

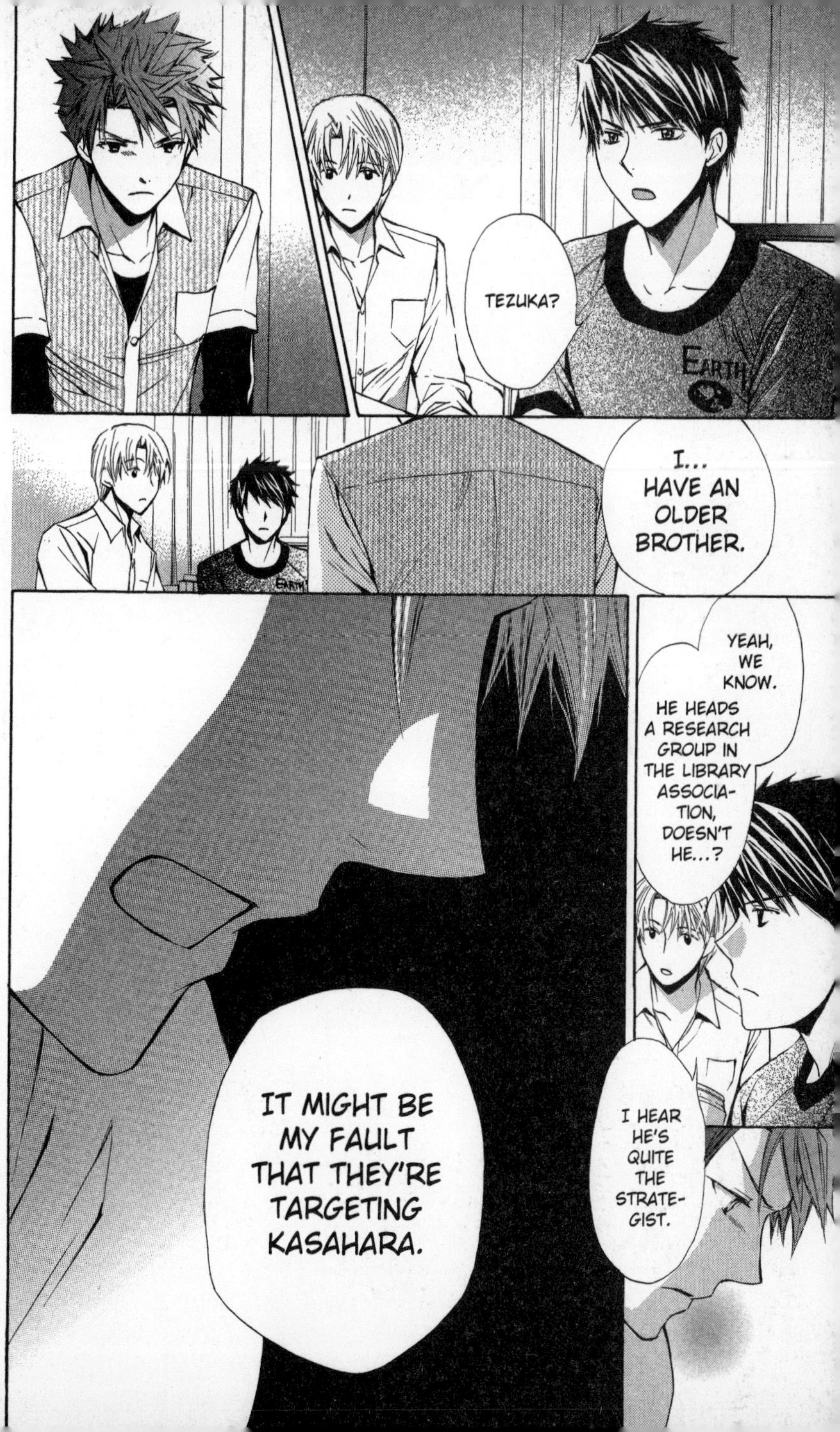
TEZUKA?
I... HAVE AN OLDER BROTHER.
YEAH, WE KNOW.
HE HEADS A RESEARCH GROUP IN THE LIBRARY ASSOCIATION, DOESN'T HE...?
I HEAR HE'S QUITE THE STRATEGIST.
IT MIGHT BE MY FAULT THAT THEY'RE TARGETING KASAHARA.

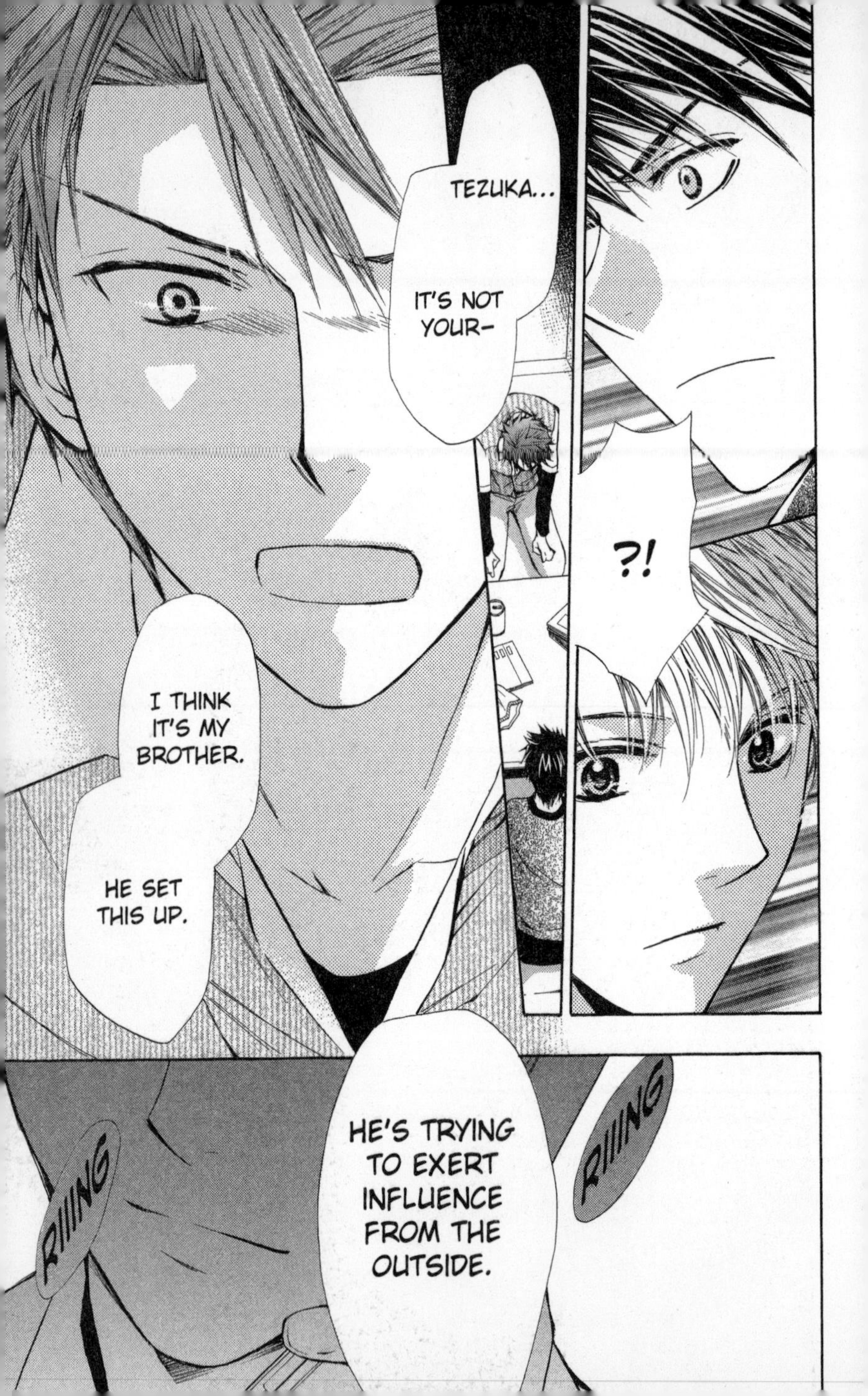
TEZUKA...
IT'S NOT YOUR-
?!
I THINK IT'S MY BROTHER.
HE SET THIS UP.
RIIING
HE'S TRYING TO EXERT INFLUENCE FROM THE OUTSIDE.
RIIING

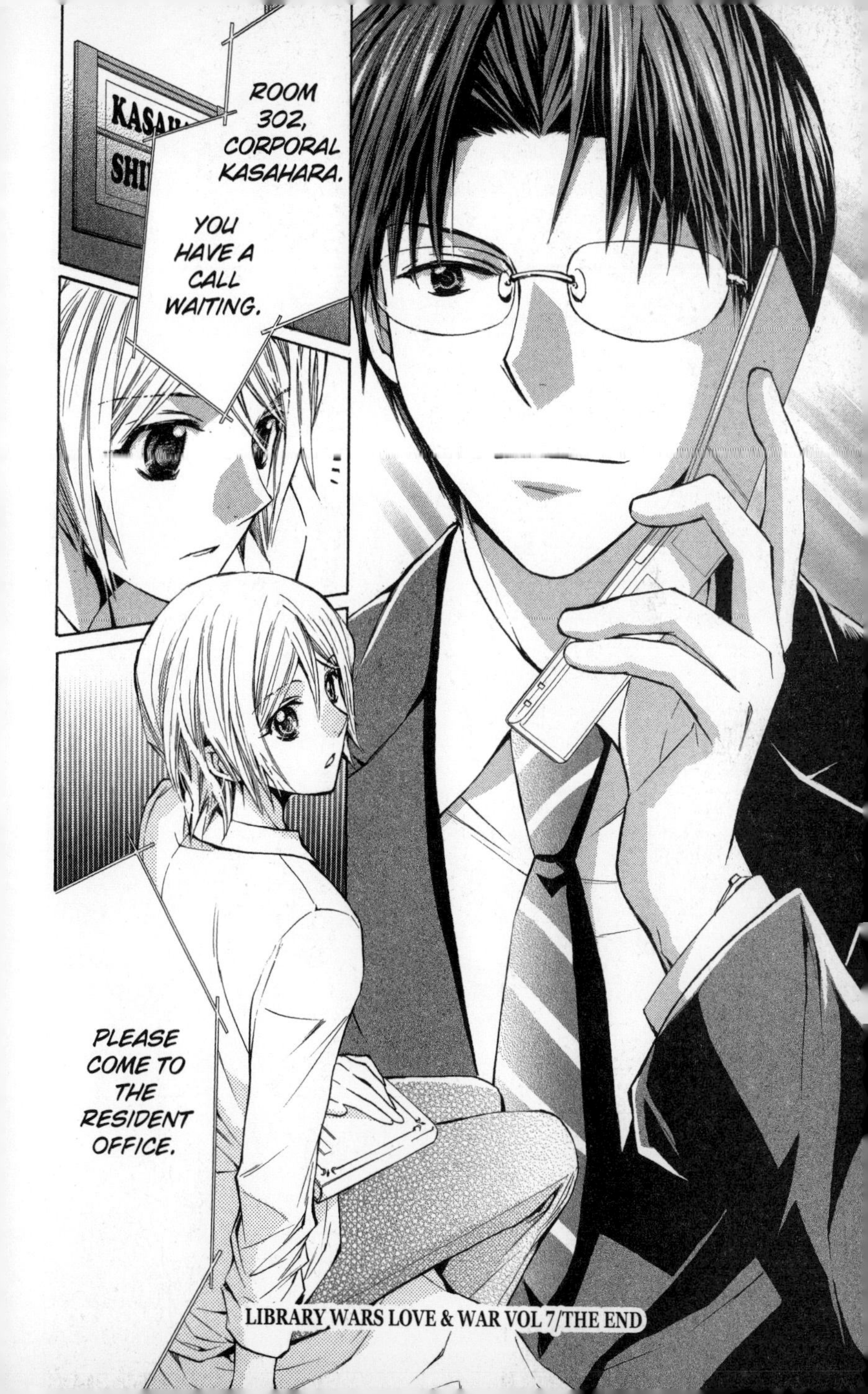
ROOM 302, CORPORAL KASAHARA.
YOU HAVE A CALL WAITING.
PLEASE COME TO THE RESIDENT OFFICE.
LIBRARY WARS LOVE & WAR VOL 7/THE END

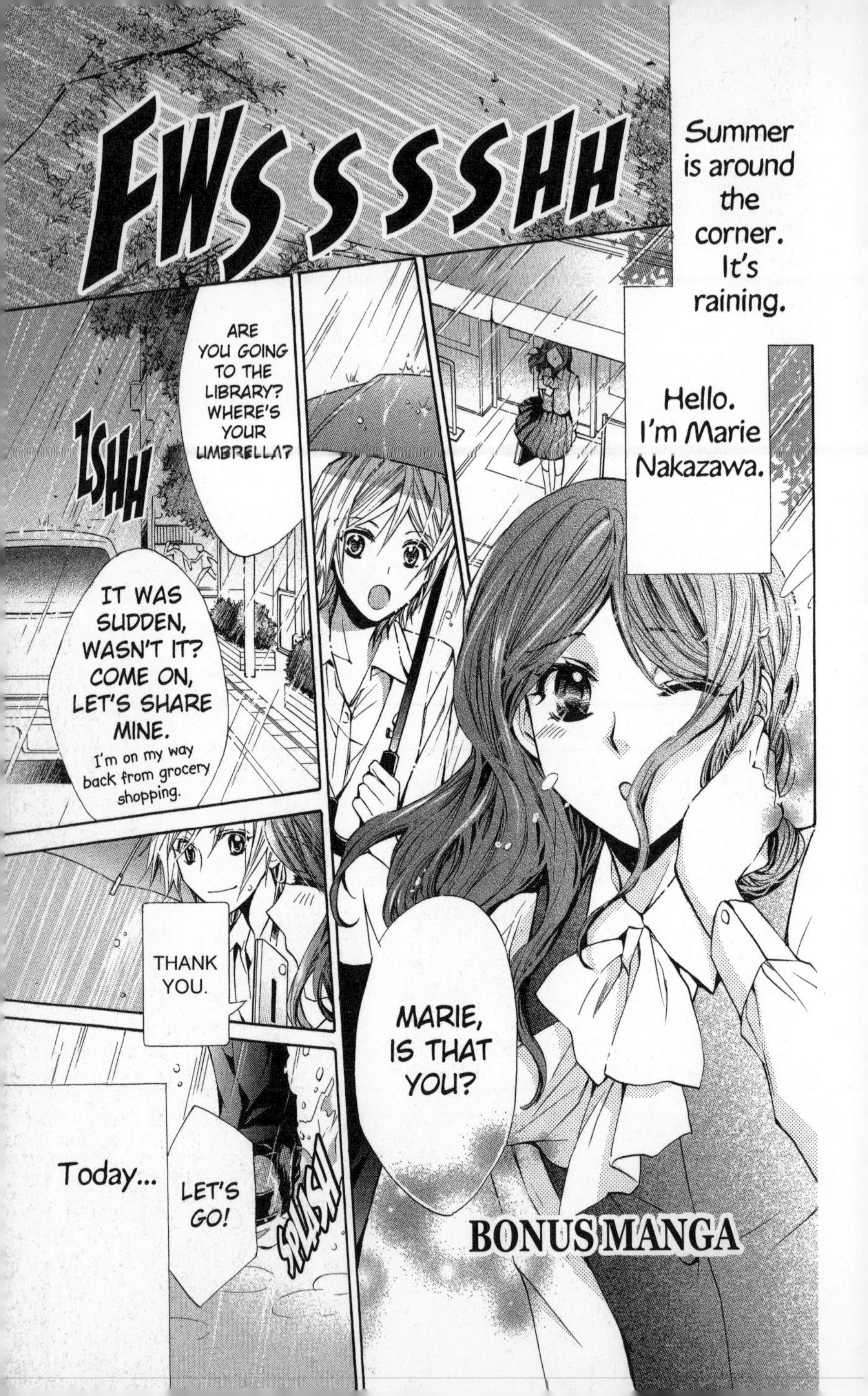
Summer is around the corner. It's raining.
FWSSSSHH
Hello. I'm Marie Nakazawa.
MARIE, IS THAT YOU?
ARE YOU GOING TO THE LIBRARY? WHERE'S YOUR UMBRELLA?
ZSHH
IT WAS SUDDEN, WASN'T IT? COME ON, LET'S SHARE MINE.
I'm on my way back from grocery shopping.
THANK YOU.
Today...
LET'S GO!
SPLASH
BONUS MANGA

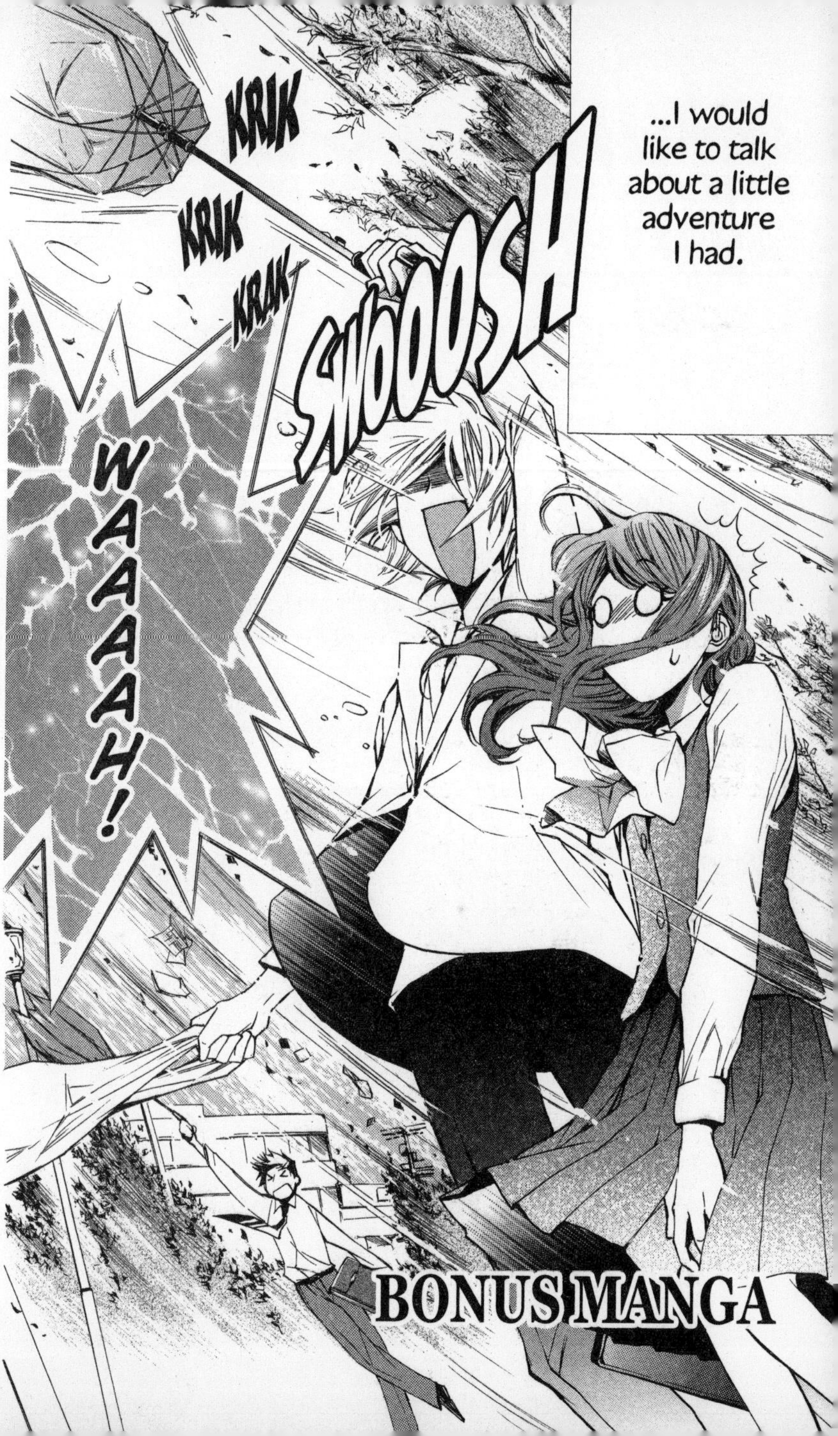
...I would like to talk about a little adventure I had.
SWOOOSH
KRIK
KRIK
KRAK
WAAAAAH!
BONUS MANGA

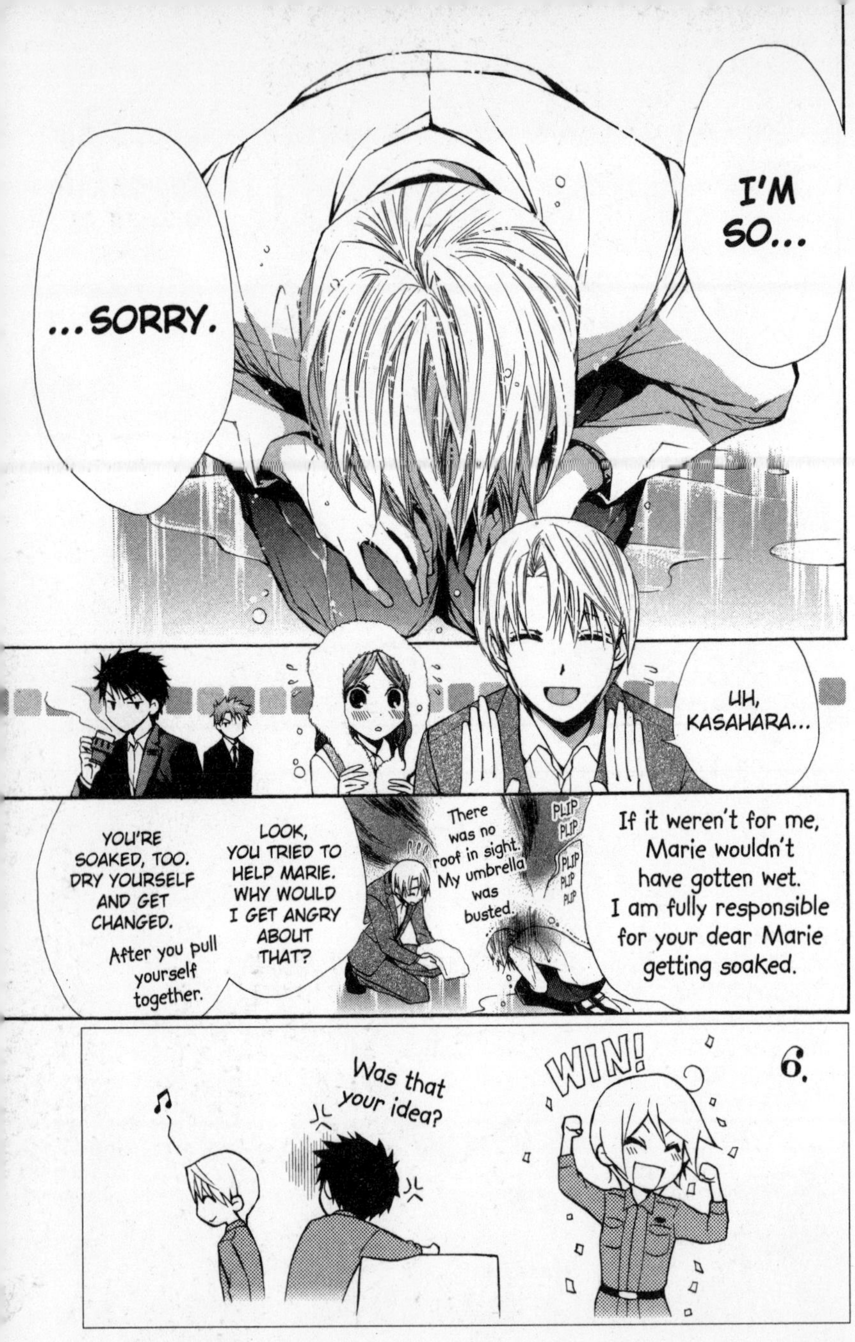
I'M SO...
...SORRY.
UH, KASAHARA...
If it weren't for me, Marie wouldn't have gotten wet. I am fully responsible for your dear Marie getting soaked.
PLIP PLIP
PLIP PLIP PLIP
There was no roof in sight. My umbrella was busted.
LOOK, YOU TRIED TO HELP MARIE. WHY WOULD I GET ANGRY ABOUT THAT?
YOU'RE SOAKED, TOO. DRY YOURSELF AND GET CHANGED.
After you pull yourself together.
6.
WIN!
Was that your idea?

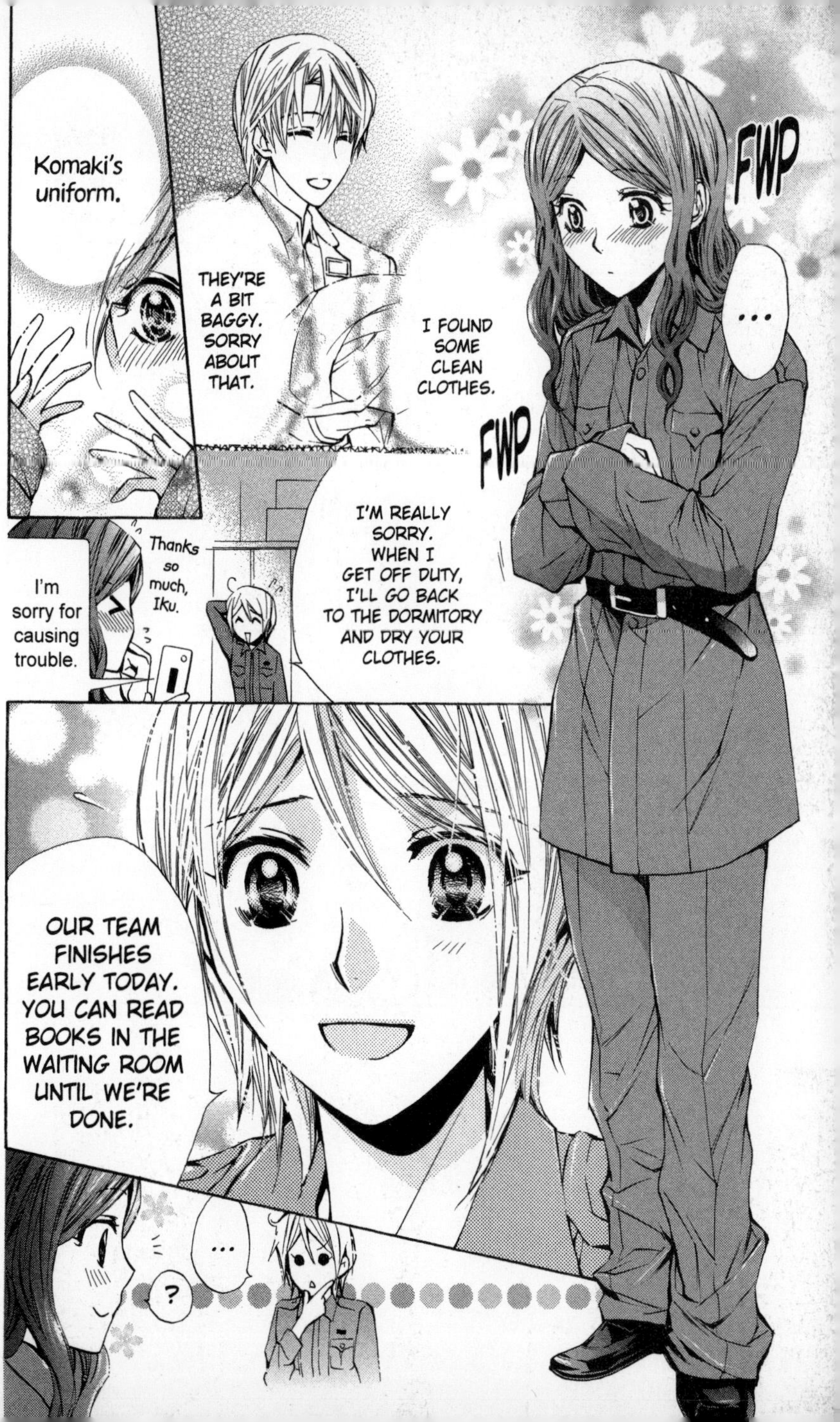
FWP
...
FWP
I FOUND SOME CLEAN CLOTHES.
THEY'RE A BIT BAGGY. SORRY ABOUT THAT.
Komaki's uniform.
I'M REALLY SORRY. WHEN I GET OFF DUTY, I'LL GO BACK TO THE DORMITORY AND DRY YOUR CLOTHES.
Thanks so much, Iku.
I'm sorry for causing trouble.
OUR TEAM FINISHES EARLY TODAY. YOU CAN READ BOOKS IN THE WAITING ROOM UNTIL WE'RE DONE.
...
?

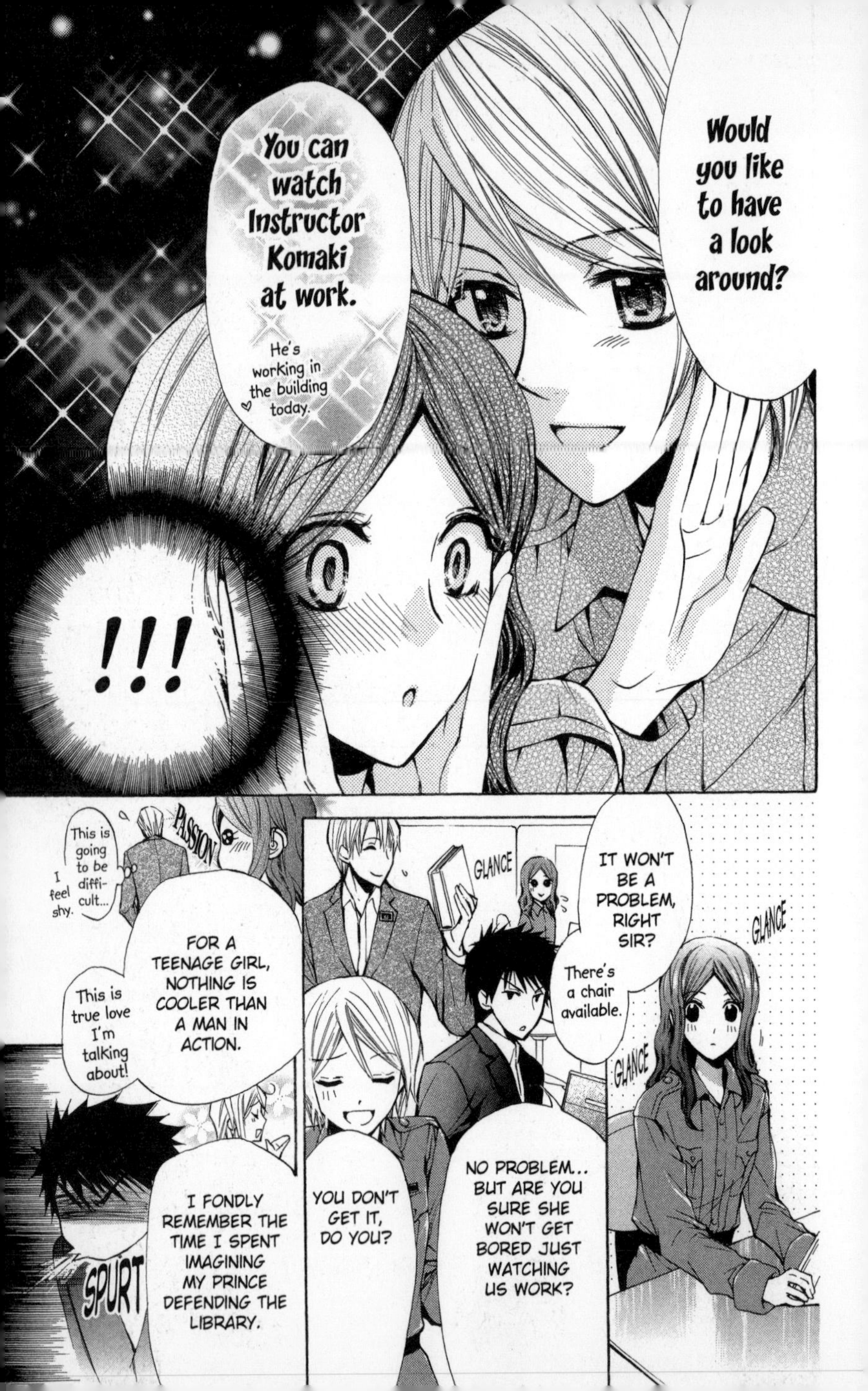
Would you like to have a look around?
You can watch Instructor Komaki at work.
He's working in the building today.
!!!
IT WON'T BE A PROBLEM, RIGHT SIR?
There's a chair available.
GLANCE
GLANCE
GLANCE
NO PROBLEM... BUT ARE YOU SURE SHE WON'T GET BORED JUST WATCHING US WORK?
YOU DON'T GET IT, DO YOU?
PASSION
This is going to be diffi- cult...
I feel shy.
FOR A TEENAGE GIRL, NOTHING IS COOLER THAN A MAN IN ACTION.
This is true love I'm talking about!
I FONDLY REMEMBER THE TIME I SPENT IMAGINING MY PRINCE DEFENDING THE LIBRARY.
SPURT

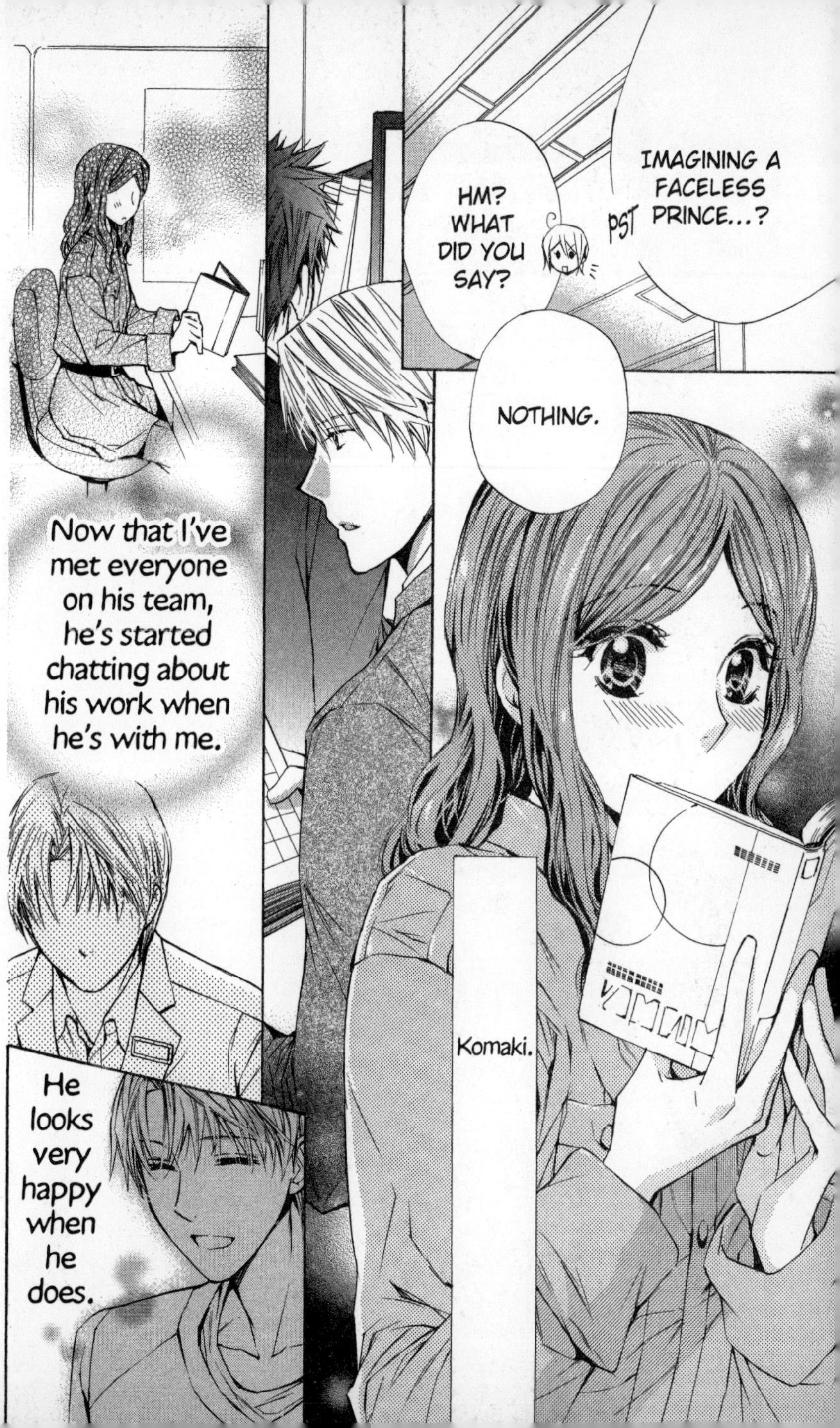

IMAGINING A FACELESS PRINCE...?
PST
HM? WHAT DID YOU SAY?
NOTHING.
Komaki.
Now that I've met everyone on his team, he's started chatting about his work when he's with me.
He looks very happy when he does.

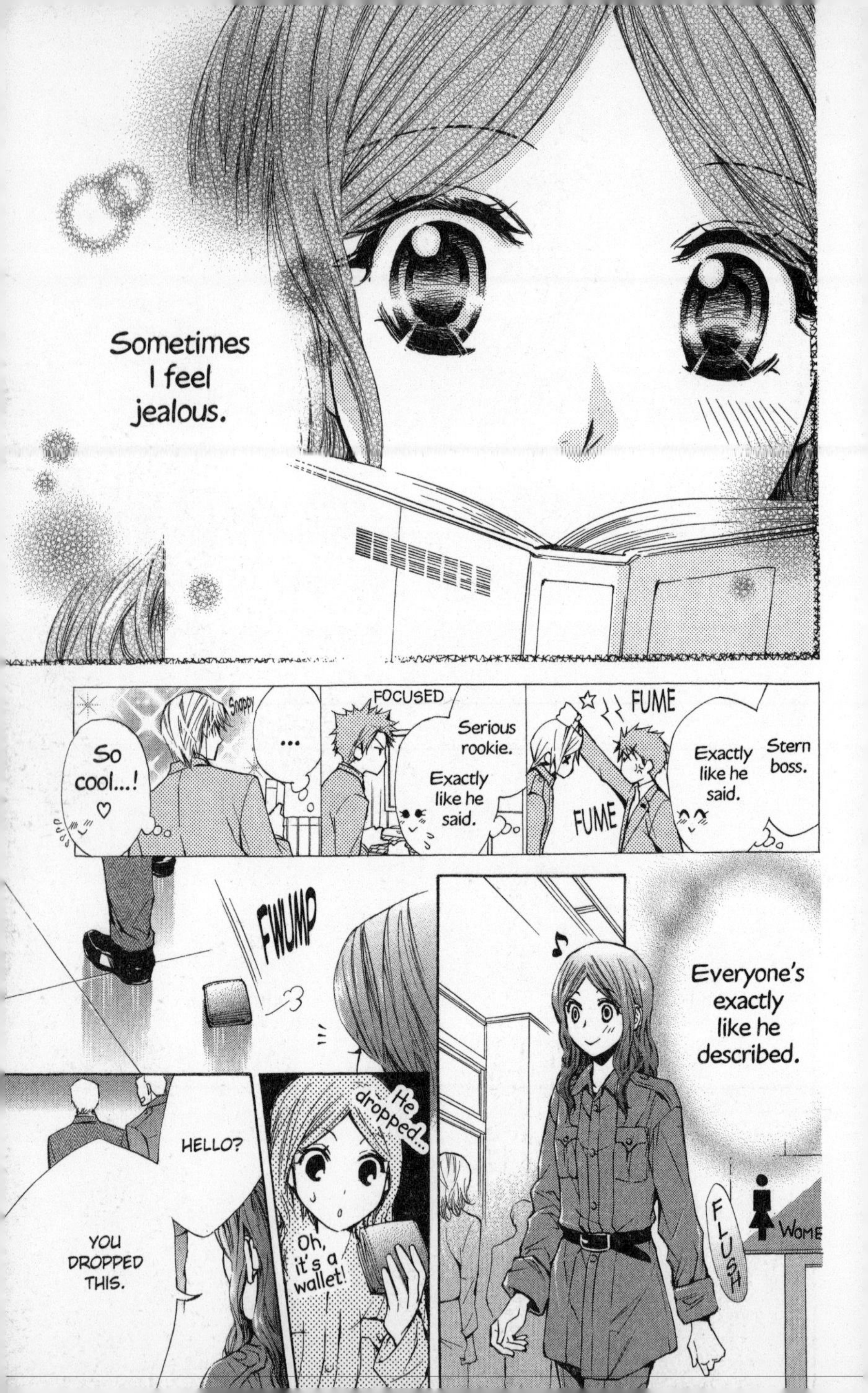
Sometimes I feel jealous.
Stern boss.
Exactly like he said.
FUME
FUME
FOCUSED
Serious rookie.
Exactly like he said.
Snappy
...
So cool...! ♡
Everyone's exactly like he described.
FLUSH
WOME
FWUMP
He dropped...
Oh, it's a wallet!
HELLO?
YOU DROPPED THIS.

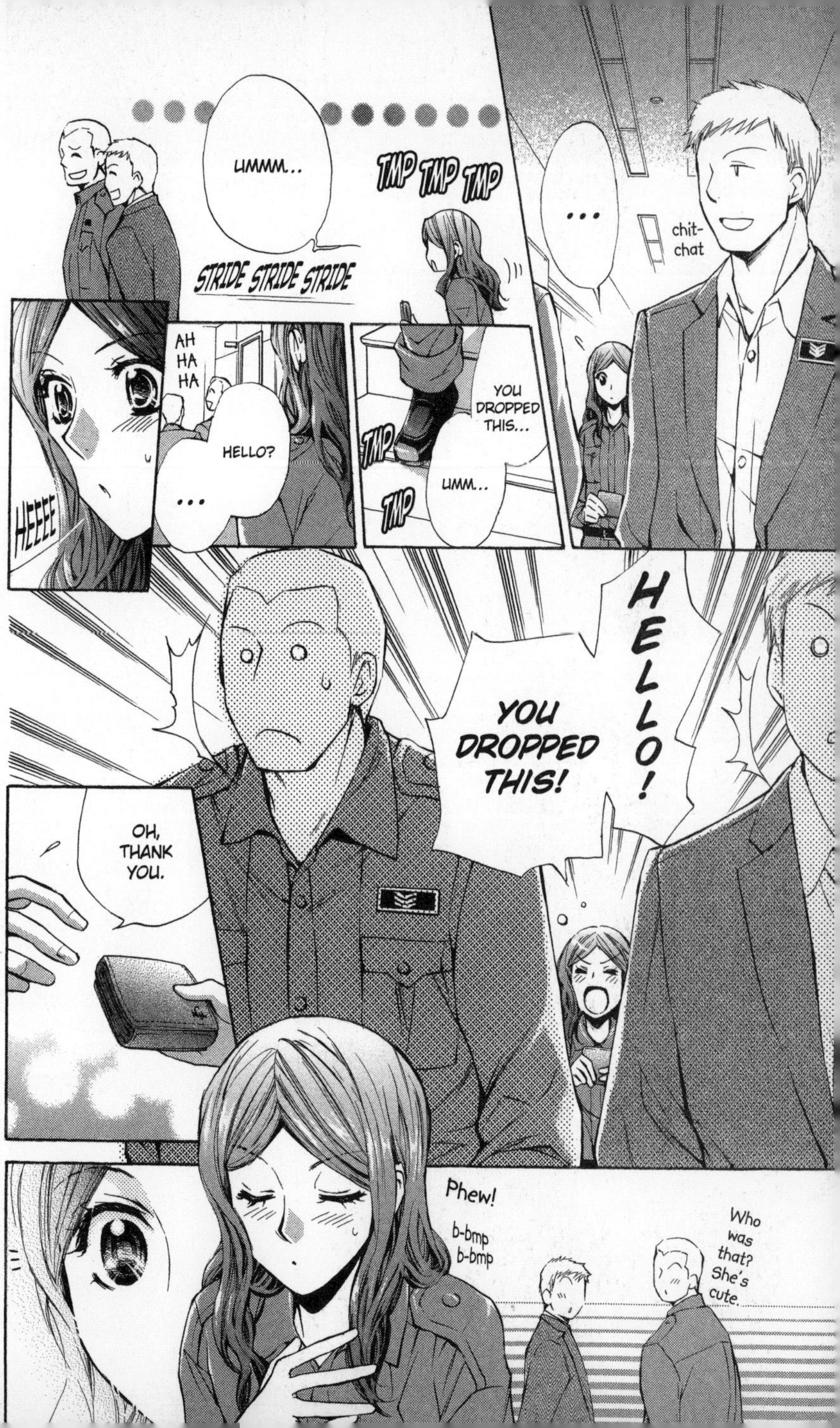
...
chit-chat
YOU DROPPED THIS...
UMMM...
TMP TMP TMP
STRIDE STRIDE STRIDE
TMP
TMP
UMM...
AH HA HA
HELLO?
...
HEEEE
HELLO!
YOU DROPPED THIS!
OH, THANK YOU.
Who was that? She's cute.
Phew!
b-bmp b-bmp

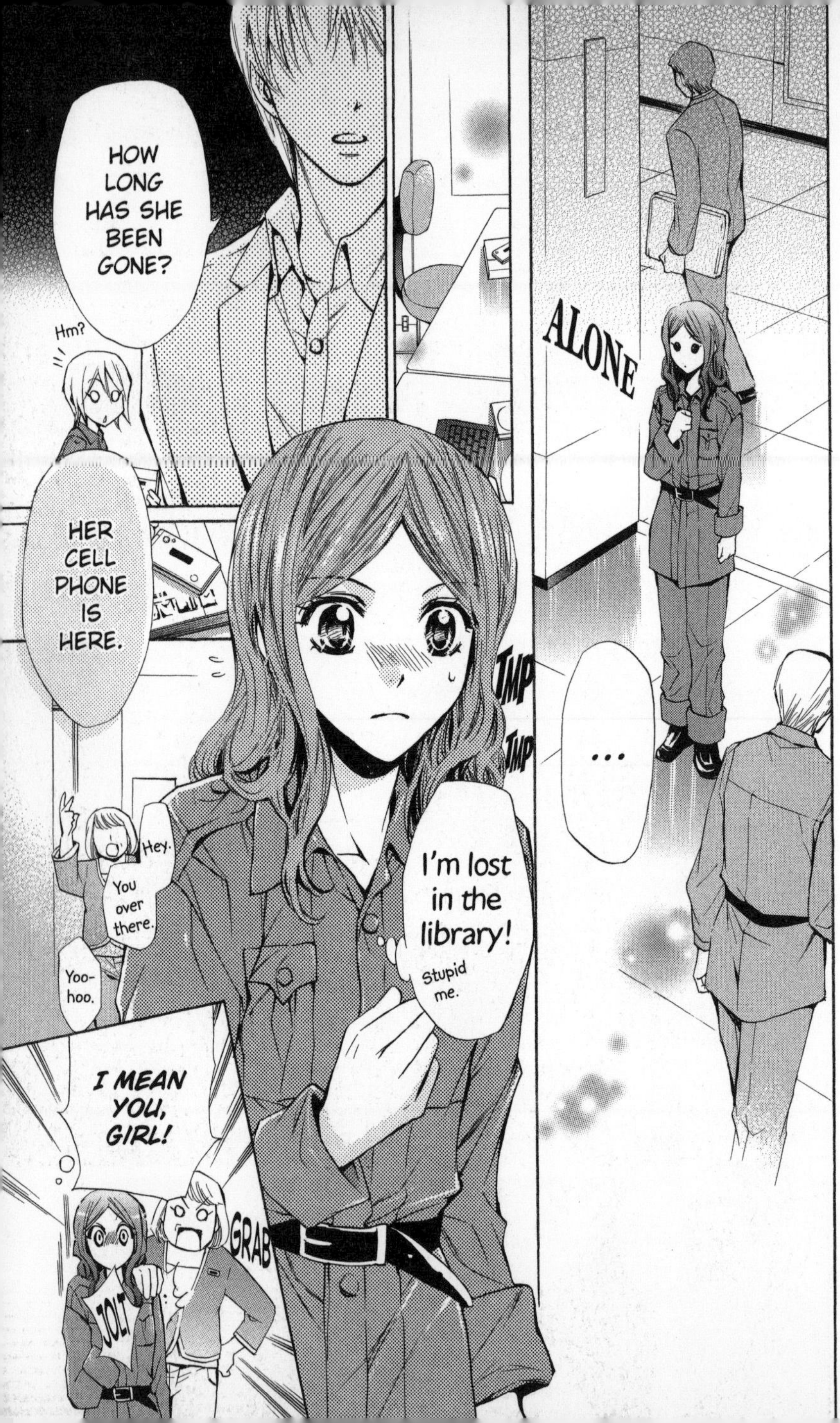
ALONE
...
HOW LONG HAS SHE BEEN GONE?
Hm?
HER CELL PHONE IS HERE.
TMP
TMP
I'm lost in the library!
Stupid me.
Hey.
You over there.
Yoo-hoo.
I MEAN YOU, GIRL!
GRAB
JOLT

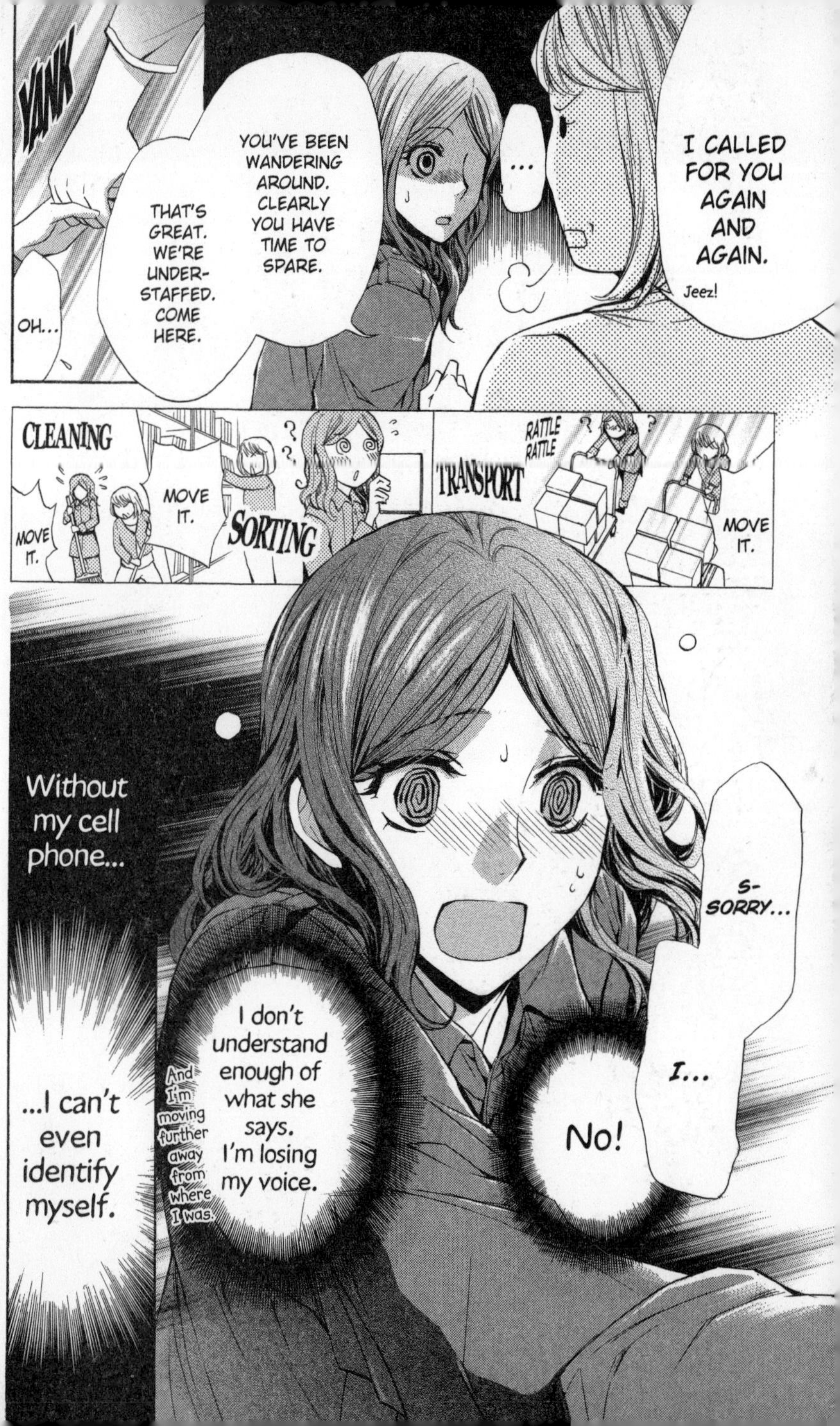
I CALLED FOR YOU AGAIN AND AGAIN.
Jeez!
...
YOU'VE BEEN WANDERING AROUND. CLEARLY YOU HAVE TIME TO SPARE.
THAT'S GREAT. WE'RE UNDER-STAFFED. COME HERE.
YANK
OH...
TRANSPORT
RATTLE RATTLE
MOVE IT.
SORTING
CLEANING
MOVE IT.
MOVE IT.
S-SORRY...
I...
No!
I don't understand enough of what she says. I'm losing my voice.
And I'm moving further away from where I was.
Without my cell phone...
...I can't even identify myself.

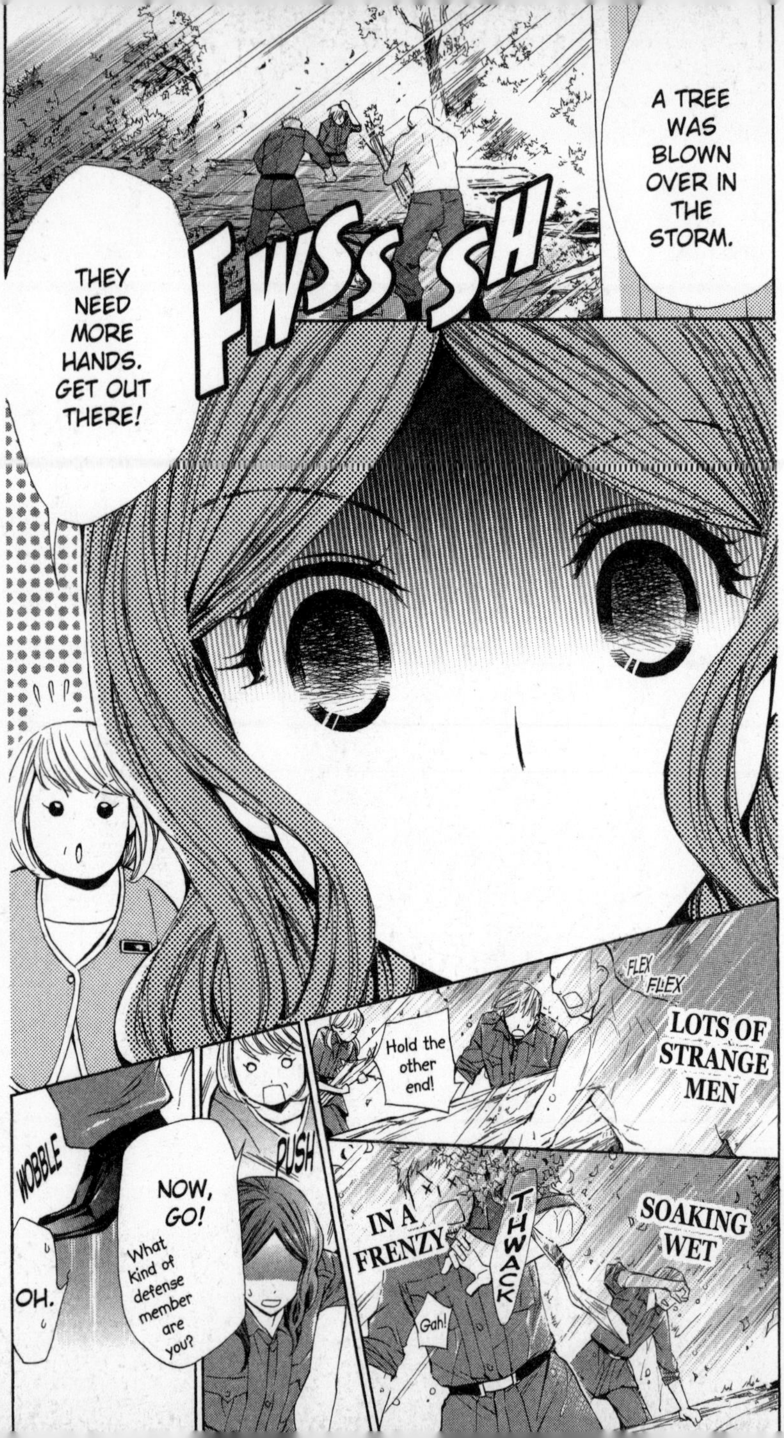
A TREE WAS BLOWN OVER IN THE STORM.
FWSSSH
THEY NEED MORE HANDS. GET OUT THERE!
FLEX FLEX
LOTS OF STRANGE MEN
Hold the other end!
SOAKING WET
THWACK
IN A FRENZY
Gah!
PUSH
NOW, GO!
What kind of defense member are you?
WOBBLE
OH.

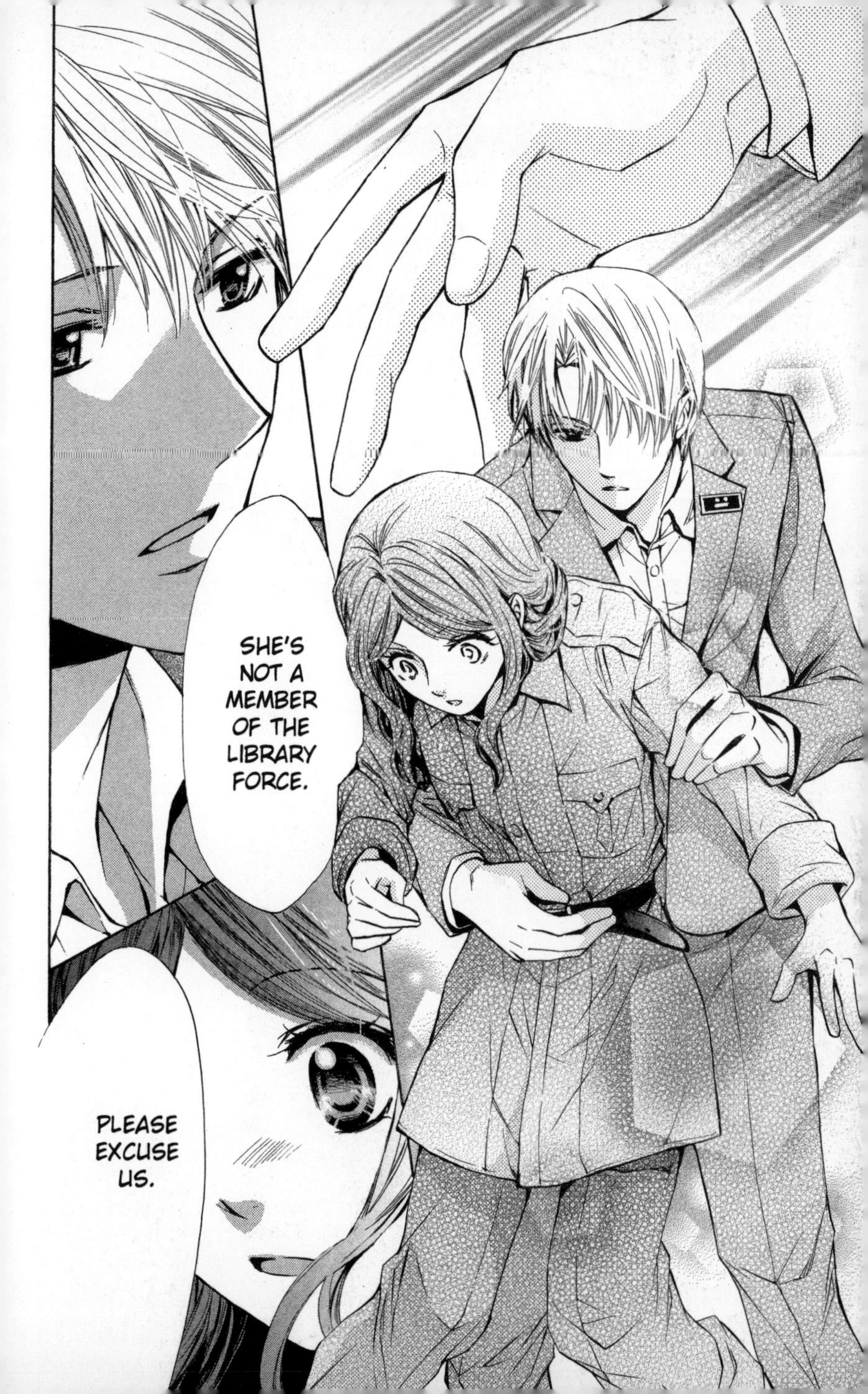
SHE'S NOT A MEMBER OF THE LIBRARY FORCE.
PLEASE EXCUSE US.

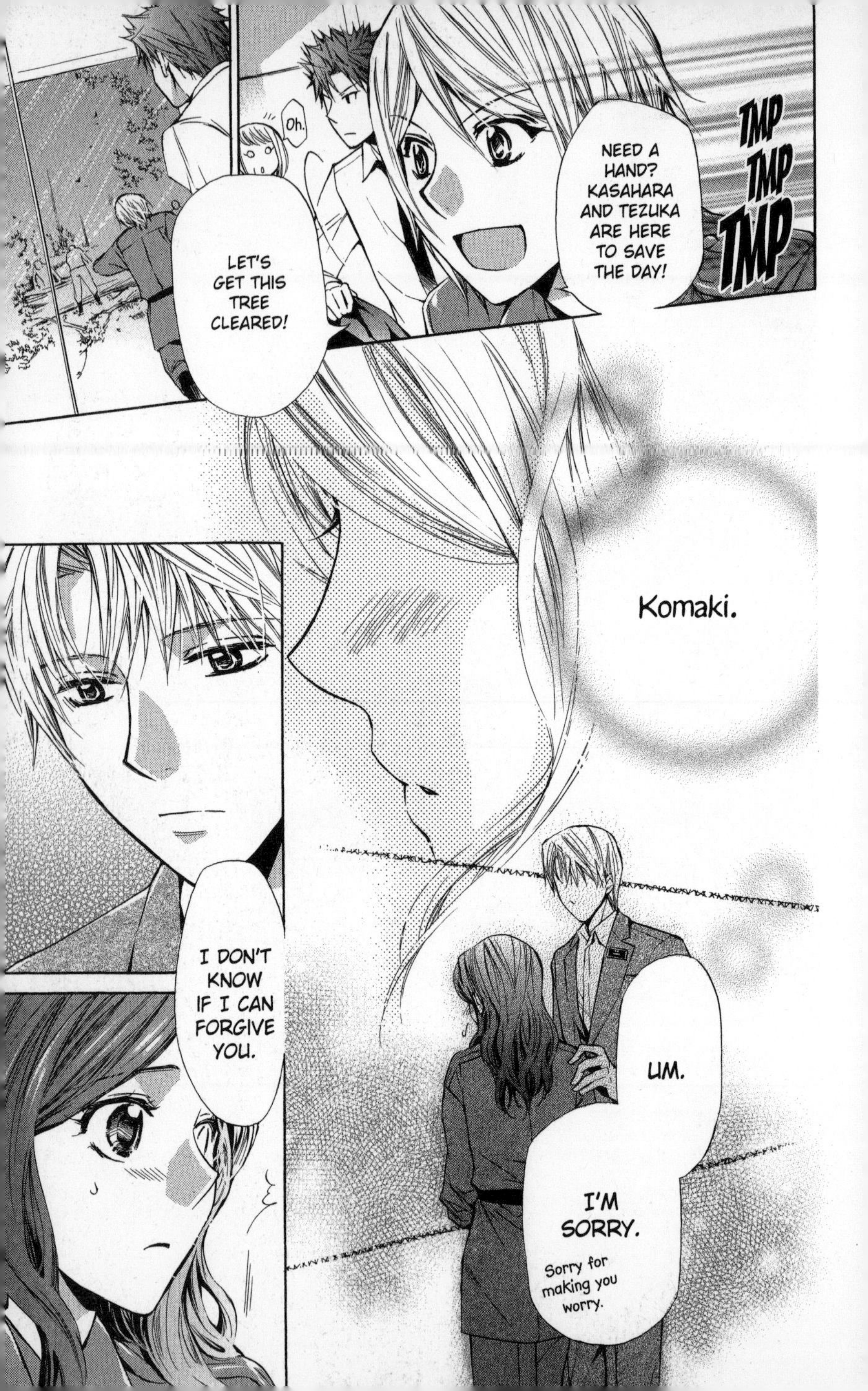
TMP TMP TMP
NEED A HAND? KASAHARA AND TEZUKA ARE HERE TO SAVE THE DAY!
Oh.
LET'S GET THIS TREE CLEARED!
Komaki.
UM.
I'M SORRY.
Sorry for making you worry.
I DON'T KNOW IF I CAN FORGIVE YOU.

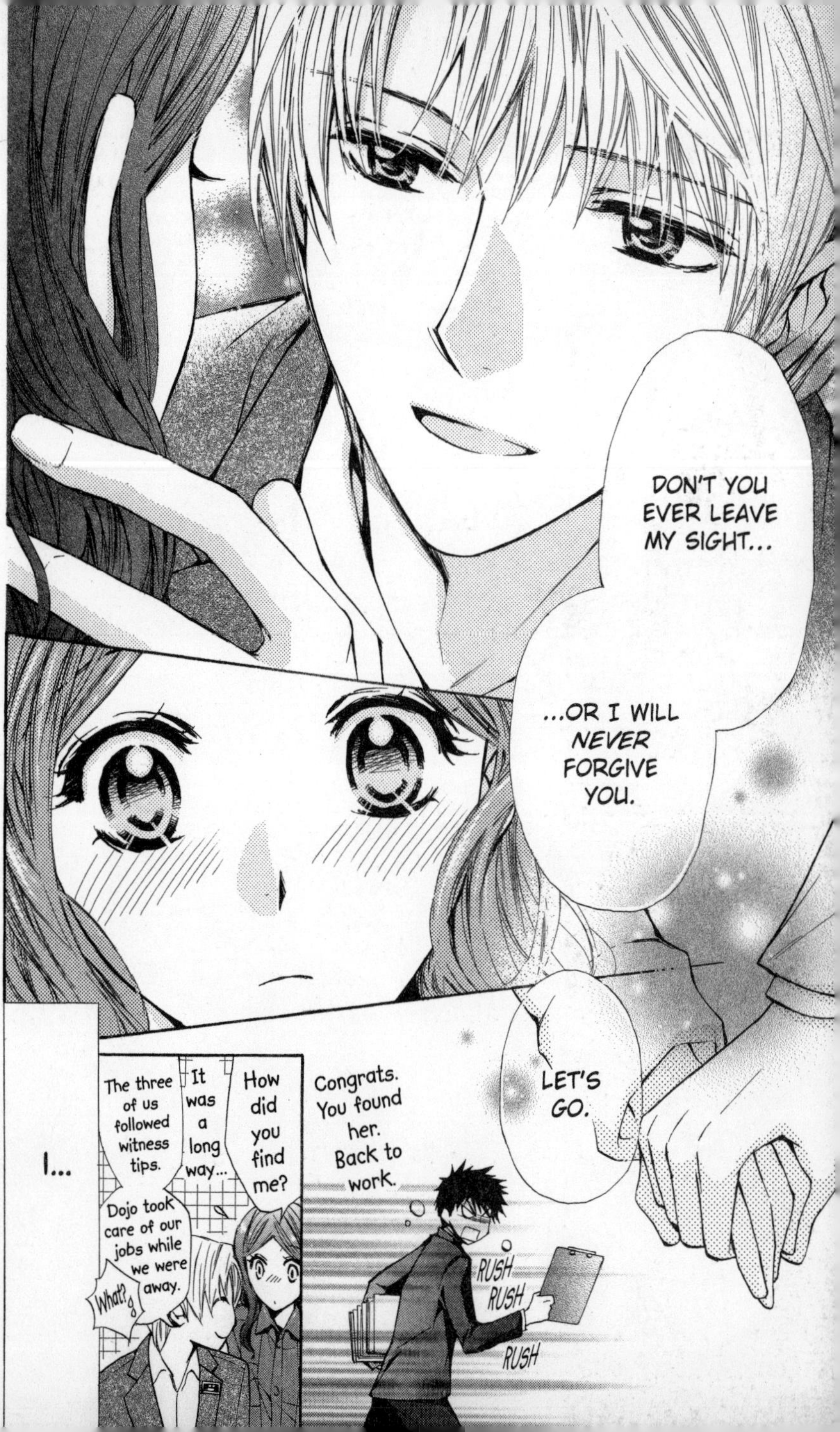

DON'T YOU EVER LEAVE MY SIGHT...
...OR I WILL *NEVER* FORGIVE YOU.
LET'S GO.
Congrats. You found her. Back to work.
RUSH
RUSH
RUSH
How did you find me?
It was a long way...
The three of us followed witness tips.
Dojo took care of our jobs while we were away.
What?
I...

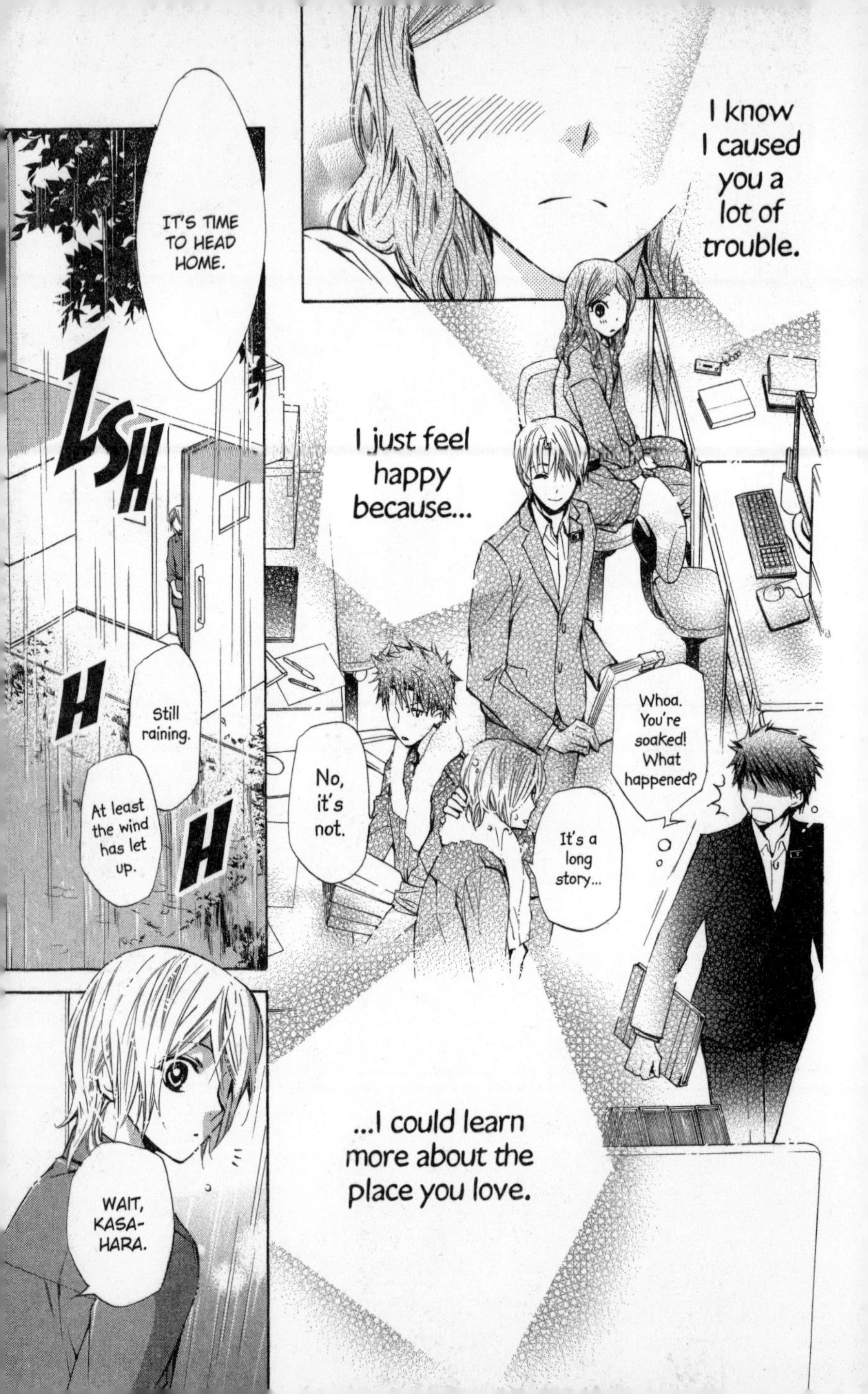
I know I caused you a lot of trouble.
I just feel happy because...
Whoa. You're soaked! What happened?
It's a long story...
No, it's not.
...I could learn more about the place you love.
IT'S TIME TO HEAD HOME.
ZSH
H
H
Still raining.
At least the wind has let up.
WAIT, KASA-HARA.

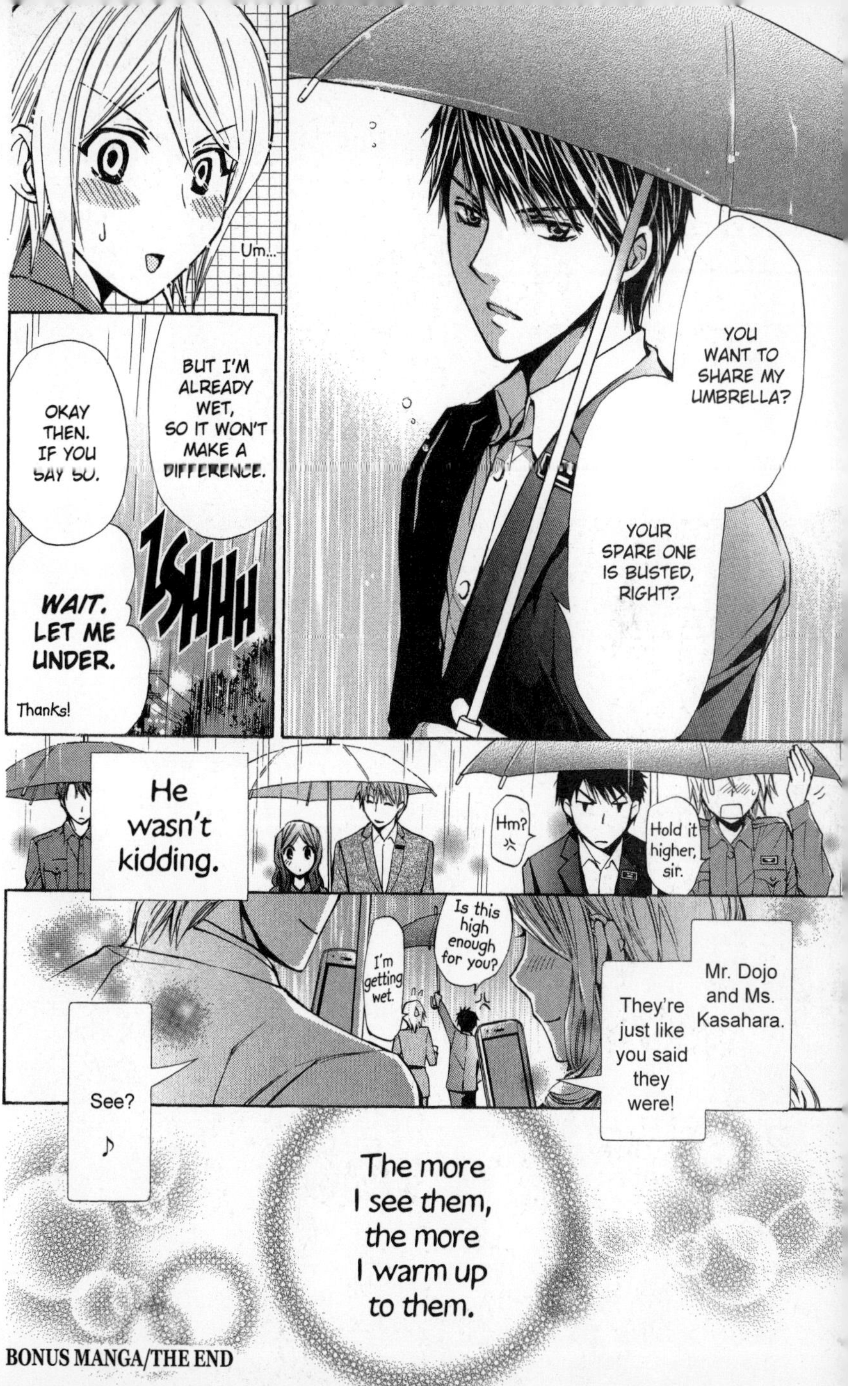
YOU WANT TO SHARE MY UMBRELLA?
YOUR SPARE ONE IS BUSTED, RIGHT?
Um...
BUT I'M ALREADY WET, SO IT WON'T MAKE A DIFFERENCE.
OKAY THEN. IF YOU SAY SO.
ZSHHH
WAIT. LET ME UNDER.
Thanks!
Hold it higher, sir.
Hm?
He wasn't kidding.
Mr. Dojo and Ms. Kasahara.
They're just like you said they were!
Is this high enough for you?
I'm getting wet.
See? ♪
The more I see them, the more I warm up to them.

BONUS MANGA/THE END

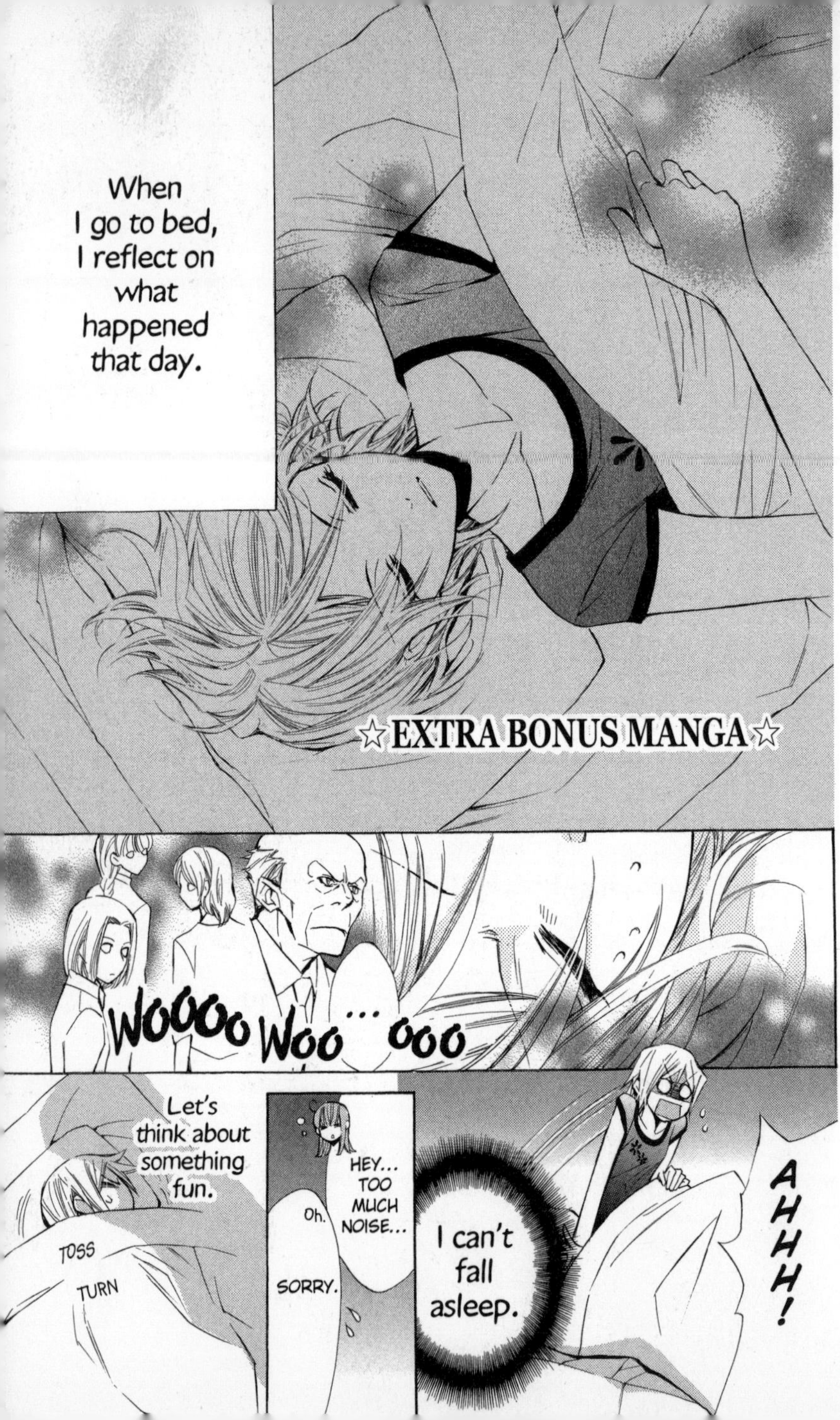
When I go to bed, I reflect on what happened that day.
☆EXTRA BONUS MANGA☆
WOOOO WOO... OOO
AHHH!
I can't fall asleep.
HEY... TOO MUCH NOISE...
Oh.
SORRY.
Let's think about something fun.
TOSS
TURN

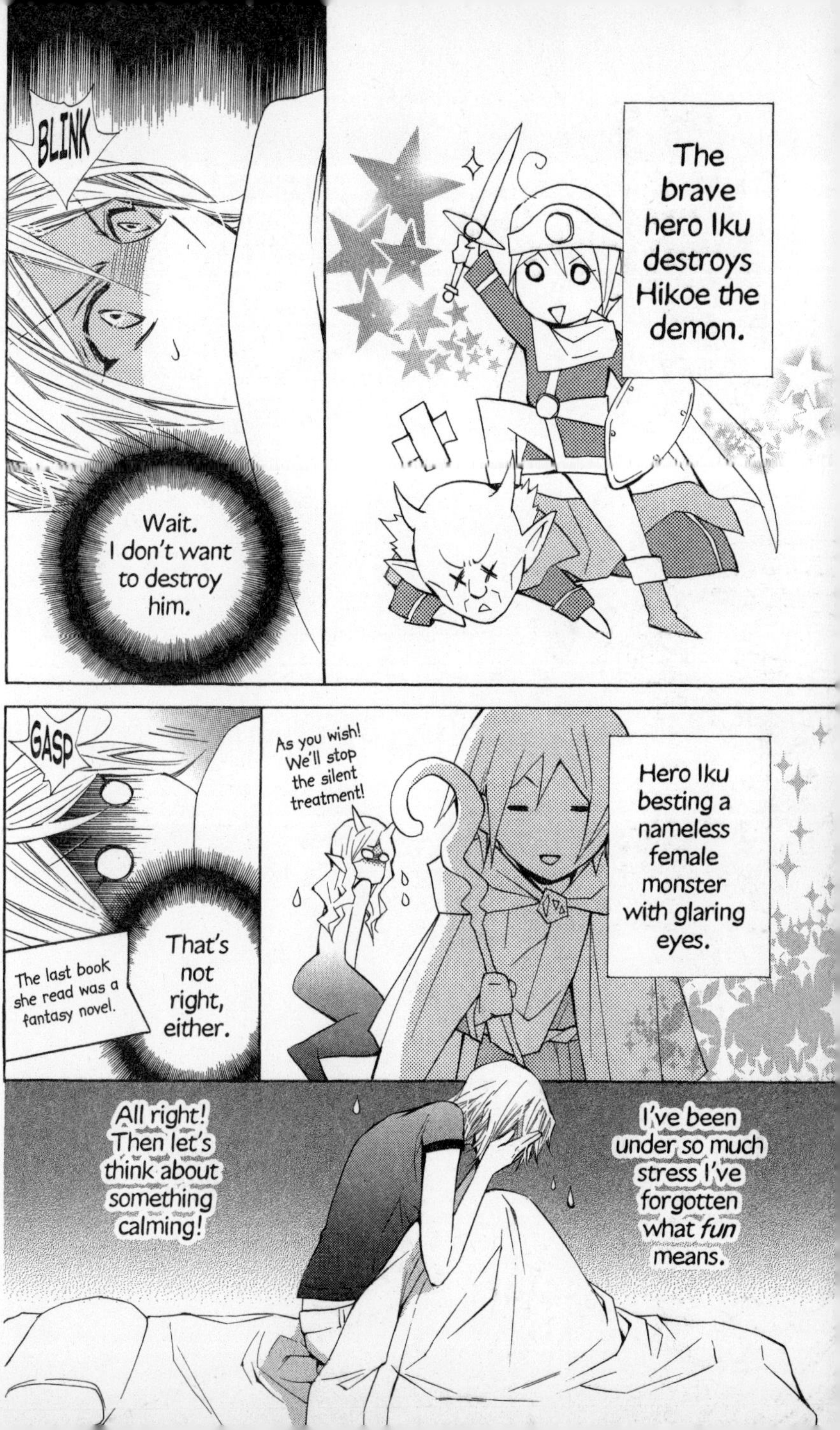
The brave hero Iku destroys Hikoe the demon.
BLINK
Wait. I don't want to destroy him.
Hero Iku besting a nameless female monster with glaring eyes.
As you wish! We'll stop the silent treatment!
GASP
That's not right, either.
The last book she read was a fantasy novel.
I've been under so much stress I've forgotten what *fun* means.
All right! Then let's think about something calming!

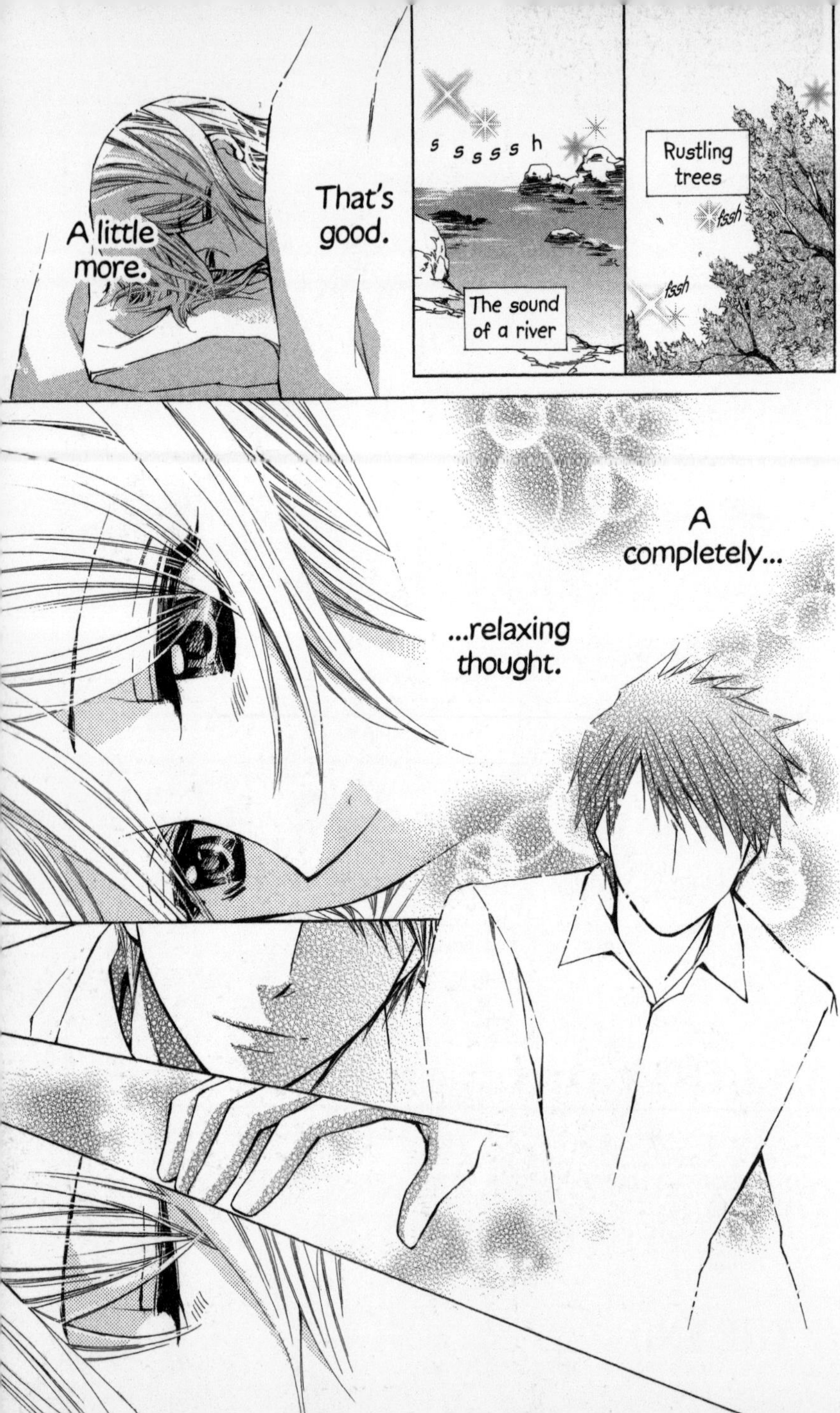
Rustling trees
fssh
fssh
s s s s s h
The sound of a river
That's good.
A little more.
A completely...
...relaxing thought.

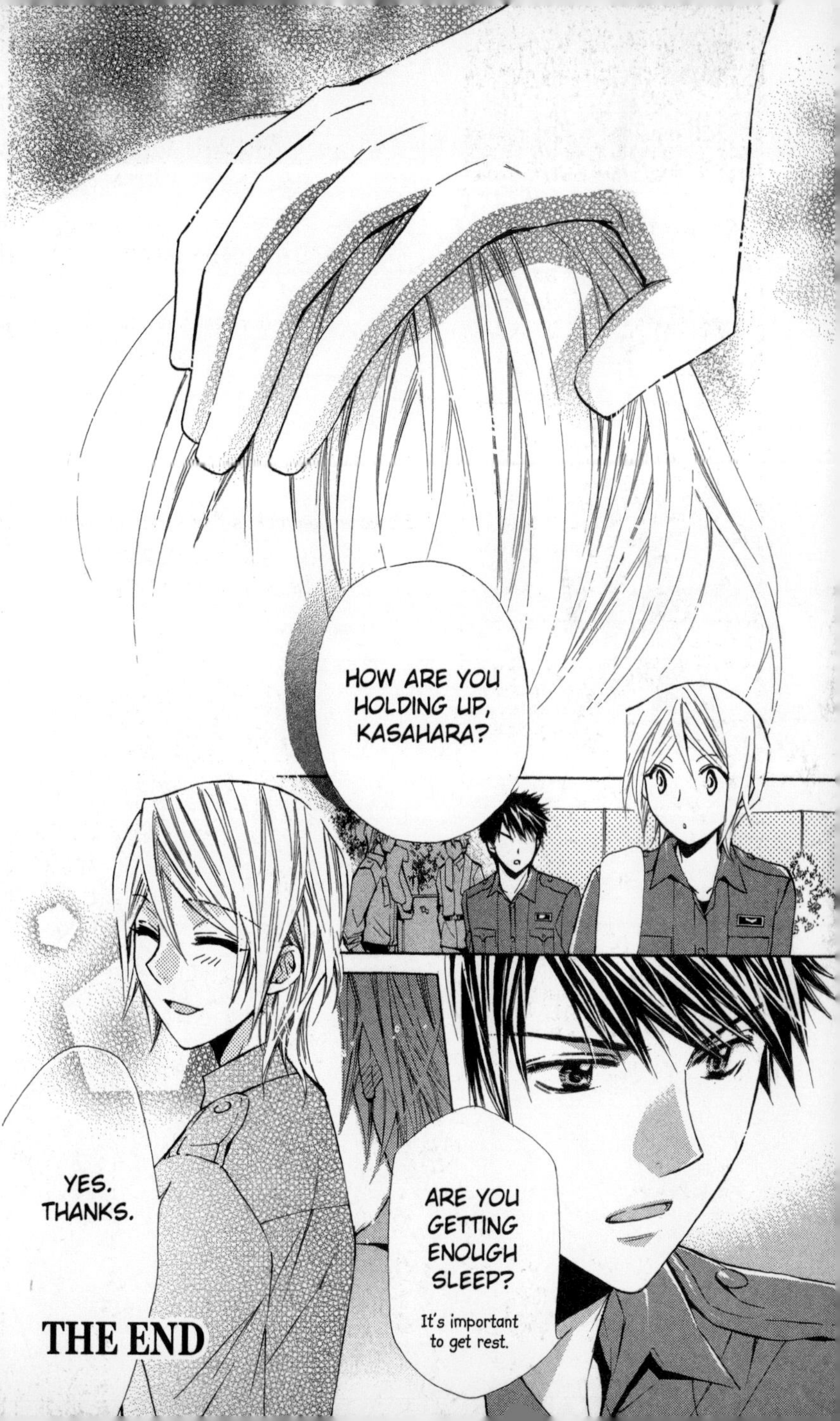
HOW ARE YOU HOLDING UP, KASAHARA?
ARE YOU GETTING ENOUGH SLEEP?
It's important to get rest.
YES. THANKS.
THE END

Special Thanks!!

Ms. Arikawa
Ms. Arikawa's editor (ASCII Media)
☆
Mamada, Murakami, Aoki
☆
My family
☆
My editor
☆
Everyone who makes this series possible.
☆☆
Thanks so much for your support!

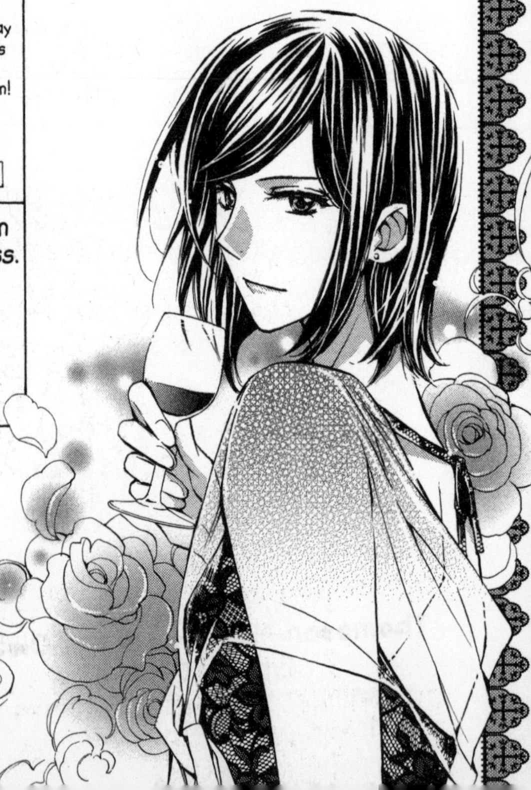

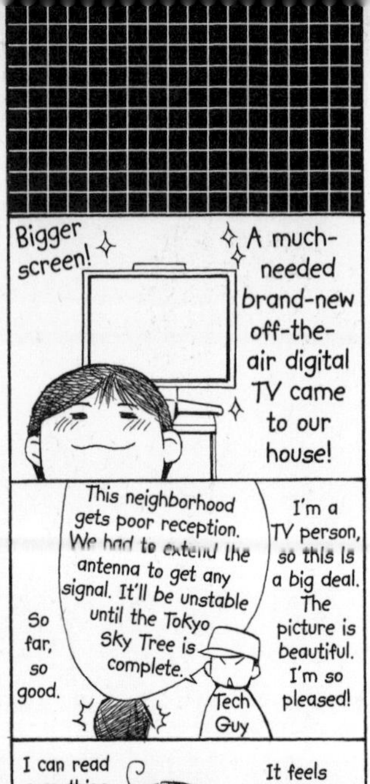
A much-needed brand-new off-the-air digital TV came to our house!
Bigger screen!
I'm a TV person, so this is a big deal. The picture is beautiful. I'm so pleased!
This neighborhood gets poor reception. We had to extend the antenna to get any signal. It'll be unstable until the Tokyo Sky Tree is complete.
Tech Guy
So far, so good.
It feels great to play videogames with this large screen!
Action Game
I can read everything now! It's incredible! Wonderful! I'm so happy!
I'm a gamer.
Motion sickness.
Wii
I got used to it after a few days.

Hope to see you in the next volume.

弓きいろ
Kiiro Yumi

End notes

Page 16, panel 4: "Prince"
Volume 1 contains the whole story on how Dojo ended up being Kasahara's mystery "Prince"!

Page 47, panel 1: Tatami
A woven mat used as traditional flooring material in Japan.

Page 48, panel 3: German Suplex
In volume 6 (page 128), it was revealed that Iku learned all about suplex wrestling moves from her brothers. The German suplex is a particularly powerful reverse body slam.

Page 111, panel 4: Spartan Agoge
This term refers to the training regimen undertaken by Spartan citizens in ancient Greece; important principles of the agoge included discipline and pain resistance.